Beyond Westphalia?

State Sovereignty and International Intervention

Edited by

Gene M. Lyons
and Michael Mastanduno

The Johns Hopkins University Press
Baltimore and London

The Johns Hopkins University Press
2715 North Charles Street
Baltimore, Maryland 21218-4319
The Johns Hopkins Press Ltd., London

Library of Congress Cataloging-in-Publication Data
will be found at the end of this book.
A catalog record for this book is available from the British Library.

ISBN 0-8018-4953-5
ISBN 0-8018-4954-3 (pbk.)

Contents

Preface and Acknowledgments

The essays in this book were first presented at a conference convened at Dartmouth College, Hanover, New Hampshire, in May 1992 under the auspices of the Rockefeller Center for the Social Sciences and the Dickey Center for International Understanding. Initially, the purpose of the conference was to examine the political and legal problems that international agencies faced in delivering humanitarian assistance in areas of civil disorder without, if necessary, the agreement of government authorities. As we prepared the conference, however, it became increasingly evident that the question of international intervention was relevant not only in the area of humanitarian assistance but also in other areas such as human rights violations, the protection of the global environment, and the control of weapons of mass destruction. It was equally apparent that the questions raised were of profound importance to students of international relations theory. The scope of the conference was thus expanded to include several areas of international intervention and a series of more theoretical issues about the nature of state sovereignty and the evolution of international society.

The conference brought together scholars who have been concerned with the implications of intervention for the future of international society and officials from governments, international organizations, and nongovernmental agencies who have had practical responsibility in the areas of humanitarian assistance, human rights, arms control, and environmental protection. We are grateful to the United Nations University, the John D. and Catherine T. MacArthur Foundation, and the Rockefeller Brothers' Fund for grants to support the conference; and to the participants for their frank and open discussion of the papers as originally presented. We want to express our special thanks to Oran Young, George Demko, Leonard Rieser, James Strickler, Jack Donnelly, James Rosenau, Friedrich Kratochwil, Thomas Weiss, and Abiodun Williams for helping to develop the structure of the

conference. Finally, we want to acknowledge the cooperation of the contributors to this book, both for their original presentations and for the time
and effort they have devoted to revising their papers for publication. We are
sure that they agree that, granted the intellectual and financial support of
others, each of us is ultimately responsible for his or her own work.

Abbreviations

AOHR	Arab Organization for Human Rights
ASEAN	Association for Southeast Asian Nations
BW	biological weapon
BWC	Biological and Toxin Weapons Convention
CIS	Commonwealth of Independent States
COCOM	Coordinating Committee on Multilateral Export Controls
CSCE	Conference on Security and Cooperation in Europe
CTB	comprehensive nuclear test ban
CWC	Chemical Weapons Convention
ECOSOC	Economic and Social Council
ECOWAS	Economic Community of West African States
EEC	European Economic Community
EU	European Union
GATT	General Agreement on Tariffs and Trade
IAEA	International Atomic Energy Agency
IBAMA	Brazilian Institute of the Environment and Renewable Natural Resources
ICJ	International Court of Justice
ICRC	International Committee of the Red Cross
ILC	International Law Commission
ILO	International Labor Organization
IMF	International Monetary Fund
INF	Intermediate Range Nuclear Forces Treaty
ITU	International Telecommunications Union
MTCR	Missile Technology Control Regime
NGO	nongovernmental organization

NPT	Nuclear Nonproliferation Treaty
NSG	Nuclear Suppliers' Group
OAS	Organization of American States
OAU	Organization of African Unity
OECD	Organization of Economic Cooperation and Development
ONUSAL	United Nations Observer Mission in El Salvador
PLO	Palestine Liberation Organization
START	Strategic Arms Reduction Talks
SUDAM	Superintendency for the Development of the Amazon
SWAPO	South West Africa People's Organization
UDR	Rural Democratic Union
UNCED	United Nations Conference on Environment and Development
UNCTAD	United Nations Conference on Trade and Development
UNESCO	United Nations Educational, Scientific, and Cultural Organization
UNITAF	Unified Task Force
UNOSOM	United Nations Operation in Somalia
UNTAC	United Nations Transitional Authority in Cambodia
WMO	World Meteorological Organization

Beyond Westphalia?

Chapter One

Introduction:
International Intervention, State Sovereignty, and the Future of International Society

GENE M. LYONS AND MICHAEL MASTANDUNO

In 1989, food and medical supplies were sent into the Sudan by international organizations in a desperate program of emergency assistance that came to be called Operation Lifeline Sudan. The objective was to sustain hundreds of thousands of people caught in a vicious struggle between rebel forces and the Sudanese government, neither of which wanted relief supplies to be distributed in areas they did not control. Similar tragic conditions developed in Somalia in 1992, when all semblance of organized authority broke down and thousands of people were threatened by starvation and rampant disease, with the international community their only hope for some slim chance to survive. In that same year, in the wake of the splintering of what had been Yugoslavia, UN peacekeeping forces were needed to provide protection for relief supplies sent from abroad into areas of Bosnia and Herzegovina under severe attack from Serbian militias fixed on a brutal campaign of "ethnic cleansing." And in 1993 the UN Security Council authorized the dispatch of a military and police mission to Haiti, intended to aid in the restoration of democratic rule and the reconstruction of a shattered economy.[1]

In keeping with current international norms, humanitarian and other assistance by international agencies should be carried out at the request of, or with the agreement of, the government that retains sovereignty in the area. In the Sudan, international relief agencies eventually reached agreement both with government officials and with rebel leaders. In Somalia and Bosnia, however, no such agreement was made, either because of the sustained opposition of the government to the distribution of supplies or because of the absence of effective political authority. In Haiti, the UN force was initially compelled to retreat before actually being deployed, threatened by violent demonstrators who were encouraged by the de facto authorities opposed to external involvement. It is these kinds of circumstances that have most pointedly raised the question of whether the international community has a "right" to intervene to respond to human suffering or political instability, with or without government agreement.

Javier Pérez de Cuéllar, then secretary-general of the United Nations, highlighted the dilemma of intervention in an address at the University of Bordeaux in the spring of 1991. "[T]he right to intervene," as he put it, "has been given renewed relevance by recent political events. . . . We are clearly witnessing what is probably an irresistible shift in public attitudes towards the belief that the defense of the oppressed in the name of morality should prevail over frontiers and legal documents." Nevertheless, he asked, "[D]oes it not call into question one of the cardinal principles of international law, one diametrically opposed to it, namely, the obligation of non-interference in the internal affairs of States?" In recognition of this tension between the necessity of intervention and the prevailing norms of international society, Pérez de Cuéllar called upon the international legal community to help develop a "new concept, one which marries law and morality."[2]

More recently, Pérez de Cuéllar's successor, Boutros Boutros-Ghali, restated the problem in his report to the Security Council on strengthening the capacity of the world organization in matters of international peace and security. "Respect for [a state's] fundamental sovereignty and integrity," he wrote, is "crucial to any common international progress." Nevertheless, he continued, "the time of absolute and exclusive sovereignty . . . has passed"; for that matter, "its theory was never matched by reality." Although the new secretary-general did not propose to resolve the dilemma, he did emphasize the need for governments to understand that sovereignty is not absolute and "to find a balance between the needs of good internal governance and the requirements of an ever more interdependent world."[3] The clear meaning was that governments could best avoid intervention by meeting their obligations not only to other states but also to their own citizens.

As Inis Claude pointed out some years ago, the UN Charter provides no guidance regarding the dilemma raised by both secretaries-general. On the one hand, the restriction on the United Nations (under Article 2[7]) not to intervene in matters that are essentially under the domestic jurisdiction of member states means "almost nothing," because ratification of the Charter by a state puts "practically every conceivable subject . . . into the international domain, so that there is precious little domestic jurisdiction left to infringe upon." Yet, on the other hand, Claude noted that the "domestic jurisdiction" restriction can be interpreted to vitiate almost the entire Charter. Claude emphasized, correctly, that the central question concerned the relationship between international society and its member states, and that over the years, the nature of that relationship had been determined politically.[4] Today, we can ask whether recent political changes—the immediate changes that have emerged with the ending of the cold war and the deeper changes that have come with increasing interdependence—have precipitated a shift in the balance between the sovereign rights and authority of states and the rights and authority of the larger international community. Are we currently witnessing the emergence and recognition of a legitimate "right" to intervene in the domestic affairs of member states in the name of community norms, values, or interests?

This question has begun to attract widespread attention beyond the corridors of the United Nations. After a comprehensive review of recent episodes, Lori Fisler Damrosch concluded that "[i]nstead of the view that intervention in internal conflicts must be presumptively illegitimate, the prevailing trend today is to take seriously the claim that the international community ought to intercede to prevent bloodshed by whatever means are available."[5] Similarly, the *Wall Street Journal* editorialized that sovereignty is not an absolute right, that starvation and wanton killing are "everybody's business," and that in such cases, "any absolute principle of nonintervention becomes a cruel abstraction indeed."[6] And reviewing a broad range of contemporary changes, an editorial writer for the *Economist* wrote that we "are increasingly concerned not just to see countries well governed but also to ensure that the world is not irreparably damaged—whether by global warming, by the loss of species, by famine or by war. . . . Increasingly, world opinion, when confronted by television pictures of genocide or starvation, is unimpressed by those who say, 'We cannot get involved. National sovereignty must be respected.'" To this, the author added, "National sovereignty be damned."[7]

The provision of humanitarian assistance involves the most immediate and dramatic confrontation between a state's right of sovereignty and the will and authority of the international community. The problem has been festering for decades in the case of millions of refugees who have sought international protection after being uprooted from their homes by armed conflict or having fled from their own countries for fear of persecution and discrimination.[8] The rights of refugees, moreover, are part of a broader set of human rights that have been continually violated by governments despite their international obligations to abide by a series of treaties that derive from the Universal Declaration of Human Rights. The continuing reports from groups such as Amnesty International, recording stories of torture and deliberate deprivation by governments, have raised questions about whether and how the international community can expand the rights of individuals to appeal beyond the state, and what active measures can be taken to compel governments to comply with their treaty obligations.

The prospect of intervention to compel compliance is also emerging in connection with arms control agreements. In the aftermath of the Persian Gulf War, the United States, Britain, and France claimed the authority to renew military action against Iraq in order to enforce the Security Council resolutions, passed at the end of the war, that called for the destruction of Iraq's facilities for the production of weapons of mass destruction. The threat of economic sanctions and possibly of military intervention provided the backdrop for negotiations with North Korea, following the latter's refusal to cooperate with the International Atomic Energy Agency (IAEA) and threat to withdraw from the Nuclear Nonproliferation Treaty. North Korea's intransigence was sparked by an IAEA effort to expand its authority at the expense of national sovereignty, by demanding the right to carry out "special inspections" that require signatories to open undeclared areas to IAEA scrutiny.[9] More generally, the pending convention on chemical weapons lays the groundwork for various types of intervention by providing for intrusive and wide-ranging international monitoring of national facilities to prevent the deployment of multiple-use chemical materials for weapons development.[10]

The question of intervention has also been raised in the context of environmental protection. The UN Conference on Environment and Development, which met in Brazil in mid-1992, for example, recommended the creation of a Commission on Sustainable Development to monitor all agreements on standards to protect the global environment. Though the commission's procedures and powers will only be worked out over time, its activities signify a more active role for the international community in ensuring that states comply with their obligations in this area.

As the above examples indicate, the tension between state sovereignty and international intervention applies to a wide range of issues and raises a series of complex practical and theoretical questions. To what extent is it meaningful to conceive of the international community as a purposive political actor? Under what circumstances can the international community intervene in the domestic affairs of states to bring governments to account for failing to meet treaty obligations, whether to provide their citizens with basic human rights and fundamental freedoms, to control the production and deployment of weapons of mass destruction, or to meet the standards and goals that the international community determines are needed to arrest the degradation of the global environment? From whence does the international community derive its authority to intervene in matters that are traditionally recognized as falling under the domestic jurisdiction of states? What principles should guide the international community when a state defies the expressed will of the larger community or when there has been a complete breakdown in political authority and the state lacks a capacity to govern? Under what conditions and under what procedures can intervention be recognized as the legitimate expression of the international community? Although these and similar questions have an immediate relevance to pressing political problems, they also prompt a deeper reexamination of the nature of international society, the rules and procedures for international intervention, the meaning and limits of sovereignty, and the role of the state in an interdependent world.

State Sovereignty and International Society

In its present meaning, the concept of sovereignty developed as an instrument for the assertion of royal authority over feudal princes in the construction of modern territorial states. Instabilities and disorder, it was believed, were severe obstacles to a stable society and could only be overcome by viable governments that could firmly establish "sovereignty" over territory and populations. Although the form of government might be monarchy, aristocracy, or democracy, what was essential was that governments maintained the capacity to provide order through the exercise of sovereignty. The concept of sovereignty was then integrated into theories of international relations through a set of ideas that evolved with the end of the moral authority of the church over the secular rulers of Europe. A historic transition was marked by the settlement of Westphalia in 1648, which ended the Thirty Years' War and opened the quest—which goes on to this day—to find a way for independent states, each enjoying sovereignty over a given territory, to pursue their interests without destroying each other or the international system of which each is a part.

That international system was initially centered in Europe and was premised on the idea that states were the central actors. All member states were to be regarded as juridically equal, and their sovereignty was to be regarded as absolute. The assumption was that states would maintain domestic order within their borders and command the resources necessary to conduct effective relations with other states outside their own jurisdiction. Nevertheless, the fact that states were necessarily unequal in dealing with one another was recognized. Four institutions eventually developed to maintain order and stability in a decentralized system of international relations in which resources are unequally distributed: a balance of power to prevent the rise of a preponderant state and to contain unlimited aggression; the codification of rules of behavior through international law; the convening of international conferences to settle major differences; and the growth of diplomatic practices through which states would maintain continuing contact and be encouraged to negotiate differences among themselves.[11] With the emergence of these institutions, the system of states was transformed into an international "society," in which members were sovereign yet recognized commonly accepted norms, rules, and obligations.[12]

The principles that undergird the international society evolved over the years as a pragmatic response to the risks and dangers of a potentially anarchical world in which sovereign states pursue self-determined interests. After the defeat of Napoleon, the leading states, meeting at the Congress of Vienna in 1815, "agreed that their society should no longer be left to the mechanistic adjustments of the balance of power, but should be directed by a diffused and balanced hegemony of the five great powers who would act in concert to manage order and change."[13] To the idea of international society was added a sense of responsibility on the part of the major states; those states agreed that they were responsible for maintaining order in international relations through a set of principles and institutions about which they basically agreed. The establishment of the League of Nations after World War I and the establishment of the United Nations after World War II were efforts to institutionalize international society to a greater extent than the loosely formed Concert of Europe had done and to extend its scope to emerging global dimensions. The League of Nations failed when the major states of Europe broke into two opposing sides, and the United Nations was, until recently, stymied by the East-West conflict. Outside of the areas controlled by the Soviet Union, however, an international society functioned under the hegemonic leadership of the United States.

The United Nations was particularly effective in drawing into international society the newly independent states that emerged out of the breakup of the European empires. Originally the concept of sovereignty was recognized as a guideline to be used by the European states in their relations with each other but not necessarily in their contacts with non-European states as they expanded their political and economic influence to other parts of the world. In Africa and Asia, the European states reserved the "right" to intervene, as the United States did in Latin America. Gradually, however, states outside Europe came to embrace the principles of international society; and the United Nations, in turn, furnished them with recognition of their sovereignty and provided an arena through which they could exercise their independence by participating in the negotiation and codification of the rules of international relations. Nevertheless, the overall position and the influence of the newly independent states remain secondary to the privileged status of the permanent members in the Security Council and to the status of the industrialized states in major financial institutions such as the International Monetary Fund and the World Bank. It is not surprising that so-called third world states, which are most vulnerable to external pressure, are also most sensitive to the possible erosion of the concept of sovereignty and are most suspicious of the development of a "right" of international intervention, which may serve to cloak domination by the major powers.

The concept of sovereignty, however, is continually evolving. In chapter 2, Friedrich Kratochwil suggests an analogy between sovereignty and property, both in their origins and in their evolution as social constructs. We own property and it is exclusively ours, but not without responsibilities and obligations. Ownership is not absolute but is subject to limits on its use and its disposition, limits that, over time, change in accordance with the overarching values of the society in which we live. Thus, there are limits on sovereignty, especially in the responsibilities that sovereign states owe to those whom they rule and to other sovereigns. By looking at the practice of sovereignty, Kratochwil observes that, in terms of responsibilities and obligations, sovereignty has evolved largely in response to developments in Eurocentric international society but is now most likely to change under the influence of the broader global experience through which international relations are moving.

The point that Kratochwil makes about sovereignty involving obligations as well as rights is evident in the UN Charter. Article 2 of the Charter begins by asserting the sovereign equality of all member states, yet goes on to caution that "all members, in order to ensure to all of them the rights and benefits resulting from membership, shall fulfill in good faith the obligations assumed by them in . . . the present Charter." Subsequent paragraphs specify what these obligations are: to settle international disputes by peaceful means, to refrain from the use of force, and to assist the

United Nations in any action it takes in accordance with the Charter. These are significant limitations on the exercise of sovereignty; as noted above, however, they are qualified, with some ambiguity, by the statement, in paragraph 7, that nothing in the Charter authorizes the United Nations to intervene in matters that are essentially within the domestic jurisdiction of any state.

It is one thing to recognize that there are limitations on sovereignty and that sovereignty carries with it responsibilities. It is quite another to determine whether or not states have met their obligations not only under the Charter but also under the treaties and agreements that derive from the broad aims of the Charter. In many respects, there is no question about the limits to sovereignty. The important question is, who determines that a state has not met its sovereign obligations and that the consequences are such that intervention to force compliance is justified? In the past, great powers often arrogated this authority to themselves. What is distinctive about the present period of history, characterized by the global expansion of international society, is not that great powers no longer intervene, but that their claims to legitimate authority are increasingly difficult to justify. What appears to be required to justify intervention, increasingly, is what might be called collective legitimation: a political decision that is made in accordance with generally accepted procedures and is consistent with generally accepted norms of behavior.

Like Kratochwil, Nicholas Onuf, in chapter 3, views sovereignty as neither fixed nor static. But perhaps to a greater extent than Kratochwil, he argues that a fundamental change is now occurring, and suggests the possibility that sovereignty's long period of conceptual stability is coming to an end. For Onuf, sovereignty derives from three notions: majesty, or the degree of respect that an institution merits; the capacity to rule; and stewardship, the idea of acting on behalf of, and for the benefit of, others. Onuf's critique of sovereignty is, in fact, a critique of the state. He argues that the state no longer holds a monopoly of respect from those it serves; that citizens now look to other institutions to provide some of their basic needs; and that most states, as constituted, have no way of fully performing the essential tasks of providing security and well-being. Some smaller, weaker states completely lack a capacity to exercise sovereignty and fail to supply their citizens with even minimal protection. Moreover, in an interdependent world economy, even the largest and most highly industrialized states must rely upon cooperative arrangements to realize economic prosperity; and such arrangements give others substantial influence, if not control, over their policy-making processes. In Onuf's view, as states lose the capacity to rule, majesty is diffused and stewardship is shared with other institutions, including international organizations and "non-state actors" such as transnational corporations. States remain necessary in that they link people to territory, but they no longer monopolize sovereignty because they no longer can meet, fully and consistently, all the responsibilities that sovereignty requires of them.

Onuf's discussion underscores a key question: to the extent that states can no longer effectively exercise sovereignty, is there an alternative basis for an international society that, at least since the Westphalian settlement, has rested on the principle of the sovereign autonomy and equality of states? Robert Jackson, in chapter 4, takes up this issue by considering two forms of international society: a community of states, and a more pluralistic community of humankind which includes not only states but also individuals as "right and duty bearing units." Jackson emphasizes the primacy of the former conception, and identifies the United Nations as the one operative community of sovereign states owing to the fact that no other international collectivity is as universal in its organization, membership, and rules. Whether the United Nations also represents the "community of humankind," in which individuals or groups of individuals, as well as states, may be meaningful actors, is less obvious. The question is significant because the current dilemma of international intervention rests, at least in part, in the tension between the community of states and the community of humankind.

If the United Nations is the one operative international community, it would seem to follow that any "collective legitimation" must result from the procedures provided in the UN Charter and be consistent with the principles and norms that flow from the purposes and practice of the organization. The emphasis on principles and norms is as important as procedures, given that the procedures of the United Nations favor the major states, especially the five permanent members of the Security Council. The "perm five," moreover, once divided by the antagonisms of the cold war, now have the potential to act in concert, not unlike the "collective hegemony" of the dominant states in the nineteenth century.[14] It is the prospect of this "concert," however, that leads others to seek the protection that the concept of sovereignty and the limits of Article 2(7) provide against the domination of the great powers.

Those who take the realist position in explaining international relations argue that, in this sense, nothing essential has changed. Whatever the changes in their capacity to govern, states matter; and powerful states continue to matter the most. Others, however, question whether the now-

pluralistic international society is giving rise to a formidable set of principles and norms to which all states, including the powerful, must respond.
This is an open question, and as part of the effort to address it, we turn first
to an examination of the concept of international intervention, and then to
a discussion of whether the practice of intervention in contemporary world
politics is altering the fundamental relationship between sovereign states
and the international community.

The Question of International Intervention

The concept of intervention is both critical and elusive.[15] Some scholars
conceive of intervention narrowly, as necessarily involving military coercion or the use of force; to others, intervention is practically the same as
international relations, in which states are always interfering in the internal affairs of other countries.[16] For the sake of analytic clarity, it is useful
to think along a continuum from intervention to the exercise of political
influence. *Intervention* involves the physical crossing of borders with a
clearcut purpose, such as transporting relief workers into the territory of a
sovereign state to deliver humanitarian assistance, or bombing a country's
nuclear or chemical facilities to stem the development of weapons of mass
destruction. Short of crossing borders and physically intervening, a group
of states may attempt to *isolate* another state by cutting off diplomatic or
economic relations, usually with the aim of precipitating a collapse of the
government or a change in its offensive behavior. The United Nations
embargoes against Iraq in 1990 prior to the initiation of Operation Desert
Storm and against the white minority government of Rhodesia after its
Unilateral Declaration of Independence are prominent examples. But before applying sanctions and isolating an offending party, states may seek to
influence another government to change its behavior through negotiations,
or by promising rewards or threatening punishment—by applying the car-
rot and the stick, as it were. Here the examples are numerous as we move
closest to the everyday character of international politics.

Although it is possible to draw these distinctions analytically, the lines
between intervention, isolation, and influence often blur in political practice. For example, in-depth investigations into human rights violations,
considered "intervention" by governments during the 1960s and 1970s, are
now accepted as standard practice, especially as more and more states
ratify human rights treaties and expect other governments to comply with
their provisions. Alternatively, what to one state looks like unobtrusive

and even benign attempts at influence may appear to another to be blatant intervention and an infringement on sovereignty.[17] This has been particularly true of smaller states that feel vulnerable to the influence of more powerful neighbors. In the nineteenth century, for example, some Latin American governments adopted, in the Drago and Calvo Doctrines, an almost absolute interpretation of the principle of nonintervention, in order to forestall larger powers, especially the United States, from intervening to protect the interests of their citizens abroad.[18] Today, the defense of sovereignty is a major element in the policies and rhetoric of developing countries that view intervention as an endemic and pervasive feature of international relations, embedded in the very structure of power relations between themselves and the highly industrialized countries of the North.[19]

The purpose of any of these three instruments is to change the behavior or capabilities of a government, or to affect the activities of political factions in a country where effective central authority has broken down. The chapters in part II, below, however, suggest that the choice of intervention, isolation, or influence may vary by issue area. The delivery of humanitarian assistance, as chapter 5, by Thomas Weiss and Jarat Chopra, demonstrates, generally requires the physical crossing of borders. Yet, as chapter 6, by Jack Donnelly, indicates, the protection of human rights is more commonly pursued by means of isolation or influence than by means of outright intervention. Similarly, it is difficult to conceive of coercive, cross-border interference as a reasonable strategy to compel recalcitrant governments to take steps to protect the environment; a more likely scenario, as foreshadowed in chapter 7, by Ken Conca, includes attempts to influence the offending governments' behavior by international condemnation and the application of political pressures by other governments and by nongovernmental environmentalists working at the levels of both international and domestic politics. Cross-border military intervention may be a viable strategy to retard the production of dangerous weapons; alternatively, Janne Nolan argues in chapter 8 that international treaties that truly reflect an international consensus and that constrain the weapons capabilities of both developed and developing states may ultimately prove more effective. Nevertheless, intervention in the form of increasingly intrusive on-site inspection may conceivably emerge as the more usual mechanism to ensure that governments abide by treaty obligations in the weapons development area.

The problem is further complicated because the use of one instrument may compromise the effectiveness of another. Robert Jackson argues that isolation may have certain advantages over intervention, in that it does not directly and explicitly violate the norm of nonintervention. Isolation, however, may be counterproductive; by stiffening the nationalist resolve of deprived populations and enhancing the popularity of besieged governments, it may render those governments even less susceptible to the influence of the international community. Similarly, as Nolan argues, reliance on military intervention to stifle would-be proliferaters may damage the credibility and effectiveness of other instruments that rely on the maintenance of political consensus, such as international nonproliferation regimes. Finally, using one instrument does not necessarily limit the use of others. As the case of Iraq illustrates, intervening states often rely on gradual escalation, increasing pressure first by attempts at political influence, then by isolation through the application of economic sanctions, and as a last resort, by applying direct coercive intervention with military force.

Whether we conceive of it broadly or narrowly, intervention has long been a routine feature of international relations. The concern of this volume, however, is not with intervention per se, but with *international* intervention. International intervention may be understood as the crossing of borders and infringements on sovereignty carried out by, or in the name of, the international community. An important difference between international and unilateral intervention involves the element of legitimacy, that is, whether and how the right to intervene has been justified, politically or legally.[20] International intervention tends to be easier to legitimize since it more credibly can be carried out on behalf of the shared values of a collectivity, rather than on behalf of the special interests of a particular state. Nevertheless, the contemporary process of legitimizing international intervention has become more complex and difficult as international society has expanded to include an increasing number of states, old and new, in a global community. In the nineteenth century, the collective approval of the major European powers was usually sufficient to legitimize international intervention. Today, intervention usually requires a more universal stamp of approval to be perceived as legitimate.

International intervention has grown in importance since the end of World War II, and particularly since the end of the cold war. The political costs of unilateral intervention have increased with the expansion of international society since 1945, and the defense of the norms of sovereignty and nonintervention by newly independent states. Not surprisingly, governments have found it desirable to justify intervention in the name of the international community in order to build up the broadest possible political support. Indeed, as Hedley Bull noted, would-be interveners "almost invariably seek some form of collective authorization, or at least *post facto* endorsement, of their policies."[21] Their ability to seek and gain that approval, moreover, has increased with the end of the cold war. The division of the world into hostile, competing blocs weakened the capacity of the United Nations to serve as a vehicle of legitimation, especially through the Security Council. As that division has ended, the Security Council has become more assertive in its own right, and the major powers have begun to rely more readily on it to initiate, legitimize, and in some cases carry out intervention.

Other developments have also enhanced the contemporary appeal of international intervention. Interdependence has made the mutual involvement of states in each other's domestic affairs necessary and inevitable. As noted earlier, the fragmentation and even disintegration of some states has also called into question the ability of their governments to meet obligations to their populations or to international society and thus to enjoy the full privileges of sovereignty. Finally, the emerging recognition among some states of common values such as the protection of human rights or the preservation of the environment has created incentives for them to broaden their conception of national interest to accommodate collective initiatives to address common problems.

It is crucial to recognize that international intervention presupposes the existence of a meaningful international community in whose name intervention may be carried out. Whether such a community actually exists, and whether, if it exists, it can be a principal agent of intervention, are fundamental yet contentious questions that divide students of international relations. On the one hand, realists are skeptical of the notion of international community and hold that international intervention can still best be understood in terms of the power and interests of particular nation-states, especially great powers, acting individually or collectively. Those states may cloak their interests in the language of the common good and may claim to be acting in the name of the international community, but ultimately they are driven by calculations of national interest rather than by the appeal of community values. In this sense, current examples of international intervention may not represent a meaningful departure from past practice. Great powers have long articulated their particular interests in the language of universal principles in an effort to persuade others to accept them.[22] Thus, what might appear to be the action of an international community is in fact a reflection of the interests of dominant states, and perhaps a vehicle for the realization of those interests. Hedley Bull speaks of "vicarious" intervention: intervention that other states may participate in, but that the great power or powers initiate and orchestrate. A great power, he goes on to add, is by definition a power that cannot be intervened against.[23] When it becomes the object of intervention, as Russia was in 1917, it ceases to be a great power.

Those in what might be called the globalist tradition, on the other hand, accept the international community as a meaningful concept. One may distinguish, as Jackson does, between the community of states, the community of humankind, and the world community (i.e., the world as a single collectivity with a common global interest). One may also accept that the one obvious operative community of sovereign states is the United Nations, and that the citizens of at least some states are members once removed. However "community" is conceived and operationalized, the key point for globalists is that the members of the community share a sense of rights, duties, values, and obligations. International intervention, in this view, is motivated by concern for, and is carried out to protect or promote, certain values, or to defend certain principles, not merely the interests and values of particular states. Globalists also stress the key role of nongovernmental organizations (NGOs), arguing that their presence and influence in international relations have increased sufficiently that it no longer makes sense to speak of states as the exclusive or even the primary actors in the international system. To globalists, the activities of many NGOs reflect the shared values of the international community; and to the extent that NGOs undertake or participate in international interventions that infringe upon state sovereignty, their behavior is further evidence of the changing nature of international society and of the enhanced role of nonstate actors.

The question of whether an international community meaningfully exists is obviously critical in determining whether and to what extent international society is undergoing fundamental change. The difficulty of resolving that question is underscored by conflicting interpretations of current examples of international intervention. Globalists point to Security Council Resolution 841 (which imposed comprehensive, mandatory sanctions to restore democracy in Haiti), and the subsequent decision to deploy UN forces in Haiti, as precedent-setting instances of a viable international community acting in accordance with values held in common.[24] Realists counter by noting that the failure of the "international community" to respond effectively to ethnic cleansing and other crimes against humanity in the former Yugoslavia reflects the fact that calculations of national interest, especially on the part of the most powerful state in the system, the United States, outweigh the appeal of even the strongest shared values. Globalists cite the involvement of the Economic Community of West African States (ECOWAS) in the Liberian crisis of 1992 as an example of legitimate intervention by the international community under the auspices of a regional organization; realists point out that ECOWAS's engagement occurred only after the United States and the Security Council made it clear they were not inclined to get involved, notwithstanding massive atrocities and the collapse of civil order in Liberia.[25] After the Persian Gulf War, Security Council Resolution 688 was interpreted, especially by the United States, as authorizing military intervention in northern Iraq to protect the local Kurdish minority from the Iraqi armed forces. The resolution broke precedent, since the council authorized intervention without securing the consent of the Iraqi government. To globalists, this signaled a change in international norms and reflected the expansion of the authority of the international community. To realists, Resolution 688 was not extraordinary when viewed in light of the history of how wars have been terminated. The victors in war often make demands that compromise the sovereignty of the vanquished; and in this context the resolution offered no new precedent or justification for international intervention.

Beyond Westphalia?

In the final analysis, the question is whether anything has changed or is in the process of changing. Intervention has always been a major characteristic of international politics, and international intervention was not uncommon under the nineteenth-century Concert of Europe. At the same time, sovereignty has never been absolute; all states—including major powers—limit their control over their own affairs by the treaty obligations that they assume and by their participation in international organizations. In contemporary international relations, moreover, states have agreed to abide by an increasing number of rules. Through their participation in international institutions, they have begun to accept common commercial practices and certain standards to avoid potential environmental risks and have committed themselves to guaranteeing the rights of their citizens to fundamental freedoms through the widespread development of treaty law in the field of human rights. Yet all of these changes have been carried out within the structure of the state-centric system that has evolved since the settlement of Westphalia. They reflect the effects of changing political and economic forces on sovereignty, and the shift from an international system to an international society. But do the many changes noted above and in the chapters that follow also amount to a qualitative shift in the authority relationship between states and the international community? Are we, in effect, moving beyond Westphalia?[26]

In chapter 9, James Rosenau argues that the line has indeed been crossed. He identifies a variety of trends and contends that they point to a decline in states' effectiveness, an erosion of their authority, and a corresponding increase in the competency of international organizations to override states' claims to full jurisdiction over their own domestic affairs. For Rosenau, these are forces for change that have been long developing, part of a "long wave" of historical transformation. The cold war only temporarily sustained the states-system, holding back a series of pressures from both subnational and transnational sources that weaken the capacity of states to perform essential functions. Ethnic and cultural loyalties had been subordinated to state allegiance in totalitarian regimes, while the major powers, rather than lose ground to their cold war antagonists, had tolerated governments that violated the rights of minorities. Now that these pressures have been released, people everywhere are demanding democratic accountability and national self-determination, even at the expense of weakening the capacity of states to function. At the same time, the transnational engines of finance and production, driven by modern science and technology and already binding together the advanced industrialized countries, are beginning to extend their impact to areas from which they had been temporarily barred. Increasingly, the need for international standards and effective cooperation to regulate economic behavior makes it difficult to operate purely national economies, and draws authority away from individual state governments.[27]

Unlike Rosenau, Stephen Krasner, in chapter 10, presents a skeptical view. Though he recognizes important changes in states' capacities to govern their own affairs and in their vulnerability to external pressures, ultimately he insists that intervention in the internal affairs of other states has been a pervasive characteristic of the sovereign state system from its very beginning and that the extent to which such intervention has compromised the autonomy of particular states depends on the distribution of power in the international system. Krasner supports his position by examining a number of cases of intervention in the past which had the effect of bringing about some "common good," such as international stability or the protection of minorities. All, he argues, came about because major powers that were capable of intervening effectively decided to do so, either in their own national interests (e.g., because they considered their own security to be endangered) or under pressure from important domestic interests (e.g., groups that opposed slavery or were appalled by discrimination against minorities in the Ottoman Empire). There is no reason to think that the changes that Rosenau enumerated alter the basic realist approach to international relations: international society is still essentially anarchical, states are motivated by what they perceive to be their interests, and behavior and outcomes are determined by the distribution of power among states.

The fact that both sides recognize changes in the contemporary international system, yet disagree with regard to the significance of those changes, leads to a conceptual puzzle: when do changes constitute a fundamental break with the past, rather than merely reflecting adaptation to a set of new political and economic circumstances? What type of test would persuasively resolve the question of whether the changes that have occurred have begun to shift effective authority away from individual states to an international community? Some suggest that these questions can best be answered definitely by reference to "critical" cases—that is, in the current context, cases in which the clear presumption is that authority should remain with the state, yet in fact authority shifts to the international community.[28] The clearest set of critical cases would involve instances in which the exertion of some form of international authority significantly constrained major powers in their pursuit of their interests.

If we look at the present processes for international decision making, however, the prospect of finding such critical cases appears to be unlikely. At the global level, the only formal decision process that is exempted from the rule of noninterference is the authority of the Security Council under the enforcement provisions of Chapter VII of the UN Charter. Yet it is here that the five permanent members retain the right of veto, which they are unlikely to use against their own interests. In other international agreements, states retain the right of withdrawal in the name of self-determined national interests, and the major powers in particular have the prerogative of interpreting their responsibilities and obligations without any real fear of contradiction or retribution. In international economic relations, the great powers also hold the upper hand through the Group of Seven, their domination of the multilateral financial agencies, and the influence that they still maintain over the large private transnational banks and corporations that have to operate within the framework of their national regulatory systems.

Others, undaunted by the absence of critical case evidence, propose an alternative test: the examination of the cumulative effect of a series of incremental changes over time. In this view, various structural changes, shifts in perceptions, and episodes of intervention—none of which appears to be critical on its own—act in combination to produce a qualitative shift in the relationship between state autonomy and the authority of the international community. Rosenau, in identifying "a variety of signals that point to a decline in the effectiveness of states," subscribes to this type of test; the challenge lies in convincing others of the point at which the line is crossed between a series of incremental developments and fundamental, qualitative change.

It all, of course, may become clearer in time; history often reveals patterns that may not have been apparent as events unfolded. But we do not yet have the benefit of historical perspective, and the contributors to this volume do not pretend to clairvoyance. Instead, they seek to clarify the central issues, track the evolution of critical concepts, and explore the empirical link between sovereignty and intervention as it has developed in various areas of international activity. In the next section, chapters by Friedrich Kratochwil, Nicholas Onuf, and Robert Jackson explore the concepts of sovereignty, intervention, and international community. Four case studies follow: Thomas Weiss and Jarat Chopra consider international intervention for the purposes of humanitarian assistance; Jack Donnelly traces the nature and extent of intervention in the case of human rights; Ken Conca takes up the question in the context of environmental protection; and Janne Nolan reviews attempts to control weapons of mass destruction. In a concluding section, the chapters by Stephen Krasner and James Rosenau offer contrasting reflections on the critical question of whether international society is in the process of fundamental change. Finally, we, as editors, provide some concluding thoughts—not in an effort to resolve debates, but to clarify how one might think about the relationship between state sovereignty and international intervention as international society continues to evolve.

Part One

Concepts

Chapter Two

Sovereignty as *Dominium:*
Is There a Right of
Humanitarian Intervention?

FRIEDRICH KRATOCHWIL

"Sovereignty" and "the state" have had their ups and down in political analysis. Having been declared fuzzy, unscientific, meaningless, obsolete, or all of the above, they have a tendency to reassert themselves again and again in the political discourse and in political practices. This resilience has two implications. It forces analysts to bring these concepts "back in" as the public debate refuses to dispense with them in spite of their problematic nature. Furthermore, given the apparent indispensability of these terms, what is their status in reality?

First, "sovereignty" is obviously not simply an observable fact that we can use as an objective yardstick for coming to an agreement. Rather, the actions and patterns we observe are part and parcel of an institution that allows us to characterize and appraise our observations in terms of certain normative criteria. This explains in a way the fuzziness of the term. Institutional behavior is hardly ever as clearly structured as in a game, and the contestability of such concepts is part of their function of mediating between the realm of "is" and the realm of "ought."[1]

Second, understanding how institutional rules function makes analysis as well as action easier, even in the face of disconfirming, and therefore confusing, evidence. For example, individuals have to make countless decisions every day regarding whether or not some things are useful for their purposes. They can proceed with their actions without being clear about the complicated nature of "property," without obtaining the advice of a legal expert, or even without first obtaining empirical evidence for the generalization of a lawlike regularity under which their action can be subsumed.[2]

Since I am concerned with the institution of "sovereignty" and with its implications for defeating and allowing claims of intervention, I want to follow the route of inquiring into the institution of property and then trying, by means of analogy, to derive criteria for assessing the (im)permissibility of intervention. Such an institutional analysis seems heuristically promising since sovereignty was developed by legal scholars such as Grotius, Pufendorf, and Selden as a rule-constituted practice analogous to private property in Roman law. While the *private* property analogy lets us grasp the central conception of the institution of sovereignty, it allows us also to examine various historical transformations. If property and sovereignty were once conceived as analogous, it would be interesting to see whether actual state practice in regard to sovereignty parallels the developments in regard to "property."

From what was said above, it should be clear that such an investigation has to proceed on the level of actual practice and on that of justification. Neither nominal definitions nor historical etymologies of the term *sovereignty* are appropriate. Nor can the development of the institution be represented necessarily in simple functional terms akin to the providential "histories" of Grotius and Pufendorf (and revived by the teleologies of rational choice theorists). Only when we consider both practice and its justification can we grasp the continuity and change of this institution without succumbing to the fallacy of structural persistence or to largely platitudinous generalizations.

In order to make good on these claims my argument will take the following steps. In the next section I will attempt to disentangle the concept of sovereignty from some cognate notions such as will, absoluteness, and possessive individualism. These notions have their root in the largely spatial representations of authority relationships familiar from Bodin and Hobbes, and from the identification of law with the "command of the sovereign."

The third section of this chapter examines the original private property analogy that was instrumental for the practice of sovereignty. The fourth shows the fruitfulness and limitation of private property analogy in the light of state practice; and the fifth critically examines normative arguments that purport to demonstrate the right of intervention for humanitarian purposes. A brief summary of the arguments concludes the chapter.

The Conceptual Puzzle: Sovereignty as Ultimate Power

It has been noted that *sovereignty* is one of the very few terms we use that does not have its roots in the classical tradition but rather emerges from the struggle of the Middle Ages. Given the conceptual apparatus of late medieval politics, claims to supreme authority arose first in the struggle for supremacy between the pope and the emperor concerning the conditions for legitimate rule, and then in conjunction with jurisdictional disputes among feudal lords, particularly when no special feudal bond of allegiance existed between them.[3]

How much the meaning of sovereignty had changed by the sixteenth century becomes clear, however, from the following brief passage of Bodin in 1577:

> It is necessary that those who are sovereigns should not be subject to commands emanating from any other and that they should be able to *give laws* [emphasis added] to their subjects, and nullify and quash disadvantageous laws for the purpose of substituting others; but this cannot be done by one who is subject to the laws or to those who have the right of command over him.[4]

Although the sovereign is still subject to natural law and bound by his conscience, he now emerges as a lawgiver who faces an (at least in this respect) undifferentiated set of subjects. He is "absolved" from law, that is, untrammeled by the laws that guaranteed "original" privileges. Gone is the notion of the sovereign as arbiter of competing jurisdictional claims, and the silence of Bodin about imperial claims to overlordship are as telling as the conception of law not as a general rule but rather as the capacity of the sovereign to make *specific* decisions legitimately on the basis of *salus publica* considerations. Finally, and most importantly, "law" is based on "will" rather than on customary understandings or reason. Thus the question of its validity is increasingly reduced to the question of whether it emanated from or was pronounced by an authoritative "source."

One particularly serious conceptual derailment flowed from the conflation of sovereignty with will. This conflation was at least empirically accurate as long as the sovereign was an actual person. Much of the *conceptual* confusion in later debates stems from the fact that sovereignty became no longer simply attributable to a real person. The confusion had two variations.

The first variation is seen in the argument that sovereignty conceived as will could not be divided and had to be clearly located in some "body." This is the familiar problem of Hobbes and his equivocation that this body need not be a concrete person but could be an assembly. But how can a "supreme" organ of government be supreme if it is dependent either upon the "people"—for instance, through the power vested in them to elect this body (Locke)—or on the rule that the majority carries in an assembly (Hobbes)? In the latter instance was only the pivotal vote "sovereign"?

From Grotius to Rousseau, this issue has led to the argument that the sovereign will can neither be alienated (Rousseau) nor be dependent upon "any other human will."[5] Similarly, Laski's debunking of sovereignty in this century consisted largely in the demonstration that parliament was not really sovereign because it was subject to various pressures or community standards.[6] Such confusions have two further mutually contradictory implications.

One plays on the equivocal meaning of "ultimate" in the notion of sovereignty. It suggests that as long as I can trace a sovereign's decision further down to some interests, the decision cannot be called ultimate. But it is pretty obvious that here the normative dimension of "ultimate," that is, being the supreme authority for making decisions, and having those decisions recognized as binding on all members, is confused with the meaning of "ultimate" in a causal sense, that is, that a particular choice is not traceable to further antecedent conditions. The question of the validity of an act, which depends on the act's conformity with certain institutional rules, has little to do with whether or not a decision cannot also be cast in terms of a causal report.

Since this way of proceeding leads to obvious absurdities, the other implication of the confusion mentioned above is that not *all* interests or antecedent causes are to be banned, but that a decision of the sovereign is legitimate only if it is based on certain factors, but not on others. Thus this implication is a modified version of the idealist position. This version has some truth to it insofar as the law might explicitly forbid certain interests to enter, such as when members of parliament or of courts have to disqualify themselves from voting because of a conflict of interests. But in the absence of a specific stipulation impairing the validity of a sovereign decision, the position comes close to an extreme natural law position: it is similar to the dubious argument that a law can only be law if it embodies the (eternal) "law" behind, or "above," the (positive) law.

Although realists are usually not known for their idealism, some of them have inadvertently become idealists of a perverse kind because they do not keep these important distinctions in mind. Consider, for example, Krasner's argument for ascertaining the autonomy of the state in making policy. He operationalizes this autonomy as a "high degree of insulation from societal pressures."[7] By conceptualizing the "autonomy" of the state as "isolation" rather than as a claim to validity by officials acting in their sovereign capacity, Krasner commits a category mistake of the first order.[8]

These last remarks raise interesting questions. If domestically sovereignty never meant supreme "power" but rather meant the quality of a claim to authority that could "bind" all subjects, then internationally sovereignty cannot be equated simply to power wielded by a self-interested (rational) actor, since part and parcel of playing the international game consists in recognizing the sovereignty of others. Claims to sovereignty are therefore inherently limited, and differ in important respects from imperial claims to authority, or from simple "rational," or maximizing, behavior. It is the task of the next section to elaborate on this point.

The Sovereignty and Property Game

Sovereignty became a distinct institution when the claim to supreme authority was coupled with a specific rule of allocation for exercising this authority. Thus, the acceptance of territorial sovereignty at the settlement of Westphalia brought to an end both imperial notions of authority and functionally defined claims to sovereignty, familiar from the "two-sword theory" of medieval times. By assigning mutually exclusive areas for the exercise of this supreme authority, the sovereigns thenceforth accepted only this form of political organization as legitimate. They also found thereby a convenient way of squaring their claims to supremacy with the mutual recognition of equality. Sovereignty thus created both the territorial state and the international system.

The template for such an arrangement was provided by the *dominium* (less often called *proprietas*) of a property holder under Roman private law. Not only could the owner of a piece of land exclude others, he could also use and convey his property freely. The restrictions on his privilege of use were few, and Roman law sharply curtailed the possibility for owners to agree on restrictions of use through private contract. Rather than unbundling the rights inherent in proprietas through the elaboration of various specific use-rights, anyone who held property jointly with others could petition for a *division*.[9] Furthermore, division was possible only along the horizontal axis, further inhibiting the possibility of the development of certain restriction on the exercise of property right. Thus, for instance, no title could be acquired for the second story of a house, or for "mineral rights" below the surface. The rule "ab inferis useaue ad coelum" prohibited such a construction of property titles.

The exclusionary character of the Roman institution of property has received proper attention in regard to its spatial exclusions because it was constitutive of the territorial order and the later treatment of the airspace and of sovereignty over resources.[10] The exclusion of challenges to exclusive "title" on the basis of alleged improper use of property, and the exclusion of challenges on the basis of conflicting use rights, seem to be equally important factors that have been neglected in the international relations literature. Certainly, even in Roman law there existed restrictions on the exercise of exclusive rights, such as the principle "sic utere tuo," which has recently become important in transborder pollution cases. Such restrictions, however, did not form part of the institution of property; rather, they were "background conditions" for the exercise of property rights.[11] In the same way, we nowadays would not consider the prohibition on running someone over with a car as a "restriction" on one's title to an automobile.

Nevertheless, one of the most important implications of conceptualizing sovereignty as an analogon to dominium is that the exercise of this right is no longer easily defeasible by moral considerations of right and wrong. The latter problem was the most important issue for medieval rulers, since their subjects were—at least theoretically—absolved from obedience in cases in which their lord violated moral precepts. Having a "right" conceived along the lines of Roman property rights simply entitled the holder of that right to "do the wrong thing" as long as he was within his territorially limited domain. In short, the boundaries of the right were no longer determined by "right use" but became dependent on the fundamental distinction between the public and private capacities of actors,[12] and by the mutual acceptance that acts of a sovereign in his public capacity are valid *prima facie* and are not "reviewable" by others. Consequently, the entitlement to exclusive possession could no longer be lost by reason of the objectionable exercise of proprietary rights, except those based on the institutionally explicit procedures providing for the acquisition or loss of title. This shift from the conception of a use right to that of an exclusive property right is well discussed in Grotius and Pufendorf, and I shall not elaborate in this paper.

There are, however, several important implications of this construction of dominium/sovereignty and international politics in general. First, property rights are neither absolute nor "natural." They are not absolute because, as mentioned above, their exercise is still governed by background conditions. Second, property rights are also defeasible by counterclaims such as eminent domain, adverse possession, or, in Grotius and Pufendorf, the "right of necessity."[13] Third, their full enjoyment may be curtailed by specific exceptions, such as the provisions in German or French law which in most cases allow individuals to leave only part of their property to whomever they choose, for the law provides for legal succession *(gesetzliche Erbfolge)*.

Fourth, property regimes can differ significantly according to the "things" owned. The distinction between articles of personal use and those of productive capacity, for example, is the basis for the socialist claim that productive resources should be owned collectively rather than privately.[14] Similarly, in the practice of states certain resources such as railroads, telecommunications facilities, and postal services were often collectively owned irrespective of whether the conditions of a "natural monopoly" actually prevailed.

Finally, rights to property are also not "natural" in the sense of existing before or outside the legal rules that constitute this institution. Even for their seventeenth-century proponents they are natural only insofar as they are part of social developments, which in the "providential histories" of Grotius and (to a lesser extent) Pufendorf become accounts of a process "whose initial steps were taken under the guidance of nature herself."[15] The present-day tendency to treat the "development" of property rights in terms of the pressures for efficient solutions to problems regarding the use of resources shows some important similarities with these highly speculative and largely justificatory histories. In the language of one commentator, "[P]roperty rights develop to internalize externalities when the gains of internalization become larger than the cost of internalization."[16]

Even though such constructions can usually amass a good deal of "confirming evidence" and thus have a certain persuasive force, the selective recording of historical data and the confirmationist bias of such constructs raise sufficient doubts to prevent their acceptance as either an adequate "theory" of institutional development or as its proper history. The main difference is that in our times, "efficiency" or the functionalist "demand for regimes" has taken over the role of God, Nature, or the Spirit.[17]

It may be true that there has been in the West, in both the common law and civil systems, the tendency to agglomerate in one legal person the exclusive right to possess, use, and convey the thing in question. Such an argument, however, is not helpful. It leaves out the countertrends toward restricting the enjoyment of property rights for purposes of protecting civil rights and the environment. It also does not help us very much in understanding the complexities that arise from the splitting and dividing of property rights without returning thereby to the old conception of use-right. If, analytically speaking, the concept of property involves the "system of rules governing the access to and control of . . . resources,"[18] then the naïve conception of property as a relationship between a thing and a person is no longer helpful for guiding our inquiry. The development of the institution of property only becomes understandable when we treat the "thing" in legal terms, namely, as legal interests in materials as well as incorporeal objects (*vide* copyrights!).[19]

Thus the ability to split the bundle of rights, which was contrary to the Roman practice of wholesale transfer or partition, has given rise to some of the most important manifestations of "property." Consider, for example, corporate ownership. In corporations the right to control is divorced from the right to manage, and from the right to receive an income from the activities of the firm. But since these rights are vested in different persons, it is difficult to locate the "owner." We are also not able to tell with confidence which of the rights is the most important, for such a judgment will depend largely on the purpose of our inquiry.

The analogies to the exercise of authority in international relations are intriguing. Thus it would be interesting to investigate whether the process of European integration can be understood as the development of a novel notion of authority. The process would be comparable to control of and access to intangible assets rather than a process in which sovereignty "moves" from national to supranational loci of "power." Aside from the limitations imposed by the spatial rather than legal representation of authority, the important point in the latter cases is that they denote legal relations that regulate a person's access to and control of resources without making him or her the owner (sovereign) in the sense of the Roman conception of dominium.

Similarly, if, as Allott suggests,[20] a revolution is taking place in the assignment of territorial rights, what implications does this unbundling of sovereign rights have for the question of exclusive dominium in a territorial order? Can a case be made for the compatibility of a right to intervention for humanitarian purposes and a notion of "sovereignty" that has changed in the same way our conception of property has?

A preliminary answer to these questions is possible only after the limits of the private law analogy have been explored and after a more detailed examination of the actual state practice has been presented, indicating to what extent indeed state behavior was institutionalized. It is the task of the next section to provide such an overview.

The Limitations of the Private Law Analogy
and the Issue of Intervention

Objections to the use of the private law analogy for explaining legal relations in international law are nearly as old as the discipline. They begin with Gentili and Montesquieu and find their strictest exponents in nineteenth-century jurisprudence, and they seem to be justified by the character of both the "persons" and the interest to be protected and regulated by the legal norms. Let us follow up on some of these arguments and see where some of their significant differences lie.

First, and most obviously, private actors could not and cannot under private law modify any part of the public order. It is, however, precisely the instrument of contract—particularly through the important lawmaking treaties—that establishes much of the order among sovereigns. Without wanting to deny the validity of this argument, the objection here is directed less to the analogy between property and sovereignty than to the certainly mistaken argument that sovereignty explains, or is constitutive of, international law in its entirety. Thus, far from invalidating the analogy, the first argument extends it to an area that is outside our present concerns in this paper.

Second, and more appropriately, Roman law did not allow for the protection of property rights against the state. Thus, though the law helped property owners to exclude others from their possessions, no remedy against interference with property rights by the public authority was possible. *Our* conception of "property," however, contains a strong component of rights against the state, so much so that the government, as an agency of the state, is seen, in Locke and others after him, as the protector of "natural" property rights.

Third, as indicated, modern property arrangements never strictly followed Roman conceptions but allowed for the unbundling of rights. Similarly, and quite contrary to the traditional notion of sovereignty as absolute, legal interference with sovereign rights, and even "abridgments" of them, have been quite common in state practice. A great deal of interference is created, for instance, by the attempts of states to extend their reach beyond their territorial boundaries by claiming the extraterritorial validity of their acts or laws. Examples of direct abridgment are the international "servitudes" and even the traditional imposition of "neutrality" on a state, divesting it of its right to contract alliances. But though the panoply of sovereign rights was thereby restricted, such abridgments were not considered to amount to a loss of sovereign status in the international game. Another classical restriction on sovereign powers concerned religious toleration.

Consider in this context the Westphalian settlement. Although in 1648 the "Cuius regio ejus religio" stipulation of the Treaty of Augsburg (1555) was adopted, the Treaty of Osnabrück made provisions for the religious toleration of minorities, which were not supposed to be deprived of rights by the settlement. Similarly, in order to secure "domestic tranquillity" within the empire the agreement hammered out at Osnabrück provided that the "one sovereign, one vote" rule would not be accepted in the German Diet in matters concerning religious freedoms. Rather, a "Calhounian" solution would prevail. Such questions were to be settled by an "amicable compromise between its two parts [corpora]," and the same arrangement was to hold true for the *Deputationstage*.[21]

Finally, classical international law knew a variety of arrangements, such as protectorates and spheres of influence, that were deliberately created as regimes allowing for the exercise of less than full sovereign powers.[22] To that extent, the sovereignty game has always been more complicated than the straightforward analogy to Roman private property suggests, notwithstanding its heuristic fruitfulness.

While the above-mentioned restrictions on the exercise of sovereign rights are imposed by explicit treaty obligations, it is also useful to inquire into the changing "background conditions" that substantially shaped the conditions of legitimate dominium. The spirit of the Enlightenment had an obvious influence in this respect. It dissolved the once-unquestioned "marriage of throne and altar" and of traditional legitimacy, and moved toward a rational-secular conception of domestic legitimacy. Rulers such as Frederick II of Prussia and Joseph II of Austria wanted to base their claim to dominium increasingly on a conception of service to the common good *(salus publica)* rather than on their feudal title to dominium. But this new conceptualization had two implications: it raised the issue of popular participation in the determination of public policy conceived as an exercise of sovereign rights, and it provided the decisive wedge to distinguish between the interest of the state (and later, of "the people") and that of the sovereign.

While the assertion of popular determination of policy led finally to the conception of popular sovereignty as the ultimate basis for legitimizing the exercise of power, it was the slow but perceptible decline of dynastic considerations during the eighteenth century that directed historical change. Quite contrary to the "state-building" literature following Hintze's or Tilly's argument for the functional imperatives driving the consolidation of states in an anarchical environment,[23] the prevailing order even in the eighteenth century was still largely dynastic. This explains why most of the decisive wars occurred when the succession to a legitimate dominium was contested. The War of the Spanish Succession, the War of the Austrian Succession, the War of the Bavarian Succession, and the problems resulting from the interminable dispute over the legitimate succession of the Polish crown (ending finally in the divisions of Poland) are all cases in point.

The point driven home by the wars of succession is not that "anarchy" (in the sense of the absence of any common norms or conceptions of legitimacy) prevailed, but rather that the dynastic property arrangements often led to the most bitter fights, quite similar to probate controversies among family members in the domestic arena. Historically there existed among "persons of sovereign authority" an awareness that territorial changes, and thereby the exercise of sovereign rights, were always dependent on some type of either traditional (dynastic) or collective legitimization.

Consider in this context the War of Spanish Succession. Although a variety of claims could be made to the Spanish crown on the basis of family relations, no unequivocal claim existed in the absence of a direct heir. Well aware of the consequences that a unification of the crowns of France and Spain would have for their own enjoyment of sovereign rights, most of the other European powers considered the question of the Spanish succession of utmost importance. In particular, they wanted to interfere with one possible conveyance: the nomination of Louis XIV's grandson as universal heir. In the treaty of 1693 between England, the States General, and France, a division of the property was proposed. The grandson of Louis was to receive Naples and Sicily, the second son of the emperor Charles was to receive Milan, and the lion's share was to go to the Bavarian Elector's son. When the Spanish king refused the division of his estate, the European powers were ready to recognize Joseph Ferdinand of Bavaria as a universal heir. However, war became inevitable when in a later testament the old Spanish king reversed himself and bequeathed all his possessions to Louis XIV's grandson, and when Louis XIV subsequently retracted his consent to the partition treaty. By asserting a property right of absolute conveyance the Spanish king had not only slighted various legitimate claims but also reversed an agreement upon which the recognition of his rights of conveyance depended.

It was only with the French Revolution that the competing principle of "popular sovereignty" fundamentally changed the background conditions for the exercise of sovereign rights. Despite the restoration at Vienna and the ominous Holy Alliance as an instrument of mutual assistance to rulers vis-à-vis their people, the Congress of Verona clearly indicated that a return to the dynastic politics of the *ancien régime* was no longer possible.[24] British reluctance to participate in the Metternichian plan to intervene in Spain on behalf of the overthrown sovereign led the way for the development of rules governing intervention by outsiders when "sovereignty" was contested. The rules governing aid to insurgents and belligerents were as much part of this effort as was the ascertainment of the precondition for recognition of a government: its ability to exercise effective authority over a people within a given territory.[25]

Although these rules were reasonably clear, their application to particular contexts became increasingly difficult. The formative influence of the "European Republic" declined, and simultaneously the notion of politics as balance and collective legitimization gave way to a conception of politics as a "struggle of the fittest." In such an atmosphere the self-interested application of norms became the standard rather than the exception. Thus Talleyrand's famous quip that "non-intervention is a metaphysical principle amounting to intervention" was now often not far off the mark. His comment was clearly not true of the Concert period—otherwise it would have lost its shock value as a witticism.

A further complication of the sovereignty game arose when, in addition to the principle of popular sovereignty, the right to *self-determination* became a competing principle for the exercise of sovereign authority. Part of this difficulty was that the original notion of "the people" had a reasonably clear meaning in its dialectical contrast to the government,[26] and in the context of universalistic conceptions of the rights of man and the rights of the citizen of a territorially bounded state. But self-determination implied that groups could make claims for political autonomy against "the people": their compatriots and fellow citizens.

Why self-determination seemed to Woodrow Wilson such a persuasive principle, one that solved both the internal legitimization problem of sovereignty and the issue of international order, is with the wisdom of hindsight difficult to fathom. Whatever the reason, it probably had less to do with Wilson's alleged idealism than with his lack of experience with the explosive force of ethnonationalism. Given that the concept of "we the people" in the U.S. Constitution was based on the myth of the "melting pot" and on the conscious rejection of old identities by most immigrants, self-determination could easily square the circle between individual rights, legitimacy, and the requirement of the international order for effective sovereign government.

However, ethnonationalism (rather than popular sovereignty) created the problem of minorities and their specific rights, which they do *not* share with all other citizens. It gives rise to irredentism and the dissolution of viable sovereign states, as the examples of Czechoslovakia in the interwar period and of contemporary Yugoslavia and the former Soviet Union show. Finally, in our time, reducing the issue of "self-determination" to a simple test of anticolonialism resulted neither in the viability of quasi-sovereign states nor in the legitimacy of their dominium, since both the "self" and the question of meaningful acts of "determination" often remain obscure. As Robert Jackson has pointed out,[27] the "self" becomes the former colony that "determines" its fate through inheriting "sovereignty" by way of the succession of states. It was precisely the recognition of the explosiveness of ethnonationalism that led Lord Acton to argue that territorial boundaries and ethnicity should not coincide.

The Issue of Intervention

How could we approach the problem of intervention from the perspective of the "sovereignty" game and its practices? While it would be unrealistic to expect this approach to resolve all of the complex issues, several points have been clarified, and three implications arise in this context.

First, intervention raises issues of justification, given that sovereignty provides a powerful prohibition. Contrary to some prevailing views that argue in favor of a moral point of view in assessing this question, the position outlined above suggests that, although moral considerations are not irrelevant to an appraisal, the relevance of such considerations is clearly bounded by the *institutional* constraints imposed by the notion of an exclusive right. This disposes of simple utilitarian justifications (intervention is justified when it is for the good of the greatest number) and the policy-oriented approaches à la McDougal. After all, it was one of the fundamental steps, in Grotius, to recognize that the question of "justice" becomes largely one of finding the various rights as soon as we move from a discourse of what *is* right, to one of *having* a right.

This argument has several corollaries. First, contrary to the view that a rights-based argument, as opposed to one based on considerations of justice, is legalistic, I suggest that "morality" itself is not a unified set of contradiction-free principles. Therefore, otherwise-unemployed philosophers cannot easily "apply" morality fresh from the shelf to concrete questions. Rather, many of the contradictions that appear in the legality-versus-morality debate are reproduced within the moral discourse itself in the debates between deontologically based and consequentialist approaches to morality.

Furthermore, due to the breakdown of an either ontologically or consensually conceived universal moral order, we have historically opted for a conception of "rights." Hence, competing considerations can normally enter the debate only via particular rule-based exemptions or exceptions, or as part of the never exhaustively specifiable "background" considerations imposing certain limits on the exercise of rights. Thus, intervention by invitation is an example of the former point, while the prohibition on using one's territory to undermine the territorial integrity of another state is an example of the latter. Attempts to construe ad hoc justification through the elaboration of an enormous "framework of appraisal" whose dominant value is "human dignity" are suspect on their own terms.[28] In McDougal's view, such assessments usually coincide with the U.S. position on virtually any issue, while some of the more radical world order proponents come to exactly the opposite conclusions.

Second, the "rights" to sovereign dominion—territorial integrity, autonomy, and noninterference—belong to the state qua participant in the international sovereignty game, rather than to the people who have delegated specific powers to the government. This conclusion follows neither from the "idealistic" premises of Hegel's *Sittlichkeit* nor from the realist perversion of conceiving of sovereignty as supreme (or even uncaused) will. It follows from the institutional analogy between property and sovereignty. As the rights of a corporation cannot be understood as a higher aggregation of those of the shareholders, so the rights of a state are not simply derivable from the rights of the citizens. The right to send and appoint ambassadors, or even the right to engage in acts of war, does not "belong" to the people but arises out of the institutional character of sovereignty. Rousseau's argument that people cannot be enemies but become so only as "soldiers," agents of the state, is apposite,[29] and it only confuses the issues when we try to think of the rights of states qua states as derived from those of individuals.

Before we object to such a conception of sovereign integrity as statist, or perhaps too grounded in the European tradition, we would do well to remember that it was precisely this argument that the U.S. Supreme Court made when it finally had to address the question of where "sovereignty" was located in the United States. The Founding Fathers had made a conscious decision not to address this issue, thus successfully avoiding both conceptual pitfalls and the allegedly dangerous consequences of leaving this question undecided and actually dividing sovereign powers among the branches of government. The question finally surfaced in the first half of this century. Since the Constitution itself was sovereign, how could the emergence of a sovereign power be conceptualized in regard to the rights that belonged to the United States qua state? Was sovereignty a "grant" from the people, or from the individual states? How was one to think about it? In phrasing the issue as a question of the "source" and transfer of this right, Justice Sutherland elaborated:

> As a result of the separation from Great Britain by the Colonies, the power of external sovereignty passed from the Crown not to the colonies *severally,* but to Colonies in their collective and corporate capacity as the United States of America. . . . The Union existed before the Constitution. . . . It results that the investment of the federal government with the powers of external sovereignty did not depend upon the affirmative grants of the Constitution. The powers to declare and wage war, to conclude peace, to make treaties, to maintain diplomatic relations with other sovereignties, if they had never been mentioned in the Constitution, would have vested in the federal government as necessary concomitants of nationality.[30]

To be oblivious to these distinctions invites problematic conclusions about the issues of intervention and nonintervention. Consider in this context the construction of a "liberation of Paris Principle," which Michael Levitin has invented since he is highly dissatisfied with what he considers a legalistic and useless approach for appraising actual interventions such as the ones in the Falklands and in Grenada. According to this principle, intervention is lawful "if the people throw flowers; if they do not throw flowers, or if they throw anything else, the invasion is unlawful."[31] This principle betokens considerable conceptual befuddlement. Not only does it leave out such minor questions as the existence of a state of war between the parties when Paris was liberated, but it also misses the point by jumping to the conclusion that violations of human rights justify intervention by an outside power. But neither of these conclusions follows.

Third, a "right" to intervention cannot be construed from the misuse of power by a government. This is because the violation of a right does not automatically vest a third person with either the duty or the right to correct the infraction. For such a situation to arise, very special circumstances have to exist. Furthermore, since by definition "intervention" involves "dictatorial interference" in a state's internal or external affairs, intervention usually implies the use of force. However, the use of force is limited not only by the nature of rights but even more so by the important special restrictions against the resort to force. Thus in the *Corfu Channel* case, the International Court of Justice (ICJ) held that the use of force is unlawful even in pursuit of rectifying the violation of a well-established right, thereby limiting "self-help" measures to peaceful means.[32] The prohibition of force, reiterated and emphasized recently in the Nicaragua case,[33] also makes short shrift of suggestions that activities directed against the "political independence" of a state have to be assessed prudentially rather than categorically.[34]

Does a right of intervention exist, and who would have such a right? Two "easy" cases come to mind. One is a case in which a right to intervention is based on the enforcement powers of the Security Council under Chapter VII of the UN Charter.[35] To that extent, the Charter clearly modified the sovereignty game of previous periods, and this modification is achieved through a multilateral treaty, although the competence of the Security Council vis-à-vis nonmembers transcends the authority conveyed by treaty. The other "easy" case could be construed on the basis of the "background conditions" of sovereignty and the system of self-help that characterizes the international legal order. Arguably there exists a residual right of states to protect their nationals under conditions of a general breakdown of law and order in a foreign country.

This residual right is narrowly circumscribed. Such intervention can be aimed only at the rescue of one's nationals, who must be clearly under the threat of mob violence while the foreign government is not able to protect them. In other words, actions cannot be aimed at the overthrow of the government or the takeover of governmental functions in the territory in question. If these criteria are met, the use of force is not in violation of Article 2(4), which provides that states shall refrain from force or threat of force when such force is "against the territorial integrity or political independence of any State," or "inconsistent with the purposes of the United Nations."

This classical position, which was first outlined by Waldock in 1952,[36] is reasonably clear as far as the applicable legal rules are concerned. While such rescue missions are obviously instruments of "self-help," I find it unnecessary to justify them by recourse to the *self-defense* exception under Article 51 of the Charter. As a matter of fact, the reference to self-defense is more likely to muddy the waters than to buttress the validity of what is quite inappropriately called a "humanitarian intervention." The legal basis of this self-help instrument is not a general authority on behalf of mankind but the limited right of the state to protect its citizens abroad. The latter is a well-established institution that also embraces diplomatic protection and the insistence on a "minimum standard" under international law. Here a moral justification—which becomes weightier the more generalized its claim is—stands in stark contrast to legal justifications that presuppose a special recognized interest in order to serve as the basis of a legitimate action. Both justifications are different from the self-defense exception of Article 51, which is based on the "inherent right" of self-defense.

To lump together missions such as the Entebbe raid and U.S. intervention in Grenada, or for that matter Argentina's dispatch of troops in the Falklands crisis, is problematic. With the exception of the Entebbe raid, none falls within the well-defined confines of the protection of nationals. In Grenada the threat to American nationals was hardly compelling, and the overthrow of the government made the characterization of this mission as "humanitarian intervention" inappropriate. In the case of the Falklands/ Malvinas war, Argentina tried to reassert a claim to sovereignty that, even if good some time ago, was certainly now of dubious quality, not to speak of the unwillingness of the local population to be incorporated into the Argentinian state.

In addition to these two universal and particularly well-established exceptions there exist various "hard" cases in which the appropriate standards are often difficult to ascertain. The most radical claims involve a universal entitlement of nations "to wage war to enforce human rights"—a claim espoused, for example, by the philosopher David Luban.[37] W. Michael Reisman put forward a similar thesis, arguing that the prohibition in Article 2(4) must be interpreted in the light of the fundamental postulate of twentieth-century legitimacy, the "enhancement of the ongoing right of peoples to determine their own political destinies."[38] Both arguments deserve some brief comments.

Although Luban claims that his thesis follows from "the cosmopolitan nature of human rights,"[39] brief reflection discloses that his claim is largely incompatible with the very notion of rights. So even if we are not bothered by the reduction of sovereign rights to the rights of the citizens, Luban's conclusions do not follow. When A sees that B's rights are being abridged by C, A has no prima facie right to take remedial steps. First and foremost, a violation of a right implies that the wronged person, not a third party, is entitled to seek redress. The systematic and persistent violation of human rights by a government gives rise to a right of resistance on the part of its people (Locke's famous appeal to heaven), but hardly to a general right of intervention by outsiders.

This is not to say that it is inconceivable that certain obligations to take measures might exist *in extremis*, analogous to the situation in which a person sees someone being beaten up by a mugger and attempts to help. But if such an obligation exists, it does not arise from A's rights or from B's rights. The reason for the confusion in this respect is the vacillation between what Grotius has analyzed as the two meanings of "right": the meaning seen in "it *is* right that," and the meaning seen in "having a right." The notion of "obligation" in the first sense is wider than that flowing from the notion of rights and duty in the second sense.[40] Furthermore, obligations derived from what is right often conflict with those resulting from "having rights." Part of the problem with the contemporary human rights debate—and with many of the human rights documents—is that there is a constant equivocation between these two conceptually quite distinct notions of "right." At the basis of Luban's argument, therefore, is some conception of a universalist order that is no "respecter of political boundaries" and that requires a "universalist politics to implement them. . . . Thus when murders, tortures, imprisonment go unchecked, more so when their perpetrators (the worst people in the world) are treated as if they are legitimate, the common humanity of all of us is stained."[41]

As obviously undesirable as is the persistence of such injustices, they are not particular to international orders but are very much part of any viable legal order. Thus the prohibition of torture, the injunction against compelling relatives to testify, the discarding of illegally obtained evidence, the principle of *in dubio pro reo*, the acceptance of jury verdicts even if they are abhorrent (as in the Rodney King case), the double jeopardy principle, and the like are all regulations that often shelter perpetrators of crimes and thus continue to stain the common humanity of all of us. Furthermore, human rights abuses might very well provide moral and legal reasons for withdrawing recognition from an illegitimate government or breaking off diplomatic relations with it, for terminating foreign aid or cooperative ventures, or even for aiding the opposition, as was done by the West in the case of Poland. But this is quite different from justifying a general right to intervention. Thus, we have to recognize that the basis for recommending a universal right to intervention is more the wrath and feeling of righteousness than the inherently limited and limiting notion of possessing "rights."

Reisman's claim is in many ways similar to Luban's argument, but Reisman is more aware of the limitations imposed by Article 2(4) of the Charter. For him, however, this article has to be interpreted in a context of "political expectation and a technological environment" that has been dramatically changed "since the end of the 19th century."[42] Not only does the classical rule of nonintervention assume "that the only threat of usurpation of the political independence of a people comes from external, overt invasion,"[43] but the reliance on Article 2(4) is also predicated upon a functioning United Nations, with the Security Council discharging its duties for the maintenance of peace. But since the latter has not become reality, Reisman argues, the situation in international politics resembles a Wild

West scenario in which a sheriff has announced that he will uphold law and order but his rule proves ineffective, forcing the people to revert again to self-help. Consequently, Article 2(4) is to be interpreted in terms of the "key postulate of political legitimacy in the 20th century. Each application of Art. 2(4) must enhance opportunities for *ongoing* self-determination [emphasis added]."[44]

Quite aside from the problematic reading of the historical record, there is something distinctly odd about the simplistic view that legal norms are simply the means to preferred worlds. Even if we accept the argument that the dichotomy between "legal" and "non-legal" norms cannot be equated with "obligatory" and "nonobligatory" prescriptions—both legality and obligatoriness might allow for further important gradations[45]—we still have to pay heed to the fact that part of the legality of norms is their firm guidance in the choice of means to a legitimate goal.[46]

Norms therefore do not fit the simple model of instrumental action. The widespread use of the death penalty might enhance deterrence and would certainly cut down on recidivism, thus enhancing the prospect of attaining a preferred world with less crime. However, norms against cruel and unusual punishment make such a maximizing choice illegitimate. Exceptions to a rule have to be based on similarly categorical norms rather than on mere considerations of efficiency in the pursuit of a desired end.

Finally, the example of self-help which Reisman gives refutes his own argument. Though the use of force in defense of one's own right might be a defensible position in the absence of an effective sheriff, concluding from the legitimacy of self-defense that the resort to force is also legitimate for a third party is patently illicit.

Thus, who has a "right" to intervene in cases of gross violations of human rights? It would seem that such a step would be justifiable only via specific stipulations circumscribing sovereignty in general, or via the background conditions that in general limit our exercise of rights. As has already been argued, the ample, but still narrowly defined, powers of the Security Council provide such a basis, and here Resolution 688 could chart new courses for action, provided that it does not remain an exception but inspires future practice. Whether a further general or particular right to intervention can be based on the changing background conditions is, however, highly problematic. If used, such a justification, de *lege ferenda*, would have to satisfy the following criteria in order to create new international custom.

First, the exercise of sovereignty would have to violate clear international obligations. The abridgment of "human rights" by the rigging of elections and even by repressive policies would not be sufficient to justify intervention, but clear genocidal activities would be. Arguments that consider illegitimate only those acts of force that are directed against the purposes of the United Nations, while asserting that the protection of human rights is one of the world organization's legitimate "purposes,"[47] are hardly convincing, given the other explicit prescriptions against the unilateral use of force. One also is hard pressed to argue that state practice gives any indication that such a construal of exceptions to Article 2(4) demonstrates an evolution of the sovereignty game in this direction.[48] It is a sad but significant fact that in the debate concerning Vietnam's intervention in Cambodia "not a single state spoke in favor of the existence of a right of humanitarian intervention."[49] Thus, while proponents of a right to humanitarian intervention can amass a great deal of evidence for their case from scholarly writings, state practice, in the legally relevant sense, does not seem to bear out their contention.

Second, as in the case of self-defense, the situation would have to be a compelling crisis, leaving either "no other choice or moment of deliberation,"[50] or occurring after the futility of alternative means of stopping these genocidal practices has been convincingly demonstrated. Many of the instances relied on by proponents of a right of humanitarian intervention seem to satisfy this criterion, at least in a prima facie fashion.[51] But again, examples from the pre–United Nations era are not by themselves compelling. What would be more persuasive is whether, in the investigation of contemporary state practice, it is found that states have increasingly tolerated unauthorized incursions into, and use of, their territory by nongovernmental organizations engaged in humanitarian pursuits. These practices could change the sovereignty game more than the alleged "right" to intervention could. They are also more likely to alleviate the problems that humanitarian intervention is supposed to solve. Furthermore, the historical examples do suggest that for an intervention to be legitimate, and not simply an action *paeter legem*, a third criterion has to be met.

This third requirement concerns some form of collective legitimization. This criterion follows neither from the "vogue of collectivism in international relations" against which Inis L. Claude has correctly warned us,[52] nor from prudential considerations, which suggest that restraint is more likely when one has to persuade others than when one can rely exclusively on a self-justifying interpretation of both the facts and the applicable norms. Rather, such a criterion seems to be required by the institutional logic of all rights, and thus, even of sovereignty. Even if the international system is only a "negative community," the exercise of sovereign rights is dependent upon mutual recognition, which serves as the background condition of its exercise. But for all the reasons given above, such a position is quite distinct from either the act-utilitarian justification of interventions or the rule-utilitarian advocacy of a right of intervention.

Conclusion

In this paper I have investigated the issue of sovereignty by providing both a historical sketch and a critical examination of sovereignty's justificatory function. Such an approach suggested itself because the generative logic of "sovereignty" prohibits intervention. This often contributes to the perpetuation of illegitimate regimes and of human rights violations. Consequently, many modern writers have argued that a right to "humanitarian intervention" exists. In assessing these conflicting claims, my argument took the following steps. First, I attempted to rescue the concept of sovereignty from some of its most egregious conceptual derailments. The identification of sovereignty with a supreme "will" and with authority "above" the law had to be discussed. By showing that the puzzles that arise in this context are the result of a category mistake (identifying validity with ultimate cause), I prepared the ground for a better understanding of "sovereignty" and its institutional character.

In the second section of this paper I investigated the analogies between sovereignty and property. Such an analogy was not introduced simply for heuristic purposes. The analogy is also justified by practice, since the historical roots of the institution of sovereignty are in the conception of exclusive property rights under Roman private law. The discussion then proceeded on two levels. One was the elaboration of the concept of property, paralleled by a discussion of the historical development of sovereignty— from the absolutism of dynastic sovereigns, to popular sovereignty and self-determination. The other examined the similarities and differences of these institutions, since only an analogy, not an identity of these institutions was claimed.

In the fifth section I returned to the issue of intervention and argued that this problem cannot be analyzed by simply taking into account the changing bases of legitimacy for the exercise of public authority. In particular, I objected to a conceptualization of sovereign rights as derivative of, or as simple delegations of, individual rights. In addition, I argued that questions of intervention necessitate a careful examination of the injunctions against the resort to force that are contained in the UN Charter. On the basis of an examination of these issues and of recent state practice, I came to the conclusion that no "right" of intervention for humanitarian purposes exists, except when such interventions are based on the institution of the protection of nationals, or on the measures taken under Chapter VII of the Charter. Finally, on the basis of the institutional logic of sovereignty, I suggested certain minimum criteria for a right to intervention that might develop *de lege ferenda*.

Chapter Three

Intervention for the Common Good

NICHOLAS ONUF

For centuries, the territorial sovereignty of nation-states has been a central, indeed a constitutive, feature of the modern world.[1] Complementing territorial sovereignty is Kantian faith in the moral autonomy of individual human beings, as manifest in their practical ability to act, by themselves and in concert, for ends they have chosen.[2]

Made for each other, the sovereign state and the autonomous individual decisively contribute to making the world what it is—and to making it seem naturally, inevitably so.[3] Sovereignty, like autonomy, implies freedom from the interference of others. "Since Nations are free and independent of each other as men are by nature," Vattel proclaimed in 1758, it is a "general law of their society that each Nation should be left to the Peaceful enjoyment of that liberty which belongs to it by nature."[4]

Nonintervention is Vattel's second general law. "The first general law, which is to be found in the very end of the society of nations, is that each Nation should contribute as far as it can to the happiness and advancement of other Nations."[5] By implication, Vattel's first general law expresses a positive duty of mutual aid, limited only by duties to one's own people, and not by the possibility that such assistance may be construed as intervention. Vattel's two general laws suggest an enduring tension in modern society, including international relations. In a purely liberal world, sovereignty entails nonintervention; the republican legacy of concern for the common good affirms the propriety of intervention inspired by larger motivations than the intervener's immediate advantage.

For more than a century liberal societies have struggled to define the conditions under which governments may intervene in people's affairs, for

43

the common good and at cost to individual sovereignty. In 1848 John Stuart Mill framed the issues by reference to "agency," as I do below.[6] Public discussion and political theory have since played their part in large changes. Comparatively little is said of the conditions under which intervention across states' frontiers is admissible and of the cost to state sovereignty. Until recently, little has changed.[7]

Dramatic events during the last few years suggest the possibility that epochal change is at hand. These and many other events have forced at least some observers to reconsider the concept of sovereignty and to reevaluate the conditions under which they believe international intervention to be admissible. What has changed most clearly is the identity of the interveners and their targets. No longer does it suffice to say that states' governments individually or collectively engage in acts of admissible or inadmissible intervention, and that these acts are directed against the governments of other states.

Interveners and their targets need not be states' governments, and increasingly are not, even though international intervention always, by definition, affects states' territorial space. Instead, interveners and targets can only be identified by reference to claims about the common good. Interveners claim to act on behalf of the common good, their targets being those who are claimed to have acted against the common good. There is nothing new about such claims, typically made in the name of humanity.[8] What is new is this: governments once were solely responsible for the common good; now they share this responsibility, and all sorts and degrees of affiliation, with other institutions operating within and across state frontiers.

That governments are no longer the only interveners identified with the common good challenges sovereignty conventionally understood as an exclusive and defining property of states. This chapter seeks to relate changes in the identity of interveners and their targets to sovereignty understood more generally as a constitutive feature of a changing world. It does so by the application of a conceptual system that I have developed elsewhere. I call this general system of definitions, conceptual categories, and propositions "constructivism."[9] Its unfamiliarity necessitates a brief recapitulation.

Deeds and Rules

Constructivism holds that individuals and societies make, construct, or constitute each other (I use these verbs interchangeably). Individuals make societies through their deeds, and societies constitute individuals, as they understand themselves and each other, through those same deeds. Some of these deeds are deliberate attempts to make, or make over, society; most are not.[10] Most deeds are responses to individuals' understandings of the choices society presents to them—choices produced by others' deeds undertaken in response to choices those others understand to be available to themselves. The co-constitution of individuals and societies has no beginning or end. From the point of view of any given individual, society is already there; from the point of view of society, at least as imagined by social contract theorists, individuals must come first. From a vantage point external to both, neither individuals nor society can have come first, for neither can be said to exist without the other.

Deeds are responses to and constituents of the circumstances in which people find themselves. People use language both to represent their deeds and in many (perhaps most) instances to perform them. Deeds performed through speech are events, real enough but elusive; they escape methodological attention unless accompanied by further deeds—deeds recording, clarifying, affirming, qualifying, or repudiating earlier deeds. Thus compounded, deeds constitute rules, which demand attention both performatively and methodologically.

A rule is a prescriptive statement applicable to some class of actions. The rule indicates whether those who perform these actions are warranted in doing so.[11] From an individual's point of view, rules constitute the conditions of choice and present opportunities for evaluating costs and consequences of alternative courses of action. From the point of view we impute to society, if only figuratively, rules regulate individuals' conduct. That conduct affects the status and content of particular rules, which is to say, it (re)constitutes them. Thus, deeds (re)constitute society through the necessary medium of rules. In shorthand, rules—all rules, at all times—simultaneously perform regulative and constitutive functions.

In contemporary scholarship, the "theory of structuration" associated most notably with Anthony Giddens closely parallels the position sketched here, and markedly influenced its development.[12] Giddens developed his position by using the term *agent* interchangeably with the terms *actor* and *structure*. Agents are always human and thus able to reflect on their acts, while structures are "virtual"—they exist only as "instantiations" in the flow of action and "as memory traces orienting the conduct of knowledgeable human agents."[13] Such a formulation gives primacy to agents. Giddens also noted that structures are "isolable sets of rules and resources."[14] Resources are functionally comparable to faculties; they give structures substance and permanence in the same way that faculties make human beings knowledgeable agents.

If resources help to offset the emphasis on agents, associating rules with resources only confuses the issue. Resources exist as such only because rules relate material conditions to social purpose, just as faculties are latent capabilities until rules harness them to social effect. Rules exist in the form of resources *and* memory traces. By making human beings into agents and material conditions into resources, rules link agents to structures, without either reducing to the other, or rules reducing to either.

Giddens acknowledged the centrality of rules for "the continuity or transmutation of structures, and therefore the reproduction of social systems"— this is "structuration"[15]—but failed to see their equal importance for the constitution of agents and the reproduction of their memories, faculties, and artifacts. In other words, Giddens's conception of the individual's relation to society leaves culture out of the equation, even as it favors the individual over society. Rules link agents and structure in a common process of constitution, but only if rules have an independent status appropriate to their dual function. Giddens accorded rules no such status because he saw them as a property of structure—and not even a material property.

Rules have properties of their own, as Giddens intimated when he related rules to linguistic practice.[16] Language gives rules an autonomous character suited to their function; through language, rules exist in their own right.[17] Furthermore, people need rules for all but their most transient exchanges. When they confront the necessity of dealing with each other without knowing if they follow the same rules, they learn what they commonly know and make what other rules they need. In other words, competence with rules is a defining feature of human cognition, and the presence of rules is a defining feature of the human condition.[18] Rules vary in degree of generality, formality, and support; none of these attributes entails the others. Informal rules may be strongly supported and rarely broken, and we tend to call the individuals for whom this is so a community, especially when the rules are quite specific in content and the individuals to whom they apply are few in number. Formal rules are frequently described as legal, especially when they are general in application and well supported. Some writers (I among them) hold that legality itself is a matter of degree; others take legality to be a formal threshold condition, specified at its most stringent to require the support of other formal, well-supported rules called sanctions.[19]

A society also consists of rules and related practices. Unlike a community or a regime of laws, a society is not defined by the degree of generality, formality, and support characterizing its rules. Instead, a society must have a rule, or set of rules, typically quite formal and well supported, stipulating the conditions of agency for that society. Membership in the society is only the most general of these conditions.[20]

Agency, Intervention, and Sovereignty

According to Giddens, *agency* refers to action understood not as "a series of discrete acts" but as a "stream of actual or contemplated causal interventions of corporeal beings in the ongoing process of events-in-the-world."[21] In this broad sense, agents are individuals whose acts materially affect the world. Yet not all individuals can intervene in particular world-making processes, or can do so even generally. Like material limitations, the rules constituting a society define the conditions under which individuals may intervene in the (social) world thus constituted.

As agent, any individual intervenes in the world—and thereupon exercises sovereignty—by responding to choices, prominently including choices offered by rules (and choices of the latter sort are always "a series of discrete acts"). If an individual is not in a position to make such choices, someone else is sovereign for the range of events covered by the rules in question. Obviously, no one is ever sovereign for all possible situations of choice. In many instances in which individuals are not in a position to make choices individually, they do so collectively. Individually or collectively they may choose someone else, an agent, to act on their behalf. If they are in a position to regain agency for themselves or to change agents, they exercise sovereignty when they do so. When their agents make choices on their behalf, the agents are sovereign. Sovereignty is relative to the rules framing relevant courses of action.

The sovereign state is a regime of laws; it is composed of individuals who have assigned agency to the state for a broad range of activities, including dealings with other states. States have rules reassigning responsibility for particular activities to agents collectively known as governments. Within a state's territorial limits, governments monopolize agency for assigned activities. Beyond those limits, other governments enjoy similar monopolies. When governments engage in activities affecting each other, they simultaneously exercise sovereignty on behalf of their states and experience intervention by virtue of the other government's exercise of sovereignty.

By dealing only with each other, governments monopolize agency for the aggregate of themselves. In so doing they constitute themselves as sovereign members of international society. By dealing with each other at all they give as they get: to act like sovereigns they give up sovereignty; to be able to intervene they open themselves to intervention. This situation is perplexing conceptually, but it is tolerable in practice because rules extensively regulate many of the interventionary activities we more neutrally call international relations and preserve a semblance of sovereignty for all states. However paradoxical the concept of state sovereignty may seem, it has stood "essentially uncontested" for two centuries or more.[22] As a highly general, formal, and well-supported rule, the principle of state sovereignty depends on conceptual stability that originally took two centuries to achieve. The concept of state sovereignty now appears to be losing its coherence, and the principle its constitutive force. Also changing are the rules concerning the admissibility of intervention.

Conceptual changes are neither simple causes nor effects. They are signs of large, complex processes of change that may, or may not, take on epochal proportions. Retrospectively, the emergence of state sovereignty as a stable concept and a constitutive principle represents an epochal change: the onset of modernity. Whether current conceptual instability represents a comparable change to a postmodern world remains to be seen. Nevertheless, a sketch of the process of conceptual change in its barest outlines—from the concept's antecedents, through its long ascendancy, to its current circumstances—can help to make sense of what otherwise may seem to be unrelated, even random, changes in rules.[23]

The modern concept of sovereignty arose from the fusion of three conceptual antecedents, each couched in a distinctive political idiom. First, in the idiom of classical republicanism, is *majestas*, not as the description of an individual but as the measure of an institution. In the degree to which the formality or dignity of an institution inspires respect, that institution possesses majesty. Even if majesty is overwhelmingly concentrated in a single institution such as the crown, it is infinitely divisible and never to be possessed absolutely. The distribution of majesty, usually skewed, reflects the operation of a rule recognizing positions in a status system. Second, in the idiom of empire, is *potestas imperiandi*, the competence to rule. Unlike majesty, the competence to rule is an exclusive grant of agency. Its measure is the territory within which some*one* rules alone or by delegation. Third, in the idiom of radical Protestantism, is a concept akin to stewardship. Rulers act on behalf of and at the sufferance of others, the people, who are ultimately sovereign. Competence to rule is thus an exclusive but provisional grant, which may be withdrawn if agents fail in their duties to others.

The principle of sovereignty distributes majesty formally and equally among states. It is permissive with respect to the internal distribution of majesty, and by locating the competence to rule within states it assures the concentration of majesty in governments acting simultaneously and indistinguishably in the name of the state and the people. Furthermore, the sovereign state has been well served by the rise of the autonomous individual and the language of rights and duties. Extended by analogy to the state in its relation to other states, rights and duties give states the appearance of living beings. As an object of awe, the sovereign state is not simply like a living person; to most people it is larger than life.

With the fusion of sovereignty's several elements the state came into its own as a majestic idea: a bounded territory within which competent officers rule for the people as a whole, and an international actor.[24] The modern concept of sovereignty links a bounded territory and the people taken as a whole, but does not link the people directly to each other. Instead, the land and the people are each linked to those agents empowered to act at home and abroad in the name of the state. In principle the state is the land, its people, and a regime of laws. In practice the state is indistinguishable from the agents authorized to act for the state, and respect invested in the state as sovereign falls to its chief agents. They give life to the state even as they become larger than life themselves.

I repeat some earlier assertions. Sovereignty entails the right of states to be free from interference. Sovereignty also confers on a state's agents the right to act on behalf of the state and implies acceptance of that right for agents of other states. In the instance of acts whose effects are narrowly confined to one state, that state's agents exercise sovereignty without affecting the sovereignty of other states. In instances where an agent's act has any effect, intended or otherwise, on other states, the result is necessarily interference incompatible with the sovereignty of those states. In a world with many sovereign states, sovereignty makes intervention unavoidable and its regulation both necessary and resisted.

In the circumstance, the most important rule for the regulation of intervention is informal and permissive. It instructs governments not to consider as interventionary whole categories of acts initiated beyond state borders. One category contains all those acts not attributable to or subject to the control of other governments. A second category contains the many acts between governments that are routine, reciprocal, and subject to innumerable, quite specific rules. The bulk of international relations fits this description. A third category contains acts that depend on special arrangement, invitation, or unexpected contingencies. Less numerous than acts

falling into the second category, these acts—for example, trade concessions, technical assistance, good offices, military support, or emergency
relief—are widely held to be the antithesis of intervention insofar as they
materially strengthen the receiving state.[25]

What remains is but a minuscule fraction of the acts that have effects
across state frontiers. Whether these remaining acts are interventionary
can be determined only by reference to still other rules. If acts are hostile in
intention and substantial in scale—enough to affect a state's "territorial
integrity and political independence," and thus its sovereignty—they are
proscribed. Typically such acts are forcible, and the relevant rule proscrib-
ing the use of force is Article 2(4) of the United Nations Charter, the text of
which provides the formulation just quoted.[26]

Article 2 of the Charter states a number of principles to which the
United Nations and its members are committed. Except for Article 2(7),
which instructs the organization not to intervene in members' domestic
affairs, the Charter says nothing of intervention. When in the 1960s the
General Assembly considered the absence of a Charter rule on intervention
in the relations of states, Western delegates argued that Article 2(4) already
established limits on admissible intervention and that any effort to identify the forms of inadmissible intervention would founder over questions
of intention.[27] The majority preferred to list the better-known forms of
intervention. In 1965 the General Assembly overwhelmingly adopted such
a list in a brief declaratory statement.[28] Soon thereafter, the General Assembly included the principle of nonintervention, and much of the language of its 1965 declaration, in a notable affirmation of seven "Principles
of Friendly Relations and Cooperation among States."[29]

Formally related to such principles as sovereignty, self-determination,
and the non-use of force, a general rule instructs states not to engage in
intervention but provides governments with only modest assistance in
determining which of their acts are inadmissible. In 1981 the General Assembly sought to provide such assistance in a more detailed declaration,
which many Western members refused to endorse.[30] Its constitutive impact is negligible. Instead, governments follow an informal rule inviting
them to weigh intentions, scale, methods, and targets in deciding whether
particular acts are admissible.[31]

The Charter is relevant to such deliberations less through Article 2 or
declarations of the General Assembly than through the list of the purposes of
the United Nations in Article 1. The first purpose is to maintain international peace and security. Though other provisions of the Charter em-
power the Security Council to intervene, massively and forcibly if neces-

sary, against members and nonmembers alike, to achieve this end, for decades the Security Council was unable to agree on such measures. The organization's other purposes are exceedingly general, even vague: to develop friendly relations among states, achieve cooperation in economic, social, cultural, and humanitarian matters, and orchestrate the attainment of goals shared by states. The Charter variously empowers UN organs to act on these goals, but hardly in the degree necessary to assure their fulfillment.

Given the Security Council's frequent inability to act even when its mandate under the Charter is clear, one might expect to hear calls for institutional innovation and an expansive interpretation of the organization's powers. In the 1960s some members moved in this direction but soon reversed themselves.[32] A number of writers have taken up a more radical form of the same argument. They presume that the organization's several purposes justify collective intervention against members egregiously thwarting common ends. If the organization is incapable of acting, then by implication members are collectively empowered to do so on its behalf.[33]

Imputing implied powers to the United Nations may contribute to the common good at cost to state sovereignty. Imputing those same powers to groups of states, acting at their own instance on the organization's behalf, may bring even greater good. Or it may invite abuse. During the cold war, symmetrically disposed superpower governments maintained spheres of influence through interventionary policies justified by reference to the common good as defined by themselves and as affirmed by international organizations under their control. The stability of these arrangements yielded informal, well-supported rules directing lesser powers within each superpower's sphere to comply with the superpower's wishes or risk intervention.[34] With the recent disappearance of one of the two superpowers and thus of spheres reciprocally necessitating each other, these rules have also disappeared.

Agency, Intervention, and the Common Good

The cold war has come to an end; and so, perhaps, has the long period of sovereignty's conceptual stability. In a time of rapid and extensive change, the elements so successfully and powerfully fused in the concept of sovereignty have come increasingly under stresses peculiar to each element. In the instance of majesty, nineteenth-century nationalism fostered an identity between state and nation, with the state both champion and beneficiary of popular commitment to the national idea. In our own time nationalism tends to promote a contrary sensibility. The well-formed nation-state is a rarity. When states and nations fail to coincide, popular opinion favors the nation with a measure of majesty no longer available to the state. Increasingly the nation as people, not land, delimits the span of rule.[35] At the same time, personality cults, ceremonial diplomacy, and constant media attention effectively shift additional increments of majesty from states to their globally institutionalized leadership.

As majesty diffuses, governments begin to lose their monopoly on agency and thus their identity as the only admissible interveners for the common good. National self-determination increasingly refers to actions taken against states that themselves achieved independence in consequence of self-determination.[36] Until recently, governments were free to invite intervention by outsiders (e.g., other governments, mercenaries) to assist in the suppression of rebellious nations within the state's borders. Rebels were not.[37] Changes now under way support the emergence of rules entitling agents of rebellious nations to external assistance in prosecuting wars of national liberation that are certified as such by international organizations, and enjoining assistance to the suppressing government. These rules would seem to involve a complex relation between the scale of hostilities and the amount and source of assistance. As the rebellion grows, assistance to the rebels is easier to justify: success legitimates the rebels' cause. If governments act collectively and, even more, do so through an international organization, higher levels of assistance are admissible than would otherwise be the case: collective judgment confirms the legitimacy of the cause.[38]

An enhanced role for international organizations follows more generally from the diffusion of majesty. The end of the superpower stalemate has already contributed to the revitalization of the United Nations. After the Iraqi invasion of Kuwait in 1990, the Security Council authorized collective intervention by UN members to restore Kuwait's sovereignty and to restore peace to the region.[39] On what powers the Security Council based its action, and how those powers are interpreted, are matters of some controversy.[40] As the organization gains in majesty, governments are likely to join progressive writers in an expansive interpretation of the organization's powers, the better to fulfill all of its purposes and not just the maintenance of international peace and security. Already, rules allowing intervention under UN auspices to curb human rights abuses and promote peaceful regime change within states are making their appearance.[41] Many other international organizations also benefit from both the diffusion of majesty and the acknowledgment that larger purpose supervenes state sovereignty and permits some measure of intervention in members' affairs.

The diffusion of majesty has even enabled private organizations to break the monopoly of agency held by governments and extended to international organizations. The respect accorded to human rights groups such as Amnesty International, coupled with the manifest inability of international organizations to deal with the bulk of human rights abuses, has prompted a rule allowing these groups to undertake a wide range of acts, including fact finding, publicity, and communication with governments and international organizations. Similar developments may be anticipated in other areas of heightened concern, such as environmental degradation and the dispersion of extremely dangerous weapons. All such rules allow intervention against governments by agents other than governments, but they do not specify the conditions of agency in any detail. At best we may infer rules of thumb (informal, contextually dependent rules) regulating the level and the form of acts generally consistent with high principles, whoever undertakes them.

The decline in the state's majesty exposes another development that has long been under way. Governments have dramatically increased in size and internal differentiation as they have acquired an ever-widening range of responsibilities calling for intervention in the affairs of ostensibly sovereign men and women. Enormous administrative apparatuses function in the name of the state, but on behalf of particular constituencies to which they are tied through elaborate sets of rules. As functional bureaucracies and functionally segmented publics have become more closely tied, the government and the public in general and the government's many parts have become less so. In due course one may speak of government, or the public, only euphemistically, as multiple, functionally oriented regimes redefine the public good piece by piece, denominate their own publics, and dominate public life. Together they constitute a regime sovereign unto itself, Michel Foucault's "régime of truth."[42]

Functional growth within states appears to strengthen rather than challenge the state, because the state tends to be credited with functional successes, and governments tend to be blamed for failures—failures to provide functionally defined goods and services, to coordinate and rationalize the range of functional activities, or to prevent the loss of personal sovereignty as separate, specialized interventions add up. While states prosper as territorial configurations, the boundaries among them become increasingly nominal because they are only territorial. Functional concerns bring agents located within the territories of different states into frequent contact. Institutional arrangements proliferate. The larger good warrants intervention not against governments, but in their place.

The coordination of economic policy for the seven largest market-oriented industrial societies (the G-7 nations) illustrates these developments.[43] Informal rules have emerged for the coordination of policy not merely through negotiation and agreement, but "by giving each government partial control over other governments' policy instruments."[44] The most important such instrument is intervention in foreign exchange markets. Finance ministers and central bankers routinely buy and sell currencies through varied arrangements reflecting degrees of autonomy for central banks. Despite consequences that other governments may not welcome, no one seems to find the term *intervention* embarrassing, for these acts are domestically executed for the good of society. Nevertheless, turbulence in the world economy threatens the good of all societies, prompting summit meetings and providing finance ministers and central bankers an opportunity to meet regularly. Their immediate subordinates also meet. Both groups evaluate economic conditions and adopt "confidential understandings" on "concerted intervention."[45] The International Monetary Fund provides staff support for "surveillance," as do ministries and central banks.[46] Governments conduct interventions according to established procedure, as if relevant policies were wholly their own.

As yet, rules for coordinating economic policies are weakly institutionalized. The political salience of these policies, difficulties in evaluation and projection, and the complexity of arrangements within governments all point to the transiency of support for these rules. They may degenerate into a series of occasional, ad hoc agreements negotiated in response to the exigencies of the moment. Or governments may acknowledge public concerns and pressure from within the ranks, and consent to further institutionalization along functional lines, thereby taking advantage of the professional standards and technical skills already found within governments and international organizations. In the latter event, a functional regime will find its place, behind the scenes, with a host of other regimes marked by functional conceptions of the common good.

No functional imperative, or logic of spill-over, should be assumed. Competence to rule remains territorially organized for some purposes, such as public security and tax collection, although it is functionally organized and transnational in scope for many other purposes. The coordination of economic policy falls somewhere in the middle. Functional growth within and beyond states is a prominent and long-developing feature of social relations in the global economy. It is likely to continue, not ineluctably, but incidentally, in response to material conditions and a vast complex of human activities.

Wherever found, functional growth entails a redefinition of the competence to rule. This consequence of long-term functional growth has become clear only because of the more recent trend toward the diffusion of majesty. When states and thus governments held the lion's share of majesty, few noticed that functional divisions in the competence to rule had progressively displaced the delegation of that competence. The "welfare state" has become an anachronism, the term an oxymoron. Agency has come to be defined in welfarist terms, at cost to governments' monopoly over agency. Public service is a generalized ideal for technically proficient personnel, whoever employs them, as they provide particular services to those that need them.

In this context, intervention is activity oriented to problem solving. So Leonard W. Doob, a social psychologist with a longstanding interest in international relations, has claimed in a particularly revealing book.[47] Doob defined this kind of activity inclusively, as ranging from the efforts of a good Samaritan to large-scale military invasion. Written largely from the intervener's point of view, Doob's book reads like an operator's manual. It provides guidelines that, if followed, would increase the likelihood that any given intervention would be effective in solving a problem. There is no presumption against intervention, notwithstanding individual autonomy and state sovereignty. Indeed, the last of Doob's "ten commandments" expressly disapproves of "nonintervention when interventions are feasible and desirable."[48]

Despite Doob's inclusive definition of intervention, he directed most of his attention to professional problem-solvers. Heading the list (symptomatically, one might say) are therapists—"psychiatrists, psychologists, physicians, social workers, clergymen, cult leaders"—followed by public authorities, diplomats, both official and self-appointed, and umpires.[49] The model for most therapy is clinical practice, the origin and diffusion of which Michel Foucault so memorably described.[50] Doob took the clinical model for granted. "Interventions follow a procedure that seeks to facilitate a solution to the problem or to reduce the conflict at hand. Patients must allow their bodies to be examined and must reply to the questions of the physician who is making the diagnosis."[51]

Like clinicians who intervene in cases of functional pathology, each an agent for the occasion, functional experts working for a variety of international organizations, government agencies, academies, and private voluntary organizations intervene where they are needed. They are invited to do so by other experts, or by presumed beneficiaries acting on the advice of experts. When intervention is resisted, experts may threaten to withdraw

welfare already extended or invoke technical and administrative rules to
the disadvantage of the reluctant party.

The recipients of functional assistance are needy people, local organizations, and governments. Even states benefit from making successful interventions, in that they gain respect for increased welfare and governmental
competence. The appearance of intervention increases, however, if the recipient is reluctant and has some claim to agency. A notorious example is
International Monetary Fund (IMF) conditionality.[52] Because in order to
receive IMF loans governments must accept conditions decided by agents
of the IMF, incensed governments and publics consider the process interventionary on its face. But because these conditions are integral to a formal
agreement, and thus are a matter of consent, however grudging, no agent
can claim that they are inadmissibly interventionary.

To generalize, the activities of functionally competent agents are per-
vasively interventionary, but they are admissibly interventionary as long as
they are consistent with rules specifying appropriate targets, forms, and
grounds for such activities. Functional regimes also have rules defining
conditions of agency, and all such rules reflect an overriding concern with
public service and technical expertise. For functionally circumscribed areas,
professional competence converges with the competence to rule. By training and circumstance, technical experts are disinclined to call attention to
themselves. Taking more responsibility than credit for the common good,
they assume the republican mantle unawares and leave the state a tattered
figleaf of majesty.

Progressive redefinition of the competence to rule and its relation to the
common good has blurred the line between the public and private spheres
of life. As the former absorbs the latter, public activities take on properties
of private activities. They are little noticed and are subject to regulation
through a panoply of petty rules, many of them informal. Agents work for a
variety of organizations, some governmental, some affiliated with governments more or less loosely, and others fully autonomous. Personnel circu-
late among these organizations freely, with no significant change in duties
and little incentive to identify with any one organization. Instead, they
internalize the functional mission of all such organizations and identify
with each other on professional or disciplinary grounds.

There is a second trend to be seen in the changing relation of the public
and private spheres. In part a reaction to the effects of functional growth, it
represents a more radical assault on the state than does the first trend.
Activities once reserved for the state are sometimes, quite conspicuously,
being organized against the state, presumably for the common good. Agency

is privatized. Public security provides a critical instance of this situation, and terrorism a most visible manifestation.

By discrediting a government's security apparatus, terrorists hope to undercut public respect for the state. Although this kind of activity is allegedly private, governments of other states find occasion to sponsor it. Terrorism also frequently slips into brigandage, thereby losing any connection with the common good. Because terrorism is typically clandestine, episodic, and media-oriented, it benefits from "outlaw" romanticization but rarely fosters the emergence of rules changing governmental powers. Often terrorists provoke state agents into symmetrically privatized responses, at greater cost to the state's majesty than terrorism can exact by itself.

Conceivably, the privatization of agency could induce the collapse of some governments and the reconstitution of some states. Unless this trend greatly accelerates, however, I doubt that it will affect the constitution of international society nearly as much as functional growth has done already. Challenging governments directly challenges them to protect their monopoly of agency. Governments have resources for doing so that far exceed the resources of their private rivals. Not the least are their normative resources—the capacity to make and use rules to advantage. If left unchallenged, governments follow rules that change as material conditions and international society change together.

Conclusion

As a principle, sovereignty earned its durability and constitutive force by granting states exclusive membership in international society and their governments a monopoly of agency. Majesty became concentrated in the state, while the government interpreted its share of agency as the competence to rule within the state's territory and assumed responsibility for the good of all people within that territory. Agency entails intervention. When governments engaged in activities affecting the land, people, or governments of other states, these activities constituted intervention, but were considered admissible intervention only if they were routine or beneficial. Activities that governments undertook ostensibly for some good other than that of their own people—the good of another people, or of all people— found enough support from writers and governments to suggest the existence of a permissive rule and enough resistance to keep the rule's status and content perennially in doubt.

To suggest the admissibility of intervention for the common good is a republican idea. Vattel, who espoused it, saw Europe as "a sort of republic." After republicanism lost its international appeal and came to be identified instead with the representative institutions of the liberal state, the rationale for international intervention grew tenuous, its practice ambiguous. Socialists took over the republican concern for the common good and drastically reconceived it in response to capitalist development and liberal indifference. As liberal states absorbed socialist concerns, and then socialist states emerged, intervention became an overwhelmingly domestic preoccupation. At the same time, functional growth enlarged governments, benefited large numbers of people, and contributed to the state's once-ascendant position in the modern world.

Functional growth has progressively undermined the monopoly that governments once exercised over agency in the name of the state. Because they link peoples to their lands, states are as necessary as ever. Nevertheless the perception of their sufficiency, and thus their majesty, has declined, as other regimes of laws perform indispensable services and claim popular attention. Frequently supported and widely condoned by governments, functional experts practice their professional skills without regard to state frontiers.

Clinically minded, these experts understand their activities to be interventionary. They justify them by reference to the common good, conceived not as the whole that Aristotle had in mind (and for which, Aristotle held, the *polis* exists as a whole), but as particular services to be provided or problems to be solved. Yet the sense of public duty that so many of these experts exhibit suggests a renewal of republicanism. So does the increasing tolerance for intervention in affairs once thought to be the state's alone. Increasingly, the rules permit agents of many affiliations to engage in interventionary activities, in the name not of the state but of the common good—or at least that share of the common good which some other regime of laws has captured for itself. With these interventions, diverse agents reconstitute the world—its structures, and its people and their aspirations; themselves; and the rules by which we know the world.

Chapter Four

International Community
beyond the Cold War

ROBERT H. JACKSON

International Community

The end of the cold war has changed the landscape of international relations to a greater extent than has any other episode in the past four decades.
What were considered permanent landmarks just a few years ago no longer
exist: the Berlin Wall has been pulled down, and Europe is no longer divided politically between East and West; America and Russia no longer
regard each other as hostile adversaries; regional superpower conflicts in
the Middle East, Asia, Africa, and Central America have been abandoned;
the Soviet Union has collapsed and its component parts have become sovereign states whose relations with Moscow are ambiguous and uneasy;
Yugoslavia has disintegrated into warring nationalities, and Czechoslovakia has split in two; communism has not only retreated but has almost
vanished as a credible rival of market economies and democracy; and the
United Nations Security Council has become actively engaged in world
politics.

For forty years international relations scholars took the great schism
between East and West as a benchmark. But the muse of history and in
particular the unforeseen revolutionary actions of Mikhail Gorbachev and
Boris Yeltsin have rendered archaic Kremlinology, Soviet studies, comparative communism, and other branches of political science which not long
ago were considered essential to any sound understanding of international
relations. The current situation thus raises a momentous question that has

agitated the minds of scholars: How should we think about international relations now that the cold war is over?[1] If the overt landscape is different, does that mean that the underlying norms also must be different? Such questions cannot yet be answered with confidence. It is still too early to discern clearly the shape and substance of the international era that is coming: the dust has not settled; indeed, it is swirling around, and the situation remains confused despite our best efforts to clarify it. The historian must wait for history. The academic folly of chasing current events in an effort to be up-to-date only to find yet another unanticipated change that destroys previous conclusions is well known. But there is another trap nearby which should also be avoided: if we wish to say something relevant we cannot do it by shying away from contemporary history and retreating to international relations theory. We cannot theorize meaningfully about human affairs, including international relations, without interrogating the goings-on of the world. Otherwise all we are engaging in is a form of scholasticism.

It may be useful at the outset to comment briefly on the concept of "international community" employed in this chapter. I conceive of all communities as human contrivances (as opposed to natural phenomena) that consist of distinctive standards of conduct or norms that express certain basic human intentions and concerns. In the case of the international community the main concern, although by no means the only one, is peace and security between states. There are of course many other kinds of political community with their own norms; perhaps the most important of these is the state itself. I follow scholars of a Grotian bent, usually referred to as "international society" theorists, who discern three conceptual elements of the international community: the community of states and citizens, the community of humankind, and the world community: that is, the world as a single collectivity with a common interest that is sometimes referred to as "the common heritage of mankind."[2] Each of these international communities presupposes different norms that can diverge and can even conflict with each other, as when the rights of sovereign states clash with human rights. Moreover, unlike national communities, which rest on deep psychological foundations, international communities are almost entirely procedural. The global patriots who march under the pale banner of the United Nations are still few and far between by comparison with the countless national patriots who hold high the colorful flags of more than 180 independent nations. Jurisprudence and not sociology is the more pertinent methodology for understanding international communities.

I will concentrate on the community of states and citizens and the community of humankind: states, citizens, and humans considered as "right and duty bearing units."[3] Although the world community is increasingly evident nowadays in global concern about the environment, it is still largely an unrealized potentiality in world politics.[4] I seek evidence of an *operative* international community and of any changes in the norms that embody and express it: international community as an element, or referent, in the conduct of states' leaders and of other agents. This normative mode of analysis basically involves interrogating real-world events to see what they can tell us about the presence or absence, and the shape and substance, of international norms. Is the international community still defined narrowly and negatively by a few basic principles of international law, such as those in Article 2 of the United Nations Charter which identify nonaggression and nonintervention as the fundamental obligations of member states? Is sovereignty still a prevailing international norm? Or is there evidence for the claim that a deeper and more active international community is coming into existence in which the independence of states is being curtailed by humanitarianism and other norms? Is the international community changing from a negative and noninterventionist regime to a positive and interventionist one?

In the next two sections I briefly outline the international community that came into existence after World War II. In later sections I consider how far its norms may be changing as we move beyond the cold war.

The Community of States

The international community, whatever else it is becoming, is still fundamentally a community of sovereign states, although it is no longer exclusively so (see below). The centrality of sovereignty in international relations is frequently questioned nowadays, but it is impossible to ignore. Even its severest critics take it as a starting point.[5] Although sovereignty is examined at length elsewhere in this volume, I will here be referring only to its meaning in contemporary diplomatic and legal *practice:* the "constitutional independence" of states. By this I mean the international legal condition in which one state's structure of authority and power "is not part of a larger constitutional arrangement."[6] For example, the moment any colony ceases to be a dependency of a (foreign) state it simultaneously and automatically becomes a subject of international law. In other words, as soon as constitutional independence occurs, the international law of sovereignty and nonintervention simultaneously takes effect.[7] At that moment the government of the newly sovereign state is legally free to make decisions and carry out policies without the authorization of any other state or international organization. But it must now observe international law, which basically involves respecting the independence of other sovereign states. I employ this definition of sovereignty not only because it is the current international practice but also because it is at the heart of the problem of community in contemporary international relations.

There is nowadays one obvious existential community of sovereign states. The year 1945 marks not only the end of a devastating world war but also the founding of a new universal collectivity of states defined by an explicit set of rules. That collectivity is, of course, the United Nations, and the rules are stated in its Charter, particularly and centrally in Article 2, which specifies the fundamental conduct requirements of the organization: equal sovereignty of all member states, forbearance from initiating the use of armed force to settle disputes among members, and nonintervention in the domestic jurisdiction of members. Article 2 also contains several related principles and requirements, including good faith, peaceful settlement of disputes, willingness of members to assist the United Nations in its actions, and compliance of nonmembers with its principles. This pretty well sums up the classical Westphalian morality of international relations. The UN Charter contains many other articles, some of which display a more active and expansive conception of international community: those pertaining to the interventionist role of the Security Council being the most noteworthy (Chapters V, VI, and especially VII). The cold war most often prevented these positive parts of the Charter from being used, but it generally did not obstruct the negative parts embodied by Article 2. On the contrary, it reinforced them.

Politically one can of course point to an international community more fundamental than the United Nations: the traditional community of diplomacy and customary international law which existed for centuries prior to the United Nations and would continue to exist if the United Nations were abandoned. That primordial international community is called into being by the existence of independent governments, which must, of necessity, live with and deal with each other. Among the norms and practices of this traditional community, some of which go back to medieval and even Roman times, are mutual recognition, adherence to treaties, safe conduct of ambassadors, condemnation of piracy, and protection of aliens.[8] But this primordial international community nowadays finds expression in formal organization, the core of which is the United Nations. If the United Nations eventually ceases to exist, some other formal institution will have to take its place, just as the United Nations in 1945 took the place of the (defunct) League of Nations. For the time being, therefore, when states and other international agents and representatives operate collectively on a universal plane, it is primarily by reference to norms sanctioned by the UN Charter. This is not to say that states always observe the UN Charter; sometimes they ignore it. But they are expected to observe it, and they are usually condemned—although not always punished—when they fail to observe it. Furthermore, states that are not members of the United Nations cannot participate fully in the contemporary international community. That is perhaps why isolating a state from the international community, or even threatening to do so, is a disciplining tool of considerable importance. Even though a state that is isolated would still retain its sovereignty, exile from the international community is a fate most statesmen and states-women would prefer to avoid if they could. They are sociable, like the rest of us, and would rather be members in good standing.

Philosophically one can point to another community more fundamental than the United Nations: the community of humankind. According to this cosmopolitan view, the community of states, whether formally organized or not, is secondary to the community of humankind, which is primary. Human beings are undeniably prior to states ontologically and historically: states, even the oldest states, are merely political arrangements fashioned and sustained by particular people at particular times. Human beings were trying to make the best of their situation long before states were invented, and they will still be trying to do so long after states have been consigned to the scrap heap of political history. Human rights—which express the community of humankind—nevertheless exist in operational fact today only by virtue of international (and domestic) humanitarian law that recognizes individual human beings as holders of rights who are separate from the sovereign states of which they are citizens.[9] Human beings have never enjoyed much of the good life unless they have successfully fashioned states to deliver the goods. Of course, it goes without saying that human life inside states and between states has always involved trials and tribulations, not the least of which have been terrible wars. But human life outside the state has statistically been shorter and poorer, and usually it has also been nastier and more brutish.[10] Consequently, although human beings are prior to states in theory and in history, whatever standing the community of humankind enjoys in practice and thus in reality nowadays usually depends on the willingness and ability of state leaders to recognize and respect human rights.

The existing international system is by far the most extensively organized of any international system in history, and there are of course many international organizations and groupings besides the United Nations.[11] Regional organizations today represent substantial segments of the world's territory and population—the European Union, the Commonwealth of Independent States, the Organization of American States, the Commonwealth, Francophonie, the Association of Southeast Asian Nations, and the Organization of African Unity are only a few that come to mind. In addition, there are various functional international organizations that deal with important specialized problems ranging from regional security to global telecommunications—the North Atlantic Treaty Organization, the Organization for Economic Cooperation and Development, the International Labor Organization, the General Agreement on Tariffs and Trade, the International Monetary Fund, the World Bank, the United Nations Conference on Trade and Development, the International Telecommunication Union, the World Meteorological Organization, and the like. Numerous other international organizations, including countless nongovernmental organizations (NGOs), also exist; a complete list of named entities would be very long indeed. All of this is historically unprecedented. But there still is no other international collectivity that is as universal as the United Nations in its membership, organization, and rules. Although sovereign states are not obliged to join this global body, virtually all of them do belong to it; new states continue to join; and its rules can be applied to nonmembers. For these reasons I believe that the United Nations nowadays best represents the "international community" in formal organizational terms, even though that community would of course exist in the absence of the United Nations or of any other international organization, provided the world was still divided into sovereign states. The United Nations should thus be seen as currently the principal international organization of the community of states.

Membership in the International Community

Membership in any association presupposes a line dividing insiders and outsiders. The criterion for inclusion and exclusion normally involves the acquisition of a fundamental status by which members can be recognized. Perhaps the clearest example is national citizenship: to enjoy the rights of citizenship in most countries one must either be born in the country or be "naturalized" as a consequence of immigration and residence for a specified period of time. The same reasoning can be applied internationally: to enjoy the rights of membership in the international community, a territorial political collectivity must be a sovereign state.[12] The rules that determine the possession of sovereignty therefore govern candidacy for membership in the international community. Territorial populations that do not possess sovereignty—such as the Kurds and other ethnonational groups, the current number of which is many times greater than the number of states—are denied candidacy.

A state may be sovereign but it still may not be represented in the international community. We must therefore distinguish (secondary) membership in the United Nations and other international organizations from the (primary) condition of being sovereign. Sovereignty is thus a necessary but not sufficient condition for membership in the community of states. South Africa was for three decades isolated by the United Nations and became a pariah state, but it did not cease being sovereign during that period. It is not regaining its sovereignty now that its government is abandoning apartheid and reentering the international community. That primary condition was never taken away. What South Africa is regaining is international legitimacy.

Contemporary practice suggests that once sovereignty is acquired, it cannot be lawfully extinguished except as a voluntary act—which is rare. In 1964 Zanzibar relinquished its independence, which it had recently acquired from Britain, to unite with Tanganyika to form the new state of Tanzania. But such cases are unusual: nowadays sovereign states hardly ever commit suicide, and they evidently can no longer be killed or die.[13] Somalia virtually ceased to exist as an organized state in the early 1990s as a result of government collapse and internecine warfare among clan warlords, but that did not extinguish its sovereignty. That could only happen if the United Nations and most other states, especially major powers, considered that Somalia was no longer an independent country and set up some kind of alternative authority to take its place—such as a UN trusteeship. This has not happened to date, and it is unlikely to happen because it invokes the negative image of colonialism. What we witness in Somalia is the extreme case of a purely notional country—a place on the map—that lacks even the appearance of a national government with which foreign powers and other international agents can deal. But they insist on pretending that Somalia still exists, because that is the norm they must observe. In short, Somalia enjoys an international juridical existence even though it is entirely lacking in national substance. This historically unusual state of affairs, which exists in less extreme forms elsewhere, is largely a postcolonial phenomenon.[14]

The fifty-one charter members of the United Nations were defined by the pattern of territorial sovereignty that existed in 1945. Almost all of these nations were jurisdictions (mostly Western states) that had been independent previously and had participated in the San Francisco Conference that founded the United Nations; many of them had also been League of Nations members. The far-flung and numerous Western colonies in Asia and Africa were of course not sovereign at that time and could not claim UN membership. A second wave of members thus resulted from the termination of overseas colonialism and the transfer of sovereignty—mainly in the 1950s and 1960s—from Western imperial states to their former colonies.[15] This transfer of sovereignty was in response partly to a sea change in international opinion, which turned against colonialism after World War II, and partly to the rise of the cold war, in which the United States and the Soviet Union (and also sometimes China) bid for the support of third world anticolonial nationalists. Hence, territorial jurisdiction within preexisting colonial boundaries (rather than some other distinction between groups, such as ethnonationality) became a second criterion for inclusion after 1945. A third wave of membership resulted from the territorial disintegration of the Soviet Union and Yugoslavia. Status as a "republic" (province) defined by the internal borders of what previously had been at least notionally a "federal" state consequently became yet another criterion for membership in the international community. Virtually all of the states acquiring or recovering sovereignty through these acts of state succession in the second half of the twentieth century have elected to become associated with the United Nations. As a result of this proliferation of sovereign statehood, the number of UN members increased almost fourfold, reaching more than 180 by 1993.

There is definite continuity in state practice since 1945 concerning the legitimacy and legality of existing national borders. When in 1990 the German chancellor questioned the postwar boundary separating Poland and a reuniting Germany, he was informed in no uncertain terms not only by the government of Poland but also by Germany's NATO allies, including the United States, that the boundary could not be questioned and must be accepted. Existing international boundaries evidently can only be redrawn with the consent of all the sovereign states that share them. This twentieth-century practice is a fundamental normative change from the basis of state jurisdiction historically, which could be determined by military force, by Machiavellian diplomacy, by commercial transaction, by dynastic marriage, and by other such means.

Determinations of territorial jurisdiction by threat or use of force, or by any means other than consent, have no legitimate place in contemporary international relations. The exceptions since 1945 are few: India changed international boundaries by force in its takeover of (Portuguese) Goa, and Indonesia resorted to the same in its occupation of (again Portuguese) East Timor. The absence of strenuous UN criticism suggests that Portuguese colonies were by that time of doubtful international legal standing, probably because of the resistance of then-authoritarian Portugal to UN General Assembly demands for decolonization. India (and to a lesser degree Indonesia) could plausibly be seen as carrying out an action comparable to that of a national liberation movement seeking to terminate colonialism by armed force if necessary. China used military force to annex Tibet, but Tibet's prior status as a sovereign state was in doubt. The separation of Bangladesh (formerly East Pakistan) from Pakistan, made possible by the intervention of the Indian army, was a splintering along preexisting boundaries and did not result in the acquisition of any territory by India.

Recent attempts to redraw the internal borders of the former Yugoslavia by force to conform to actual ethnic patterns rather than to juridical divisions of the former Yugoslavia constitute a more important exception. But it is again noteworthy that the inherited internal borders of the former Yugoslavia have been regarded by the United Nations, the European Union, the Conference on Security and Cooperation in Europe (CSCE), the major Western powers, and most other states as the only legitimate and lawful points of reference in such matters, until such time as the parties agree to change them. The London Conference (1992) placed great emphasis on this norm. They were still the recognized borders at the time of writing (1993), but there were growing and already strong signs that this would change. If Bosnia-Herzegovina's borders were changed as a result of acquiescence to the armed occupation of territory by Serbian and Croatian militias, that would of course indicate a return to an older, pre-1945 norm. Observers will also be looking at the former Soviet Union to see if any successor states, such as Georgia or Azerbaijan, splinter in the same way along ethnic lines. Then it will be interesting to see if there are any reversions to the older norm in other parts of the world where state borders conflict with ethnonationalism.

In short, candidacy for group membership in the international community has been confined to territorial political entities that either were sovereign in 1945 or were the juridically demarcated colonies or provinces of such sovereign entities. There has been a continuity of sovereign state jurisdiction and succession since that time. Extant (historical) territorial jurisdiction has (so far) triumphed over culture, religion, language, ethnicity, or any other nonjuridical definition of statehood in international relations. The basic norm of the UN Charter concerns the recognition of such boundaries and a pledge not to infringe upon them without lawful cause.

An effect of this norm has been to elevate citizenries of sovereign territorial jurisdictions into members of the international community once removed. The community of states nowadays is in certain important respects a community of citizenries. This latter community could be expanded if in the future democracy becomes a necessary ground for claiming and enjoying international legitimacy in the community of states. A huge step forward would be taken if, for example, Russia succeeds in becoming a genuine democracy; a big step has already been taken in the as-yet-imperfect democratization (or, in some cases, redemocratization) of Eastern Europe. As I indicate below, this has significant implications for the present and future conduct of international relations. For if we now vest sovereignty not only in the governments but also in the citizens of democratic states, that will affect not only how international relations theorists should think about the international community but also how international practitioners ought to conduct foreign policy on such questions as humanitarian intervention. In the final section of this chapter I deal with some of the theoretical and practical implications of the notion of citizens as members of the international community once removed.

A last category of membership in the international community which commands notice is the category of humanity, or rather, individual human beings. The standing of human beings in international relations is not new: the protection of fundamental human rights across international frontiers dates from at least the early nineteenth century, when attempts were made, initially by Britain and later by the Concert of Europe, to abolish the slave trade. One could go back much further, to the Spanish conquests in the Americas, where the aboriginal people, by virtue of their humanity, were held by some to possess rights that had to be respected by sovereigns.[16] However, human rights have acquired unprecedented international legality only in the present century, and particularly since the end of World War II, as disclosed by (for example) the Nuremberg war crimes tribunal (1946), the Universal Declaration of Human Rights (1948), the Geneva Conventions (1949), the European Convention on Human Rights (1950), the UN human rights covenants (1966), the American Convention on Human Rights (1969), and the Helsinki Final Act (1975), which established the CSCE. One cannot overlook the support of human rights by NGOs that have proliferated mainly (although not exclusively) in Western countries since Amnesty International was founded in 1961. These covenants and activities imply that human beings have normative standing in international relations independent of their status as subjects or citizens of particular sovereign states.

To sum up: there is a discernible international community centered on the United Nations which is defined by operative standards of conduct (specified by the Charter) and a historical criterion of membership through sovereign state succession. The citizens of states are surfacing as members once removed: the community of states is becoming in certain respects a community of citizenries. And, finally, individual human beings have acquired standing in international law, however limited and qualified that standing may as yet be in practice. But after all is said and done, the international community is still fundamentally a community of sovereign states.

Beyond the Cold War

Contemporary events give some indication that in the future the international community may not be as narrow and negative as it has been in the past. Let me therefore turn to a question of prime concern: whether the fundamental norms and practices of the international community outlined above—particularly those embodied by Article 2 of the UN Charter—are changing or can be expected to change as we move beyond the cold war. Is the international community changing from a negative and noninterventionist to a positive and interventionist regime? I address this issue in relation to the following topics, all of which were at the forefront of international concern in the last decade of the twentieth century: intervention, democracy, human rights, and refugees. These unfolding issues were examined using data available in the first half of 1993, and my account of them is of course limited by that historical fact.

Intervention and Nonintervention

The question about intervention is not only whether it will continue to be committed for reasons of expediency and interests, but also whether it is legitimate and legal. Of course, states have in the past intervened in the domestic jurisdiction of other states because it was expedient to do so. To expect that states will continue to act in that self-interested manner in the future is only reasonable. There is a longstanding Machiavellian applied science (realpolitik) on the subject.[17] However, here I am interested in knowing not when intervention may be opportune but, rather, when it may be justified—which is a legal and moral question.[18] I am also interested in determining whether the norms for justifying intervention may be changing.

In the jurisprudential logic of the UN Charter, nonintervention is the norm, and intervention is what must be justified. The fact that the Soviet Union and the United States infringed upon this rule during the cold war is not sufficient to nullify it as an operative international norm. Even though the legitimacy and legality of some of those superpower interventions is dubious, to say the least, the superpowers both still tried to justify them in terms recognizable to international law. When the Soviets intervened in Afghanistan in 1979 they claimed that their action was solicited by the government in Kabul, which was at the time a pro-Moscow regime. Because solicited intervention by a sovereign state is lawful, the real question was the legality of that government, which had seized power not long before. However, many armed interventions during the cold war were genuinely (rather than spuriously) of the solicited rather than the imposed variety, which is consistent with the UN Charter.[19] For example, the Soviet Union and France frequently intervened in sub-Saharan African states at the invitation of sovereign governments. The United States did the same, although on at least one occasion it succumbed to the cold war temptation to do otherwise where an allegedly "communist" government was involved: that was in Angola in 1975, where the United States intervened on the side of antigovernment rebels. One must therefore draw a firm distinction between solicited and unsolicited intervention: only the latter poses a normative problem for the international community.

White South Africa repeatedly violated the rule of nonintervention in black Africa during the cold war, probably because the Organization of African Unity, and specifically its "frontline" states, were on record as seeking the destruction of the apartheid regime. This goal of the OAU disclosed a principle of international legitimacy which white South Africa defied: namely, the principle of African majority rule. This led to the isolation of Pretoria on an international legitimist ground that nevertheless did not deprive white South Africa of sovereignty. I believe that this case sets a precedent for the imposition of isolation and sanctions on grounds of illegitimacy rather than illegality, and this merits further investigation. (Some preliminary thoughts on the practice of isolation are presented in the final section of this chapter.)

There is no reason to expect any change in the requirement that states should refrain from the illegal use of armed force to settle disputes. Any actions by states in violation of this norm would be widely condemned by members of the international community. The almost universal negative reaction to the invasion of Kuwait by Iraq underlines the point. This case is particularly interesting, however, because it was the first time since the Korean War that the UN Security Council sanctioned military action against a state that had flagrantly violated Article 2 of the Charter. Here is at least one instance of a more positive and active international community resorting to sections of the Charter (Chapters V and VII) that could not be used during the cold war. Of course, it is impossible to tell merely from this one case if there will be a recurrent willingness of the Security Council to enforce this principle. For the time being, however, the council's action in the Kuwaiti case stands as a deterrent to any belligerent state that might contemplate similar actions in the future.

The wars in Croatia and Bosnia-Herzegovina cast some doubt on this conclusion. The Security Council, the European Union, and major outside powers, including the United States, Britain, and France, were extremely reluctant to intervene militarily other than by supporting a more active variety of humanitarian peacekeeping. However, one must keep in mind fundamental differences between the two cases: the Iraqi invasion of Kuwait was an unambiguous act of external aggression as defined by the UN Charter, and there was a profound and legitimate international interest in the security of the region and its oil supplies. By contrast, the wars in Croatia and Bosnia-Herzegovina began within what had recently been the state of Yugoslavia: they have earmarks of civil and ethnic warfare, and it is therefore more difficult to conceive of them strictly in terms of aggression. That is perhaps evident in the fact that humanitarian aid rather than international security is usually cited as a basis for military intervention in Bosnia-Herzegovina to stop the slaughter of civilians. (The issue of humanitarian intervention is discussed below.)[20]

However, these wars were very different from the civil wars of the cold war era, in many of which outside military powers, particularly the superpowers, participated as military suppliers, supporters, agitators, and even, in some cases, instigators. In the Balkan conflicts, major powers (and other states) were concerned to prevent external supply and support of the warring factions, if necessary by international sanctions, in order to limit the spread of the conflicts and conceivably bring about an earlier end to the hostilities. The international community, acting through the United Nations (and also the European Union, the CSCE, and other bodies), attempted to censure and isolate the warring parties, particularly the Serbian militias and their backers in Belgrade, while at the same time providing humanitarian aid for noncombatants. That is a noteworthy change from the cold war, during which external meddling in civil wars by the superpowers, expediently justified by their own interests or ideologies, often fanned the flames and prolonged the suffering.

Nonintervention and Democracy

If members of the international community are defined as sovereign citizenries and not merely as sovereign states, that will affect the way in which we reason about the practice of nonintervention. At first glance it might seem that such a definition would expand the grounds for unsolicited intervention. Sovereign states that were not democracies could not claim the same rights of nonintervention. Democracies might have a right, possibly even a duty, to intervene—within limits determined by circumstances and prudence—to promote the freedom and welfare of citizenries that are oppressed by their rulers. Although this reasoning appeals to our democratic sentiments I do not believe there is much virtue in it. Of course, it is lacking in realism, but that is not the problem with which I am concerned here. It is also flawed in its conception of what democracy presupposes about sovereignty and intervention.

To bring democracy into existence in a country by the efforts and resources of outsiders has only been possible in unusual circumstances, such as the successful democratization of Germany after World War II. Even in that case, influential German leaders, such as Konrad Adenauer and Willy Brandt, were energetic collaborators in postwar democratic reconstruction. The far more typical historical experience we ought to keep in mind is the failure of the British and the French to develop democracy in most of their Asian and African colonies. One also cannot overlook the frustrated American attempts to build democracy in the Philippines and South Vietnam. Foreigners cannot give people in other countries democracy: that is not in their power. People must acquire democracy and keep it by their own efforts. Foreign powers can only encourage people in other countries to pursue democracy, and assist them in whatever ways they can. I believe that this is the main lesson of history and political theory on the issue.[21] However, circumstances may encourage or discourage the spread of democracy, and today they are more encouraging because democracy no longer has to compete with state socialism and communism as a world political ideology. Islam is a regional but surely not a global competitor. Samuel Huntington's thesis about a new conflict between Islamic and Western civilizations displacing the old one between communism and democracy exaggerates the status and appeal of Islam as an international ideology.[22] There is no question but that democracy is today unrivaled as a world ideology and is spreading beyond its ancestral home in what previously was "the West," although it is not clear how far or fast it will travel in other parts of the world.

Let us nevertheless assume that a revolution is under way in which democracy is becoming an international norm even though most states still are not democracies. How should that affect our normative reasoning about intervention and nonintervention? If we are now dealing with a community of citizenries (and not merely a community of states), we are going to have even more difficulty in justifying intervention. This is due to the normative logic of democracy, which is that of self-determination and self-government: in a democracy the people (and nobody else) are ultimately responsible for their government and its actions. If sovereign governments cannot purchase, conquer, or colonize foreign countries nowadays, neither can they save foreign populations from their own rulers—or from themselves. Paternalism is antithetical to democracy. Making the world safe for democracy goes against the spirit of democracy. If we justify unsolicited intervention in a country on the grounds that we are helping the people who live there to build democracy, we are getting involved in something strongly reminiscent of colonialism.

The conception of the international community as a community of citizenries does not alter the classical rules of nonintervention contained in Article 2 of the UN Charter. On the contrary, it reinforces them: there is even more reason than before not to intervene. An international community of democratic states would be minimalist, and not expansive, in its legitimate grounds for intervention, owing to the fact that political responsibility would be more firmly rooted within the citizenry of a state. Such a citizenry would bear all the rights and all the duties of sovereignty. In a democracy we cannot separate the state and the citizen and ultimately hold only the former responsible—at least, we cannot do so if citizenship involves what it surely must involve in a bona fide democracy: self-determination and self-government. Arguably, a world of democracies would be a world of general nonintervention and nonaggression.[23]

If democracy is becoming an international norm, then we should expect that even fewer acts of international intervention would be justifiable than was the case previously. For example, if we view the current Balkan conflicts as popular wars of ethnic self-determination, then the justifiable grounds for intervening are more restricted than if we view them as armed struggles of ambitious warlords who are preying upon innocent people. As indicated, perhaps some of the international uncertainty and hesitation regarding international intervention in Croatia and Bosnia-Herzegovina derived from a widespread perception of the conflicts as popular wars of ethnic self-determination. Those who called for international intervention in the Balkan conflicts on humanitarian grounds were more inclined to locate responsibility in the warlords. This latter view conceives of the Balkan peoples not as responsible parties to the conflicts but, rather, as innocent victims of them. Such a view was evident in the response of the United Nations and the "coalition" states, including the United States, to Iraq. Washington time and again declared that its enemy was not the Iraqi people but only the regime of Saddam Hussein. That made sense to the extent that Iraq was a ruthless personal dictatorship. But it may not make as much sense in the former Yugoslavia, where "the people," in the shape of mutually hostile ethnonational groups, have been asserting conflicting rights of self-determination against each other.

Intervention and Humanity

Human rights and humanitarianism normally compete with sovereign (and citizen) rights as grounds for intervention. That is particularly so if by human rights we mean the classical natural rights of individual human beings not to have their persons or liberties interfered with against their will: as is the case with torture (and other kinds of physical torment), imprisonment (without a fair hearing and trial), enslavement, forced exile, and so forth. The right not to be willfully or negligently deprived of food and other necessities that would otherwise be available must also be included as a bona fide human right.

As indicated, for most of the classical period of positive international law there were few recognized humanitarian grounds for curbing states' rights. Although that has been changing in recent decades there are still legal limits to international human rights—usually indicated by derogation clauses in human rights covenants which relax certain obligations to protect human rights in exceptional circumstances, typically during wars or other public emergencies. This normative logic merely recognizes the reality that there will be times when the interest of a state or its citizens— utilitarian ethics—must "trump" individual human rights. As long as the international system consists substantially of sovereign states that are invested with independent normative value as collectivities (and I see no sign that this will soon change) there will be no complete escape from this reality. We must therefore reason about humanitarian intervention in these terms for the time being.

However, suppose the international community determines that human rights are being violated in a member state that has ratified international human rights covenants without any reservations and cannot claim that the violation is warranted by exceptional circumstances. Consider as a case in point the warring clans in Somalia whose warlords in 1991–92 willfully obstructed the importation and distribution of food, thereby exacerbating existing problems of drought and civil war and thus causing even greater suffering to the population. Here is a case in which the state has collapsed into a chaotic condition that Hobbes would characterize as a "state of nature."[24] Common morality and international humanitarian law tell us that, if possible, something should be done to stop the suffering. Suppose armed intervention could be justified in this case on humanitarian grounds. Leaders of foreign states would still bear the heavy responsibility of deciding whether or not they should send their people into the country. Such a decision cannot (and should not) avoid the question of prudence: would it be wise to intervene in Somalia in circumstances of armed anarchy even if it could be justified? The first duty of a sovereign government in such circumstances is to protect its own people, soldiers as well as civilians. After that it can try to protect whomever else it can.

Both the Bush and Clinton administrations, and predominant opinion in Congress and among the American people, operated with roughly that reasoning in regard to Somalia: the United States intervened on humanitarian grounds in December 1992, but when a Somali warlord began to inflict casualties on American troops and UN troops from other countries, their safety, and not the plight of Somali civilians, became the fundamental concern. The case of Somalia seems to indicate that democracies are highly concerned about the welfare of their own people and will be reluctant to engage in armed intervention in foreign countries if it involves putting their people at risk, and if there is no real security threat from that quarter which would justify taking such risks. Unfortunately, and perhaps even paradoxically, this "realist" logic made it possible for a Somali warlord, with limited power resources but a lot of audacity, to thumb his nose at the world's greatest power. But perhaps this only underlines the point that ultimately it is up to the Somali people to get rid of their warlords; they cannot expect others to do it for them.

Here is the operational dilemma confronting a humane and democratic leader of a state in an international community that recognizes a right of humanitarian intervention in appropriate circumstances but does not (and cannot) make it a duty. Humanitarian intervention cannot be a duty because that would terminate the primary obligation of such leaders to their own citizens. It boils down to a question of normative choice: either sovereigns and citizens remain primary members of the international community and human beings remain secondary members, or the reverse. I believe that the choice between protecting their own citizens and protecting human beings in other countries can in certain circumstances be a genuine dilemma for leaders of states; maybe that has been the dilemma facing Western governments in the case of Bosnia-Herzegovina. They could not ignore the suffering, but they lacked solid political or military reasons for intervening: there was no threat to their security. I do not see how democratic governments could sacrifice their own people if such sacrifice was necessary to protect human rights in foreign countries but nothing else was at stake.

It may be useful to speculate briefly about ways to resolve this problem. I certainly cannot see the international community eliminating the dilemma by transforming itself into primarily a community of humankind in which human rights would always have priority over all other normative considerations: that would be extremely far-fetched. Perhaps an all-volunteer UN armed force whose personnel were willing to risk their lives to enforce human rights is a non-Utopian way around the problem. Perhaps the major powers could arm, equip, and train special regiments formed by volunteers from other countries for military operations under the UN flag: international foreign legions. That would overcome both the moral problem of putting one's own people at risk and the political problem of risking a loss of domestic political support when the "body bags" are brought home.

But even if UN members were prepared to pay for such international brigades—a very big "if"—it is still far from clear how, exactly, the armed humanitarian intervention of such a force in the domestic jurisdiction of a UN member state could be justified. If such intervention were a real option—if those brigades were as capable as the French Foreign Legion—it would raise well-founded fears in the minds of the leaders of militarily weak countries in which human rights were being violated on a major scale. According to reports by humanitarian NGOs there are more than a few such countries at the present time, mostly in the third world. And if such humanitarian interventions were actually embarked upon, it would mean that a new form of international paternalism had come into existence, one in which particular states would in certain circumstances temporarily, lose the protection of Article 2, and thus their sovereignty. That would be a fundamentally different international community from the one that exists at the present time: a new regime of international humanitarian trusteeship that would have more than a little resemblance to colonialism.

In sum, the operative definition of the international community will affect the normative logic of intervention. If that community is primarily a community of states or citizenries, the (existing) rule of nonintervention must take precedence; indeed, a community of citizenries arguably raises the barrier against unsolicited foreign intervention even higher. If that community is primarily one of human beings, then it is nonintervention rather than intervention which must be justified. That makes intervention normatively easier in theory, but I cannot foresee the latter rule becoming operative any time soon in a political world that is still most accurately conceived in normative terms as fundamentally a community of states and citizenries.

Refugees and Migrants

This normative analysis can be extended to another problem that confronts the international community at the present time: refugees and illegal immigrants.[25] A refugee (in the proper use of the term) is someone who has not committed any recognized crime but has fled to a foreign country to escape persecution at home. Refugees are involuntary exiles from states: people who are not criminals in the ordinary sense of the word but whose persons or liberty would be at extreme risk if they did not flee from their homeland. Someone who crosses an international border illegally to escape arrest after having committed a crime, or to search for a better life, cannot be considered a bona fide refugee. If someone is a criminal or an economic opportunist, he or she may justifiably be sent back. But if someone is a bona fide refugee the morality (and, in some countries, also the legality) of sending him or her back can be questioned. Much of the time of national refugee tribunals in Western Europe and North America is taken up with adjudicating this question.

If the international community is *exclusively* a community of sovereign states, and if those states have not entered into any legal obligations to the contrary, then someone crossing an international boundary illegally cannot claim a legal right to be granted refuge. If people flood across a border, and if the receiving state has enacted no law or signed no treaty to the contrary, then it does not have a legal obligation to admit them and can do whatever is necessary or expedient to deal with them. That includes such measures as physically blocking entry, arresting and detaining intruders, and forcibly sending them back—as the government of Turkey did in 1991 in reaction to an influx of Kurds fleeing from Iraq after their unsuccessful uprising against Saddam Hussein's regime following the end of the Persian Gulf War. Other pragmatic responses are also conceivable—such as diplomatic measures to encourage the exporting state to prevent the exodus, or development aid to encourage economic migrants to stay at home. About the only thing a receiving state cannot do is kill or injure such people—which indicates the existence of a fundamental norm of human rights.

Does this normative logic change if we assume that the international community is a community of citizenries? Clearly not. A citizen is someone with civil and political rights in a particular state; ordinarily one cannot be a citizen of more than one country at the same time. Nor does citizenship in one country bestow some kind of international citizenship. If we are citizens of the world it is only a metaphorical citizenship; real citizenship is always national. What if the country left behind patently is not a democracy but the receiving country is a democracy? Again, the normative logic does not change: a democratic government is one that is accountable to its own people but not to the people of other countries—even if they are persecuted by their own governments. Unless a sovereign government has incurred a legal obligation to admit such people, it is at liberty to deny them entry or residence.

To address the problem of refugees, what is required is some moral notion, such as human rights, that transcends international boundaries and impinges upon the freedom of sovereign states and citizenries. The human right in question is the right to escape from persecution or from the well-founded fear of persecution—even if the persecutor is one's own government, and even if it is a democratic government. The 1951 Convention on Refugees and its 1967 Protocol recognize this human right in international law. As far as I can make out, it is also recognized in domestic law by most Western democracies, which have tribunals that endeavor to identify bona fide refugees. Most of this accommodation of refugees appears to be domestically (rather than internationally) driven by capable humanitarian NGOs in these countries. But if the influx (or threatened influx) is on a large scale, giving refuge is unlikely to be the response of most countries, including democracies with refugee laws and tribunals. Western European governments admitted substantial numbers of refugees from wars in the former Yugoslavia, with Germany taking in the largest number, approximately 275,000. But these numbers pale in comparison to the approximately 2 million displaced persons within the former Yugoslavia at that time, with almost 600,000 in Croatia alone.

When the Italian government was confronted by an inrush of Albanians in 1991, most of the migrants were arrested and, as far as I have been able to determine, were immediately sent back without refugee hearings. However, the Italians also provided substantial development aid to assist the Albanian authorities to improve economic conditions and thus prevent future exoduses. But this appeared to be a mass movement of economic migrants rather than of refugees. A similar case is the American government's encouragement of foreign investment in Mexico to help stem the flood of illegal Mexican immigrants into border states, particularly California and Texas. In the early 1990s the European Union was contemplating a substantial increase in development aid for certain North African and Middle Eastern countries for the same purpose: to reduce the flow of unwanted illegal immigrants. The following refrain was widely heard in Western Europe at about the same time: either allow the Eastern European countries to export their goods into the European Union economies or risk a flood of illegal economic immigrants.

What, if anything, do these cases tell us about international norms? I think it is that there are definite limits to the numbers of illegal immigrants and refugees that Western democracies are prepared to accept. Governments that face an influx of such people feel justified in repatriating them if they cannot for political, economic, or cultural reasons absorb them. Humanitarian organizations that deal with refugees may despair and even protest at this, but such conduct is consistent with the normative logic of a community of sovereign states or citizenries. In such a community we may be our brother's keeper—but brotherhood for most purposes is limited to common nationality.

One recent episode casts some doubt on this conclusion: the military intervention by certain Western powers in northern Iraq following the Persian Gulf War to protect the local Kurdish minority from the Iraqi armed forces. A portion of Iraqi territory was occupied under the authority of the UN Security Council, and "safe havens" were established for the Kurds who lived there. Under the existing refugee regime, international efforts to deal with human calamities involving massive dislocations of people require the consent of the governments in whose sovereign territories they are conducted. This intervention appears "to have bent the rules" by not securing the consent of Iraqi authorities. It was an "*ad hoc* response on the part of Western governments, stung by intense public pressure and disquiet at the abandonment of the Kurds to the Iraqi military." Nevertheless, as N. Van Hear points out, it was effective in accomplishing its limited goal: providing sanctuary for the Kurdish population in northern Iraq.[26]

Because this unsolicited intervention by the UN Security Council was an unprecedented action against a UN member state, it could be an important sign of international normative change. But one fundamental feature of the episode should not escape our notice: it is the sort of action one would expect in the aftermath of a war in which the victors could claim military rights to intervene in the territory of the defeated state, independent of any humanitarian justification. Iraq was an aggressor and therefore a violator of the UN Charter, and could thus be considered to have forfeited, for the time being, some of its rights to control all its territory. The UN-sanctioned coalition massively intervened elsewhere in Iraq for military purposes. This interpretation makes the humanitarian intervention in northern Iraq less exceptional than it might otherwise appear, and really not very different from humanitarian actions by the Allied powers in Germany at the end of World War II.

Intervention or Isolation?

In contemporary practice states and citizens, and not humans, arguably are still the fundamental right- and duty-bearing units of the international community. Nonintervention continues to be a preemptive international norm, and intervention is what requires justification. This means, among other things, that it may not be particularly promising to search for humanitarian grounds to override the norm. The "solution" to current international humanitarian problems should perhaps be sought elsewhere.

One practice that immediately comes to mind is that of isolation, a practice that recognizes that there is (as yet) no general agreement about humanitarian intervention in international relations and assumes that the international community is still legally grounded in a few cardinal principles of equal sovereignty and nonintervention embodied in the UN Charter. Human rights law is still secondary to this international *Grundnorm*, the heart of which is Article 2. The logic of isolation recognizes that except for these few universal legal rules the international community is pluralistic in its values. According to this logic, the system of sovereign states has succeeded in becoming a global institution because it can accommodate a diversity of civilizations, cultures, religions, ideologies, and the like. In other words, the Grundnorm is indifferent to the particular domestic values of member states, *as long as they do not interfere with the values of other states and the states-system.*[27] This will be recognized as the old Westphalian principle of international toleration, *cujus regio ejus religio,* which is still the main normative obstacle to humanitarian intervention in a community of sovereign states and citizens.

This traditional principle is not an obstacle to a policy of isolation, which is lawful because it does not trespass upon the sovereignty of a state; such a policy merely makes a state pay a price by making it a social outcast from the international community. The policy of isolation thus escapes from the noninterventionist restrictions of Article 2 of the UN Charter. The target state retains sovereignty—its borders are not violated—but it is denied association and intercourse with the international community (and member states) until such time as it changes the domestic policies that are offensive to the norms of the international community. International law does not forbid the quarantining of a sovereign state from the international community by methods such as economic sanctions. It only forbids armed economic blockade, the modern version of siege warfare, which can be justified only if the target state has committed aggression or some other fundamental violation of the UN Charter which threatens the peace. In the longer term, diplomatic and economic isolation could prove to be more effective and lasting than armed intervention, because it seeks to secure a responsive change from within a country rather than to impose change from without.

A policy of isolation is now more feasible because the recently expanded West is again the central reference group of the international community, and its values and institutions set the standard for the world. The United States may be declining as a hegemon, and regionalism may be on the increase in international economics, with great trading blocs emerging in Europe, North America, and Asia. But the West, which encompasses the countries in two of these blocs as well as others outside, especially in Eastern Europe, is the unrivaled normative center of the international community; its norms are the ones that really count. That makes policies of isolation from the West more practical and effective than they were during the cold war, when international society suffered from a split personality of competing norms. Isolation is a viable strategy insofar as all major powers nowadays either openly espouse the same basic values—human rights, liberal democracy, and market economy—or are no longer in rebellion against those values even if they do not yet affirm them, as is the case with China. The key is Russia. Its declared support of these values—arguably beginning with Gorbachev's 1988 speech to the UN General Assembly affirming the legitimacy of human rights in the classical, natural-law meaning of the term—makes their promotion and protection a practical international option that cannot be undermined in the way that international humanitarian action during the cold war was scuttled by ideological and political discords between East and West. If Yeltsin's Russia turns away from the foregoing values, as it well could, and again becomes an ideological rival of the West, then the policy's efficacy will of course decline accordingly.

But until that happens isolation will be a practical option. The obvious precedent is the isolation of white South Africa. That nation was not subjected to military intervention by the Security Council, and it retained its sovereign immunities. But it was eventually quarantined by the international community, a move that was effective because the West and the

Communist bloc cooperated to make it so. When South Africa's government took the decision to abandon apartheid and began to institute democracy and human rights, one of the main reasons it gave to justify its actions was a desire to return to the international community.

As the South African example and the above remarks indicate, isolation requires a united international community to be effective. Only in such circumstances could quarantine be applied to a state with some promise of success. It could not of course be applied effectively to a large and self-sufficient state, as the failed history of Western attempts to isolate revolutionary Russia and China clearly indicates. Nor could the isolated states outnumber the isolators, for that would make the quarantined states a rival bloc of outcasts who could support each other: the efficacy of isolation would be reduced accordingly. At the time of writing, Iraq, Iran, Libya, and Serbia were under international quarantine intended to persuade their governments to alter domestic policies that were offensive to fundamental norms of the international community. It still remained to be seen how successful the policy would prove to be in these cases. In the case of Serbia, economic sanctions were having substantial adverse effects on that nation's economy, although it was still far from certain that they would eventually oblige Slobodan Milošević to make peace with the other warring parties in the Balkans.

A policy of isolation does not mean that states can be compelled to change their policies. Rather, it is a way of avoiding the use of military force, respecting the traditional doctrine of nonintervention, and upholding the value of self-determination while still sanctioning human rights and other emergent international standards of conduct. A government could still refuse to go along with the international community and accept the consequences of isolation. But the decision could be a costly one if the members of the international community were prepared to make it so, as they were in the case of white South Africa and as they recently have been in the cases of Iraq and Bosnia. That still would not deter a leader who was determined to defy the international community—someone like Saddam Hussein. The citizens would then suffer from the hardships of isolation, and the hope would be that their pain would sooner or later persuade them to change their leader and begin to institute the normative standards that the international community was seeking. That is the political logic of isolation. If we conceive of sovereignty as ultimately rooted in the people and not merely in the government, it is possible to justify the pain imposed on ordinary citizens by such a policy. That is the moral logic of isolation.

The policy of international quarantine might or might not produce the desired change of domestic policy in the target state. But even if it did not produce that result, it would still draw an important normative line in international relations between domestic conduct that was generally acceptable to the international community and domestic conduct that was not. During the cold war such a line could not be drawn, with the unfortunate consequence that normative discourse in international relations relating to the question of sovereignty and nonintervention (Article 2) usually collapsed into relativism or sterile ideological debate. Thus, drawing such a line is a normative step forward of considerable significance. It would mean that the concept of the international community as an important part of global civilization had been restored after several decades of normative confusion on that issue.

To sum up: Isolation is, within limits, a practical and not merely a theoretical way of responding to humanitarian problems in international relations. First, it is not hedged in by existing international law: because it belongs to the sphere of international legitimacy and not international law, it does not require fanciful interpretations of the UN Charter to justify itself. Second, it is not paternalistic: it leaves it up to sovereign states and citizenries to conform to the new standards of international legitimacy. They are still free to reject those new standards and suffer the consequences of increased isolation. Third, it is feasible, both in the sense that the expanding Western-centered international community is today the sole major repository of prestige and in the sense that the costs of exclusion, especially the economic costs, would be substantial and thus not easy to contemplate and even less easy to accept. Fourth, it opens a door for international humanitarianism without undermining the sovereignty of states and the self-determination of their citizens. Thus it is an evolutionary development of Westphalian international society that expands humanitarianism while still upholding the traditional values of the states-system, values that for three centuries, and longer, have been fundamental to the political achievement of the good life. But lastly, it also signals a rejection of moral relativism and an affirmation of civilized standards of conduct, which states may repudiate but not without paying a price.

Part Two

Cases

Chapter Five

Sovereignty under Siege:
From Intervention to Humanitarian Space

THOMAS G. WEISS AND JARAT CHOPRA

In the bloody aftermath of the Persian Gulf War, two major relief operations, "Safe Haven" and "Provide Comfort," materialized in spite of host government hostility and widespread reluctance in the region and in some United Nations circles. Approximately thirteen thousand U.S. troops and ten thousand soldiers from twelve other nations delivered 25 million pounds of food, water, medical supplies, clothing, and shelter to protected areas carved out of northern Iraq. Several observers considered these efforts "humanitarian intervention" or "humanitarian war,"[1] resuscitating a conceptual debate about sovereignty and the relative rights of governments and of innocent civilians, and stimulating essays in this volume.

There had emerged in Western public opinion a widespread sense of outrage against African countries where both governments and rebels had deprived innocent civilians of international relief as part of their war efforts. Further questions have been raised in the wake of efforts to respond to the humanitarian crisis in Somalia, as well as in the former Yugoslavia and elsewhere.[2]

Sovereignty is a shibboleth whose debate proves divisive. During the 1991 General Assembly, for example, representatives of developing countries were particularly concerned that reform of the UN humanitarian machinery might be a "Trojan horse" for great-power intervention after the cold war.[3] Yet, the erosion of sovereignty by human rights concerns continues, in spite of dissent from the third world. Expansion of the Security Council's scope of activities was affirmed in January 1992 for the first time by heads of state: "The non-military sources of instability in the economic, social, humanitarian and ecological fields have become threats to peace and security."[4] And the newly elected secretary-general, Boutros Boutros-Ghali, expeditiously reorganized UN humanitarian mechanisms in February of that year by creating a new Department of Humanitarian Affairs as part of his inner circle.

Like private ownership, sovereignty implies absolute rights to territory and the prohibition of trespass by others. The enclosure of territory by sovereign boundaries separates internal from external space. "Internal space," in this sense, means that within a territory there is unity of control, or some final point of authority, whose influence extends from the center to the borders. Moreover, unification of territory is achieved through linkage with the single identity of the *state* (as distinct from the *nation*, of which there may be many in this space); and the population is similarly unified through a common citizenship and passport, expressed in the misnomer "nationality."

Paradoxically, the identity of populations is being conceived at levels below and beyond the level of nationality, and it is the intersection of these trends that presents opportunities for international action.[5] Such subnational and ethnic particularism as that of the Basques, the Eritreans, the Tatars, and the Tamils has exerted pressure toward the dissolution of national borders that do not coincide with the presence of a self-defined ethnic group.

At the same time, and more importantly from the point of view of new international norms, the identity of populations is also expanding beyond nationality to be all-inclusive of the human species, irrespective of origin. This is the basis of a developing global humanitarian space, which is significantly eroding the distinction between concepts of "internal" and "external." Because humanitarian space is not linked to territory and transcends sovereign boundaries, it becomes increasingly difficult to speak of "*intervention*" within it. Consequently, humanitarian assistance shifts from being a potential violation of sovereign rights to being a safeguard for fundamental human rights. This process is in transition, and the term *intervention* has yet to be erased from the lexicon of international affairs.[6]

The conceptual gap between conventional notions of sovereignty and ascendant human rights was dramatically illustrated by UN member states debating in the aftermath of the Persian Gulf War the passage of Security Council Resolution 688, which insisted "that Iraq allow immediate access by international humanitarian organizations to all those in need of assistance in all parts of Iraq and to make available all necessary facilities for their operations."[7] Supporters of the resolution could not reconcile sovereign inviolability with the need to defend human welfare. They retreated to the position that Resolution 688 was upholding both; they did not try to redefine either, and argued that the protection of human rights was not a violation of sovereignty. They did, however, link human rights with international peace and security by asserting that failure to protect the Kurds would threaten the security and sovereignty of neighboring countries.

Humanitarian values are becoming a catalyst for international relations scholarship about interdependence in the 1990s,[8] in much the same way that earlier analyses of the environment, transnational corporations, and debt served to expose the weaknesses in Westphalian concepts.[9] Although hardcore realists still cling to the notion that states are supreme, they nonetheless admit that the stage is shared with a vast array of non-sovereignty-bound actors whose activities modulate the behavior of states.

The analytic significance of humanitarianism is that it reflects not a change in technology or phenomena but rather an evolution in perception. This qualitative shift from "material interdependence" to "moral interdependence" necessitates an ethical vision in which human values supersede state rights. This essay contends that the development of guidelines for the forcible delivery of emergency assistance, building upon both historical and recent experience, can break the human rights–sovereignty deadlock that so often paralyzes debate as well as decision making in a system where states remain the principal actors.

Sovereignty has traditionally excluded external interference in local affairs and has therefore prevented effective international responses to such atrocities as genocide by the Khmer Rouge, and the Iraqi government's gassing of Kurds. The cold war as a rivalry between superstates contributed to the preservation of a statist international order. Statism was taken particularly seriously in the newly independent and fragile countries of the developing world, "where even if the state acted unjustly or genocidally against its own people, the prevailing wisdom was that this was not an affair for outside powers."[10]

The creation of havens in Kurdistan in 1991 was a watershed indicating the extent to which sovereignty was under siege. However, although this precedent forecast the continued erosion of sovereignty and the expansion of humanitarian assistance, it is still not yet the norm. There is reluctance regarding these developments because of the role of power politics and the fear that humanitarian interventions would be undertaken for self-interested motives.

The voting results for Resolution 688—Cuba, Yemen, and Zimbabwe voted against the measure, while China and India abstained—indicated how uneasy third world countries were about violating absolute sovereignty within state boundaries. At best, they considered Kurdistan an exception to the rule. Deep suspicion of the event highlighted the practical inadequacies of humanitarian intervention, because there is no mechanism in place to differentiate truly humanitarian intentions from camouflaged and biased national interests. In short, a way should be found to distinguish interventions reflecting power politics from those safeguarding lives.

In his last annual "Report on the Work of the Organization," UN secretary-general Javier Pérez de Cuéllar called for reinterpretation of the Charter principles of sovereignty and noninterference in domestic affairs to allow for intervention on humanitarian grounds, as well as identification of the objective conditions under which it should be carried out.[11] Nevertheless, special interests in the Security Council in December 1992 converged unanimously to break the impasse in Somalia.[12] Third world delegations supported Resolution 794 because the situation was regarded as "unique," since the local government had disappeared. However, given the prevalence of micronationalism and "failed states,"[13] this fiction obscures the need for the third world to consider supporting humanitarian intervention under less unusual conditions.

In the past, debate about humanitarian intervention had been primarily among legal scholars, who affirmed the validity of the concept but disagreed on whether or not to codify the objective conditions under which it should be carried out.[14] The principal shortcoming was vulnerability to abuse: powerful states with ulterior motives would be able to intervene in weaker states on the pretext of protecting human rights.

Current debate has, however, moved beyond lawyers to include politicians, diplomats, military officers, and political scientists. Most of these practitioners and analysts have little understanding of the essential legal quality and background of humanitarian intervention. Our working hypothesis is that greater familiarity with international legal arguments would not only clarify debate but also assist in the development of a legitimate mechanism to guarantee, by force if necessary, the access of innocent civilians to international assistance.

Generally, this chapter concerns the legal framework of humanitarian action. Particularly, it notes that the terms *humanitarian* and *intervention* are contradictory when viewed through the prism of sovereignty. But we contend that the two can be reconciled by examining closely the sources of underlying authority for both sovereignty and human rights.

The argument proceeds in five parts. First, we examine a shift in the debate, largely since the Persian Gulf War, away from a legal emphasis on humanitarianism and toward a political focus on a general prohibition against intervention. Second, there follows a discussion about conceptualizing sovereignty and its diminished relevance in current policy preoccupations with intervention. Third, human rights are scrutinized as a means to bridge the contradictions of humanitarian intervention. Fourth, we suggest some criteria to regulate international humanitarian operations, criteria that reconcile sovereignty and human rights through common standards and collective action. We conclude with what we postulate is a growing role for international norms in the "new world order."

The Debate Shifts

Although battles are rarely won by relying on lessons from previous wars, new international principles necessarily build on past experience. The current—largely political—debate about humanitarian intervention represents a step backwards from the conceptual progress made during an extensive legal debate two decades ago. The present focus is on "intervention" per se, and therefore sovereignty, while previously domestic jurisdiction as an issue was considered secondary to preventing the misapplication of humanitarian norms. This preoccupation with "intervention" is something of a red herring. It ignores the more feasible task of developing adequate measures to prevent states from using the rhetoric of human rights to camouflage ulterior motives. It also disregards the UN Security Council's constitutional powers to decide to intervene on the basis of humanitarian needs, particularly when the intervention is represented as a response to threats to international peace and security.

Legal debates in the 1960s and 1970s concerned mainly the codification of rules and objective criteria for humanitarian intervention. They paralleled earlier arguments about the definition of "war" in the 1928 Kellogg-Briand Pact,[15] and the definition of "aggression" in the 1945 UN Charter.[16] Since no definition can be sufficiently comprehensive, it was argued in both cases that potential aggressors would be able to navigate between provisions and circumvent the letter of any prohibition. In fact, without defined parameters states were able to contravene without difficulty the spirit of the prohibition. For example, in 1931 Japan invaded Manchuria and declared that since a formal state of "war" did not exist, its actions were not inconsistent with the 1928 pact. Similarly, Italy invaded Abyssinia in 1936 without any formal declaration.

Whether the Kellogg-Briand Pact prohibited only formally declared "war" or also prohibited measures involving force short of war, Article 2(4) of the

UN Charter sought to rectify this discrepancy by forbidding "the threat or use of force." It still permitted and described exceptions in cases of self-defense (Article 51) and collective action (Articles 39–50). Unacceptable aggressive uses of force were not defined more specifically because of the fear that states would abuse such a definition, and also because the Charter's more general prohibition was thought to redress the restrictiveness of the term *war*.

In the absence of specificity in the Charter, states were able to avoid the international characterization of their actions as "aggression." This was possible partly because the generally accepted conception of "aggression" did not match a new world reality. Following World War II, the nature of conflict changed; increasingly, there were fewer interstate territorial disputes and a larger number of more complex internal insurgencies.[17] The decolonization process that began in Africa and Asia continues not only in the former Soviet empire but also within newly independent states, as ethnic particularism and subnationalism surface to dominate the agenda.[18] Foreign economic and political coercion has often replaced massed armies, and interventions have been based on requests from governments with questionable legitimacy. Superpowers intervened militarily in their spheres of influence (the United States in the Americas and Vietnam, and the Soviet Union in Eastern Europe and Afghanistan), as did lesser powers in theirs (for example, Cuba in the Caribbean and Africa, and India on the subcontinent). War "by proxy" entered the practice of international relations. In these instances, states resorted to justifying their interventions as assistance to legitimate governments.

Efforts to clarify what was meant by the "threat or use of force" which was prohibited under Article 2(4) included the 1974 passage of General Assembly Resolution 3314 on the "Definition of Aggression," which proved not to be comprehensive and excluded disputed categories of force in the interest of consensus. Nevertheless, states encountered difficulty in manipulating the provisions to their use and have instead relied on elastic interpretations of entirely separate, lawful justifications for using force, such as self-defense or invitation by host governments. Since states have had to flout the definition openly, unilateral uses of force have sometimes been easier to condemn since the first determination of "aggression" by the Security Council in 1976, when South Africa invaded Angola. In this way, definitions restrict and can thereby reduce incidents. Although determined efforts cannot be deterred by rules, coordinated responses to the clearly labeled Iraqi "aggression" against Kuwait dramatically illustrate what condemnation can entail in the post–cold war era.[19]

The legal debate concerning humanitarian intervention was remarkably similar, particularly the debate concerning whether objective criteria for such intervention should or could be codified. Comprehensiveness and fear of abuse were as prevalent as in earlier debates about war and aggression. There are essentially four lines of reasoning employed against codification:[20]

1. Whatever the rationale, interventions have not usually had humanitarian results. For example, the Crimean War was provoked by Russia's asserting in 1853–54 the right to protect Christians persecuted by the sultan of the Ottoman Empire. Far from supporting Russia, Great Britain and France intervened to protect Turkish sovereignty and independence. In 1931, Japan justified its invasion of Manchuria on humanitarian grounds. Hitler invaded Czechoslovakia in 1938 to protect ethnic Germans, who he claimed had been denied the right of self-determination and were suffering mistreatment. More recently, the Indian Army intervened in the Jaffna Peninsula to provide aid to the besieged Tamil minority; but airdrops and the presence of some fifty-five thousand troops failed to produce anything other than continued civil war in Sri Lanka and are more readily explained by Indian domestic politics than by purely humanitarian sentiments.

2. Codification would lead to further abuse, as states could base their actions on interpretations of legal provisions rather than on rhetorical proclamations. Thus law could be used by the strong against the weak and would serve power politics.

3. Whatever the objective conditions identified, it would still be impossible to distinguish between action sincerely based on humanitarian grounds and action based on ulterior, self-interested motives. Intentions cannot be identified without access to the policy-making *mind* of the state, which is hardly accessible in multilateral diplomacy.

4. The value of codification is minimal because legal systems allow for mitigating circumstances. In fact, humanitarian intervention by an interested state would not be inconsistent with existing international norms, which seek to restrict only harmful conduct. It is further argued that the prohibition on the use of force and intervention under Article 2(4) of the Charter is fragile enough and is so often breached that the codification of another exception would only erode it further.

At the same time, there are four arguments, largely mirror images of the above, conventionally used in favor of codification:[21]

1. The concept of humanitarian intervention has not been sufficiently tested precisely because there have been no agreed-upon, objective criteria. Besides, there have been a number of successes. As early as 480 B.C., Prince Gelon of Syracuse demanded that the Carthaginians halt child sacrifices to Saturn,[22] and more recently there has been successful international arm-twisting in the Sudan.[23]

2. Clearly defined parameters would inhibit states from easily rationalizing their abusive actions as driven by humanitarian considerations. Codification would make it possible to demand a high degree of proof from states claiming the right to intervene. Thus, powerful states would be restricted and the weak protected from intervention driven by insincere motives.

3. Moreover, if an intervention fulfilled the objective criteria stated in the codification, it would not matter if state action had been motivated by a concurrent self-interested policy.

4. Like any law, codification would restrict abuse, not merely affirm acceptable conduct. By further clarifying what conduct was unlawful, codification would strengthen the general prohibition on the use of force. If the terms *territorial integrity* and *political independence*, which figure so prominently in Article 2(4) of the Charter, were not interpreted to include the protection of human rights, they would be inconsistent with the spirit of the Charter. In fact, without such codification there is a glaring contradiction in the Charter, rather than protection of both domestic jurisdiction and human rights.

This legal debate was largely forgotten during the 1980s, but the aftermath of the Persian Gulf War placed the issue prominently on the global political agenda. Although the right of humanitarian intervention had dropped from sight, human rights commanded international interest. In the decades after the signing of the UN Charter and the adoption of the Universal Declaration of Human Rights, the boundaries of state sovereignty became more porous, as any number of technical, economic, and environmental challenges demonstrated. Moreover, areas that formerly had been considered largely domestic, such as minority and individual rights, became legitimate subjects of external scrutiny in much the same way that slavery, prisoners of war, and colonial relations had previously become matters of international rather than domestic concern.[24] This led to a growing body of international conventions, rules, and norms aimed at regulating the behavior of states. Following the creation of several prominent nongovernmental organizations, including Amnesty International, Jimmy Carter placed human rights at the center of his presidential platform.

Moreover, the internationalization of human rights has been recognized. Despite persisting controversy, human rights have become viewed as less Western and more universal, particularly when they are expanded to include not only civil and political rights but also economic, social, and cultural rights.[25] Until recently, though, the international community has had little capacity to respond when these norms are violated.

However, 125 years of practice by the International Committee of the Red Cross (ICRC) and four decades of the passage of international human rights treaties within the United Nations have led to the possibility of and the need for the implementation of norms. While disagreements continue over precise definitions and practical means for implementation, there is an overwhelming consensus even among governments that the subject of human rights is an appropriate one for international debate.[26] Hence, theoretical questions about the acceptability of humanitarian intervention have remained secondary to the practical problem of how such intervention should be conducted.

In December 1988, the General Assembly adopted Resolution 43/131, which formally recognized the rights of civilians to international aid and the role of nongovernmental organizations in natural and man-made disasters. Two years later, General Assembly Resolution 45/100 reaffirmed these rights and provided specific access corridors of "tranquility" for humanitarian aid workers. With the passage of Security Council Resolution 688 four months later, the issue of humanitarian intervention was thrust squarely onto the international political stage when the acute needs of some 1.5 million Kurds were interpreted as a threat to international peace and security.[27]

This trend continued with the first summit of the Security Council in January 1992, which reflected the expanding role of the United Nations in a variety of tasks—including election monitoring, promoting human rights, and humanitarian affairs—that had formerly been considered beyond the competence of the Security Council. In the following weeks, the deployment of UN troops into Yugoslavia and Cambodia, where cease-fires were tenuous and humanitarian needs great, indicated that the next generation of multinational military operations was developing.[28] Finally, in September and December 1992, the Security Council authorized the use of force to deliver humanitarian assistance in Bosnia (Resolution 776) and Somalia (Resolution 794).

In this process, however, the finely tuned legal debate has been overlooked in the defensive reactions of many developing countries. The old shibboleths of noninterference in the domestic affairs of governments and the inviolability of sovereignty have been cited instinctively, with increasing frequency and inadequate reflection and at higher and higher rhetorical decibel levels.

Can the protection of human rights justify setting aside these inherent organizing principles of the international system? Bold proponents of the cause, including the former UN secretary-general, call for limited acceptance of the idea. However, the global community has taken a step backwards. Moving forward with codification has become secondary to determining whether or not the basic right of humanitarian intervention exists. In the heat of political debate, delegates have lost sight of plausible answers to the following questions: What has sovereignty been, and what is it now? What is its relation to human rights? And what are the objective criteria of humanitarian intervention? It is to these questions that we now turn.

Sovereignty

Sovereignty features pivotally in the question of whether or not to intervene on humanitarian grounds. Intervention implies violation of or intrusion upon local authority; and though authority, like sovereignty, is an abstraction, its concrete form consists of territorial boundaries. Controversy over the crossing of borders occurs not only because borders represent the extent of local political control but also because the right to this control is a sacred underpinning of international order as currently understood. Hence, significant legal instruments have been concluded which prohibit action that is considered threatening to the overall system.[29]

There has always been a tension, however, between state sovereignty and other values that call into question its primacy.[30] Sovereignty is a legal fiction that continues to evolve. It is not an immutable feature of the human condition: the family, the tribe, and the city functioned quite well without it. In fact, the Permanent Court of International Justice pointed out in 1923 that "the question of whether a certain matter is or is not solely within the jurisdiction of a state is an essentially relative question; it depends on the development of international relations."[31] Gradually, issues that were once considered "domestic"—such as slavery, prisoners of war, and colonies—became matters of "international" concern. There is no permanent demarcation between domestic and international, no absolute rule that defines in perpetuity what is and is not permitted to a government.

Yet the widespread view persists that sovereignty is the only feasible mechanism for global organization in what Hedley Bull labeled the "anarchical society."[32] The inability of sovereignty to reflect adequately the self-development of international society has already relegated it to doubtful conceptual and practical relevance in such fields as trade, finance, and the environment.[33] For the protection of human rights, too, there has been a perceptible movement away from the anachronism of exclusive domestic jurisdiction. The Geneva Conventions and Additional Protocols are voluntary commitments by states that concede elements of sovereignty to ensure the protection of civilians and prisoners of war.[34]

States have been the principal building blocks of the international system, and their measure of legitimacy has been the attribution of sovereignty. As the only abstraction, sovereignty is special in the list of the criteria for statehood. The 1933 Montevideo Convention on the Rights and Duties of States lists three other, concrete criteria: a permanent population; defined territory; and a government. Although a state, like any collective construct, is something more than the sum of its parts, sovereignty transforms it into an absolute. Hinsley points out that sovereignty is not a fact, like energy or power; it is a quality of a fact.[35] Sovereignty is a characteristic of power that relegates its holder to a place above the law. A sovereign is immune from law and is only subject to self-imposed restrictions.

The birth of sovereignty in the nation-state is customarily dated from the end of the Thirty Years' War in 1648.[36] Essentially, after three decades of war between Catholics and Protestants, the Peace of Westphalia sought to separate the powers of church and state. In so doing, it transferred to nation-states the special godlike features of church authority. States inherited sovereignty, and with it an unassailable position above the law that has since remained the central element of international relations.[37]

Whether or not the power structure of nation-states ever accurately reflected textbook characteristics, sovereignty is no longer sovereign; the world has outgrown it.[38] The exclusivity and inviolability of state sovereignty are mocked by increasing interdependence. The atomic age has dramatically extinguished the boundaries between destruction and the destroyer. That the nations with the most powerful economies in the world, the Group of Seven, must now act in concert on major policies reflects increasing awareness of global financial integration.[39] Electronic communications and media have fostered conscious and unconscious identification with humanity. Convenient and accessible transportation has facilitated mass movements of people and the increasing psychological and physical de-linkage of populations from territory. Satellites and pollution penetrate space above territory, regardless of sovereign rights over air spaces and the proscription against intervention.

The language of international diplomacy increasingly reflects these realities. "The common heritage of mankind," enshrined in the 1979 Convention on the Moon and Other Celestial Bodies and the 1982 Convention on the Law of the Sea, "marks the passage from the traditional postulate of sovereignty to that of co-operation."[40] It is also the harbinger of an internationalization of "state-territory as a species of property."[41] Interconnectedness has entered the consciousness of public opinion and has been expressed through popular concern for the environment, human rights, and health—including the AIDS epidemic. The United Nations Conference on Environment and Development (UNCED) debated an "Earth Charter."

At the same time, the fiction of absolute sovereignty has remained surprisingly intact. States have been the only *members* of the international community, and individuals do not exist independently of states. Yet, the direct application of international law to individuals has begun to evolve and to penetrate the once-impermeable membrane of sovereignty.[42] This is the principal consequence of attributing *rights*, as well as *duties*,[43] to human beings. Also, there is direct participation by individuals in the international system: bodies such as the International Court of Justice (ICJ) and the International Law Commission (ILC) are composed of specialists who, "whilst appointed by governments, sit in their individual capacities as experts."[44] The UN secretary-general has an independent capacity under Article 99 of the Charter, which has been inadequately utilized in the past but which assumes new poignancy after the cold war.

Other nonstate actors also have become influential participants in international processes. The personality of international organizations, and their capacity to enter into relations with other subjects of international law, has been affirmed and has grown in the last four decades.[45] Business corporations have enjoyed limited status as persons under international law.[46] The mandate system of the League of Nations, the UN trusteeship system, and the concept of self-determination are expressions of the personality of *non*-states, or more precisely, *pre*states. National liberation movements—the Palestine Liberation Organization (PLO) and the South West Africa People's Organization (SWAPO) prior to Namibian independence—were given observer status in the General Assembly. In addition to expanding roles for transnational corporations, the proliferation of nongovernmental organizations (NGOs) in the last few decades has resulted in a certain privatization of diplomacy and the realization that local citizens cannot be excluded from the international system.[47] In October 1990, the UN General Assembly admitted the International Committee of the Red Cross as the first NGO with observer status, while many others hold consultative status with the Economic and Social Council.

Revolutions in technology and information, as well as the appearance of important actors lacking the attributes of state sovereignty, have shifted the criteria of statehood to include more qualitative and subjective standards,[48] and not only the objective characteristics of territory, population, and government. Is there a willingness and ability to observe international law? Is the regime racist or unlawfully constituted? That a state's legitimacy can determine its sovereignty gives the term *sovereignty* new meaning.

The supremacy of state sovereignty is untenable. Sovereignty as a transcendent source of law is supposed to operate hierarchically between ruler and ruled; it is not supposed to function horizontally, or relatively with other sovereigns. Sovereign equality supposedly prevented the development or legitimation of a *primus inter pares*. The basic flaw in the theory of sovereignty is that sovereignty was a unitary concept operating in a community: mutual respect implied not being sovereign at all. Thus it is universally recognized that in conflicts between the laws of a national sovereign and international law, the latter prevails.[49]

International organizations have further contributed to the erosion of textbook notions of state sovereignty. The earlier principle of requiring unanimity in votes in the League of Nations became decision making by majority in the United Nations, which means that sovereign states can be bound against their will by the votes of other states. The veto power of the permanent members of the Security Council vitiates the sovereignty of all other members because, by definition, one state cannot be "more" sovereign than another. Rapid decolonization led to the creation of a third world sensitive to domestic jurisdiction; at the same time the newly emerging states were often weak and had to rely on community laws for security, thus weakening the concept of sovereignty. In any case, the natural-law tradition within international legal thought always perceived the ultimate source of law as supranational, for only the law is sovereign: "[T]he public interest (state necessity, reason of state, or whatever) cannot be invoked against the law, except to the extent that the law itself so allows."[50]

What, then, has sovereignty become (or perhaps, what has it always been)? There are two interpretations, legal and political. Under international law, there are no degrees of sovereignty; it either exists or it does not. The narrow standard of traditional sovereignty forms a threshold: once a nation achieves a kind of critical mass, it is catapulted to a transcendent status through recognition by other members of the club of sovereign states. Legal sovereignty cannot be partially redefined or refined. Even when international lawyers account for factual challenges, they retain the classic formula. Reisman's concept of "popular sovereignty" is no less traditionally conceived than state sovereignty.[51] If the standard of definition is not met, sovereignty does not exist.

When NGOs, corporations, and revolutionary movements interact directly with states, both the nonstates and the states are considered to operate as legal equals. Employing the logic of the law, either both or neither are sovereign. Fear of attributing recognition explains the general hesitation of government officials and senior staff members of international secretariats to meet with insurgents or to consider national liberation movements entitled to protection under the humanitarian laws of war.[52]

When nonstates gain personality, statehood is no longer exclusive; and sovereignty loses its special meaning altogether. Moreover, if collective enforcement under Chapter VII of the UN Charter is acceptable intervention, states are not absolutely inviolable, and therefore they are not sovereign. Even if sovereignty is still the working assumption at the highest levels of government, current challenges to the concept lead to the conclusion that it is becoming a dead letter of international law.

In contrast, political scientists and international relations theorists have formulated a corruption of sovereignty, which they perceive in terms of degrees. Sovereignty is not considered incompatible with individual rights, nonstate actors, or permeable boundaries. For these scholars it is possible to be *more* sovereign or *less* sovereign. *Sovereignty* becomes an elastic term that refers to a category of social and political organization that is linked geographically to delimited territory. In contrast to the objective and largely standardized threshold of international law, political scientists view limits as determined subjectively and contextually. Humanitarian interventions can be classified as yet another exception to the anomaly of sovereignty.

Proponents of humanitarian intervention can, and usually do, rely on one of two arguments, both of which lead to the same conclusion. On the one hand, to maintain the traditional legal interpretation of sovereignty is to accept its obsolescence and recognize that the emperor has no clothes; if sovereignty is dead, humanitarian intervention does not violate a sacred principle. On the other hand, if humanitarian intervention is permitted as part of an expanded definition of sovereignty and solidarity, then it does not conflict with what remains of sovereignty.

Eliminating sovereignty from the lexicon of international relations in the foreseeable future is unlikely; state-centric structures will not agree easily to part with the basis for their status quo. Moreover, slights of hand and redefinitions that include humanitarian intervention would actually perpetuate the fiction of sovereignty and continue to slow the acceptance of such rapidly developing concepts as cross-boundary environmental protection, which are discussed elsewhere in this volume. One way to circumvent sovereignty altogether is to explore why human rights constitute a legitimate justification for intervention, and how codifying the rules of intervention could prevent abuse. We now turn to this issue.

The Conceptual Conflict between the Terms
Humanitarian and *Intervention*

Future acceptance of humanitarian intervention is linked to a conceptual conflict that reflects two contradictions or tensions running through the UN Charter: sovereignty and human rights; and peace and justice.

Explicit provisions in the Charter illustrate the first contradiction. Paragraph 1 of Article 2 bases the organization on the principle of sovereign equality of all member states; paragraph 4 prohibits the threat or use of force against any state; and paragraph 7 prohibits interference in "matters which are essentially within the domestic jurisdiction of any state." At the same time, preceding these provisions are the first words of the preamble: "We the Peoples of the United Nations determined . . . to reaffirm faith in fundamental human rights, in the dignity and worth of the human person, in the equal rights of men and women." Article 1(3) then states that "[t]he Purposes of the United Nations are: . . . To achieve international co-operation in solving international problems of an economic, social, cultural, or humanitarian character, and in promoting and encouraging respect for human rights and for fundamental freedoms for all without distinction as to race, sex, language, or religion." Under Articles 55 and 56, members are committed "to take joint and separate action in co-operation with the Organization" for the promotion of "equal rights and self-determination of peoples," including "universal respect for, and observance of, human rights." In Article 68, the Economic and Social Council "shall set up commissions . . . for the protection of human rights." Article 76(c) states that a basic objective of the trusteeship system is "to encourage respect for human rights and for fundamental freedoms for all."

The contradiction is apparent in the following questions: Are human rights exclusively within the domestic jurisdiction of states, or are they an international concern with community jurisdiction?[53] What is the separation of powers? Should the prohibition on using or threatening to use force against states be applicable to violence against human beings? Or, for that matter, is the threat or use of force against states permissible for the protection of human rights? Which authority is superior, a state's jurisdiction over individuals within its boundaries, or international jurisdiction over inalienable human rights?

In addition, there is the perennial tension between peace and justice, stability and change. The avoidance of war, or at least the control and centralization of violence, is central to the Charter. Order, ideally maintained through the enforcement mechanisms of Chapter VII, was considered the best means to maintain peace. However, order frequently amounted to the maintenance of the status quo, which enabled "those who already 'have' to secure their privileges and . . . encourage[d] the 'have nots' to accept their lot."[54] Seeking justice often implied disorder, instability, and therefore the scourge of war. Order and the hope for peace normally outweighed the concern for justice.

The concept of humanitarian intervention could not have developed if respect for sovereignty (and the prohibition against intervention) always superseded human values. The evidence of forty years suggests that human rights have grown steadily in clarity, strength, and breadth, and that this trend will continue. Although human rights do not systematically outweigh sovereignty, occasionally they do. And the intervention on behalf of the Kurds was a milestone that will serve to modulate behavior. There is as yet no pattern of human values overriding domestic jurisdiction, but the event was a dramatic harbinger reflecting the quickening pace of humanitarian developments and the extent to which sovereignty is under siege.

Human rights are now more clearly a justification for action than ever before, and norms are reaching a point at which they can be implemented and enforced.[55] In the last decade, the United Nations "has developed an impressive array of new enforcement machinery—machinery that is not widely known but that has fundamentally changed what the United Nations can and does accomplish to aid individual victims of human rights violations."[56] This machinery includes

—the establishment of a variety of specialized theme mechanisms (a working group and several independent rapporteurs) to take effective action (often on an emergency basis) wherever there are problems regarding several critical human rights violations that affect individuals: disappearances, summary executions, torture, and religious intolerance;
—the appointment of numerous special rapporteurs (or representatives) to examine conditions in individual countries (Afghanistan, Chile, El Salvador, Iran, and Romania are among the current ones);
—the establishment and expansion of the activities of new supervisory committees that monitor compliance with human rights treaties, sev-

eral of which have new optional complaint mechanisms through which
individuals can seek redress;
—the substantial expansion of the advisory services program that provides
technical assistance in human rights; and
—the development of a major initiative to expand UN public information
on human rights in a world campaign designed to advance awareness
of rights and of the UN machinery through which individuals can
claim their rights.

Moreover, in August 1991 the United Nations Observer Mission in El
Salvador (ONUSAL) became the first military-civilian operation with the
task of monitoring human rights abuses, a process that made an essential
contribution to the January 1992 cease-fire and peace treaty. Also, at the
World Conference on Human Rights, in 1993, the importance of human
rights was highlighted in proposals to restructure the secretariat, including
the creation of a commissioner for human rights who would cooperate
with the undersecretary-general for humanitarian affairs. Although there
is still an operational distinction between humanitarian and human rights
issues within the United Nations, the organization's future activities will
need to integrate the two areas to be more effective.

However, reversing the conventional hierarchy that places sovereignty
over human rights would not automatically reconcile internal contradictions in the term *humanitarian intervention.* In practice, the concept of
intervention would still imply violating sovereign authority without having identified a higher authority on which the supremacy of human rights
rests. Questioning the source of authority for human rights invites responses from many sides of a traditional split in jurisprudence: positivism
considers international law to be derived fundamentally from the will of
states,[57] while natural law maintains that there is a higher authority than
sovereignty. For positivists, human rights exist only because states permit
them to exist; and as sovereignty is the source of rights, it will always be
the higher authority. This contravenes the spirit of the movement toward
increased respect for human rights. As a formulation it is self-defeating.

Natural law is a suitable and logical means by which state abuse of
human rights can be challenged. But one of the reasons that human rights
have not yet gained primacy is that their source of authority is more difficult to identify than the concrete mechanisms of states. Identifying the
source of natural law is an ancient problem, but one that merits increased
attention today in order to deduce the legitimacy and authority for the
concept of human rights, as well as for their protection.

Although both sovereignty and the source of natural law are absolutes, they differ in their formulations. The former is quantified in secular terms and manifested as the state; the latter is a qualitative determination of basic goods.[58] Thomas Aquinas's "treatise on law" in the *Summa Theologiae* consolidated much of the earlier thought on this subject since Plato's *Republic* and Aristotle's *Nicomachean Ethics*. Aquinas encapsulated his definition of natural law in the condensed phrase *participation legis aeternae in rationali creatura:* the participation of the eternal law in rational creatures. It is an operation between our capacity to understand and existing universal laws. This principle is comparable to the Tao, or way, of Lao Tzu; Confucian rites or "style of life"; Hindu and Buddhist dharma, or right action; Islamic Sunna, or model behavior of the Prophet; and Japanese giri, or rules of behavior.[59] Aquinas's "account of the source of natural law thus focuses first on the experienced dynamisms of our nature, and then on the intelligible principles which outline the aspects of human flourishing, the basis values grasped by human understanding."[60]

The authority for natural law is what *ought* to be. It is very much the purpose of law to restrict possible destructive action. Allott summarizes: "Law constrains or it is a travesty to call it law. . . . Law transcends the power of the powerful and transforms the situation of the weak or it is a travesty to call it law."[61] While what human rights ought to be has been enumerated, clarification of how they ought to be enforced has only begun. It is to the notion of collective enforcement that we now turn.

Common Standards and Collective Action

There is no disagreement about whether or not, in principle, humanitarian intervention is acceptable. The crux of the issue is fear of abuse (*raisons d'état* couched in humanitarian terms) and the question of how the danger can be mitigated to make the pill of intervention easier to swallow, in theory and in practice. This problem has become more, rather than less, acute in the wake of interventions in Kurdistan, the former Yugoslavia, and Somalia.

Swallowing is particularly difficult for third world countries.[62] Their representatives draw obvious parallels to imperialists who intervened on the basis of questionable "principles" such as "civilization," the "white man's burden," and "manifest destiny."[63] The fact that in the present international system those with the resources to intervene in the third world are former colonial powers or large and traditionally obtrusive neighbors does not foster confidence among the governing elites of vulnerable developing countries, who have an "obsession with security."[64]

Nonetheless, there are two starting points for dialogue and decision making. The first is the need to codify objective criteria governing the circumstances in which humanitarian intervention is justifiable. The second is the need to ensure that decisions about humanitarian intervention be exclusively and genuinely collective.

Some authors have attempted to identify lists of objective criteria.[65] Lillich enumerates five factors that would validate humanitarian intervention: the immediacy of the violation of human rights; the extent of violation of human rights; invitation to use forcible self-help; the degree of coercive measures employed (i.e., proportionality); and the relative disinterestedness of the intervener.[66] Moore adds five qualifications: an immediate and extensive threat to fundamental human rights, particularly a threat of widespread loss of human life; a proportional use of force which does not threaten a destruction of values greater than that posed by the existing threat to human rights; a minimal effect on authority structures; a prompt disengagement, consistent with the purpose of the action; and immediate full reporting to the Security Council and appropriate regional organizations.[67]

In the context of relief for man-made disasters, Minear has set down nine operational principles governing aid that is truly humanitarian: there should be a recognition of the importance of safeguarding human life; the motives for assistance missions should be transparent, to affirm legitimacy; there should be consistent response to assistance needs in each case, and therefore assistance should be automatic and not selective; comprehensive assistance should be provided to all categories of persons in need, without reference to artificial distinctions such as those between "refugees" and "displaced persons"; the success of assistance operations should be dependent on local popular participation, or mutuality; there should be a preference for civilian management in civilian humanitarian initiatives; there should be increasing fidelity to international law; disaster prevention measures and methods of peaceful conflict resolution should be fostered to avoid the need for intervention after the fact; and there should be accountability by the assistance donor, as well as by host governments to their own populations.[68]

An essential problem with codification has reemerged in the current debate: the dilemma about specificity. The enumeration of appropriate circumstances might exclude unforeseen situations requiring assistance which do not fall strictly within any agreed-upon categories. Although exhaustive definitions can become too restrictive, flexible provisions are open to abuse.

One observer has noted that "humanitarian intervention is something of a chameleon,"[69] with its colors changing and reflecting the tints of both self-interest and altruism. States that have intervened by force—for instance, India in East Pakistan (1971) or Sri Lanka (1987), Vietnam in Kampuchea (1979), or the United States in Grenada (1982) and Panama (1989)—have mixed strategic and economic objectives with humanitarian concerns. It is difficult to separate unilateral humanitarian intervention from anything more than a type of realpolitik.

Therefore, a practical way to reduce the danger of abuse is to restrict humanitarian intervention involving the use of military coercion exclusively to the category of collective action as understood in Chapter VII of the UN Charter. Prohibiting humanitarian intervention as a form of self-help would circumvent the unreliability of unilateral interventions. Oscar Schachter stopped short of referring to Resolution 688 as an authorization for humanitarian intervention: "It is unlikely that most governments would approve a broad right of the United Nations to introduce troops for humanitarian purposes against the wishes of the government."[70] But, he argued, the United Nations could override reluctant host governments by invoking enforcement procedures under Chapter VII of the Charter.

To impede the resort by states to illegitimate justifications, the UN Security Council should have sole responsibility for determining the existence of humanitarian crises that warrant outside intervention, in the same way that it has sole authority under Article 39 to "determine the existence of any threat to the peace, breach of the peace, or act of aggression." Like interventions by states, interventions by regional organizations have not been immune from bias. Although constituted multilaterally, regional forces are invariably dominated by a local hegemon.[71] Only a universal forum such as the United Nations can hope to avoid the kind of charade performed by the United States in Grenada (1982) and by Nigeria in Liberia (1991), under the reluctant auspices of the Organization of Eastern Caribbean States and the Economic Community of West African States (ECOWAS), respectively.[72]

While weak governments and developing countries fear a powerful Security Council, the alternative is unbridled big-power politics. A former permanent representative of the United States to the United Nations, Thomas Pickering, expressed this clearly:

Before the Security Council is ready regularly to serve as global crisis manager, there needs to be a reasonably clear and predictable consensus on how and to what extent it should address threats to international security arising from internal situations . . . [T]hough no such consensus now exists, we have seen a more dramatic narrowing of differences on this issue in the last year of the UN's existence than in the previous 45 . . . [S]o long as sharp political differences of view remain, we must stay open—as the UN Charter provides—to alternative regional and even unilateral tools.[73]

To strengthen collective resolve and avoid disputes in the face of crisis, an independent humanitarian commission could monitor potential catastrophes and bring them to the attention of the Security Council through the secretary-general. Although humanitarian action would not be guaranteed, the Security Council, even its permanent members, would find embarrassment and difficulty in remaining aloof from extensive violations of human rights. They would at least have to justify publicly their hands-off stance when military force is required and an independent body calls for action.

Independent monitoring could be a task for regional organizations. Although many call for enhancing such organizations' operational role in humanitarian intervention,[74] watchdog monitoring—for example, through the creation of an African or Asian "ICRC" or an independent "Humanitarian Aid Watch"—seems more plausible and more likely to be efficacious.[75] Regional organizations have traditionally remained mute on internal conflicts and have demonstrated even more deference to domestic jurisdiction and state sovereignty than has the United Nations. Furthermore, they have a poor track record, a history of interventions that have exacerbated rather than pacified conflicts: the Organization of African Unity in Chad and the Western Sahara; the Arab League in Lebanon; the Organization of American States in a variety of conflicts; the European Union in Yugoslavia; ECOWAS in Liberia. However, at the diplomatic level they have a comparative advantage. Particularly in monitoring humanitarian crises and violations of individual rights, they might be criticized less for "outside imposition" of "foreign values and traditions" than groups based in Geneva or New York would be.

As in the gradual escalation of provisions under Chapter VII, outside intervention should not be based on the use of military force as a first recourse. The international declaration that a crisis was a threat to international peace and security would facilitate the right to provide less threatening assistance from neighboring territories. Only worst-case scenarios would justify coercion, and the entire array of more subtle humanitarian diplomatic measures should be resorted to first.

Many NGOs and even some governments claim that the right to intervene in humanitarian emergencies exists separately from the Charter. However, a Chapter VII–style graded response would provide a workable compromise and help overcome the reluctance of most governments to consider international action. While the danger of politicization exists, and no action could be taken against the will of a permanent member of the Security Council, the advantages of a genuinely international decision-making process to determine when outside humanitarian interventions are justified would outweigh the disadvantages. The alternative is the conscience of single individuals, single organizations, or single governments; and such unilateralism is not a sufficient guarantee against abuse.

The direction or conduct of humanitarian operations should ideally be a United Nations activity, particularly when military force is used. In the absence of agreements under Article 43 for a standing UN force and provisions for an adequate international military capacity, however, more thought needs to be given to clarifying the exact meanings of "collective action" and "subsidiary organ."

"Collective action" must entail the subordination of command and control of sovereign armed forces to a centralized instrument, authorized to act by the larger community in the event of a crisis in which coercion is required to enforce international decisions.[76] Action through international organization, or multilateralism, is distinct from multinational action, which amounts to individual states independently cooperating in a particular venture, effectively as a form of self-help. Collective action must be conducted according to standard operating procedures that have been devised and agreed upon prior to a crisis and are consistently applied.

The importance of "collective action" is not necessarily in the conduct of an operation, which may be executed by one, two, or many states, but in the decision to act as well as the continued direction of an operation. Given the United States–led coalition's prosecution of the Persian Gulf War and the lack of reporting once the decision to authorize "all necessary means" was taken,[77] the nature of centralized command and control has assumed vital importance for future humanitarian interventions as well as for other enforcement actions. The United States–led Unified Task Force (UNITAF), or "Operation Restore Hope," was an important step, since it was under greater international scrutiny and subject to a number of procedures that enabled the UN secretary-general to monitor and participate in the direction of the operation. However, the transfer of responsibilities to the United Nations–controlled UN Operation in Somalia (UNOSOM II) verged on operational disaster.

United Nations command and control has traditionally reflected three shortcomings. First, on the technical level, communications have been erratic owing to multiple languages, procedures, and equipment; and problems have been exacerbated by the lack of common training for individual contingents. Second, operations have suffered from multiple chains of command within a theater, and between the military and civilian sides of the UN secretariat. Third, the conventional tendency of contingents to seek guidance from their own capitals is intensified by complexity and danger in the field, such as reflected by the multiple strains in the former Yugoslavia.

A collective alternative to the ideal security system envisioned in the Charter is the appointment and direction by the Security Council of agents with the military competence to ensure compliance with international decisions. Under Article 7(2) of the UN Charter, the principal organs of the organization, including the Security Council, can appoint an agent or establish "such subsidiary organs as may be found necessary." The Charter nowhere defines "subsidiary organ," but Kelsen argues that it can include a collegiate body, a single individual or member state, or a group of members.[78] This raises the question of whether the Security Council can delegate the execution of enforcement measures—as a category of tasks distinct from others—to a "subsidiary organ." Although the Charter is unclear, it would seem that the answer is affirmative if three conditions are met.[79] First, it should be clear that the state or group of states is acting on behalf of the world organization and that the link between the two is direct. Second, since command of the operation is not functionally part of the United Nations' own administration, the instructions from the organization to its agents must be clear, specific, and incontestable. Third, and finally, the agent must be directly responsible to the authority of the organization.

The inadequate contact between the United Nations and allied forces in the Persian Gulf after Resolution 687, as well as in Kurdistan after Resolution 688, and the mixed experience with U.S. forces in Somalia, has made imperative the formalization of "sub-contracts" for humanitarian relief to subsidiary organs. The United States may choose to permit its forces to operate only under U.S. or NATO command and control, ceding them to the UN secretary-general only for safer and smaller operations, as in Macedonia. If NATO command structures, such as those in the former Yugoslavia, are strengthened and become more comprehensive, relations with the United Nations will have to be clarified.

In the longer term, the United Nations needs to develop a professional capacity to conduct such operations on its own and also revive and modify the Military Staff Committee, or its equivalent, in order to mitigate disputes as to the collectivity or legitimacy of actions called for by the Security Council. The conceptual framework for multilateral military undertakings is being developed through such efforts as the secretary-general's *Agenda for Peace*, the veritable cottage industry of peacekeeping analyses, and the new thinking in many staff colleges and defense ministries.[80] However, there have been too few operational improvements within the United Nations. Efforts to establish a Situation Room and the Task Force for Stand-By Agreements have had little success and have not fostered much confidence in the armed forces of major powers about placing the United Nations in charge of combat missions.

However, the United Nations might begin by strengthening its humanitarian assistance mechanisms for interventions not involving the use of force. Coordination of assistance efforts is a significant step toward collective action. General Assembly Resolution 46/182 called for the appointment of a single humanitarian aid coordinator with the authority, at least in principle, to respond to governments and opposition groups that deny assistance to suffering civilians. It also laid the groundwork for new and potentially useful institutional mechanisms, including a special $50-million emergency fund, a standing interagency committee in Geneva, unified appeals, and a new roster of international experts.

Observers have often criticized the United Nations for inefficiency and duplication in its emergency assistance, because individual agencies seemingly are often more concerned with their particular objectives and fundraising needs than with effective delivery. The harmonization of efforts among intergovernmental and nongovernmental organizations was seen as an imperative in the aftermath of problems in the Persian Gulf War.[81] The new coordinator and institutional machinery, when backed by the secretary-general and the five permanent members of the Security Council, should be in a position to manage operations more effectively than in the past.

Ethical Norms and the New World Order

The struggle toward a law of humanitarian intervention is a twofold task: to mollify contradictions between human rights and intervention; and to codify norms and procedures so that humane values cannot be used to justify unacceptable and self-interested interventions.[82] Overcoming the abuse of humanitarianism as a smokescreen for ulterior motives provides a common ground in debate. Drawing upon analyses of humanitarian intervention as well as reexamining legal meanings in a political context provides the means not only to frame the question more accurately but also to build bridges and act. The previous UN secretary-general, Javier Pérez de Cuéllar arrived at a similar conclusion: "We need not impale ourselves on the horns of a dilemma between respect for sovereignty and the protection of human rights. The last thing the United Nations needs is a new ideological controversy. What is involved is not the right of intervention but the collective obligation of States to bring relief and redress in human rights emergencies."[83]

In spite of setbacks, there still remains a rare opportunity to place long-standing humanitarian concerns at the center of international decision making as policy makers come to grips with the new dynamics of international peace and security. As the heads of state at the January 1992 Security Council summit declared: "The members of the Council agree that the world now has the best chance of achieving international peace and security since the foundation of the United Nations."[84]

While the Persian Gulf War was a dramatic illustration, humanitarian concerns have been central to evolving UN operations in the former Yugoslavia, Cambodia, El Salvador, and Somalia, as in virtually every other regional conflict. The continued erosion of sovereignty and the emergence of a human rights regime converge when it is finally possible to enforce the growing recognition of an individual's right to humanitarian aid, irrespective of a government's permission. Although sovereignty distinguishes between interstate and intrastate conflicts, the applicable humanitarian provisions for civilians and for prisoners of war are the same in all conflicts. Under the provisions of the Fourth Geneva Convention of 1949 and the two Additional Protocols of 1977, protection is extended to civilians not taking an active part in hostilities.

Half a million civilians died or were wounded in fighting among the clans in Somalia between 1991 and 1993. In Yugoslavia in the same period, there were some two hundred thousand deaths and numerous atrocities perpetrated among civilians, as well as approximately 1 million refugees and 3 million persons internally displaced.[85] This is adequate testimony to the need for vigorous and timely action.

Missing, however, is what critics refer to as a moral authority for humanitarian intervention. Recent thinkers have looked beyond sovereignty toward social organization based on culture or society defined in their widest senses.[86] As these undermine sovereignty, we must better understand the human desire for absolutes, inherent in both individuals and communities.[87] To transcend the dictates of sovereignty, we must articulate an ethical vision and so reshape human relations with authority.[88]

While human needs do not as yet override sovereignty in all instances, recent actions by the General Assembly and the Security Council nonetheless represent a significant milestone along the path toward ensuring the welfare of war-afflicted civilian populations. This process is an extension of Henri Dunant's founding of the Red Cross in the nineteenth century and of continued efforts to convince states to cede sovereignty in order to protect innocent civilians or soldiers *hors de combat.*

Dramatic actions contributing to the reconceptualization of the limitations of sovereignty have been taken by nonstate humanitarians. In the last few decades, humanitarian NGOs have taken matters into their own hands and resorted to cross-border operations that were "illicit"—in terms of the narrowest interpretation of international law, if not in terms of morals—while intergovernmental organs were struggling to define the rights of innocent civilians in war zones.[89]

As a minimum, the moral and political arguments in favor of humanitarian intervention have grown stronger. The complacency on the part of the international community which formerly permitted states and insurgent movements to repress their own populations or to starve them to death is being called increasingly into question. In fact, the United States was far less bullish in Kurdistan than was France. In sponsoring Resolution 688, Bernard Kouchner, then France's minister for humanitarian action, had persuaded the Mitterand administration that the right of peoples had to take precedence over the preservation of the order of states.

Modern humanitarian operations frequently require violating international boundaries. This reality led to a much-publicized debate between the International Committee of the Red Cross and Kouchner.[90] Much of the rhetorical fireworks can be explained by differences in style (discreet versus high profile) and tactics (prudent and deliberate versus audacious and confrontational). Bitterness had grown continuously since Kouchner broke with the ICRC over policy in the 1968 Biafran civil war and founded the "Médecins sans Frontières" and later the "Médecins du Monde."

However, both agree on the existence of the principle that individuals have a right to international assistance and that aid agencies have a right to reach innocent civilians. It is preferable to employ terms such as *humanitarian access* or *humanitarian space,* which are less provocative than *humanitarian intervention* or *humanitarian interference.* Conceptually, the provision of humanitarian assistance is not intervention or interference but an accepted part of international law. Guaranteeing the room to maneuver for both aid providers and recipients, becomes obligatory for a de facto or de jure government. If it fails to do so, and life-threatening suffering results, an international police action can result. Artificial spatial boundaries of states are not relevant for solidarity among human beings; humanitarian space is required.

Disagreement arises in the absence of a resolution such as Resolution 688 or Resolution 794, which remain at present exceptions rather than rules. As the guardian of international law, the ICRC strives to ensure that parties agree to respect commitments, whereas others (like Kouchner) champion the position, taken by some officials of NGOs and UN organizations, that no permission is necessary. Civilians have rights, and aid agencies have a "duty" and a "right" to intervene. Analytically, NGO action should be distinguished from activities by intergovernmental actors, whose "intervention" is normally passive and low-level (for instance, the collection of information, the investigation of complaints, the monitoring of compliance). The actual delivery of humanitarian relief by many NGOs routinely ignores borders and amounts to a new conception in which human values predominate over narrow definitions of domestic jurisdiction.

The media are another nongovernmental actor playing a crucial role on the global humanitarian stage. Their ability to communicate the plight of innocent civilians has also exposed domestic jurisdiction to new pressures from international public opinion. Although publicity can in the short term hurt the cause of humanitarianism,[91] it usually forces governments to react to public opinion; and even nondemocratic regimes are sometimes sensitive to such pressures.

Observers often point to the BBC television special in 1984 that catalyzed a dramatic reversal of the public and private lethargy that had characterized reactions to the Ethiopian famine. Moreover, the arm-twisting to which the Khartoum government and the insurgents of the Sudanese People's Liberation Army (SPLA) were subjected in 1989 was made possible in this way, as was the more dramatic intervention in Kurdistan in 1991. In these cases, as a result of media-induced pressures from public opinion, donor governments and aid agencies had to respond more quickly and energetically than they themselves would have wished.

The international humanitarian interventions in Iraq and Somalia represent an intergovernmental turning point. Earlier actions taken under Chapter VII of the UN Charter—the 1966 and 1968 binding economic sanctions against the white minority regime in Rhodesia, and the 1977 arms embargo against the Republic of South Africa—had been harbingers of enforcement action. When a consensus emerged about the need for action in the light of a widespread violation of basic human rights, the international community could act.

However, by comparison with the use of economic sanctions, the use of multilateral military force is a significant escalation in enforcement. Previously, the use of military forces to rescue the nationals of one's own country from foreign territory where they were endangered was the only form of military intervention for humanitarian purposes that was widely accepted.[92] In other cases, governments had treated humanitarian intervention as they had treated euthanasia,[93] unwilling to legalize it for fear of abuse, but willing to look the other way under exceptional circumstances. However, since 1945 such exceptions have become more widespread and have included a number of armed interventions in which a primary, albeit not exclusive, concern has been humanitarian: India's intervention in East Pakistan in 1971; Vietnam's in Kampuchea in 1978; Tanzania's in Uganda and France's in the Central African Empire in 1979; India's in Sri Lanka in 1987; and finally the United States–led interventions by coalition forces in Kurdistan in 1991 and in Somalia in 1992–93. It is ironic that some of the countries that initiated these interventions are among the developing countries that have most vociferously defended the sanctity of sovereignty in international forums.

The international community now appears to be perched on the brink of a new era and is moving toward codification of principles and identification of the appropriate conditions under which humanitarian imperatives can override domestic jurisdiction. Intervention to protect one's own nationals has, over time, also evolved to include coercive action in another state on behalf of non-nationals when egregious violations of human rights occur. In particular, humanitarian access has become an accepted principle of international law; and access to suffering civilians can be legitimately guaranteed by force, if necessary, with a decision by the Security Council under Chapter VII.

Given pressures on governments to address domestic concerns and the proliferation of crises that require outside help, humanitarian enforcement may be rare, but it should at least halt genocide or the mass slaughter of civilians. Given the lack of resources and military professionalism on the part of the United Nations, the use of force to protect human rights may be postponed until the world organization's record on enforcement of humanitarian delivery is more firmly established. Operationally, such decisions should be made by the Security Council, but effective command and control may be under the major power providing the bulk of the military resources or under a regional organization.

Sovereignty is under siege from many sides. But the nature and weight of humanitarian values may provide a framework and new "teeth" for the concept of a new world order. Humanitarianism provides a very apt lens through which to examine the turbulent evolution of the international system as the twenty-first century approaches.

Chapter Six

State Sovereignty and International Intervention: The Case of Human Rights

JACK DONNELLY

Human rights, as they have traditionally been understood, regulate certain relations between individuals and the states of which they are nationals. But if sovereignty means, roughly, that what a state does to its own nationals (and other resources) on its own territory is its own business, a state's human rights practices are prima facie protected exercises of sovereign prerogative. This orthodox understanding has changed significantly over the past half century. States now operate in an environment of formal and informal legal and political constraints on their human rights practices. I will argue, however, that sovereignty remains the central norm in the politics of international human rights. "The international community," except in rare circumstances, does not have the right to exercise the power to intervene on behalf of human rights, nor has it been willing to do so. Although human rights have become an accepted, if still controversial, subject of bilateral, multilateral, and transnational international relations, they have not been, and are not likely to become, a standard subject of coercive intervention.

Defining Terms

The crucial terms in my argument are controversial. In fact, this volume contains chapters devoted to exploring the meanings of *sovereignty, inter-*

vention, and *international community.* Therefore, I need to begin with definitions of these terms, as well as of *human rights.*

Human Rights

Human rights are ordinarily understood as the rights one has simply because one is a human being. They are held equally by all human beings, irrespective of any rights or duties individuals may (or may not) have as citizens, members of families, or parts of any public or private organization or association. They are also inalienable rights, because being human is not something that can be renounced, lost, or forfeited. In practice, not all people *enjoy* all their human rights, let alone enjoy them equally. Nonetheless, all human beings *have* (the same) human rights and hold them equally and inalienably.

For the purposes of international relations, philosophical controversies connected with human rights can be largely ignored. Virtually all states agree that the 1948 Universal Declaration of Human Rights and the 1966 International Human Rights Covenants, sometimes referred to collectively as the International Bill of Human Rights, provide an authoritative list of internationally recognized human rights. (See table 1.)

Given the concerns of this volume, one of the most interesting aspects of human rights, as they are ordinarily understood, is their special relation to the state. Although people may be prevented from enjoying the substance of human rights by a wide range of individuals and organizations, "human rights" are usually taken to have a special reference to the ways in which states treat their own citizens in their own territory. For example, domestically we distinguish muggings, private assaults, and ransom kidnappings, which typically are not considered to involve human rights violations, from police brutality, torture, and arbitrary arrest and detention, which are violations of human rights. Internationally, we distinguish terrorism, famine, war, and war crimes from "human rights" issues, even though they also lead to denials of life and security.[1] In other words, state sovereignty is built into our ordinary understanding of international human rights.

Sovereignty and (Non-)Intervention

To be sovereign is to be subject to no higher power. For the past two or three centuries, international relations have been structured around the legal fiction that states have exclusive (sovereign) jurisdiction over their

Table 1.
Internationally Recognized Human Rights

The International Bill of Human Rights recognizes the rights to
  Equality of rights without discrimination (D1, D2, E2, E3, C2, C3)
  Life (D3, C6)
  Liberty and security of person (D3, C9)
  Protection against slavery (D4, C8)
  Protection against torture and cruel and inhuman punishment (D5, C7)
  Recognition as a person before the law (D6, C16)
  Equal protection of the law (D7, C14, C26)
  Access to legal remedies for rights violations (D8, C2)
  Protection against arbitrary arrest or detention (D9, C9)
  Hearing before an independent and impartial judiciary (D10, C14)
  Presumption of innocence (D11, C14)
  Protection against ex post facto laws (D11, C15)
  Protection of privacy, family, and home (D12, C17)
  Freedom of movement and residence (D13, C12)
  Seek asylum from persecution (D14)
  Nationality (D15)
  Marry and found a family (D16, E10, C23)
  Own property (D17)
  Freedom of thought, conscience, and religion (D18, C18)
  Freedom of opinion, expression, and the press (D19, C19)
  Freedom of assembly and association (D20, C21, C22)
  Political participation (D21, C25)
  Social security (D22, E9)
  Work, under favorable conditions (D23, E6, E7)
  Free trade unions (D23, E8, C22)
  Rest and leisure (D24, E7)
  Food, clothing, and housing (D25, E11)
  Health care and social services (D25, E12)
  Special protections for children (D25, E10, C24)
  Education (D26, E13, E14)
  Participation in cultural life (D27, E15)
  A social and international order needed to realize rights (D28)
  Self-determination (E1, C1)
  Humane treatment when detained or imprisoned (C10)
  Protection against debtor's prison (C11)
  Protection against arbitrary expulsion of aliens (C13)
  Protection against advocacy of racial or religious hatred (C20)
  Protection of minority culture (C27)

Note: Includes all rights enumerated in two of the three documents of the International Bill of Human Rights or having a full article in one document. The source of each right is indicated in parentheses, by document and article number. *Abbreviations: D,* Universal Declaration of Human Rights; *E,* International Covenant on Economic, Social, and Cultural Rights; *C,* International Covenant on Civil and Political Rights.

territory and its occupants and resources. Most of the fundamental norms, rules, and practices of international relations rest on the premise of state sovereignty. Even many characteristic violations of sovereignty are themselves rooted in state sovereignty, that is, in the absence of political power or legal authority above states.

Nonintervention is the duty correlative to the right of sovereignty. Other states are obliged not to interfere with the internal actions of a sovereign state. A state's actions are a legitimate concern of other states only if they impinge on the sovereignty of those states. This technical legal sense is fully consistent with ordinary usage. For example, the first definition of *intervention* in the *Oxford English Dictionary* is "The action of intervening, 'stepping in,' or interfering in any affair, so as to affect its course or issue. Now frequently applied to the interference of a state or government in the domestic affairs or foreign relations of another state."[2]

The rights of sovereignty and the duty of nonintervention are, of course, only a starting point for international relations. They may be eliminated, restricted, or infringed upon by formal legal processes, by legally unregulated action that falls short of intervention, or by the use of power contrary to law.

States, in the exercise of their sovereign prerogatives, are free to relinquish their legal immunity from international interference. International law records the restrictions that states have accepted on their sovereignty, typically through treaties and similar contractual agreements. If the party authorized to interfere is a multilateral agency, the resulting shift in authority from states to the international community would be of special relevance to the concerns of this volume.

States (and to a lesser extent nongovernmental organizations [NGOs] and some intergovernmental organizations) are also legally at liberty to use the ordinary instruments of foreign policy short of coercive intervention. This domain of unregulated interference is, as we shall see, the principal area of international human rights activity. It does not, however, involve a significant transfer of power or authority to the international community.

We should also note that states often violate or fail to discharge their international obligations, including the obligation of nonintervention. In practice, however, we can point to few instances of illegitimate coercive intervention on behalf of human rights. The United States and the Soviet Union during the cold war era regularly engaged in what might be called antihumanitarian intervention, but we can point to extraordinarily few instances of humanitarian intervention in the past century.[3]

Different means of intervention also need to be distinguished. In particular, we need to distinguish between strong, or coercive, and weak, or noncoercive, means of influencing the affairs of another state.

All of international relations involves attempting to influence the behavior of states (as well as that of intergovernmental organizations and various transnational actors). This involves "interfering" in political processes to alter international outcomes. But if we are to count even private diplomatic expressions of concern as "intervention," the concept is of little interest. Only when the interference is coercive do we have a type of international practice that can be usefully distinguished from the rest of international relations. In particular, only in strong, or *coercive,* interference in the internal affairs of states do we have restrictions on or infringements of sovereignty.[4]

Of course, "coercion" is itself a contested notion, and a concept with strong and weak senses as well. The threat or use of force is certainly coercive, as is an economic embargo backed by military force. But what about a reduction in foreign aid, or calls to boycott trade? Although at the margins the line between sovereignty-respecting, noncoercive interference and coercive intervention may be ambiguous, the conceptual distinction is basically clear. Furthermore, it is essential to assessing the relative balance of power and authority between states and the international community. Only legitimate multilateral coercive interference involves a significant transfer of political authority from states to the international community.

Combining this distinction between coercive and noncoercive interference with the distinction between authorized, unregulated, and prohibited interference yields six categories of intervention. In practice, though, very little noncoercive interference is prohibited, and few acts of coercive interference are unregulated. Therefore, we will be concerned primarily with four possible types of "intervention":

1. Authorized coercive interference. This involves a transfer of authority from states to the international community, resulting in a redefinition of the range of sovereignty.[5] The security zones in postwar Iraq are striking examples.
2. Prohibited coercive interference. Such actions unambiguously involve a violation of sovereignty. The invasion of the Dominican Republic by the United States in 1965 and the invasion of Czechoslovakia by the Soviet Union in 1968 are good examples.
3. Authorized noncoercive interference. Human rights treaties that establish mandatory reporting procedures fall into this category.
4. Unregulated noncoercive interference. Official public expressions of

concern over the suspension of parliamentary government in Peru in the spring of 1992 are a good example.

Approaching the question from the perspective of sovereignty rather than intervention yields a complementary picture. Kratochwil's chapter uses a property metaphor to conceptualize sovereignty. Of special interest are the rights of use and of exclusion. International human rights standards in effect seek to regulate certain "uses" of a state's population, and international human rights activities challenge states' rights of exclusion.

Illegitimate coercive intervention is a violation of a state's sovereign right to exclude others, a violation of a state's sovereignty. Such exercises of power without international authorization on behalf of human rights would be of considerable interest in the context of this volume. As we shall see, however, they are exceedingly rare.

Noncoercive endeavors on behalf of the human rights of foreign nationals fundamentally respect a state's sovereignty. Legitimate coercive intervention also respects state sovereignty: it is legitimate, and thus not a violation of sovereignty. At the same time, however, it reflects a redefinition of the property rights of states, a limitation on the abstract "primordial" right of unrestricted use and exclusion. The extent of such transfers of authority provides the crucial evidence for testing claims about the balance of authority between states and the international community.

Finally, for the purposes of this volume, we need to distinguish unilateral or bilateral intervention from multilateral intervention. Multilateral intervention is clearly the crucial category (except in the very rare cases in which a state acts unilaterally on behalf of the international community). Therefore, unless otherwise explicitly noted, by "intervention" I will mean only multilateral intervention. Furthermore, for simplicity I will assume that action by permanent or ad hoc multilateral bodies represents action by the international community, even though in fact it may be more accurately described as the action of powerful states.

The International Community as Reflected in Three Models of International Human Rights

Combining the preceding accounts of human rights and sovereignty yields three models of international human rights, which reflect fundamentally different conceptions of the international community.

The traditional statist model sees human rights as principally a matter of sovereign national jurisdiction.[6] Contemporary statists certainly admit that human rights are no longer the exclusive preserve of states, and that the state is no longer the sole significant international actor, if it ever was. Statists nonetheless insist that human rights remain principally a matter of sovereign national jurisdiction and a largely peripheral concern of international (interstate) relations. For statists, there is no significant, independent international community, especially when questions of human rights are at issue. International intervention on behalf of human rights is not to be expected. If it occurs, it rests on state power, not legitimate authority.

A cosmopolitan model starts with individuals, who are seen more as members of a single global political community (cosmopolis) than as citizens of states.[7] In fact, states are problematic, and often "the problem," for cosmopolitans. Cosmopolitans focus on the ways in which the state and its powers are challenged both from below, by individuals and NGOs, and from above, by the truly global community (not merely international organizations and other collective enterprises of states). Cosmopolitans often see international organizations and certain transnational NGOs as representatives of an inchoate global community of mankind. International intervention on behalf of human rights is relatively unproblematic in such a model. In fact, cosmopolitans typically reverse the burden of proof, requiring justification for *non*intervention in the face of gross violations of human rights.

If the statist and cosmopolitan models lie at the end points of a continuum of international orders, the space toward the center is occupied by what we can call internationalist models. Internationalists accept the centrality of states and of sovereignty in international relations, but stress international social practices that regulate interstate relations (such as international law, the rules and procedures of diplomacy, and spheres of influence). This body of formal and informal restrictions on the original sovereignty of states creates an international social order, an anarchical society of states.[8] The international community, in an internationalist model, is essentially the society of states, supplemented by nonstate actors that participate in international politics. Intervention on behalf of human rights is permissible to the extent that it is authorized by the society of states.

Much of the rest of this chapter is in effect devoted to showing that a relatively weak internationalist model, including only modest and primarily normative international societal constraints on state sovereignty, describes international human rights practices over the past half century and is likely to continue to do so throughout the 1990s. The cosmopolitan model, to the extent that it is more than a prescription about what is desirable, is largely a prediction about the direction of change in world politics. The statist model, although accurate prior to World War II, today is at best a crude and somewhat misleading first approximation.

The Emergence of Human Rights as an International Issue

The following three sections examine multilateral human rights practices up to the end of the cold war. They present the evidence for the claim that international human rights policies during the cold war era can be accurately described by a weak internationalist model. The post–cold war era will be the subject of the penultimate section.

Prior to World War II, human rights practices were generally considered an internationally protected exercise of the sovereign prerogatives of states. The European great powers and the United States did occasionally intervene in the Ottoman and Chinese Empires and in Latin America and the Caribbean to rescue nationals caught in situations of civil strife or to establish or protect special rights and privileges for Europeans and Americans. Rarely if ever, though, did they intervene to protect foreign nationals from their own governments. Likewise, the "humanitarian law" of war, expressed in documents such as the 1907 Hague Conventions, limited only what a state could do to foreign nationals, not how a state treated its own nationals (let alone subject peoples over whom it exercised colonial rule).

The principal exception was slavery, a subject of multilateral diplomacy as early as the Congress of Vienna in 1815. But even here, a comprehensive treaty to abolish the slave trade was not finally concluded until 1890, and a major international treaty to abolish slavery had to wait until 1926. In the interwar period, the International Labor Organization (ILO) dealt with some limited workers' rights issues and the League of Nations established its Minorities System to protect the rights of ethnic minorities in areas where boundaries had been altered following the war. Except for these marginal exceptions,[9] though, when World War II broke out human rights simply was not a topic of international relations. In other words, modern international relations, until relatively recently, treated international human rights in accord with a very expansive statist understanding of sovereignty.

The catalyst that made human rights an issue in world politics was the Holocaust,[10] which simultaneously shocked the conscience of the international community (at least after the obsession with victory was overcome) and yet was not clearly prohibited by international law. At the Nuremberg War Crimes Trials (1945–46), leading Nazis were prosecuted under a novel charge: crimes against humanity. It was in the United Nations, however, that human rights really emerged as a subject of international relations.

The Covenant of the League of Nations did not even mention human rights. By contrast, the preamble of the UN Charter expresses a determination "to reaffirm faith in fundamental human rights." "Encouraging respect for human rights and for fundamental freedoms for all" is listed as one of the organization's major purposes in Article 1. Article 55 explicitly includes human rights among the responsibilities of the Economic and Social Council (ECOSOC). And the United Nations proceeded to elaborate a strong set of explicit and fairly detailed international human rights standards.

On December 9, 1948, the Convention on the Prevention and Punishment of the Crime of Genocide was opened for signature. On the following day, the General Assembly unanimously adopted the Universal Declaration of Human Rights.[11] The cold war, however, largely put an end to this spurt of international activity. By 1953 the treaty intended to give binding international legal force to the Universal Declaration was tabled, and it languished for a decade.

The principal exception to the cold war paralysis of the human rights machinery of the United Nations was decolonization. And success in decolonization profoundly altered the membership of the organization. By the mid-1960s, the Afro-Asian bloc was the largest group in the United Nations. These countries, which had suffered under colonial rule, had a special interest in human rights issues. They also received a sympathetic hearing from some Western European and Latin American countries. The United Nations thus again began to give priority to human rights questions. Most significantly, the International Human Rights Covenants were finally completed in December 1966.[12]

The covenants, however, mark the high point of the standard-setting work of the United Nations. Further major progress in international action on behalf of human rights would have to come primarily in the implementation (or in the monitoring of the implementation) of these standards, an area in which the United Nations had made no headway in its first two decades. Although states had agreed that they ought to follow international human rights standards, they most definitely did *not* agree to let the United Nations (or anyone else) enforce implementation of these norms. Norm creation was fully internationalized by the mid-1960s, but implementation of those norms remained almost entirely national.

This began to change, very slightly, in the late 1960s. In 1967 the UN Commission on Human Rights received authority to discuss human rights violations in particular countries, and in 1970 it was authorized to investigate complaints of human rights violations. In 1968, a Special Committee of Investigation was created to consider human rights in the territories occupied by Israel after the 1967 war. In the same year, the Security Council imposed a mandatory blockade on the white minority regime in Southern Rhodesia. The United Nations was at last beginning to move, however tentatively, from merely setting standards to examining how those standards were implemented by (at least a few) states. And such efforts continued in the 1970s. In response to the 1973 military coup in Chile, an Ad Hoc Working Group on the Situation of Human Rights in Chile was created. The international campaign against apartheid in South Africa intensified. And in 1976 the International Human Rights Covenants, with their supervisory machinery (discussed below), finally entered into force.

The 1970s also saw human rights explicitly and systematically introduced into the bilateral foreign policies of individual countries, beginning in the United States with congressional legislation in 1973 and 1975 that linked U.S. foreign aid to the human rights practices of recipient countries. The 1970s was also the decade in which human rights NGOs emerged as a notable international political force, as symbolized by the award of the Nobel Peace Prize to Amnesty International in 1977.

These trends toward increasing multilateral, bilateral, and nongovernmental action on behalf of human rights continued, more or less steadily, through the 1980s. New treaties on women's rights, torture, and the rights of the child were completed (in 1979, 1984, and 1989, respectively). The Human Rights Committee began to review periodic reports submitted under the Civil and Political Covenant. The Committee on Economic, Social, and Cultural Rights was created in 1986 to improve reporting and monitoring in this important area. The Commission on Human Rights undertook "thematic" initiatives on disappearances, torture, and summary or arbitrary executions, and subjected a larger and more diverse group of countries to public scrutiny. And the process of incorporating human rights into bilateral foreign policy accelerated and deepened in the 1980s, even in the United States, despite the early efforts of the Reagan administration to force international human rights to the sidelines or to transform them into just another instrument for waging the new cold war.

The stronger versions of the statist model, at least, simply do not provide an accurate or illuminating picture of the place of human rights in contemporary international relations. Human rights have become a standard subject of international relations. Furthermore, there are well-established international normative constraints on the human rights practices of states. The question that remains, however, is how far these restrictions on sovereignty extend.

Multilateral Implementation Machinery

A fairly extensive array of multilateral human rights monitoring bodies has been established. In this section, we will look at the two most important, the UN Commission on Human Rights, and the UN Human Rights Committee. In addition, we will look at the work of the International Labor Organization on workers' rights, the first and most developed single-issue human rights regime, and the international campaign against apartheid, the most extensive and elaborate example of multilateral international human rights activity.

In considering the question of the transfer of power and authority from states to the international community, it is crucial to distinguish not only between coercive and noncoercive interference but also between international norms and international procedures. Human rights norms have been thoroughly internationalized. The Universal Declaration of Human Rights and the International Human Rights Covenants are recognized as authoritative by virtually all states. But the internationalization of norms does not necessarily entail the internationalization of implementation procedures. Although the international human rights obligations of states are normatively strong, procedurally, as we shall see, they are extremely weak.

The United Nations Commission on Human Rights

The UN Commission on Human Rights, a permanent subsidiary body of the Economic and Social Council, is the single most important international human rights body. The Universal Declaration of Human Rights and the Human Rights Covenants, along with all the major single-issue human rights instruments, were drafted by the commission. Its powers to supervise the implementation of these norms, however, are extremely weak.

Until 1967, the commission was not authorized to discuss human rights conditions in particular countries publicly. Until 1970, it was not even authorized to see the details of the thousands of human rights communications received by the United Nations. ECOSOC Resolution 1503, however, gave the commission the authority to conduct confidential investigations of "communications" (i.e., complaints) that suggested "a consistent pattern of gross and reliably attested violations of human rights and fundamental freedoms."

The 1503 procedure is administratively cumbersome, involving three levels of scrutiny before a situation even reaches the full commission. It also is limited to "situations" rather than individual cases. Nonetheless, it often operates with considerable impartiality, in large part because the members of the subcommission, where the process begins, are independent experts, not state representatives.

The 1503 procedure, however, is strictly confidential, although its confidentiality has been partially circumvented by annually announcing the countries that are actively being considered. Although this is better than no publicity at all, the weakness of this "blacklist" as an enforcement mechanism is evident.

The 1503 procedure is also very slow. Because the subcommission and the commission each meet just once a year, the procedure cannot be brought fully into play in less than two or three years after complaints are received (which may be some time after serious violations began). A state can almost always add a year to the process by pretending to cooperate, as, for example, Argentina did in 1979 and 1980. Political considerations often stretch a case out even longer.

Finally, the 1503 procedure is ultimately simply weak. "Enforcement," at its strongest, means making publicly available the evidence that has been acquired, along with the commission's views on it. At most the 1503 procedure provides a certain degree of semi-independent international monitoring. And less than half a dozen cases have even reached this final stage of public disclosure.

In the late 1970s, a revitalized Western bloc, led by countries such as Canada and the Netherlands, joined by third world states such as Senegal, began to develop a coalition pressing for a more aggressive commission. New initiatives were undertaken on a "global" or "thematic" basis. Rather than examine the full range of abuses in individual countries, the commission addressed particular types of violations globally, (more or less) wherever they occurred.

The decisive step was the creation in 1980 of a Working Group on Enforced or Involuntary Disappearances. In its first decade, the working group handled more than nineteen thousand cases. In roughly one case in ten, government responses to working group inquiries established the whereabouts or the fate of the missing individual. Urgent action procedures, for disappearances within the past three months, have resolved about one case in five.

A Special Rapporteur on summary or arbitrary executions was appointed in 1982. S. Amos Wako, a Kenyan national and secretary-general of the Inter-African Union of Lawyers, has aggressively pursued his mandate. For example, his 1990 report noted more than fifteen hundred alleged cases in forty-eight countries. In 1985, Peter Kooijmans of the Netherlands, the outgoing chair of the commission, was appointed special rapporteur on torture. In addition to approaching governments (thirty-three in the first year alone) with information on alleged torture in their countries, Kooijmans—who in 1993 left his position to become foreign minister of the Netherlands—developed urgent action procedures similar to those of the working group on disappearances and also made official visits to a number of countries, including Guatemala, South Korea, Peru, Turkey, and Zaire. A promising Working Group on Arbitrary Detention was also created in 1991. Additional special rapporteurs on religious intolerance (appointed in 1986) and human rights violations by mercenaries (established in 1987) have been much less significant.

All of these activities reflect significant growth in the highest levels of multilateral human rights activities. Although many targets of these actions have denounced them as unjustified intervention in their internal affairs, these same states usually have supported similar, and often even stronger, "interventions" against other states (especially South Africa and Israel). The activities of the Commission on Human Rights clearly reflect an internationalist, not a statist, perspective.

All of these procedures, however, essentially respect sovereignty, as they involve only unregulated noncoercive interference. They do not represent a significant transfer of power or authority from states to the international community. They reflect weak rather than strong internationalism, and the continuing (although not unchallenged) priority of sovereignty in multilateral human rights politics.

The Human Rights Committee and International Reporting

A number of human rights treaties have created supervisory bodies to monitor their implementation. The most important of these is the UN Human Rights Committee, a body of eighteen experts established to supervise the implementation of the International Covenant on Civil and Political Rights.[13]

The committee's principal activity is to review periodic state reports on compliance. The questions posed by members of the committee are often penetrating and critical. When the responses of state representatives are serious and thoughtful, the result can be an exchange of information and views that provides a real element of international monitoring. Cooperation by the state, however, is entirely voluntary: the representative need not answer any question, let alone provide an answer that the questioner finds satisfactory. The committee may ask for additional information, but states actually provide only what they choose. Sometimes this is little more than extracts from laws and the constitution, or obviously evasive claims of compliance. The committee cannot even ensure the timely submission of reports. Zaire presents an extreme example: its initial report, due in 1978, was not submitted until 1987. Furthermore, the entire process applies only to the parties to the covenant, which numbered 124 at the end of 1993.

Reporting procedures cannot force recalcitrant states to alter their practices. This does not, however, mean that they are of no value. Conscientious preparation of a report requires a national review of law and practice that can uncover areas where improvement may be needed or possible. Reporting also assures that there will be at least one international body periodically looking over the shoulders of those responsible for implementing internationally recognized human rights. The reports of some countries may even provide ideas or models for other countries, as may the comments of the supervisory committee.

Reporting as an implementation technique functions primarily through the good will of reporting states. As a result, supervisory bodies must walk a delicate line during their review of reports. "Weaker" and less adversarial techniques thus may actually have a greater positive effect, at least in relatively favorable circumstances. In addition, states whose records are less bad, or even are relatively good, are particularly promising targets for international action. These states have, by their behavior, given concrete evidence of relatively good intentions. They are also likely to be more open to international suggestions and more concerned about their international human rights reputation.

Multilateral procedures for coercive intervention to enforce international human rights obligations simply do not exist. Recalcitrant states usually can violate human rights with impunity.[14] But even a country with a relatively good record may still violate human rights. And any victim (or potential victim) who is helped is a victory for international action, wherever that person resides.

Reporting systems fall far short of coercive intervention. They do not even involve the strongest forms of noncoercive interference. Nonetheless, in some cases at least, they can influence national human rights practices.

The Human Rights Committee may also investigate complaints from individuals in states that are parties to the covenant's First Optional Protocol. Although half of the countries that are parties to the covenant have accepted the optional protocol, the majority of the countries of the world still are not covered. Nonetheless, the optional protocol provides a strong system of monitoring. Although the list of countries on which action was

taken is hardly representative of the world's major human rights violators—
Bolivia, Canada, Colombia, the Dominican Republic, Ecuador, Finland,
France, Italy, Jamaica, Madagascar, Mauritius, the Netherlands, Peru, Sweden, Uruguay, and Zaire—there is some geographic diversity. Furthermore,
complaints are pursued relatively aggressively, as evidenced by the committee's innovative decision to treat a state's failure to respond as an admission of culpability.

The limitations of the optional protocol procedure, however, are no less
noteworthy. After the committee states its views, the process is concluded.
Not only is there no coercive enforcement of the findings of the committee, but the committee's judgments are not even technically binding on
states. Furthermore, most major human rights violators, not surprisingly,
have elected not to be covered. This is the overriding problem of treaty-
based enforcement mechanisms. Obligations apply only to parties to the
treaty; and states, in the exercise of their sovereign rights, are free to
choose not to accept these obligations. The stronger the monitoring and
implementation procedures, the fewer the states that are willing to be
covered. The First Optional Protocol thus presents a striking example of
the typical tradeoff between the strength of international procedures and
their coverage.

Machinery for the Enforcement of Workers' Rights

The first international human rights regime of any sort was the workers'
rights regime developed in the International Labor Organization after World
War I. Important ILO conventions have dealt with freedom of association,
the right to organize and bargain collectively, forced labor, migrant workers,
and indigenous peoples, as well as a variety of technical issues of working
conditions and workplace safety. And ILO monitoring procedures, which
date back to 1926, have been the model for the international human rights
reporting systems discussed above.

The ILO Committee of Experts meets annually to review periodic reports submitted by states on their implementation of ratified conventions.
Following this review, the committee may issue a Direct Request asking
for additional information, or even for changes in policy. Over the last two
decades, more than a thousand requests have resulted in changes in national policies. If the problem remains unresolved, the committee may
make "Observations"; that is, authoritative determinations of violations of
the convention. In addition, special complaint procedures exist for cases
involving freedom of association or discrimination in employment.

The Conference Committee, composed of ILO delegates rather than independent experts, provides an additional level of scrutiny. Each year, it selects cases from the report of the Committee of Experts for further review. Government representatives are called upon to provide additional information and explanation.

No less important than these inquisitorial procedures is the institution of "direct contacts." Since 1969, the ILO has pursued an extensive program of consultations and advice. It is a leader in using this method of cooperation to resolve problems before they reach international monitoring bodies.

Part of the ILO's success can be attributed to its unique tripartite structure. Virtually all other intergovernmental organizations are made up entirely of state representatives. NGOs may participate in deliberations, but they have no decision-making powers. In the ILO, however, workers' and employers' representatives from each member state are voting members of the organization. It is therefore much more difficult for states to hide behind the curtain of sovereignty. The transideological appeal of workers' rights has also been important to the ILO's success.

The principal resource of the ILO, however, remains publicity, and the principal power available to the organization's supervisory bodies is the power of persuasion. The ILO has influenced labor conditions and policies in a number of states over several decades. Nonetheless, it lacks coercive enforcement powers.

The Campaign against Apartheid

Apartheid is the human rights issue that has received the most extensive multilateral action over the past three decades. In 1962, the General Assembly called on states to break off diplomatic relations with South Africa and boycott all trade with that nation. The decisions of the General Assembly, however, are only recommendations. And until the 1980s, these particular recommendations were largely ignored by most powerful states. The Security Council, which does have the authority to impose mandatory sanctions, established only a voluntary arms embargo in December 1963. A mandatory arms embargo had to wait until November 1977, after the Soweto riots following the death in detention of Steve Biko. Although efforts over the following decade failed to establish a more comprehensive trade embargo, several states did undertake a variety of actions to reduce or eliminate their diplomatic, cultural, and commercial relations with South Africa.

The Special Committee on Apartheid, created in 1962, coordinated and promoted a broad international campaign against apartheid. National support committees were formed and opinion leaders in several countries were specially targeted. Material assistance was also provided to victims by organizations such as the United Nations Educational and Training Program for Southern Africa, established in 1964, and the United Nations Trust Fund for South Africa, established in 1965.

The 1973 International Convention on the Suppression and Punishment of the Crime of Apartheid, which came into force in 1976 and had ninety-eight parties at the end of 1993, attempts to establish international criminal liability. No prosecutions, however, have occurred. Furthermore, the "Group of Three," which receives reports on and makes recommendations with respect to the implementation of the convention, has had no discernible impact.

Reiteration of antiapartheid norms, and associated condemnations of South Africa, became a regular feature of most international organizations. Some specialized agencies such as the ILO and the World Health Organization gave particularly close scrutiny to South African policies in their area of competence. Others adopted the alternative strategy of excluding South Africa; the first to do so was the International Telecommunications Union, in 1965. The South African government was prevented from taking its seat in the UN General Assembly from 1970 until 1992. The norm of isolation was applied particularly effectively in sports, culminating in the 1985 International Convention against Apartheid in Sports. Less systematic efforts were also made to deter, monitor, and adversely publicize concerts and other cultural contacts.

The principal impact of the antiapartheid effort probably was the support, encouragement, and justification it provided for individuals and national and international NGOs trying to alter the foreign policies of individual states. These campaigns had some success in a number of Western countries in the 1980s. The resulting initiatives, including boycotts and embargoes, even crossed into the realm of coercive intervention.

All of this international activity clearly played a role in the process of reform that led to the March 1992 decision of the white electorate to abolish the race-based social and political system in South Africa. But international pressure only went as far as breaking relations, a strategy that still largely respected South African sovereignty. In particular, no Western state seriously contemplated the use of force against South Africa. South African governments were able to resist even these unusually strong international pressures for thirty years. And South Africa is clearly the exception, not the rule.

Regional Human Rights Regimes

So far, we have looked at international procedures that in principle cover or are open to all countries. Regional human rights regimes operate among smaller, more homogeneous groups of states. The one case of genuine international enforcement of human rights that exists anywhere in the world is the European regional regime. Regionalism, however, is no guarantee of strong international human rights procedures. The inter-American regime is no stronger than the procedures we have discussed above. The African regime is significantly weaker. And there are no regional regimes at all in Asia and the Middle East.

Europe

A very strong regional human rights regime exists for the twenty-three (primarily Western European) members of the Council of Europe. Article 3 of the council's Statute requires each member to "accept the principles of the rule of law and of the enjoyment by all persons within its jurisdiction of human rights and fundamental freedoms." Such provisions have been treated seriously enough to keep Spain and Portugal from being members until after the fall of those nations' fascist military governments in the mid-1970s. Furthermore, Greece (in 1969) and Turkey (in 1981) have been suspended for systematic human rights violations.

The European Commission of Human Rights receives, reviews, and evaluates "applications" (complaints) from individuals.[15] Once a case is accepted, the commission pursues it vigorously, and a majority of cases end with a decision against the state. The commission's decisions, although not technically binding, are usually accepted. Furthermore, the European Court of Human Rights has made legally binding decisions on more than 150 cases dealing with a great variety of issues, including such sensitive questions as public emergencies and the treatment of prisoners in Northern Ireland. In addition, there have been six complaints by one state against another, including cases involving British interrogation practices in Northern Ireland and torture in Greece and in Turkey.[16]

Special procedures also exist under the 1987 European Convention for the Prevention of Torture and Inhuman or Degrading Treatment or Punishment. The Committee for the Prevention of Torture is authorized to visit *any* place within the territory of a party to the convention where even a single individual might be detained, either legally or illegally, even by military authorities. Such on-site inspections, at the discretion of an independent monitoring committee, are unprecedented.

The European human rights regime has also influenced national political reforms. For example, new constitutions in Greece, Portugal, and Spain were explicitly written with the European Convention in mind. Decisions of the commission and the court have led to constitutional revisions in Sweden and the Netherlands. On a day-to-day basis as well, an additional level of regional scrutiny may subtly influence national political processes.

There is also a human rights dimension to the activities of the twelve-member European Union (EU), especially the European Economic Community (EEC). Economic integration in recent years has been accompanied by some efforts to harmonize social policy. Because policies tend to be standardized not according to the lowest common denominator but on the basis of the better performers, these efforts have often had a positive impact on economic and social rights. The EU has also incorporated human rights concerns into its external relations, although the means used have been relatively weak (except for the suspension of a special agreement between Greece and the EEC from 1967 until 1974, in protest against military rule).

The powers of both the Council of Europe and the EU are voluntarily agreed to by the member states. Nonetheless, they involve what I have called authorized coercive intervention. In Western Europe there has been a significant transfer of authority from states to the regional community of states, which has redefined the limits of sovereignty. Human rights practices, which previously were an area of sovereign prerogative, are now subject to coercive regional enforcement. But the special conditions of relatively similar cultural and historical backgrounds, generally excellent human rights records, high levels of economic development, and high levels of regional and subregional cooperation on economic and other matters suggest that the European experience is unlikely to be replicated elsewhere.

The Americas

Like the European human rights regime, the inter-American human rights regime revolves around a commission and a court. The Inter-American Court of Human Rights, however, has decided only two cases (dealing with a disappearance in Honduras and a military attack on two journalists in Peru). The real heart of the regime is the seven-member Inter-American Commission of Human Rights. The commission was established in 1959 as a part of the Organization of American States (OAS), and thus its authority does not rest on a separate human rights treaty (although there is a 1948 American Declaration of the Rights of Man, and a 1969 American Convention on Human Rights). The commission is like the UN Commission on Human Rights in that all members of the organization may in principle come under its scrutiny.

Although the Inter-American Commission of Human Rights receives about five hundred complaints a year, its decisions have usually been ignored, in sharp contrast to the situation in Europe. The primary reason for this is the very different domestic human rights environment in the region.

Almost all of the countries in the European regime have excellent human rights records, and a strong desire to maintain them. Communications thus typically deal with narrow or isolated violations, which are inherently unthreatening to the government. Even when there are serious systematic violations, as during the period of military rule in Greece, the government involved is seen as aberrant, and if it persists it is treated as a pariah.

Most countries in the Americas, by contrast, have suffered repressive military rule within the past generation. In fact, until recently, at any given time several OAS member states typically were ruled by dictatorial governments. As a result, many communications have concerned systematic human rights violations that represented an important element in the government's strategy to keep itself in power. In such circumstances, it is hardly surprising that the findings of the commission have usually been ignored.

A more important activity of the Inter-American Commission has been the production of studies and reports on human rights situations in more than twenty countries. For example, the commission's series of reports in the 1970s and 1980s on Chile were an important element in the international campaign against the Pinochet government.[17] Although such efforts to generate international publicity fall far short of coercive intervention, their significance is perhaps best attested to by the diplomatic effort states exert to avoid such publicity. For example, both Argentina and Chile devoted considerable diplomatic effort in the late 1970s and early 1980s to avoiding public criticism.[18] In addition, international publicity may aid individual victims, even if the overall situation in the country remains repressive. States often respond to adverse publicity by releasing prominent victims or improving the way they are treated.

In at least one case, though, the OAS has had a systematic impact on human rights. The Inter-American Commission's 1978 report on Nicaragua substantially increased the pressure on the Somoza government. And when the OAS General Assembly called on Somoza to resign in June 1979, it clearly shook his political confidence and seems to have hastened his departurè.[19] Although this was not coercive intervention—the action was purely verbal and the sanction entirely normative—it is noteworthy.

In the end, though, reports and resolutions require additional action by states to have any real impact. The regional community can call on states to act in certain ways. During the cold war era, however, except in the case of the politically motivated embargo on Cuba, the OAS did not intervene coercively on behalf of human rights.

Africa, Asia, and the Middle East

A third regional human rights regime has been established within the Organization of African Unity (OAU) under the 1981 African Charter on Human and Peoples' Rights. Its implementation procedures, however, are extremely weak. The eleven-member African Commission on Human and Peoples' Rights, in addition to reviewing reports, may consider communications. Only situations may be discussed, however, not individual cases. In addition, an in-depth study of a situation requires permission from the OAU's Assembly of Heads of State and Government. This is by far the most politicized regional or international human rights complaint procedure.

The commission's initial reviews of state reports have not been promising, and the reports themselves have had little substance. No public action had been taken on any of the more than one hundred communications that have been received. Nonetheless, the African commission does seem to be approaching its task with seriousness, and it has not merely permitted but encouraged NGO participation.

The Permanent Arab Commission on Human Rights, established in 1968, has been notably inactive, except for occasional efforts to publicize human rights violations in Israeli-occupied territory. There are not even authoritative regional norms. Little more has been done in Asia and the Pacific. For example, the only substantial result of a 1982 United Nations–sponsored seminar in Colombo, Sri Lanka, seems to have been a decision to abandon a broad regional approach in favor of either the global institutions discussed above or subregional groupings. Only the Pacific Island subregion shows much promise for the development of a subregional regime.

In such an environment, NGOs become especially important. Human Rights Internet's recent *Human Rights Directory: Asia and the Pacific* lists more than one thousand. Although most operate only domestically, they and their transnational colleagues play an important role, especially in countries with relatively good human rights records. Even in extremely repressive countries, international human rights NGOs, such as New York–based Asia Watch, engage in considerable, and occasionally successful, efforts to assure that human rights violations are not ignored by the international community.

In the Middle East as well, NGOs have tried to compensate for the absence of a functioning regional regime. For example, the Arab Organization for Human Rights (AOHR), founded in 1983, issues annual reports on human rights conditions in the countries of the Arab world. In 1989—through a joint initiative of the Arab Lawyers Union, AOHR, and the Tunisian League for Human Rights,[20] with the support of the UN Center for Human Rights—an Arab Institute for Human Rights was established in Tunis to provide information and training for governmental and nongovernmental personnel.

The general environment in the Arab world, however, is unusually hostile. For example, AOHR operates out of Geneva, rather than an Arab country. The general hostility of governments, however, only increases the importance of the activities of national and transnational human rights NGOs. They can help to keep the idea alive and at least on the fringes of the political debate. NGOs also are likely to be important in probing the limits of political tolerance and attempting to take full advantage of what limited political space exists for action on behalf of internationally recognized human rights.

As private entities, NGOs can operate free of the political control of states. And unlike even states and international organizations that are actively concerned with international human rights, they do not have broader policy goals that may conflict with their human rights objectives. NGOs, however, must rely on the power of publicity and persuasion. They lack the resources of even weak states. And states remain free to be unpersuaded. Once more, we have only modest measures of noncoercive interference.

The Helsinki Process

A hybrid sort of human rights regime exists within the Conference on Security and Cooperation in Europe (CSCE), an organization made up of all the countries of Europe, plus the United States and Canada.

The principal Soviet objective in the initial CSCE negotiations was formal recognition of the cold war division of Europe. The Western Europeans, however, pressed hard for incorporating human rights provisions, under the notion of domestic security for citizens. The resulting Helsinki Final Act of 1975 is a marvel of diplomatic compromise. Three very differ-

ent "baskets," dealing with political and military issues, economic relations, and humanitarian relations, respectively, are held together in a delicate political balance.

Our concern here will be solely with "Basket III" ("Co-operation in Humanitarian and Other Fields") and Principle VII ("Respect for human rights
and fundamental freedoms, including the freedom of thought, conscience,
religion or belief"). Basket III deals solely with "human contacts" (especially family contacts and reunification), the free flow of information, and
cultural and educational cooperation. Principle VII, however, includes a
general agreement to "promote and encourage the effective exercise of
civil, political, economic, social, cultural and other rights and freedoms."
Much of the history of the Helsinki process during the cold war era was in
effect a struggle over the relative priorities of these two provisions.

The Helsinki process can be seen, with the benefit of hindsight, as a
chronicle of the gradual demise of the cold war and Soviet-style communism in the face of increasing national and international demands to implement internationally recognized human rights. The Helsinki follow-up
meetings in Belgrade (1977–78), Madrid (1980–83), and Vienna (1986–89) provided a forum in which the West could pressure the Soviet bloc regimes.
Even more important, though, was the legitimation that the Helsinki Final
Act gave to the activities of dissident groups in the Soviet bloc.

The Final Act recognized the "right of the individual to know and act
upon his rights and duties," and Basket III included provisions relating to
the free flow of information. In May 1976, eleven leading Soviet dissidents
established what soon came to be known as the Moscow Helsinki Group. Its
stated purpose was "to inform the governments that signed the Final Act in
Helsinki, as well as the publics of those countries, of cases of direct violations of the humanitarian articles of the Final Act in the Soviet Union."[21]
They issued more than 150 reports and provided a focal point for national
and international human rights activities.

From the outset, members were intimidated into leaving the group or
accepting exit visas from the Soviet Union. By 1980, the group's principal
activity had become monitoring the cases of their colleagues. By August
1981 only three members remained at liberty in the country. In September
1982, the group was finally forced to disband.

In Czechoslovakia, the coming of the Belgrade follow-up meeting helped
to spur Charter 77, a manifesto signed in January 1977 by 242 people,
including Vaclav Havel. Over the succeeding decade, Charter 77 became a
powerful local human rights group with more than thirteen hundred public adherents. As in the Soviet Union, though, official harassment was

swift and continuous. In other Soviet bloc countries, the situation was no better, and was often worse. The Polish Helsinki Committee was forced underground during martial law. In countries such as Bulgaria and Romania, repression was so effective that monitoring groups could not even be formed.[22]

Nonetheless, the immense international publicity generated by the activities of monitoring groups in the Communist world both embarrassed the authorities and helped to mobilize private and public political pressure in the West. The formal Helsinki meetings also provided a regular, well-publicized forum for airing human rights grievances. And in Czechoslovakia, Charter 77 provided much of the leadership for the Velvet Revolution of 1989.

The Helsinki process also spurred international human rights activities outside the Soviet bloc. In the United States, Helsinki Watch was founded in 1979. This became the model for the creation of new regional watch committees: Americas Watch, Asia Watch, Africa Watch, and, most recently, Middle East Watch. Operating out of New York under the general umbrella of Human Rights Watch, they have become an important source of information and a major human rights lobby in the United States. In other countries as well, local and transnational NGO monitoring activities were spurred by the Helsinki Final Act and the model of the Moscow Helsinki Group. The various national Helsinki groups now cooperate within the framework of the International Helsinki Federation for Human Rights.

Repressive governments can almost always ignore the pressure such NGOs bring to bear. They may even choose to apply the power of the state to weaken or eliminate human rights NGOs. Nonetheless, such behavior has international costs, especially if the victims are prominent or have developed good international contacts. There may be domestic political costs as well. Rarely will the consideration of such costs be politically decisive. In some cases, however, NGO activities, especially when coordinated with intergovernmental and bilateral state initiatives, have made at least some human rights violations less burdensome to their victims. Real international influence has been exerted, even though it falls far short of coercive intervention. It must be noted, however, that there is no transfer of authority from states involved in such activities of NGOs, even where their activities are part of a broader process of delegitimizing the ruling regime.

Human Rights in a Post–Cold War World

The preceding sections largely chronicled the cold war experience. We live in a world, though, of exciting international change. Most dramatic, of course, has been the end of the cold war and the dissolution of the former Soviet Union. These changes followed a decade of democratization in Latin America and seem to have helped speed liberalization in Africa and Asia. The hopes embodied in these changes have led to much talk of a new world order. I will argue, however, that the emerging post–cold war order is unlikely to be characterized by a significant transfer of power or authority in the field of human rights from states to the international community.

In a recent article,[23] I developed such an argument in some detail. Here I will briefly sketch the outlines of my position. I will then consider recent activities in some of the institutions discussed above, and certain recent events that might be taken as counter-evidence. My contention is that we should expect continued modest growth in international human rights activities, but that coercive intervention is likely only in very limited and specific circumstances.

At the level of the structure of the international system, the crucial change in recent years has been the end of bipolarity. This change, coupled with the rise in importance of economics and new issues such as human rights and the environment, has caused an increasing fragmentation of international politics. With the elements of power increasingly separated— most dramatically illustrated by the military might and economic weakness of Russia, and the economic prowess but military weakness of Japan and Germany—international political processes and outcomes now vary dramatically from issue to issue. Well over a decade ago, Keohane and Nye described this type of international system as one of "complex interdependence."[24] The end of the cold war has furthered this process.

Although the end of U.S. (and Soviet) hegemonic leadership may create new opportunities for progressive international action, complex interdependence makes it dangerous to generalize across issue areas. In particular, we must be careful not to infer that the changes in international economic relations which are challenging entrenched notions of economic sovereignty will necessarily be accompanied by comparable changes in international human rights.

For all the talk of a new world order, most states today still jealously guard their sovereign prerogatives in the field of human rights. Consider, for example, how weak the multilateral human rights procedures discussed above seem in contrast to, say, the procedures of the General Agreement on

Tariffs and Trade and the International Monetary Fund. Even in Europe, the relatively strong regional human rights system pales in comparison to the restrictions on state sovereignty achieved through regional economic institutions. And nowhere are states advancing new proposals for major enhancements of the power of existing human rights bodies (except perhaps the CSCE) or the creation of new bodies with strong powers.

Helsinki

Although the inherent sensitivity of human rights issues helps to explain the persistent strength of the commitment to sovereignty, a considerable part of the explanation lies in the qualitative difference between the material interdependence that underlies international economic cooperation and the moral interdependence underlying international cooperation in human rights. Although neither less real nor less important than material interdependence, moral interdependence does typically lead to different sorts of national and international political processes, which makes international cooperation more difficult to achieve. Because the costs and benefits of the human rights practices of other states are largely intangible— a sense of moral disgust or satisfaction rather than a loss of income, a deterioration in one's quality of life, or a reduction in perceived security— they are likely to have a relatively low priority in the policy of most states (and most individuals), especially when human rights concerns conflict with material interests.

Although the end of bipolarity has not changed the impediments to effective international human rights policies rooted in an international system of sovereign states, the demise of the superpowers' ideological rivalry, the other defining feature of the cold war order, does suggest significant human rights progress. Whatever the ultimate motivations of American (and Soviet) foreign policy, ideology played a significant part in the justification of numerous interventions that had as their consequence the systematic violation of human rights. Although U.S. intervention in the third world certainly will continue in the post–cold war era, without the overarching appeal to anticommunism American administrations will find it much more difficult to muster domestic support for repressive foreign regimes. In addition, it will be easier to treat local political conflicts as local, rather than as manifestations of global ideological rivalry. These changes imply major improvements in the international human rights environment.

They do not, however, necessarily imply support for stronger international human rights procedures. There is no necessary connection between a decline in foreign policy actions that harm human rights abroad and the development of positive international human rights policies. To date there have been few if any new developments of significance. Since the end of the cold war, neither the president nor Congress has been willing to expend substantial political or financial capital on behalf of international human rights. Elsewhere as well, satisfaction at recent changes has not spurred new endeavors to develop stronger international human rights procedures.

There has been modest progress at the regional level. The Council of Europe's new program of human rights assistance for the countries of Central and Eastern Europe is clear evidence of a desire to begin to prepare the former Soviet bloc states for entry into the European human rights regime. And because good human rights practices are a major condition of acceptance into "Europe," with its associated symbolic and material benefits, these efforts are likely to have a significant impact, at least in the more progressive states of Central Europe. This represents a geographic expansion of the coverage of the existing European human rights regime, rather than an increase in that regime's powers. Furthermore, one may question whether setting conditions for providing a benefit desired by the other party is really coercive intervention. Nonetheless, these developments are of considerable importance.

In the Americas, the overall environment has improved dramatically: elected (although not necessarily democratic) governments were in office in all the mainland countries of the hemisphere throughout 1991. The OAS General Assembly, which in the early 1980s refused to even discuss the practices of gross and persistent human rights violators, has become willing to act on behalf of human rights. The increasingly restrictive embargo against Haiti and the rapid criticism of the suspension of parliamentary government in Peru are also promising developments.

It is too early to say whether this will be a new pattern or a temporary interlude. It is unclear how the OAS will respond to the imposition of military rule on the mainland, or to a series of coups or quasi-coups, rather than single, isolated occurrences. Furthermore, there is no evidence of a new political commitment to a more aggressive pursuit of human rights violations by elected governments. The activities of the Inter-American Commission of Human Rights in the near future, and in particular the responses the commission receives from the OAS and affected states, are likely to be an important indicator of whether the characteristic U.S. confusion of elections and human rights is being transcended in the hemisphere. Clearly, though, the overall picture is one of modest progress, with the realistic possibility of continued incremental growth throughout the rest of the decade.

Much the same is true of the CSCE. The CSCE meetings at Copenhagen and Paris in 1990 expanded and deepened the normative dimensions of the

CSCE. But proposals to make the CSCE a much more active supervisory body for the monitoring of human rights have met with little enthusiasm from the major states.

Perhaps the clearest sign of human rights progress in the United Nations is the United Nations Observer Mission in El Salvador, which has unprecedented authority to engage in extensive on-site monitoring of human rights practices. This is indeed a significant transfer of authority to the international community. It is, however, an intrusion that El Salvador voluntarily accepted. There is no indication that many other states will permit similar interventions. Furthermore, it is only a temporary measure, agreed to as part of a broader political settlement, intended to help smooth the transition to a new government. It should not be confused with human rights monitoring in more settled situations. In particular, the political dynamics that make a UN monitoring role acceptable, or even desirable, in such transitional situations are not likely to be replicated once a supervised election has been held.

This distinction between "normal" situations and transitional ones, or other extraordinary situations, raises broader questions about the international human rights significance of some other often-cited examples of transfers of authority or power from states to the international community. Consider, for example, the aggressive efforts to provide humanitarian assistance in Somalia. There has been a modest but very real coercive element in these UN actions. But the actions were undertaken in a situation in which the Somali state had largely disintegrated into a struggle between warring clans and factions. They thus represent not so much an intervention or even a temporary transfer of authority to the international community as an international response to a breakdown of national political authority. Although the United Nations has obtained unprecedented, if temporary, authority in Somalia, the political processes leading to this result are unlikely to be replicated in more settled situations.

Consider also the United Nations Transitional Authority in Cambodia (UNTAC), which recently completed its task of managing an electoral transfer of power. The extensive UN role in the decolonization of Asia and especially of Africa is the real precedent for such action. In effect, the United Nations helped to manage the end of Vietnamese imperialism in Cambodia—imperialism that, ironically, began with a Vietnamese intervention (to remove the Khmer Rouge) that had a substantial humanitarian component. But the political dynamics that make a UN monitoring role acceptable, or even desirable, in such transitional situations are not likely to be replicated once a supervised election has been held.

Such cases suggest that the United Nations will have a role only where there are fundamental gaps or breakdowns in standard patterns of sovereignty. During decolonization, the transition involved a fundamental formal change in legal status. (There are certainly a number of possible areas for UN or regional action of a very precisely analogous character, most notably in the former states of Yugoslavia and the Soviet Union.) In contemporary cases such as Somalia, Cambodia, and El Salvador, civil war created a breakdown of authority. The United Nations has stepped into that void, providing humanitarian assistance in Somalia and transitional assistance and monitoring in Cambodia and El Salvador. But just as the decolonization activities of the 1960s had no direct spill-over into new human rights activities of a more standard type, there is little reason to expect such a spill-over today.

Where sovereignty has become problematic, as in El Salvador and Somalia, the United Nations may (although it will not necessarily) have an opportunity to intervene coercively. We should not belittle the importance or local impact of such interventions. Nonetheless, to the extent that coercive interventions remain restricted to cases of this sort, they actually underscore the centrality of sovereignty. What has changed is not so much the balance of power between states and the international community as the opportunities for action. The end of the cold war has made it possible for (states to allow) the United Nations to act in such former areas of superpower rivalry. This does indeed result in greater authority for the international community. But the transfer of authority is of a peculiarly limited sort.

Much the same is true of recent interventions in Iraq and Bosnia. In each case, the international community has treated the conflict as an interstate conflict, despite the assertions to the contrary of Iraq and Serbia. The UN security zone in northern Iraq is the result of a cease-fire agreement. It has the consequence of protecting the human rights of Iraqi Kurds. But it provides absolutely no precedent for multilateral military protection of endangered minorities in more normal circumstances.[25] Likewise, the Bosnian intervention has been conceived of as assistance against aggression, rather than as human rights intervention, even if the result is to protect the lives of many Bosnians from a force that claims to be their government (but whose claim is rejected by the international community).

Somalia also reminds us of the distinction between humanitarian assistance, the subject of a separate chapter in this volume, and international human rights policies. Emergency aid to victims of natural or man-made disasters is a noble and important international activity. The intervention in Somalia does involve an unprecedented augmentation of the authority of the international community in the field of humanitarian assistance. But we have no reason to expect a spill-over into international human rights activities, as they have been conventionally understood.

Even during the cold war, massive famine usually provoked an international response that largely transcended politics. The Reagan administration's assistance to Ethiopia, one of the world's most reprehensible Marxist-Leninist regimes, is perhaps the most striking example. But there has been a huge gulf between the provision of disaster relief and the provision even of food aid, let alone international human rights intervention, once the immediate crisis is over. We have no reason to believe that there has been any fundamental change in perceptions or behavior in the so-called new world order. Therefore, the value of Somalia as a precedent for human rights activity by the United Nations is likely to be negligible. Much the same is true of Bosnia.

I do not want to belittle the importance of these interventions. Lives are being saved in ways that just a few years ago would not have seemed possible to most observers. I do, however, want to insist that these cases have few or no implications for intervention on behalf of human rights; that is, intervention in response to direct violations of internationally recognized human rights by recognized governments in control of their states. We may be witnessing modest expansions of the authority of regional communities in Europe and the Americas (but not in Africa, Asia, or the Middle East). I see little or no evidence, however, that any transfer of power or authority from states to the international community is occurring in the post–cold war world.

Human Rights, Sovereignty, and Intervention

In summary, let me address directly the questions posed in the introduction to this volume. There is indeed evidence that foreign states and the international community are taking an increased interest in restricting the domestic freedom of action of states according to authoritative international human rights norms. There has been a slow, but steady and clearly discernible, growth of interest over the past two decades. This has been accompanied by modest and slow, but steady, growth in the willingness of states and intergovernmental organizations to exert international influence short of coercive intervention on behalf of human rights. One might even argue that there is a growing desire to impose new restrictions on sovereignty, although I think that this is largely restricted to pariah regimes such as Iraq. There is, however, no evidence of a growing willingness of states or intergovernmental organizations to act to impose international human rights norms on recalcitrant states.

The underlying motive for the development of new international human rights policies by states, intergovernmental organizations, and NGOs alike is moral, not material. Governments that respect human rights may be more attractive and trustworthy friends and allies. Repressive regimes may not make good customers or markets in the long run. Such arguments, however, usually are peripheral and even after the fact in policy debates. International human rights policies rest largely on the fact that they seem to be demanded by morality. The harm that they try to avoid is material harm for others, but a largely moral harm for oneself.

This central role of moral interdependence is crucial to explaining the weakness of most international human rights policies. States are often, perhaps even increasingly, willing to accept the cost of strained relations. On very rare occasions, they may even accept a modest loss of trade. They are sometimes willing to provide renewed or increased foreign aid to reward improvements in human rights practices. But almost never are they willing to sacrifice significant material interests. And coercive intervention always has material costs.

The evidence I have reviewed suggests that the threshold of coercive intervention is likely to be crossed only when the case stops being seen as a human rights issue and becomes a more conventional international conflict (as in Iraq) or involves the breakdown of the authority of the state (as in Somalia). If it raises the imminent danger of mass starvation, the chance of intervention is further enhanced. The end of the cold war probably has created more such cases. (To the extent that this is true, of course, the new world order is a more dangerous one.) It has not, however, altered the apparent willingness of states and the multilateral organizations that they control to intervene on behalf of human rights in ordinary circumstances.

Authoritative collective international human rights norms do exist. Global intergovernmental organizations, regional organizations, NGOs, and even states (especially the United States and the Nordic states) have established relatively effective procedures for gathering information about the protection and violation of such rights. The foreign policy of many states has incorporated a concern for international human rights—as a secondary, but nonetheless real, element. There are thus multiple channels through which states and NGOs can attempt to exert influence on behalf of international human rights. But, as we have seen, these procedures have not led, and are not likely to lead, to authoritative international enforcement (except in Europe).

States retain primary responsibility for implementing human rights. Norms and the process of norm creation have been almost completely collectivized. Monitoring has been substantially collectivized, especially if one includes the activities of NGOs as part of a collective international political process. But implementation and enforcement remain almost exclusively national. The priority of the rights of sovereign states, not the international community, remains—and is likely to remain—the governing principle in the law and politics of international human rights.

Chapter Seven

Environmental Protection, International Norms, and State Sovereignty:

The Case of the Brazilian Amazon

KEN CONCA

> Especially with the ecological imperative, the entire world now realizes that modern progress threatens our survival. In our interdependent world, everyone senses that we need "global standards" and "universally binding ethical norms. . . ." The ethical goal for the third millennium is "planetary responsibility." That is the slogan for the future.
>
> —*Hans Küng*

> The Earth is one but the world is not.
> —*World Commission on Environment and Development*

Emerging Norms for Environmental Protection

The state of the global environment is an issue that governments can no longer ignore. As awareness of environmental problems deepens and spreads, it has become apparent that many of the most pressing threats to survival and well-being are international or even global in scope. Not surprisingly, the result is pressure on governments to take action, including collective action. For evidence of this growing awareness and the political pressure it creates, one need look no further than the daily newspaper of any major city in the world.

Pressures on the state to respond to environmental problems are not new. John Perlin reports that severe wood shortages led to conservation efforts in Babylonia during the time of Hammurabi.[1] Zuo Dakang and Zhang Peiyuan cite measures to protect wetlands in the Huang-Huai-Hai plain of northeastern China during the sixth century A.D., in recognition of their importance as sources of fish, game, and fuel.[2] Air-quality crises in London during the early stages of the industrial revolution eventually led to the formation of smoke-abatement societies advocating legislation.[3] Countless other historical examples could be cited.

What *is* relatively new is the emergence of a global discourse on environmental problems. Beginning with the 1972 UN Conference on the Human Environment, held in Stockholm, the past two decades have seen the emergence of an increasingly influential paradigm of global environmental management. The central premise of this paradigm is expressed in the introduction to *Our Common Future,* the 1987 report of the World Commission on Environment and Development:

> In the middle of the 20th century, we saw our planet from space for the first time. Historians may eventually find that this vision had a greater impact on thought than did the Copernican revolution of the 16th century, which upset the human self-image by revealing that the Earth is not the centre of the universe. From space, we see a small and fragile ball dominated not by human activity and edifice but by a pattern of clouds, oceans, greenery, and soils. Humanity's inability to fit its doings into that pattern is changing planetary systems, fundamentally. Many such changes are accompanied by life-threatening hazards. *This new reality, from which there is no escape, must be recognized—and managed.*[4]

Although there are many ways of characterizing the environmental problematique, this passage reflects several features of what is emerging as the dominant discourse on global environmental problems. These features include the use of a global, socially undifferentiated level of analysis, the powerful invocation of planetary symbolism, the appeal to modern science as a frame of reference, and the call for active, coordinated management of global-scale natural systems.[5]

The pressures that this and other forms of environmental awareness exert on governments have complex implications for national sovereignty. Obviously, modern states are ecologically interdependent, and agreements that recognize this fact can and do limit the autonomy of action of individual governments. Such limits only scratch the surface of the sovereignty-ecology relationship, however, for several reasons. One reason is that such constraints on action are rarely distributed equally; states have never enjoyed equal measures of sovereignty over their own natural resources and the ecosystems lying within their borders. The lack of such control was a defining feature of colonialism, and environmental agreements negotiated in an unequal world clearly do not impose an equal loss of autonomy on all parties.[6]

A second complicating factor is that sovereignty looks inward as well as outward: it finds its basis not only in autonomy relative to external actors but also in the state's power over civil society. Historically, the ability to control the rules of access to the environment and natural resources—to define who may alter, and to what extent, which specific natural materials, systems, and processes—has been a central component of state authority and legitimacy.[7]

Emerging norms of planetary ecology may undermine sovereignty in this inward-looking sense if they weaken the rule-making authority of the state, the scope of the state's reach, or the degree of legitimacy accorded to the state by its citizens. However, to the extent that environmental regulation becomes codified as a responsibility of the state, aspects of state authority, legitimacy, and control could indeed be strengthened. The very notion of a "global commons," for example, legitimizes the sovereign state system, by defining it as the institutional norm to which global environmental problems do not conform (hence their status as problems).[8] Seen in this light, pressures on the state to respond to environmental problems could also have the effect of strengthening the principle of sovereignty, and with it the sovereignty of at least some states.

The interplay of sovereignty and ecology is also complicated by the fact that environmental protection is a broad and ambiguous theme, subject to widely different constructions and interpretations.[9] The content, the symbolism, and the imagery of environmental discourse can be, and routinely are, appropriated for a broad range of social and political purposes. Thus the emergence of international environmental norms must be seen in part as a definitional struggle, and one that cannot be separated from the more general structures that create power and authority in the international system.

These preliminary observations raise a series of questions about emerging norms for environmental protection: How do such norms define the rights and responsibilities of states? Who controls or shapes the process of norm definition? Do such norms simply reflect current patterns of power and authority in the international system, or do they challenge those patterns? How are the resulting consequences distributed in an unequal world? In this paper, I consider these questions on three separate levels. I begin by

examining the evolution of environmental discourse with regard to national sovereignty over the past two decades—a period bounded by two
major global conferences on environmental themes. The discussion then
turns to the question of tropical deforestation, an issue area in which the
sovereignty debate has been particularly contentious. Finally, the chapter
examines the specific case of the Brazilian Amazon, which provides an
important example of concentrated international pressure and complex
state responses.

Ecology, Sovereignty, and Environmental Discourse

Environmental discourse has changed dramatically in the two decades
since the seminal UN Conference on the Human Environment, held in
Stockholm. The current emphasis on "global change" and on the integrity
of global-scale environmental processes differs in important respects from
the paradigm of "limits to growth" that prevailed in the early 1970s.[10] The
central claim of this earlier paradigm was that population growth, mounting resource scarcity, and accumulating environmental pollution would
combine to limit expansion of the world economy—that there were, literally, limits to growth.[11] The more recent concept of "global change" stresses
instead the disruptive impact of human activities on global-scale ecological services (climate regulation, atmospheric screening of solar radiation,
water and nutrient cycling, maintenance of biological diversity). Comparing the declaration of principles that emerged from the 1972 Stockholm
Conference to that of the Rio Earth Summit twenty years later illustrates
the differences between these paradigms. Most of the twenty-six principles
in the Stockholm Declaration stress problems of overconsumption of natural resources. Only passing reference is made to what would be the primary
concern of the Earth Summit two decades later: the problem of collective
management of global-scale natural systems.[12]

It is important to recognize that the ecology-sovereignty debate in international politics predates the relatively recent emergence of "global change"
as the dominant paradigm of environmental discourse. Because the earlier
"limits to growth" paradigm challenged resource-intensive development
strategies, it provoked third world fears that environmental concerns would
become obstacles to development. These fears were fanned by suspicion
that Northern governments were seizing upon environmental rhetoric as a
way to limit industrialization in the South.

This brought the sovereignty question into clear and contentious focus at the 1972 Stockholm conference. The polarization of Northern and Southern views on the relationship between environment and development found its expression in a debate over the rights and responsibilities of individual states.[13] Third world governments insisted upon several clauses, couched in terms of the sovereign rights of states, that rejected the use of environmental protection as a barrier to economic development. As a result, the Stockholm Declaration of Principles focuses almost exclusively on the individual rights and responsibilities of states, rather than on the need for coordinated collective action. Principle 21 of the Stockholm declaration expressed the core tension surrounding the sovereignty issue:

> States have, in accordance with the Charter of the United Nations and the principles of international law, the sovereign right to exploit their own resources pursuant to their own environmental policies, and the responsibility to ensure that activities within their jurisdiction or control do not cause damage to the environment of other States or of areas beyond the limits of national jurisdiction.

By posing the problem in this manner, the Stockholm declaration established sovereign rights and responsibilities as the central frame of reference for future debates on international environmental protection.

"Global change" discourse emerged well after the Stockholm conference had established this sovereign-state framework. The rise of the global-change paradigm can be attributed to a combination of scientific and political developments in the 1980s. Although great uncertainties persist, the past two decades have seen enormous growth in scientific understanding of globally linked environmental processes.[14] This deepening understanding carries with it a growing tendency to view the earth as a single integrated system, with multiple interconnections and feedbacks linking oceans, atmosphere, land, and biosphere in complex fashion.[15]

A second force contributing to the rise of global-change discourse has been the globalization of the environmental movement itself, in both symbolic and organizational terms. U.S. and European environmentalists made a concerted effort to raise the profile of "global" issues such as climate change, destruction of the atmospheric ozone layer, and declining planetary biodiversity. In doing so, they began to forge links with a broad range of third world organizations and movements mobilized by local resource and environmental concerns.[16]

Notably, both the scientific emphasis on global-scale interconnections and the globalizing politics of the environmental movement rely on a fundamentally physical notion of what is global. Phenomena such as climate change, biological diversity, and depletion of the ozone layer, which are "globally" linked in an immediate, physical sense, are generally interpreted as global problems. At the same time, localized, cumulative developments such as soil erosion are not typically assigned "global" status within global-change discourse, and are therefore relegated to a secondary level of concern.[17] The ability of individual sovereign states to claim jurisdiction is thus a key determinant of whether particular problems or trends are accorded "global" status.

This way of differentiating what is global from what is not steers the focus away from international-scale social structures that link localized forms of environmental damage occurring around the planet. Many of the social, economic, and political forces that drive the "local" phenomenon of soil erosion, for example, are transnational in extent.[18] At the same time, soil erosion has many effects that clearly go beyond the "local," including its impact on world food markets and its role in creating border-crossing environmental refugees. Global-change discourse stresses the "global" character of certain physical systems but not of economic, social, and political institutions.

Both the sovereign-state frame of reference and the ascension of "global" issues can be seen in the most influential post-Stockholm attempts to formulate international environmental principles. The 1980 World Conservation Strategy, although asserting a global interest in the conservation of biological diversity, proposes a strategy based on individual national and subnational efforts.[19] Similarly, the 1985 Tropical Forest Action Plan, put forward by the World Bank, the UN Food and Agriculture Organization, and the World Resources Institute, called for international funding of national forestry plans.[20] The series of agreements on protecting stratospheric ozone, widely cited as a breakthrough in international environmental cooperation, is premised on national-level implementation of negotiated reductions in the use of ozone-destroying chemicals.[21]

Our Common Future, the highly influential 1987 report of the World Commission on Environment and Development, marked an intellectual watershed in the evolution of international environmental norms. Although most often cited for its embrace of the concept of "sustainable development," Our Common Future also stressed the sovereign-state framework as the key to effective international environmental governance. The report set out a list of "proposed legal principles for environmental protection and sustainable development."[22] Although Principle 1 asserts, "All human beings have the fundamental right to an environment adequate for their health and well-being," each of the remaining twenty-one principles focuses on the rights and responsibilities of nation-states. Indeed, each of the subsequent principles begins with the same two words: "States shall . . ." Although stressing the importance of international law and multilateral financing, *Our Common Future* is principally a model for environmental regime building based on principles of sovereignty, collective action, technology transfer, and information sharing.[23] These principles in turn informed the regime-building efforts of the 1992 Earth Summit in Rio de Janeiro (formally known as the UN Conference on Environment and Development, or UNCED). They can be seen in the regimes on climate change and biological diversity born at Rio, as well as in the failed effort to create a regime for the preservation of tropical rainforests (discussed below).

In summary, both the North-South debate on environment and development and the recent ascension of global-change discourse stress the need to define the collective duties and responsibilities of individual, sovereign states. This way of framing the debate tends to skirt the issue of whether national sovereignty and environmental protection are fundamentally incompatible in a tightly interconnected world. Some observers have argued that the shift from limits to growth to a global-change paradigm reflects a growing willingness among environmentalists to accommodate rather than challenge capitalist forms of economic growth and development.[24] Much the same can be said with regard to sovereignty: characterizing "global" in this fashion carries with it an implicit but powerful endorsement of national sovereignty as part of the solution to "global" problems. Emerging principles and norms of environmental protection are thus taking institutional form as a hodgepodge of relatively narrow efforts to build functional, issue-specific international regimes, in ways that do not pose a more direct challenge to the sovereign rights of states.[25]

Thus, in their most common form, emerging international environmental norms embrace the principle of sovereignty as the foundation for international policy responses, even as they complicate the exercise of specific sovereign rights. Under these circumstances, pressures for ecological responsibility have complex and often contradictory implications for the practice of national sovereignty. This pattern can be seen in the general debate surrounding tropical deforestation and in the specific case of the Brazilian Amazon.

Tropical Forests and Global Environmental Protection

Forests cover more than one-fourth of the earth's land surface, a larger fraction than is occupied by any other terrestrial ecosystem. Tropical moist

forest, also referred to as tropical rainforest, makes up about one-third of
the world's total forest cover. The remaining two-thirds is split approximately evenly between temperate-zone forests and tropical dry forests.[26]
Most of the world's tropical rainforest is found in a relatively small number
of countries: Brazil alone accounts for more than one-fourth of the global
total, and three countries (Brazil, Indonesia, and Zaire) together account for
roughly half.

It is generally agreed that deforestation is currently proceeding much
more rapidly in the tropics than in temperate-zone forests.[27] Data on the
rate and extent of tropical forest destruction are highly uncertain and controversial, however. One often-cited study estimates that deforestation claimed
on the order of 142,000 square kilometers of moist tropical forest in 1989,
which the author estimates to represent about 1.8 percent of the remaining
expanse.[28] The same study estimates that the annual rate of tropical deforestation was 90 percent greater at the end of the 1980s than it had been a
decade earlier.[29] Such estimates are highly uncertain and hotly debated.

The causes of tropical deforestation are complex; they include land clearing (for grazing or crops), commercial logging, the expansion of human
settlements, and local and regional fuelwood demand.[30] Underlying these
immediate causes is what William B. Wood describes as a web of "inter-
locking socioeconomic and political factors: inequitable land distribution,
entrenched rural poverty, and rapidly growing populations which push landless and near-landless peasants on to forest lands that contain infertile
soils; government-subsidized expansion into forest regions by plantations
growing export crops, timber companies, and cattle ranches; and government-sponsored population relocation to frontier regions."[31] Many observers
would add to these local processes a list of transnational forces, including
foreign debt, international market pressures, and the dependent linkages
that characterize most third world economies. Within this complex causal
web, the relative importance of particular forces may vary over time and
from region to region. Timber harvesting for export has been a major cause
of deforestation in Southeast Asia, for example, but a lesser (albeit growing) factor in Latin America.[32]

The consequences of tropical deforestation also operate on scales ranging from local to global. Like all forest systems, forests in the tropics play
an important role in maintaining the health of local ecosystems and the
stability of regional climates. Deforestation can lead to or exacerbate soil
erosion, flooding, and even desertification, and can also yield changes in
local and regional climate patterns. The impact of such changes is social as
well as environmental: the World Bank estimates that half a billion people

depend directly on forests for their livelihood.[33] Forests around the world have thus become the focus of intense and at times violent local jurisdictional disputes. The reasons for this are several: the many potential economic, ecological, and sociocultural uses of forest resources are often incompatible or contradictory; the impact of deforestation on local peoples is usually severe; and the agents of forest destruction are often outside forces whose goals conflict directly with local interests and livelihoods.[34]

Tropical deforestation also has global consequences. Habitat destruction is by far the leading cause of species extinction worldwide, and tropical rainforests are by far the planet's richest storehouses of biological diversity.[35] Rainforest destruction is also implicated in the problem of climate change. Although combustion of fossil fuels in the industrialized countries remains the predominant human source of greenhouse gases, the burning of tropical rainforests does release substantial amounts of carbon to the atmosphere.[36]

The controversies surrounding tropical deforestation are a good test case of the power of emerging environmental norms to reshape traditional conceptions and practices of national sovereignty. There are at least five reasons for this. First is the combination of intense local interests and mounting global concerns: strong interests in stemming the tide of forest destruction collide with powerful forces propelling that destruction. Second, the rainforest controversy reflects the complex distribution of interests, and the resulting definitional struggle over questions of jurisdiction, authority, and legitimacy, that typically mark environmental politics. Where first world environmental organizations see a global ecological concern, third world governments see a national economic asset. The governments of the industrialized countries often find themselves on both sides of the issue—reaping tangible benefits from the transnational economic relations that propel deforestation, but also facing mounting public pressures to take action against the well-publicized tide of destruction. Grassroots organizations and local communities represent still another pole in the debate; such groups, which frequently go unheard in international policy debates, stress threats to local economies, ecosystems, communities, institutions, and ways of life.[37]

Third, tropical deforestation also brings the sovereignty debate in international environmental politics into particularly sharp relief, for the simple reason that deforestation takes place within the territory of individual sovereign states. As Andrew Hurrell points out:

Tropical forests, like the ozone layer or the atmosphere, provide benefits for all and are in this sense a collective good. They are therefore characteristic of commons in terms of the functions that they perform. On the other hand, unlike the ozone layer, the oceans, or Antarctica, forests are located firmly within particular sovereign states and do not share the typical characteristics of collective goods: indivisibility and non-excludability. . . . Forests are thus both a "global commons" providing a collective good from which all benefit and the "property" of an individual state.[38]

Fourth, the tropical deforestation controversy shows that mainstream environmental policy debates are embedded in a more fundamental discourse on sovereignty, as alluded to earlier. To be sure, close links to "global" issues of climate change and biodiversity mean that saving the rainforests has emerged as a central theme of global-change discourse; this in turn generates often intense pressures on rainforest states to act in the interests of the "international community." Nevertheless, the international policy debate over rainforest management has generally been framed within the discourse of states' rights and responsibilities laid down at Stockholm. This can be seen clearly in the principal efforts to date to institutionalize some form of international management. The International Tropical Timber Organization, which seeks to coordinate and balance the concerns of tropical timber producers and consumers, is a state membership organization. The Tropical Forest Action Plan, established in the mid-1980s to support tropical forest conservation, is a multilateral funding mechanism for national forestry-sector plans (including many that have little or nothing to do with forest conservation). As discussed below, a more ambitious effort to create an international forestry regime at the Earth Summit collapsed under the weight of sovereign resistance by key producer states.

Fifth, and finally, tropical deforestation represents a good test case in that the debate has taken on the type of North-South polarization typical of international environmental politics more generally. North-South disagreement was an important element in the collapse of talks on a proposed forestry regime during the preparatory conferences for the Earth Summit. Many third world governments opposed separating forestry issues from climate-change negotiations, fearing that concrete concessions on forest destruction would not be balanced by concessions on fossil fuel use in the industrialized countries. Also, the governments of several leading rainforest countries insisted that the regime negotiations be broadened to include temperate-zone forests as well, a position opposed by the United States.

These general features are reflected in the specific set of disputes surrounding deforestation in the Amazon, to which the discussion now turns. Strong interests in preventing deforestation collide directly with strong interests in resisting change; appeals to national sovereignty and international community represent important resources for actors struggling to shape forest futures. The resulting pattern, however, is by no means simply one of "international" pressure in the name of community norms and "national" resistance in the name of sovereignty. A more complex pattern emerges: pressures emanating from the international environmental community quickly spread to distinct domestic, bilateral, and multilateral political channels; and responses, though typically framed as defenses of national sovereignty, have also sought to exploit international pressures for a range of domestic economic and political purposes.

The Brazilian Amazon

Although the Amazon rainforest spans nine countries of South America, about 60 percent of it lies within Brazilian national territory.[39] The data on deforestation in the Brazilian Amazon are disputed and controversial; official government figures, which some observers contest, suggest that in 1990 nearly 10 percent of the original forest cover was gone.[40] In spite of these disagreements, several facts are not in dispute: very little forest was cleared prior to the 1970s; the rate of deforestation increased rapidly in the late 1970s and 1980s; and the regional distribution of deforestation has been highly uneven, with the most extensive destruction taking place in the eastern state of Pará and the southwestern state of Rondônia (the latter on the Bolivian border). Most observers also agree that there has been a decline in the annual rate of deforestation since the late 1980s. The specific causes of this decline remain unclear, but seem to include changing governmental policies, economic recession, and perhaps even unusually wet weather.

Analysts disagree as to the root causes of deforestation in the Amazon.[41] Some stress penetration of the region by multinational capital. Others point to the concerns of Brazil's military government (1964–85), which sought to occupy the region geopolitically and use it as a safety valve for venting social pressures that were mounting elsewhere in the country. Still others cite Brazil's foreign debt, which is said to generate pressures for the export of natural-resource commodities.[42]

In spite of these diverse and sometimes conflicting interpretations, a general picture of the dynamics of deforestation has emerged. The principal driving force behind deforestation has been a series of state-led efforts to promote the occupation, colonization, and economic development of the region.[43] These efforts, which began in earnest in the mid-1960s, have often involved international financing. They include several broad categories of economic activity:

—Large-scale resource-development projects, including the Grande Carajás mining project in the eastern Amazon and the construction of massive hydroelectric facilities throughout the region
—Colonization schemes intended to attract landless peasants to the region and establish agricultural communities
—Subsidized corporate-scale enterprises in cattle ranching, agriculture, and industry
—State investment in infrastructure development, road building, settlements, and land and mineral surveys

Although the particular type and mix of activities has varied over time, one feature that has remained relatively constant from the mid-1960s until recently has been the key role of state policies.[44] One indicator of the crucial role of the state is that, although the social and ecological toll of these activities has been massive, the economic gains have been minimal when compared to the level of public investment.[45] In essence, the state used subsidies, tax incentives, land surveys, and infrastructural investments to stimulate activities that would typically have been unprofitable or infeasible without such support. In doing so, the Brazilian government set in motion processes of frontier expansion, land speculation, and forest destruction that have proven difficult to steer, adjust, or otherwise control.

The Domestic Politics of International Pressure

The complex Brazilian response to the mounting international outcry must be seen in historical context. The recent pulse of international concern does not mark the first time that Brazilian ecology has been shaped by external pressures. Such pressures can be traced back to the European conquest of the Americas, which brought with it—indeed, depended upon— a revolutionary transformation of indigenous flora and fauna.[46] Horses, cattle, pigs, sugar cane, coffee trees, and other introduced species literally drove to extinction countless varieties of plants and animals. The transformation was social as well as ecological: mining and monocrop agriculture replaced food security and ecologically sustainable survival strategies as the dominant principles of social organization.[47] The impact on indigenous peoples was devastating: in the Amazon alone, disease, enslavement, and habitat destruction reduced an indigenous population estimated at between 2 million and 5 million at the start of the sixteenth century to a population that today consists of a few hundred thousand people.[48]

In Brazil and throughout the region, deforestation was a central instrument in this transition. The colonial sugar economy that emerged in northeastern Brazil in the sixteenth century brought with it destruction of the once-vast Atlantic forest. The expansion of agriculture and the discovery of gold pushed both development and deforestation southward. The state of São Paulo, site of the nineteenth-century coffee boom and later the heart of Brazil's industrialization, has seen its once-vast forest cover reduced to less than 10 percent of the state's land area.

If this process of ecological incursion is the dominant theme of Brazilian environmental history, a second and closely related theme links territorial control, economic dependence, and the catalytic role of the state in provoking environmental change. As Susanna Hecht and Alexander Cockburn point out, vulnerability to world-market fluctuations and concerns over the minimal presence of the state in the region have been recurring themes in the various boom and bust phases of Amazonian development.[49] From the start, shortages of labor and capital forced the colonial state into an active role in fostering economic development. Wary of the threat of incursion from other European powers, and seeking to weaken the influence of the church in the interior, the Portuguese colonial regency began to promote agricultural development in the region as early as the late eighteenth century.[50] The rubber boom of the nineteenth century raised the issue of sovereignty, dependence, and territorial control in even starker form. The 1866 Treaty of Ayacucho defined the border between Brazil and Bolivia in such a way that the poorly mapped territory of Acre fell to Bolivia. When Acre emerged as a rich rubber-producing region in the late nineteenth century, a complex struggle for control ensued, involving Bolivian, Brazilian, and North American actors.[51] After a revolt, a failed effort by a Bolivian–North American syndicate to consolidate control, and a brief period of independence, Acre became part of the Brazilian Republic in 1903.

During the nineteenth century, the emerging Brazilian state found its interests frequently in conflict with those of traditionally powerful rural oligarchs, over whom the state exerted only limited control.[52] As the modern bureaucratic and military institutions of the state developed, centralization of authority and effective occupation of territory emerged as recurring concerns. This process of state-building unfolded, however, within the context of a resource-extractive economy highly vulnerable to fluctuations in international markets and often dependent on foreign political and economic power.[53] This leads us to a third crucial historical theme: the state has often been forced to rely on international tools and resources to promote domestic changes. The Revolution of 1930, for example, brought to power a new coalition of industrializing, modernizing interests led by Getúlio Vargas. As part of a larger effort to promote national integration, industrial development, and westward expansion, the Vargas regime sought to revive the sagging Amazon rubber economy in the 1940s. The principal instrument was an infusion of U.S. development funds, intended to boost production and meet the wartime surge in demand for rubber.[54]

Amazon policy under military rule in the 1960s and 1970s also reflected the tensions between the Brazilian state's growing political strength and its enduring economic dependence. By federalizing much of the region and promoting state-led capitalist development, the military regime's policies extended state control. But many of the tools at the regime's disposal—foreign development assistance, foreign investment, export-oriented growth policies—had the effect of internationalizing the region.[55] At the same time, regime policies undermined the traditional elite, exacerbated local land conflicts, and politicized local disputes—greatly complicating efforts to consolidate federal control.[56] The deepening of the state's presence in the region created both internal and external dynamics that greatly complicated the problem of state control.

To summarize: the themes of national sovereignty, international vulnerability, and territorial control were deeply embedded in Amazonian history long before the world focused its attention on the rainforest in the 1980s. Three patterns emerge from that history: the state has long been a central agent of environmental change in the region; Amazon policies have often been guided by more general domestic political purposes of the state; and in promoting activities that had environmental effects, the state has often had to rely on international tools and resources. These patterns provide the key to understanding the responses of recent civilian governments to international environmental pressures.

The 1980s: Mounting International Pressures

As evidence of the mounting ecological toll accumulated, rainforest destruction in Brazil and elsewhere quickly rose to a prominent position on the agenda of the international environmental community. The most effective catalyst for international concern, however, was not specific to Brazil or tropical forests but emerged instead from a more general campaign against ecologically harmful development projects. In 1983 an international coalition of nongovernmental environmental groups launched a

highly publicized campaign against the lending practices of the multilateral development banks, and of the World Bank in particular.[57] The
campaign sought to force the banks to stop financing ecologically destructive projects and to make environmental considerations central in development financing.

By targeting a few large projects with particularly destructive ecological
consequences, the campaign sought to generate public pressure focusing on
the World Bank and the donor governments sitting on its board of directors.
A handful of the bank's projects in Brazil quickly emerged as leading symbols in the campaign: the Polonoroeste project of road paving and agricultural colonization in the state of Rondônia, the Carajás mining complex
in the eastern Amazon, and the massive Altamira dam project on the
Xingú River.

A key result of the antibank campaign was that North American and
European environmentalists became more aware of organized local opposition to deforestation. Although local opposition and social conflict have a
long history in the Amazon, such groups began to emerge in more organized form in the 1970s—often linked to rural trade unions, the progressive
wing of the Catholic Church, and the emerging political opposition to
military rule.[58] In the region affected by the Polonoroeste colonization
program, for example, local rubber tappers had already established a tradition of struggle against land takeovers, rural violence, forest destruction,
and poor working conditions. Rubber tappers in the state of Acre began to
unionize in the mid-1970s, and played a key role in forming the National
Rubber Tappers' Council in 1985. Indigenous peoples also emerged as an
organized form of local opposition. The Union of Indian Nations, an autonomous association of indigenous groups, was formed in 1980. Direct action
by some of the better-organized indigenous groups began to yield gains in
the 1980s (although, as David Treece points out, such gains have been "few
and scattered in comparison with the concentrated manpower and resources
at the disposal of landowners, mining companies, and the State").[59]

By the mid-1980s, both local and international groups opposing deforestation had seen the potential power of coordinating their opposition. Local
struggles came to be couched more explicitly in "environmental" terms,
while international pressures came to focus more explicitly on the fate of
forest peoples.[60] Chico Mendes, a leader among the Acre rubber tappers,
received a series of international environmental awards and made a number of appearances in the United States and Europe to increase international attention.[61] When Mendes was assassinated by local ranchers in
December 1988, the international uproar over his death further escalated

pressure on the Brazilian government. Similarly, members of the Kayapó nation traveled to Washington, D.C., in July 1988 to meet with members of the U.S. Congress and publicize their protest against proposed hydroelectric development in the Xingú River basin.[62] José Lutzenberger, an internationally prominent Brazilian environmental scientist, testified before the U.S. Congress on the local effects of the Polonoroeste project.

As a result of the anti–World Bank campaign, alarming estimates of accelerating deforestation, and then the Mendes assassination, pressures on the Brazilian government spread in the late 1980s from the environmental movement to other political channels. One such channel was the World Bank itself, which provided Brazil with nearly $5.5 billion in funds in 1986–90.[63] Under pressure to "green" its lending practices, the bank began to call for change in those state policies that were most obviously promoting deforestation. The bank also exerted pressure for more careful ecological "zoning" in choosing project sites, and for more effective state regulation and enforcement. Although many environmentalists criticize the new environmental awareness of the multilateral development banks as superficial and unsubstantial, changes in the development banks' policy did generate tangible pressure on the Brazilian government.[64] The World Bank suspended its lending for the Polonoroeste program in early 1985, and the Inter-American Development Bank followed suit in 1987. In 1990 the World Bank also came forward with new loan proposals to control environmental destruction in the region of the Polonoroeste project; these included funds for the establishment of extractive reserves and protected lands.[65]

Direct government-to-government dialogue emerged as a second new channel for pressure, albeit a more ambiguous one. The United States, France, and the Netherlands put forward proposals for "debt-for-nature" swaps, in which a portion of Brazil's foreign debt would be retired in return for conservation projects.[66] At its 1990 meeting the Group of Seven (G-7) announced a five-year, $1.57-billion project to finance sustainable development in the Amazon.[67] Given the key role of multilateral financing in some of the most destructive large-scale projects, the willingness of the G-7 to also fund environmental programs essentially placed it on both sides of the issue.[68]

Thus pressures that began with the international environmental community quickly spread to three distinct, albeit overlapping, channels: North-South environmental coalitions, the development dialogue with multilateral lending institutions, and direct government-to-government discussions. Thus "intervention" came both in the form of the empowerment of previously weak and marginal actors in Brazilian domestic politics, and in the form of financial incentives for alternative development strategies and policy changes. First world governments and press sources have tended to characterize such incentives as "assistance." But given the political and economic context—the conditions attached to assistance, the close association to the sensitive issue of Brazil's foreign debt, and the already significant influence of multilateral organs such as the IMF and the World Bank in Brazilian economic policy—such "assistance" also set the stage for a nationalist backlash.

The Sarney Era: "Our Nature"

Brazil's 1985 transition from military to civilian rule added a further complication. The military retained a strong influence on Amazon policy after withdrawing from formal power. One vehicle for this influence was the Calha Norte program, which sought to enhance the military's presence in the border regions of the Amazon.[69] The program, which was developed and implemented in an atmosphere of military secrecy, around the time of the political transition, included a series of investments in physical infrastructure, improved border demarcation, and military operations in the region. Calha Norte also sought to seed resource-extractive economic development and assert greater control over local (and in particular indigenous) populations. The premise was that establishing a military presence and encouraging particular forms of economic development would pull the remote border regions into the orbit of state authority.

There is little or no evidence to suggest that Calha Norte was conceived as a response to growing international criticism per se. Rather, by starting with the national borders and working inward, the program represented a new approach to what the Brazilian military saw as a very old problem: the effective occupation of remote regions of national territory, for purposes of "national integration." In political terms, however, the program also ensured that under civilian rule the military would remain influential on Amazon policy. The post-1985 period also saw growing political organization among rural landowners, seeking (among other things) to block proposals for land reform in the Constituent Assembly.[70]

As the euphoria of the transition to civilian rule faded, the transitional government of the civilian president José Sarney found itself in an increasingly difficult political position. With the faltering of its economic program, the Sarney government grew increasingly dependent on the military for political support. These developments meant that where the Amazon was concerned, the Sarney government was caught between growing inter-

national pressure for change and powerful domestic forces seeking to resist
such pressures.

In October 1988 Sarney ordered a suspension of Amazon subsidies and
tax breaks, and announced that a new overall policy for the region would be
forthcoming. When the details of this new policy were announced six
months later, the situation had polarized considerably. The death of Chico
Mendes greatly escalated the international outcry, and a series of high-
profile events in early 1989—including the visit of a U.S. congressional
delegation and a major demonstration by indigenous groups against the
Xingú hydroelectric project—provoked an increasingly nationalistic backlash, led by the military and rural landowners.

The new policy, dubbed Nossa Natureza (Our Nature), sought both to
defuse international pressure and to help boost Sarney's sagging political
position. Shortly before the announcement, Sarney made a speech to the
high command of the armed forces, in which he fanned the flames of
nationalist sentiment: "Brazil is being threatened in its sovereign right to
use, exploit and administer its territory. . . . Every day brings new forms of
intervention, with veiled or explicit threats aiming to force us to take
decisions that are not in our interest."[71] In announcing the new policy,
Sarney also rejected the use of "debt-for-nature" swaps on the grounds that
they were an infringement on Brazilian sovereignty, stating, "We accept
international aid, but we don't accept conditions."[72] The plan also rejected
the calls to repeal tax credits for cattle ranching, the activity most often
cited as the leading cause of deforestation.

The plan did contain a number of concessions to international pressure,
however. The centerpiece of Nossa Natureza was a proposed five-year,
$100-million program to undertake agro-ecological "zoning" of the region,
which would allegedly reconcile economic uses with ecological realities.[73]
To carry out this task and related tasks, the plan created a new Brazilian
Institute of the Environment and Renewable Natural Resources (IBAMA).
Sarney also called for the creation of new nature reserves, the demarcation
of indigenous lands, and upgraded investment in environmental protection. Funds for these purposes were not forthcoming, however, and when a
court order prohibited miners from invading territories inhabited by indigenous peoples, Sarney signed a decree reinstating partial access.

The Collor Government: Change and Continuity

The administration of Fernando Collor de Mello, Brazil's first elected
president in three decades, took power early in 1990. The Collor govern-

ment, like the Sarney government, illustrated the possibility of channeling international pressures for domestic political purposes. But whereas Sarney had exploited such pressures to boost his sagging political fortunes via nationalist sentiment, Collor pursued a very different agenda. Collor's Amazon policies were instruments in a larger agenda for political change, both within Brazil and between Brazil and the industrialized countries.

Collor gained considerable backing from conservative rural landowners during the election campaign. Though initially wary, senior military circles also came to see Collor as the preferred (though perhaps not the ideal) candidate, particularly when his opponent in the run-off election proved to be the candidate from the Workers' Party. Candidate Collor tended to echo Sarney's nationalistic tone, but the Amazon was not among the major issues of the campaign. Press accounts following Collor's victory characterized him as a "mystery" on Amazon policy, a theme echoed by many Brazilian environmentalists.[74]

Collor moved quickly, however, to defuse international pressure and establish a new policy on the Amazon.[75] He appointed an internationally respected Brazilian environmentalist, José Lutzenberger, to head a newly created environmental secretariat with cabinet-level rank. A $117-million loan for environmental projects from the World Bank, followed by a $150-million grant from the German government, bolstered the new secretariat.[76] Collor also took a conciliatory tone on environmental issues during a visit to several European capitals shortly before taking office.[77] Once in power, the new government moved to expel the estimated forty thousand gold miners operating on indigenous lands in the northern state of Roraima. Collor also indicated a willingness to consider the sensitive issues of debt-for-nature swaps, in which Brazil's foreign debt would be reduced in return for environmental protection measures.

Additional steps were announced during Collor's second year in office. A June 1991 decree blocked tax subsidies for farming and cattle-ranching projects (which had previously been suspended).[78] At that time Collor also fired the military reserve officer whom Sarney had appointed to lead the Indian protection agency (FUNAI), blaming him for delays in demarcating the territory to be reserved for the Yanomami indigenous group. Shortly thereafter, the Brazilian government unveiled to the G-7 a proposal in which it sought more than $1.5 billion in foreign assistance, for forest protection and sustainable development.[79]

These aggressive efforts to defuse international criticism and seize the environmental initiative must be seen in the context of Collor's overall political and economic program. From the start, the Collor government adopted as its central foreign policy goal the improvement of relations with the industrialized countries (and the United States in particular). Under these circumstances, the Amazon controversy came to be seen primarily as a barrier to better relations on the more fundamental issues of trade, debt, investment, and technology transfer. Importantly, however, the Amazon was also seen as a political resource, in that Northern concerns provided Brazil with a certain leverage on issues that could be linked to deforestation, such as development assistance or international debt.

These international political goals converged with the Collor regime's program to redefine the economic and political role of the Brazilian state. Ben Ross Schneider described this program as "conservative modernization": it was conservative in that it did not challenge the highly unequal "basic property and power relations" in Brazilian society, but it was also modernizing in that it sought to "redistribute power within the elite from the old to the modern."[80] The result was a political agenda combining privatization, bureaucratic reform, and trade liberalization with several of the traditional hallmarks of the Brazilian state, including broad use of executive powers and a heavily technocratic philosophy.

This basic approach can be seen in attempts to reduce the state's role as the stimulus for economic activity and investment choices in the Amazon, while simultaneously strengthening the state's regulatory capacity throughout the region. This enhanced regulatory capacity involved continuing an active military presence, using the facilities and infrastructure established in the Calha Norte program.[81] The government also increased air patrols in the region and used the monitoring capacity of Brazil's fledgling space program to enforce restrictions on forest burning.

Collor thus had some successes in exploiting international pressures to promote domestic change. These initial steps toward a more liberal regulatory model for the state further polarized regional politics, however. On the left, the combination of Collor's actions and the growing linkages to international environmental groups empowered local environmentalists and social movements (as did the build-up to the Earth Summit, which Brazil hosted).[82] On the right, the 1990 gubernatorial and congressional elections produced a solid victory throughout the region for conservatives opposed to the preservationist agenda. Many of the new governors advocated traditional development-oriented policies for the Amazon, setting the stage for a renewed struggle to define regional policies.

A final observation about the Collor period is that international pressures show a marked tendency to follow a "path of least resistance" in Brazilian politics. This pattern can be seen clearly in issues related to land tenure. At least three separate land-tenure disputes are directly linked to deforestation: the struggle to establish extractive reserves for the sustainable production of nontimber forest products (such as rubber or Brazil nuts); the controversy over demarcating indigenous lands; and the question of land reform. In the first two instances, protecting the traditional practices of forest peoples is seen as a key to protecting the forest itself; in the third instance, the highly skewed pattern of land distribution is generally recognized as one of the main pressures on peasant colonists to move into the forest.

International environmentalists have pushed for all three measures, but with very different results. Extractive reserves have proven to be the most tractable issue, for several reasons: the creation of reserves can enhance the regulatory power of the state; international financial resources can help minimize conflicts with local landholding interests; and the reserves fit well with the traditional project-oriented mentality of multilateral lending agencies such as the World Bank.[83] Demarcating indigenous lands has proven more difficult, principally because of nationalist opposition. Collor bowed to international pressure on the politically charged case of the Yanomami territory on the Venezuelan border, but progress was much slower on defining boundaries for less high-profile groups or enforcing any boundaries that were defined. Effective land reform in agricultural regions has seen the least movement toward change: redistribution of productive lands is adamantly opposed by powerful interests, and remains a closed subject.[84]

Conclusion

The Amazon case shows that governments can be subjected to intense pressures to make their policies conform to emerging global environmental standards. Not surprisingly, however, the process by which such "standards" are defined reflects several enduring features of world politics. The particular set of "global" issues that has emerged at the forefront of international environmental discourse reflects the ability of the developed world to define the environmental agenda. Also, there is a strong tendency for both North and South to frame the debate in terms of the rights and responsibilities of states—underscoring the principles of national sovereignty, collective action, and regime building rather than more direct forms of intervention. Finally, because the "incentives" (aid, investment, trade, and technology transfer) that can be used to stimulate participation or compliance are themselves highly contested issues, the global environmental debate tends to recreate the basic disputes over political economy and global governance that divide North and South.

These basic features notwithstanding, the international environmental movement is emerging as an important catalyst for intervention. Environmentalism actually represents a diverse collection of social movements, driven by a complex mix of ethical and material concerns. Whether environmentalists appeal to a sense of moral or of material interdependence, their ability to generate domestic political pressure has been the key to mobilizing national governments and international organizations. As the Amazon case illustrates, pressures emanating from the environmental movement can spread quickly to multiple political channels; these channels include not only government-to-government dialogue but also the multilateral development-assistance network and those domestic opposition groups mobilized or strengthened by international linkages.

The implications that such pressures have for national sovereignty are complex. In Brazil, the policies that led to deforestation in the Amazon did strengthen the state's presence in that remote region. But the price of this heightened presence was to set in motion social forces that ultimately complicated the exercise of sovereign control. The outlines of the same general pattern can be seen in the more recent push for forest preservation. The preservationist agenda is enhancing the state's regulatory capacities and creating a new role for the state as environmental manager. But that same agenda has also mobilized local groups, across the entire spectrum of Brazilian politics, in a way that will be difficult for the state to control.

In examining the longer-term implications for the state, a useful distinction can be drawn between what has been termed the "despotic" and the "infrastructural" components of state power.[85] According to this distinction, despotic power is the state's ability to act independently of constraints imposed by civil society, whereas infrastructural power is the state's ability "to penetrate society and to organize social relations."[86] International pressures to stop deforestation have clearly undermined the state's despotic power in Brazil. But those same pressures may be reinforcing the state's infrastructural power by strengthening its regulatory capacity, expanding its role as environmental manager, and making it the agent of internationally financed policy responses.

Perhaps the most important question—the question of what ramifications these potential changes in state power will have for state legitimacy—remains more speculative. Consider, however, the following commentary in the leading Brazilian newsweekly *Veja*, which refers to the highly publicized murder of a group of indigenous people at the Haximu settlement.

Here the state's inability to protect the lives and land of indigenous peoples is directly linked to its other widely perceived inadequacies: "The Haximu massacre shows that, in reality, protection of these minorities is accomplished with the same courage and efficiency that guard the public hospital network and the pensions of the retired."[87] That the consequences for state legitimacy may be diffuse should not obscure the fact that the stakes are high, as the capacity to draw this sort of connection illustrates.

Finally, we turn to the question of the effectiveness of intervention. In this case two complicating factors can be identified. First, both domestic and international actors can and do seize upon environmental pressures to promote more fundamental political and economic goals. Second, existing domestic political structures channel international pressures, often in unpredictable ways. The result may be consistent with the environmental protection agenda, as appears to be the case in some of the Collor government's efforts to reorient the Brazilian state. But this is not inevitable, as illustrated by the nationalist backlash encouraged by Sarney, and the complex consequences for land-tenure issues.

As long as national sovereignty, collective action, and regime building constitute the dominant approach to global environmental governance, the state will be the key agent in implementing environmental protection strategies. Thus the effectiveness of this type of intervention hinges on the state's ability and willingness to play the role of environmental manager. It may be that states can develop the complex bureaucratic, legal, and technical institutions needed to accomplish this task, but this is far from certain. And given the role of natural-resource control and environmental transformation in historical processes of state-building, the willingness of states as currently constituted to address the underlying causes of environmental destruction must also remain in doubt.

Chapter Eight

Sovereignty and Collective Intervention:
Controlling Weapons of Mass Destruction

JANNE E. NOLAN

Imposing international controls on national military forces is an unnatural act for sovereign governments. Military capabilities are the ultimate symbol of state power, nationalism, and sovereign status. The ability to produce and deploy advanced weapons is viewed as a sacrosanct objective in both industrial and industrializing countries, the sine qua non of independence and modernity. A country's defense industrial base, in turn, typically is jealously protected by its leaders, shrouded in secrecy, and willingly supported and paid for by patriotic citizens. For a state's leaders to make a conscious decision to forgo weapons that could enhance the state's power and prestige, by contrast, especially when the decision entails the intrusion of international authorities to enforce compliance, runs counter to all traditional instincts of national security.

However, efforts by the international community to control so-called weapons of mass destruction—nuclear, chemical, and biological—along with certain advanced conventional technologies have been part of the diplomatic landscape for decades. Controls on chemical and biological weapons date back to the early 1920s, when forty-one nations signed the 1925 Geneva Protocol prohibiting the use of these weapons in any future conflict.[1] In the intervening decades, states have devised several methods to restrict particular weapons and the technologies needed for their manufacture. One of these methods is the use of formal treaty regimes, such as the 1970 Nuclear Nonproliferation Treaty (NPT) and the Chemical Weapons Convention (CWC) currently under negotiation. Another is the use of multilateral or bilateral supplier cartels designed to limit the export of key technologies useful for weapons development; these cartels include the Australia Group, established to restrict third world access to materials needed for chemical weapons, and the Missile Technology Control Regime (MTCR), which controls the trade in ballistic and cruise missiles. Also used are less formal, ad hoc arrangements to deny states overall military capabilities, such as the longstanding United Nations arms embargo against South Africa; and explicitly coercive efforts to disrupt or destroy states' military capabilities, such as the Israeli destruction by air strikes of an Iraqi nuclear reactor in 1982, or UN Security Council Resolution 687, the blueprint for the dismantlement and destruction of Iraq's unconventional weapon arsenal initiated after Desert Storm.[2]

The agreements that pertain to various limitations on weaponry differ in the degree to which they are cooperative: they may include incentives to elicit states' support, or they may be more coercive in nature. The spectrum of agreements ranges from wholly consensual arrangements to limit national arsenals (such as the United States–Soviet Union Strategic Arms Reduction Talks [START]), through agreements among some states to deny certain military capabilities to others through trade restrictions (such as the Missile Technology Control Regime), to wholly coercive initiatives (such as UN Resolution 687), which intrude directly on states' sovereignty without their consent.

Most international agreements include a mixture of cooperative and coercive elements, intruding to a lesser or greater degree on state sovereignty. Agreements between sovereign states to limit their respective arsenals typically impinge on sovereignty only on behalf of very specific objectives—for example, on-site verification of missile dismantlement under the terms of the U.S.-Soviet Intermediate Range Nuclear Forces Treaty (INF). By contrast, measures imposed without the consent of the targeted states, including "challenge" or surprise inspections of suspect nuclear sites by the International Atomic Energy Agency (IAEA) or preemptive military attacks against a country's weapons infrastructure, are in direct confrontation with sovereign prerogatives.

Axiomatically, formal treaty regimes such as the NPT or the CWC contain more intrusive enforcement mechanisms (which can impinge on sovereignty) than do consensual supplier cartels; these mechanisms may include broad authority to monitor participants' technological developments, or to impose stringent economic or other penalties on violators.

Supplier cartels such as the Missile Technology Control Regime rely instead on the political will of consenting states, have no formal interna-

tional verification or enforcement mechanisms, and were designed specifically to mitigate intrusion on members' domestic autonomy so as to reduce political controversy. These arrangements are coercive in the sense
that they discriminate against countries outside of the cartel, which are
denied the right to acquire proscribed technologies and may be subject to
punitive measures if they do not comply.

Obviously, the most coercive approach to nonproliferation is the use of
unilateral or collective force to destroy military facilities in countries perceived to be on the threshold of acquiring destabilizing weapons. The coalition war against Iraq following the latter's invasion of Kuwait was intended
in large measure to destroy Iraq's ability to produce unconventional weapons.
Beginning in early 1992, there was considerable discussion about the possible use of military instruments to force Iraqi compliance to Resolution 687
or to eliminate the nascent North Korean nuclear infrastructure.

To illustrate various ways in which sovereignty and collective intervention can come into conflict, this chapter discusses international efforts to
control weapons of mass destruction. The discussion focuses predomi-
nantly on the recent increase in the international community's interest in
the use of coercive measures to enforce nonproliferation objectives, although less intrusive enforcement instruments are discussed as well. The
analysis is organized around five key questions: (1) to what extent is there
in the international community increased interest in imposing restrictions
on weapons arsenals, coercively if necessary? (2) what is the basis for this
interest? (3) what factors transform an interest in controls into collective
intervention to stop states' military ambitions? (4) what are the norms,
procedures, and practices that inform the collective intervention regime,
and how are these legitimized? and (5) what is the relative effectiveness of
various kinds of intervention in changing state behavior?

The Extent of International Interest
in Restricting Weapons Arsenals

To what extent is there evidence of increased interest on the part of the
"international community" in imposing restrictions on how states tend to
their domestic affairs in this area? Is there a desire to impose such restrictions even against the will of the government of the host state?

Beginning in the late 1980s, the international community confronted
a dramatic example of its failures to monitor and control the traffic in
weapons of mass destruction. Iraq's massive investment in a defense indus-

trial base capable of developing, modifying, and/or producing a wide range of unconventional military capabilities demonstrated the consequences of a laissez-faire approach to global military commerce. Following Iraq's invasion of Kuwait in August 1990, which precipitated the United States–led conflict Desert Storm, every industrialized country participating in the military coalition was forced to confront weapons or military potential that it had previously provided to Iraq—from Soviet SCUD missiles, to French Mirage aircraft, to the German chemical materials that were believed to have found their way into Iraqi chemical artillery shells and ballistic missile warheads. Despite its tradition of strict adherence to nuclear nonproliferation controls, even the United States found that it had assisted Iraq's nuclear program with a variety of commercial and dual-use products.[3] The increasingly porous nature of the international technology market, Iraq's immense wealth and ambition, and the industrialized countries' tendency to favor Iraq over Iran had allowed Saddam Hussein to buy a formidable array of weapons, weapons technology, and expertise—much of it through legal channels.[4]

The latter part of the 1980s was a low point for nonproliferation regimes. It was a time in which increasingly fiscally constrained defense industries in the West competed vociferously for exports to almost any nation that could pay; when third world weapons producers, such as China, North Korea, and Pakistan, were coming of age, demonstrating growing capabilities to develop and export weapons without interference from the industrial world or international law; when it was no longer possible to ignore the weaknesses of longstanding treaty arrangements, especially the NPT, to which Iraq, North Korea, and other proliferaters are signatories; and when the long-held illusion that third world states could never pose a serious military threat to the United States or its allies was left to languish in the sands of the Iraqi desert.

In addition to Iraq, at least four states—India, Pakistan, North Korea, and Israel—are believed to have achieved significant progress in their nuclear weapons and ballistic missile development programs since the mid-1980s.[5] Others, such as Iran, are moving more slowly, but they still are part of the unmistakable reality that existing control regimes are not fully keeping up with the pace of the global diffusion of technology. Following the disintegration of the former Soviet Union, moreover, the risk that former Soviet nuclear scientists, engineers, or military officials would sell skills or hardware to renegade states has become a major focus of security concerns.[6]

The aftermath of Desert Storm galvanized international attention in nonproliferation. At least at the rhetorical level, interest among governments has never been higher. U.S. officials began to state publicly that the proliferation of weapons of mass destruction is the gravest risk to U.S. security, and to take steps to improve the domestic and international apparatus for stemming the spread of destabilizing technologies.[7]

Explanations for Interest in Weapons Restriction

The majority of weapons control regimes derive from a mixture of normative and practical considerations, based on a common perception that particular military capabilities are inherently destabilizing and/or immoral. This kind of categorization depends on several variables, including the degree to which certain military capabilities (e.g., nuclear, chemical, and biological weapons) pose risks to noncombatants because of indiscriminate effects; normative concerns about the way in which a weapon inflicts injuries or casualties (death by poison gas or biological toxins is viewed as more horrible than death by conventional means); a perception that a system (e.g., ballistic missiles) is particularly useful for preemptive, offensive operations; and/or the belief that the use of particular weapons poses risks of sufficient gravity to countries well beyond the possessor's territory that such weapons cannot be seen as purely national instruments.

How weapons become subject to international opprobrium is a fairly subjective exercise, but depends to a significant extent on the military value accorded to particular capabilities by states that possess them. Because of their operational limitations, chemical and biological weapons have never been central to developed countries' military doctrines, and thus have proven relatively less difficult for these states to renounce unilaterally. Nuclear weapons, conversely, have served as the core of the superpowers' security paradigms for decades, and only recently has it been possible to even discuss serious reductions in nuclear arsenals—let alone the more remote prospect of nuclear disarmament.[8]

At the same time, the degree of interest in limiting certain categories of weapons stems from the perceived threats these weapons could pose to the forces or territories of the large powers. In recent years, the possession or use of even crude nuclear or chemical forces has come to be seen as potentially "equalizing" third world countries' military strength to the superior military capabilities of the industrial world. Nonproliferation efforts, as such, are driven by the desire on the part of the developed world to slow the dissemination of weapons that could undercut its dominant military (and political) stature.

The lessons of Desert Storm helped to reinforce existing international concern about the dangers of chemical weapons and ballistic missiles. For weeks, the populations of countries not directly involved in the conflict— Israel, in particular, but also Saudi Arabia and the other Gulf states—were vulnerable to Iraqi missile strikes. The fear that these systems might be armed with chemical weapons underscored the reasons for having an international taboo on indiscriminate weapons whose lethality cannot be contained on the battlefield. The heightened interest in nonproliferation of these systems, like the interest in nuclear nonproliferation, is thus far more material than normative in nature.

The Threshold for Collective Intervention

What is the threshold at which increased interest is transformed into collective intervention? What factors (e.g., public opinion, the influence of outside states) raise or lower it?

There have been many instances in which collective intervention has impinged upon national sovereignty. Most commonly, the international community is galvanized after a conflict has ended, when the vanquished and the victorious are easily distinguishable. With few exceptions, ensuing disarmament regimes are inherently coercive, and absent plans for indefinite occupation they are necessarily temporary. Eventually, rearmament is inevitable without some other source of security that replaces sovereign arrangements for the defeated state. In this century, there are multiple examples of collective intervention in defeated nations, including Germany after World War I. After World War II, Germany, Italy, Japan, Rumania, Bulgaria, Hungary, Austria, and Finland all signed peace treaties or adopted constitutions limiting rearmament. Most recently, Iraq was obliged to accept the U.S.-led coalition's terms for a cease-fire in the wake of the Persian Gulf War.[9]

Current efforts to compel Iraq to forsake all weapons of mass destruction and their companion delivery systems have some parallels to the Allied program to disarm Germany following World War I. They are similar in that both disarmament regimes are coercive, intrude on national sovereignty, and call for the complete destruction of the weapons under consideration.[10]

Japan's unconditional surrender and its occupation by the Allies after World War II is a different case of a country's forswearing the acquisition of certain military capabilities as a result of international intervention.[11] Japan's conversion is extraordinary, however, in that the disarmament regime imposed following demobilization was not enforced by explicit military pressure or contractual arrangements, but was instead adopted voluntarily by the Japanese Diet: international political pressure, total defeat in World War II, and cooperative security arrangements were sufficient incentives for the Japanese government to fundamentally change its military posture and strategic goals.[12]

The international community's interest in collectively intervening to stop proliferation in recent decades has been sporadic and idiosyncratic. Although existing regimes are intended to embody universal guidelines that apply equally to all states in the system, in practice the enforcement of restrictions has varied according to the political status of the violating state, the perceived threat that a violation poses to international stability, and a judgment about how effective punitive measures would prove if imposed on a particular government.

Traditionally, concerns about proliferation have been subordinate to other foreign policy priorities. Successive U.S. administrations have tended to look the other way in the face of obvious violations by countries that are allies or trading partners. The United States has been extremely reluctant to question Israel about its nuclear force development, for example.[13] The Reagan and Bush administrations refused for years to adopt a confrontational policy toward Pakistan in response to that country's nuclear program, until forced to do so by U.S. legislation.[14] Congressional pressures to impose comprehensive sanctions on China, in the face of Beijing's repeated violations of its own pledges to abide by international nonproliferation norms, have been resisted by the executive branch.

International sanctions are rarely applied to states believed to be geostrategically important, partly because of the fear that such actions would only serve to antagonize a government rather than persuade it to change its behavior. Maintaining cordial relations with key clients such as China and Israel, as well as with allies who may be violating international laws, as in the case of German and French nuclear and chemical assistance to Iraq, may always take precedence over more abstract nonproliferation objectives. Unpopular states such as Libya, Iran, and North Korea, by contrast, have been subject to punitive sanctions, sometimes without regard to the effectiveness of these policies.[15]

The international community becomes motivated to act collectively on behalf of nonproliferation objectives usually only after a crisis, such as the Iraqi invasion of Kuwait. The crisis, in turn, has to be perceived as militarily significant in order to remind states of the dangers that uncontrolled proliferation poses to their own security. Traditionally, nonproliferation was seen as more of a political priority than a military one, with accordingly lower status in policy making.

Public opinion may play a role in prompting or sustaining attention to nonproliferation in some instances, but is rarely persuasive in changing government policy before a crisis has occurred. It is not clear that public opinion played a role in the Israeli decision to attack the *Osirak* reactor, for example, even though the decision was taken in a context of implicit support from the international community for Israeli objectives. In the case of Iraq, countless efforts by private analysts and members of Congress to draw attention to the pattern of military acquisitions by Saddam Hussein were routinely rebuffed by the Bush administration. A decade earlier, calls for restraint on arms sales to Iran under the Pahlavi regime were ignored until a new American administration briefly embraced this stance to appeal to domestic constituencies, a policy that did little to hinder U.S. arms sales to Tehran until the overthrow of the shah in 1980.

In recent years, a number of developing states have chosen to acquire chemical and possibly biological armaments as substitutes for nuclear weapons. However much they may decry it, supplier states have indirectly contributed to this trend by imposing lax export controls or even by direct promotion of exports in some cases. In the late 1980s, it became clear that firms in Germany and other Western nations had assisted Libya, Egypt, Iran, Iraq, and Syria with chemical weapons programs.[16]

Even the ongoing effort to disarm Iraq under UN Security Council Resolution 687 demonstrates a less-than-enthusiastic support of nonproliferation priorities within the international community. The UN special commission that was appointed to implement the plan is underfunded and underequipped, and in its first year it was even vilified by competitive institutions for its apparent failure to bring this operation to a quick conclusion. Just as the IAEA was blamed for the failure to detect nuclear developments in Iraq, the commission was targeted as a scapegoat for the world's reluctance to accord sufficient resources and leadership to make this venture a success.

Norms, Procedures, and Legitimization of Collective Intervention

The nuclear nonproliferation regime has adapted various forms of noncoercive instruments over the years in its attempt to stem the global spread of nuclear technologies. Immediately after World War II, the United States was the sole possessor of nuclear capabilities, and was determined to maintain this monopoly indefinitely. However, after the first Soviet test of an atomic bomb in 1949, followed three years later by a British test of an atomic device, the Eisenhower administration recognized that its efforts had failed.

In 1953, the administration proposed instead to trade U.S. assistance in civilian nuclear research for states' willingness to forswear the development of nuclear weapons. This was to be accompanied by countries' acceptance of routine inspections of their nuclear facilities. Known as "Atoms for Peace," this program introduced the concept of promoting legitimate uses of advanced technology while controlling and monitoring the application of that technology to avoid its diversion to military purposes. This set a precedent for what was to become a mainstay of future nonproliferation efforts: the provision of access to some kinds of legitimate technology in return for pledges not to pursue proscribed military ambitions. It also began the practice of conducting on-site inspections in recipient countries to monitor the disposition of exported products and to verify compliance— a practice known as safeguards.[17]

Ever since negotiations for a formal nuclear nonproliferation treaty began in the mid-1960s, the treaty has been plagued by controversies about the degree of intrusion to be permitted in safeguard inspections, and about how to manage nonnuclear states' demands for equity in the regime.[18] Some states have resisted safeguards altogether, claiming that the safeguards are a form of unwarranted infringement on their perceived sovereign right to autonomy and secrecy in their military establishments. Partly in response to these political sensitivities, less formal mechanisms, such as coordination of export policies by consent among producers of controlled technologies, are far more prevalent in existing nonproliferation regimes.

The overwhelming preponderance of controls on weapons and weapons technologies consists of initiatives undertaken by the larger powers to restrict access by smaller states to proscribed technologies, while still preserving the right to retain these weapons in their own arsenals. This is certainly the case with respect to nuclear weapons, but it also pertains to various conventional armaments, and until just recently, chemical weapons.[19] While invoking the interests of global security, nonproliferation arrangements ratify the right of the technologically powerful to impinge on the sovereignty of lesser states.

The nuclear nonproliferation regime suffers from the basic incompatibility between the near-sacrosanct status accorded nuclear weapons by the superpowers and those powers' attempts to declare these weapons illegitimate in the rest of the world. Nuclear weapons and ballistic missiles have long been seen as a barometer of enhanced sovereign status in the international system. The key political vulnerability of the NPT, not uncommon to other supplier control regimes, is the difficulty of sustaining an international norm against the development or use of a particular weapon once the industrial countries have declared that their own security is critically dependent on that weapon.[20]

The industrial countries have never hesitated to assert their sovereign right to develop weapons of mass destruction as needed for "deterrence" and self-defense. Industrial countries with declared nuclear arsenals tend to believe that they are uniquely able to deploy such capabilities responsibly, especially since they claim to have no aggressive or hegemonical ambitions. The NPT, in short, is unabashedly designed to protect a hierarchical international system whose underpinnings are eroding steadily.

Until the early 1990s, moreover, the United States pledged its support for the CWC only on the condition that it could retain 2 percent of its own chemical stockpile pending ratification of the treaty by all states possessing chemical weapons. By appearing to continue to value its chemical weapons, the Bush administration weakened the case for delegitimizing these systems internationally.[21] Control of the diffusion of chemical production capabilities is already complicated by the ready availability of the products and equipment needed to produce chemical agents, by the many legitimate civilian uses of such products and equipment, and by an eroding normative consensus against chemical weapons among some developing countries. The difficulties of assuring legitimate commerce while prohibiting development of weapons-usable materials are even more pronounced in the CWC than the NPT.[22]

Efforts to eliminate biological weapons have been under consideration for more than two decades, and include the Biological and Toxin Weapons Convention (BWC), which entered into force in 1975.[23] The agreement seeks to eliminate all development, production, stockpiling, and acquisition of biological weapons. Like the nuclear and chemical regimes, the BWC tries to provide for legitimate commerce in dual-use technologies, encouraging open exchange and international cooperation in permitted biological and toxin research. Many of the materials needed to develop rudimentary biological weapons are available to any country with a reasonably well developed pharmaceutical industry. The biological convention does not have a body comparable to the IAEA to implement formal verification or enforcement provisions in order to protect against diversion of civilian biological capabilities to military use.[24] Efforts to implement more formal measures were attempted during several review conferences in 1980, 1986, and 1991. Despite evidence of possible violations of the BWC as early as the mid-1970s, however, only voluntary confidence-building measures, such as annual data reporting requirements on biological research programs, have proven possible.[25] It is left to the United Nations to investigate reports of violations.[26]

The spread of weapons of mass destruction may be exacerbated as advances in chemical and biological research yield more effective methods of weapons development. The use of biotechnologies in research on vaccines, for example, contains both the promise of vast improvements in the prevention of common diseases and the possibility of far more lethal and usable materials for developing biological weapons. The maturation of developing countries' economies, coupled with the growing commercialization and internationalization of the technology market, virtually guarantees that countries determined to acquire these capabilities will do so.

Efforts to tighten controls on selective technologies may prove beneficial in the short term, but the global diffusion of technology and technical capability may eventually render such controls ineffective for all but the most advanced products. The exclusive focus on controls on the supply of technology will have to give way to consideration of controls on the application of technology, verified by strict end-use provisions. Governments currently place blanket prohibitions on products and technologies that have legitimate uses, for instance, space launch vehicles, but when forced for political reasons to make exceptions they lack the means to monitor the disposition of those products and technologies after sales take place. To ensure that end-use assurances are being honored, more coercive arrangements and greater intrusions on sovereignty may be required.

To the extent that the failures of existing regimes are attributable to loopholes in their mandates and the absence of effective enforcement, there are several well-publicized problems. The intentional proliferation of civilian nuclear technology, for example, not only failed to dissuade determined military proliferaters and/or to attract key states to join the regime but also helped to make dual-use nuclear technology, infrastructure, and expertise more readily available worldwide.[27]

The IAEA is one example of a regime that in recent years has suffered from operational shortcomings and from its lack of sufficient power to carry out its evolving mandate. The discovery of Iraq's clandestine nuclear weapons program, a program that proved far more sophisticated than intelligence reports had previously indicated, prompted changes in IAEA methods and standards of inspection. Before the Persian Gulf War, the IAEA's success was measured by the quantity of nuclear material that it was able to place under international safeguards.[28] The IAEA would routinely conduct two inspections of declared sites in each non-nuclear-weapons state annually, providing a substantial warning period to the host government before each inspection. Iraq complied with these procedures. After the revelation of secret, undeclared sites in Iraq that were not subject to IAEA inspections, however, the standards changed. The current goal is to monitor and keep informed of all nuclear-related activities in member countries in hopes of minimizing the possibility of covert nuclear development programs.

Since 1991, the NPT and IAEA regimes have been strengthened by a number of specific events and new measures.[29] First, the UN special commission and the IAEA proved initially quite successful in revealing the extent of Iraq's undeclared chemical and nuclear weapons capabilities, and in dismantling Iraq's ballistic missiles. Throughout the process, IAEA and special commission activities were bolstered by the Security Council's heightened interest and its more active role, which were manifested through the Security Council's credible threat to inflict further sanctions on Iraq should Iraq abrogate the terms of the cease-fire.[30]

The IAEA's overall authority to impinge upon national sovereignty has also increased in the last two years. IAEA "special inspections," otherwise known as challenge inspections, which require limited prior notice to host governments, have been reactivated.[31] In addition, U.S. intelligence, the main source of nuclear-related information for the IAEA, has been improved by the creation of a one-hundred-employee non-proliferation center at the CIA.[32]

Several other events also have improved the IAEA's credibility. The Security Council joint communiqué issued in 1992 expressed strong support for nonproliferation efforts, including specific reference to Chapter VII of the UN Charter, which allows for economic sanctions and the use of force in order to inhibit proliferation. Additionally, both China and France acceded to the NPT, in March and August 1992, respectively. In July 1991, South Africa became the first nation in history to voluntarily yield its previously undeclared nuclear arsenal to IAEA inspections and restrictions as a nonnuclear state. Even given these enhanced powers, however, concern remains about how much authority the IAEA will exercise to order special, short-notice inspections of suspect sites, including those that are not declared facilities.[33]

Critics of the NPT have noted particular shortcomings in the implementation of export controls. The Nuclear Suppliers' Group (NSG), which monitors the traffic in technologies potentially useful for weapons development, has no formal mechanisms for monitoring and enforcing its guidelines, and significant violations by companies in participating countries have occurred since its inception.[34] Despite strong U.S. pressures, the NSG does not formally require developing states to accede to full-scope IAEA safeguards as a condition of nuclear supply, although Australia, Canada, Sweden, and the United States chose to impose this requirement on their own exports.[35] And the NSG's trigger list is not consistent with the NPT's Zangger Committee list, aggravating confusion and dissonance in export practices. Finally, the NSG has been singled out for special criticism by third world countries, which see it as a particularly egregious form of supplier discrimination aimed solely at keeping developing countries technologically and militarily inferior.

The Nuclear Nonproliferation Treaty, the chemical and biological conventions, and the Missile Technology Control Regime are all accurately depicted as agreements that lack early warning and enforcement authority and cannot stop determined violators. The record of these regimes is mixed, with some successes and some notable failures. It is obvious, however, that the regimes all have one thing in common: they lack clout, money, authority, and sufficient international support.

Given the historically circumscribed powers and limited resources granted the IAEA by the international community, for example, blaming this institution for failing to stop proliferation is meaningless. Even if it had adequate resources and the authority to conduct challenge inspections in suspect countries, the IAEA still could not be held accountable for the high demand for weapons which is threatening to undercut the nuclear nonproliferation regime.[36] The institutions that have the mandate to control other types of weapons of mass destruction are even weaker, less well funded, and less likely to prove equal to international trends.

A growing international desire to impose restrictions on proliferating countries more forcefully was certainly evident in the early 1990s. But while there might be an obvious interest in making nonproliferation regimes more intrusive, there is still no consensus internationally about the means by which to do so. UN Security Council Resolution 687, the blueprint for the dismantlement of Iraq's arsenal, is a remarkable precedent in this regard. But in cases in which a country's sovereignty has not been so severely compromised by international action, devising legitimate ways to force its government to change its behavior is far more problematic. Whether the resolution turns out to be an experimental policy specific to Iraq or a "pilot plan" for future nonproliferation efforts remains to be seen.

Efforts to impose more intrusive measures on NPT violators face similar constraints. Under its existing mandate, the IAEA is not yet fully empowered to subject countries to inspections without some degree of cooperation from the host government; and the agency must respect fairly stringent limits on the scope of its inspections of industrial facilities. While obligating signatories to accept IAEA safeguards on their nuclear installations, for example, Article 4 of the NPT specifically grants states "the inalienable right to develop research, production, and use of nuclear energy for peaceful purposes without discrimination."[37] As military and commercial enterprises increasingly converge, conducting requisite inspections of military activities without interfering with legitimate business will become even more difficult.

Another example of the conflict between sovereignty and collective intervention emerged recently as part of the negotiations for a chemical weapons treaty. The draft treaty proposes various kinds of verification inspections, ranging from routine visits to declared facilities to short-notice, "anywhere, anytime" challenge inspections of suspect sites to detect and prevent violations.[38] Problems arise in trying to balance desired levels of intrusion against the need to protect the privacy of defense installations and commercial enterprises engaged in other kinds of sensitive activities.

After years of insistence that challenge inspections be permitted "anywhere, anytime," the United States recently decided that such an arrangement would pose undue risks to the security of highly classified U.S. weapons research and development activities. By choosing to defer to U.S. military planners and contractors at the expense of achieving a verifiable chemical weapons ban, the United States is believed to have impaired chances for reaching a meaningful agreement.[39] It also discovered the limits on its own willingness to sacrifice sovereignty on behalf of a collective security goal.

The most controversial instrument under discussion is the use of force to destroy problematic military facilities. The basic legitimacy of this approach is obviously in question, as such actions are seen by some countries as the ultimate compromise of their sovereign and territorial integrity. Legitimacy aside, the notion that the West can arm itself to remove unwanted military facilities when it deems it necessary is probably naïve.

There has been considerable debate since early 1993 about the need for collective intervention to stop North Korean nuclear developments, for example. In this case, American opinion has been divided about the best means by which to pursue such an objective; and there have been only a few, albeit vocal, advocates in Congress and the executive branch urging military destruction of suspected nuclear sites. Other U.S. officials, as well as key U.S.

allies such as Japan and the members of the Association of South-East Asian Nations (ASEAN), have stressed the potentially self-defeating nature of military measures. At a minimum, the risks to South Korea posed by North Korean retaliation seem to preclude the successful use of military instruments to contain North Korean military ambitions.

Another contentious issue currently is the question of the appropriate collective response to a potential disintegration of central control over weapons of mass destruction in the Commonwealth of Independent States (CIS). Although the European Union's actions to date have not been overly ambitious in this regard, the United States was seen by many in the early 1990s as remarkably reluctant to devote leadership and resources to help sustain vital institutions in the CIS or to lend assistance to CIS governments to reduce the dangers of theft or compromise of nuclear weapons and other weapons of mass destruction. The U.S. Congress reluctantly approved the nominal sum of $400 million in 1991 to assist CIS states in dismantling nuclear weapons—a commendable effort, given that the administration opposed any funding at all. Appropriations for these tasks have continued to increase in subsequent years, but not by an amount commensurate with the impending security risks.

The Effectiveness of Various Forms of Collective Intervention

The fact that the vast majority of NPT signatories have abided voluntarily by the agreement and refrained from developing nuclear weapons is frequently cited as the clearest indicator of the NPT's success as a consensual arrangement. The number of states that are seeking to subvert the regime is actually quite small.[40] By formalizing states' investment in the nuclear status quo, it is argued, complying states have been protected from the threat of uncontrolled global proliferation which might otherwise have induced them to develop their own nuclear arsenals.[41] The embodiment of the nuclear nonproliferation regime in a formal treaty arrangement, moreover, has helped give it more clout and more international stature than are evident in less formal arrangements. The fact that many countries share strong norms against nuclear weapons in itself helps to deter or at least complicate cheating, and provides a court of international opinion to publicize and penalize violators.

Critics of the NPT, conversely, argue that the number of signatories that are in compliance with the treaty is not necessarily meaningful, as most of these states chose for their own sovereign reasons to willingly forgo nuclear weapons development. If the credibility of the NPT regime is judged by the regime's ability to fully deter determined violators, it obviously falls short. Significant states that remain outside the regime (for instance, Israel, India, and Pakistan) now have nuclear programs that are fairly well advanced. Of even greater concern are the dedicated proliferaters that are NPT signatories, including Iran, Iraq, Libya, North Korea, and Taiwan.[42]

The occasional use of collective military intervention for nonproliferation objectives, however, has not proven to be a decisive or reliable instrument. One legacy of the *Osirak* strike was to drive Iraqi military programs into clandestine, underground installations that could resist destruction. As was discovered in Desert Storm, it is not easy to destroy a military infrastructure of this kind, however superior one's forces.

Even if supplier states were able to successfully inhibit access to technology, making weapons development projects prohibitively costly or selectively destroying facilities in pariah countries, some states would still eventually succeed in acquiring proscribed technologies. Even Iraq demonstrates that there are limits to the effectiveness of coercive instruments. Were all of its current weapons stockpiles to be dismantled or destroyed under Resolution 687, Iraq could still pose a military threat by resuming military production programs once it is out of the international spotlight. The core of Iraq's and other third world countries' military power is entrenched in a growing industrial capability, human capital, and ability to attract suppliers. These are not readily susceptible to change by external intervention.

As a political message, what has come to be known in Washington as "coercive arms control" (usually stated with no trace of Orwellian irony) is also not consonant with a policy seeking to promote global military restraint. The idea that a few states have the right to eliminate military capabilities in states of which they disapprove will not help the West's credibility in its quest for international acceptance of nonproliferation objectives. Although military options may remain one of several instruments that could be used to punish those who violate treaties in extreme cases, such options are unlikely to be a long-term or widely applicable solution.

Intrusive inspections can help deter and detect illegal activities, but there is a limit to the degree of intrusiveness that individual countries and the international community will accept. And the effectiveness of inspections, even very intrusive ones, is not assured. Despite its status as a dispossessed power whose sovereignty is now virtually beholden to international authorities, Iraq still succeeds in thwarting or deceiving UN inspection teams.[43] The technological maturation of many third world states and their increasing ability to tap into the international technology market has meant that many dual- or multiple-use technologies can be purchased without interference from, or even oversight by, international institutions. The problem seems even more formidable in the case of nuclear weapons expertise.

The structural changes in the international technology market, including the breakdown of sovereign government control over technological innovation, has exacerbated the difficulty of stopping proliferation through external coercion or denial. Iraq demonstrated that the most vital indicator of a state's military potential is its access to international commerce. Supply networks for many military and dual-use technologies have become multinational commercial enterprises, sometimes operating out of several different countries under the guise of front companies. Industrial mercenaries—cadres of engineers, technicians, and arms brokers who owe allegiance to no government or international law—are beginning to replace government-sponsored technical assistance as a source of technology and expertise.

Nonproliferation regimes are likely to be effective only when they have the benefit of strong political leadership and a coherent institutional structure, and when they become part of a broader regime that includes incentives for consumer states to perceive that they have a stake in cooperating. The imposition of penalties on suppliers, or external intervention, will have to be bolstered with efforts to lessen the demand for proscribed military activities, which reflects states' sovereign security interests. To retain any credibility, the global nonproliferation regime must be adhered to by a larger group of nations, eliciting the support of developing as well as developed states. Developing states, in turn, are more likely to work consensually with an impartial, international body such as the United Nations than with supplier cartels or treaties from which they feel excluded. In the end, the adequacy of any control regime is determined by the number and the degree of compliance of its adherents.

It is in this context that regional confidence- and security-building measures are vitally important. Intervention to control access to weapons technology must be accompanied by efforts to accommodate developing states' sovereign security concerns. Regional agreements have played too small a role in nonproliferation regimes, although these seem to hold the most promise for creating enduring agreements and there have been recent signs of progress in this sphere.[44] Building on agreements such as the 1968 Treaty of Tlatelolco and the 1986 Treaty of Rarotonga, which established nuclear-weapons-free zones in Latin America and the South Pacific, initiatives that originate among the governments in a particular region are likely to be much more readily supported and enforced by those governments.[45] Such arrangements would require far greater levels of transparency in the international trading system, and a system of cooperative enforcement among like-minded states to verify compliance and to isolate and penalize violators.

Most states abide by at least some of the nonproliferation regimes willingly, concurring with the premise that the spread of weapons of mass destruction endangers their security. But other countries deliberately do not, trying instead to circumvent restrictions in order to reassert sovereignty and press for greater equity in the international system.[46] The Achilles heel of nonproliferation initiatives, as such, is emerging regional powers' perception of discrimination in a system that continues to place a high value on weapons of mass destruction as an indicator of state power and prestige, even while trying to promote the global prohibition of such weapons.

Part Three

Syntheses

Chapter Nine

Sovereignty in a Turbulent World

JAMES N. ROSENAU

Like all relationships, political balances are endlessly in a process of becoming. Sometimes the process is erratic and sometimes it is unerring, but it is always evolving and it is never fixed, as each point on the evolutionary trendline subsumes dynamics that generate immediate or eventual movement on to the next point. To assess the nature of a prevailing political balance is thus to focus on a convergence of diverse causal streams, a convergence that is bound to change as the streams sustain their momentum into the future.

The law introduces a degree of intermittency into the evolutionary nature of political balances. When a particular balance is codified and legally sanctioned, the evolutionary process enters a period of intermittent pause, a period that lasts as long as the new legal codes are effective and sustain the balance between the opposing forces that press for a resumption or reversal of the prior trendline. Viewed in this way, codified legal arrangements—such as those that define sovereignty in any era—are end points of numerous and diverse nonlegal developments. Their codification reflects the premises that underlie those moments of convergence wherein past changes are synthesized in the hope of achieving a respite from uncertainty and a measure of stability. And for a while the law does stabilize relationships and institutions as its precepts evoke compliance and introduce regularity into public affairs. But eventually the political side of the balance resumes its evolution, at which point habits of compliance begin to attenuate, ambiguity begins to spread, and the legal arrangements begin to undergo recodification.

This conception of change and continuity serves as a backdrop for the

ensuing inquiry into the balance between the sovereign rights of states and
the rights of international communities of states to intervene in states'
affairs. It is a conception that enables us to treat sovereignty as the culmination of complex psychological and sociopolitical processes rather than
as simply an unwavering legal principle. It allows us to stress that the
present state of the state—of sovereignty's reach—is in flux and that a
variety of signals point to a decline in the effectiveness of states, an erosion
of their sovereignty, and a corresponding increase in the competency of
international organizations to ignore, override, or otherwise circumvent
the longstanding claims of states to full jurisdiction over their own domestic affairs. More than that, the conception of sovereignty as intermittently
ensconced in a process of becoming facilitates a perspective in which both
the aspiration to maintain collective legitimacy through statehood and the
impulse to serve human needs through collective intervention are acknowledged as powerful determinants of behavior, neither of which is morally
superior to the other and both of which are deeply rooted in the human
psyche.[1]

The Analytic Challenge

However the concept of sovereignty may be approached, the task is
bound to be difficult. Its use can be traced back to Aristotle, but its formulation in subsequent eras has varied widely. And many of the formulations
have been marked by ambiguity, contradiction, and the lack of a consensual perspective. For some purposes sovereignty is exclusively a legal concept that can be understood by probing the materials of international law. It
is also a political concept that requires focusing on the conduct of states.
For other purposes it can be treated as a psychological concept with which
to explore the behavior of ethnic groups, nationalism, and peoples' sense of
community and territoriality. Within each of these analytic traditions,
moreover, the concept of sovereignty has taken on diverse meanings at
different historical junctures as different elites evolve different stakes in
the contents and applications of the concept.

The ambiguities and difficulties inherent in the analysis of sovereignty
seem especially challenging at this time of profound and rapid change. For
not only do states and their sovereign prerogatives seem ever more vulnerable to the demands of both domestic constituents and international organizations, but they also have to contend with the advent of new global
actors and processes that confound their roles, constrain the limits of their

authority, and undermine their territorial appeal. The boundaries of states no longer confine the flow of information, goods, money, and people. Instead, the processes of globalization have become predominant and perhaps even permanent.[2] Markets are worldwide, gaps in the ozone layer are hemispheric in scope, multinational corporations provide global services, the Cable News Network offers the same news to all, tourists and human migrations are everywhere, and fax machines ignore national boundaries, as do computer modems, satellites, and VCRs. As one analyst put it, "Commercial pilots, computer programmers, international bankers, media specialists, oil riggers, entertainment celebrities, ecology experts, demographers, accountants, professors, athletes—these compose a new breed of men and women for whom religion, culture, and nationality can seem only marginal elements in a working identity."[3] In some deep and significant sense, in short, the authority of states has, like money, moved offshore.

Yet, just as the foundations of sovereignty have been eroded by the centralizing processes of globalization, so have they been diminished by decentralizing tendencies wherein people are shrinking the definition of "we" to include only like-minded others and enlarging "they" to include everyone else. Subgroupism, tribalism, nationalism, ethnicity—however they are labeled—these simultaneous inclinations to resist globalization by reverting to close-at-hand ties have the consequence of further challenging those who aspire to clarify the bases of modern-day sovereignty.

Normatively, too, sovereignty has long been varyingly appraised. For some it is a dangerous illusion that inhibits international cooperation and is conducive to conflict. For others it is a positive stimulus to a shared sense of community, a feeling of collective independence. For still others it is mostly a neutral means of specifying legal and geographic jurisdictions. There is some utility to all three of these perspectives. To the extent that states hide behind their sovereign prerogatives as a reason for resisting or avoiding collaborative international projects, sovereignty does become dangerous, either by serving as an illusionary symbol of independence that blocks a full accommodation to the realities of interdependence or by providing an excuse for responding aggressively to neighbors who are said to be a "threat." Likewise, to the extent that people have a need for community and a sense of independence, the achievement and maintenance of sovereignty for their nation does serve important human longings.[4] And to the extent that governments, courts, and philosophers need a framework for differentiating among political entities with competing claims to ultimate authority, the sovereignty concept has proved its worth for centuries. Whatever the merits of these diverse normative perspectives, the problem is that they all derive from very different purposes and thus arrive at very different interpretations of the same phenomenon.

Given the ambiguous and contradictory understandings of sovereignty in a rapidly changing world, it can easily be argued that the concept ought to be abandoned and replaced by new, more elaborate analytic equipment and a new, more appropriate vocabulary. That is, since the concept is under siege by phenomena that do not fit readily under its traditional rubric, it is misleading, to say the least, to continue using the concept as if its contents were self-evident. What is needed, this reasoning concludes, is new terminology derived from a fresh conceptualization that more incisively differentiates among the emergent processes and values that, in the absence of any other conceptualization, tend to be subsumed under the sovereignty label.

Unfortunately, however, we are ill-equipped to begin afresh. Our habitual forms of analysis are so state-centric that we tend to view worldwide markets, television, corporations, and the other dynamics sustaining the processes of globalization as problems for sovereign states to manage and accommodate to, rather than as indicators of a historical breakpoint that requires the development of new conceptual equipment. For globalization is not so much a product or extension of the interstate system as it is a wholly new set of processes, a separate form of world politics, initiated by technologies that have fostered new human needs and wants. Confronted with such unfamiliar activities stemming from such unfamiliar sources, students of world affairs understandably have been slow to make the necessary theoretical adjustments. It is much easier to fall back on the tried and true, on the notion that no change is so sharp as to render long-standing analytic traditions obsolete. One analyst, for example, acknowledges that the sovereignty claims of states "have changed across time and over countries," but nevertheless concludes that the institution of sovereignty is presently so entrenched in world politics that it is "difficult to even conceive of alternatives" to it, "regardless of changed circumstances in the material environment."[5] If this is so, if it is the case that our imaginations are paralyzed by the sovereignty concept, there are good reasons to pause and ponder the implications of the observation that since the "prevailing modes of analytic discourse lack the vocabulary to articulate change in the very system of states, . . . we are not very good as a discipline at studying the possibility of fundamental discontinuity in the international system."[6]

The Sovereignty Continuum

Although elsewhere I have tried to break with habitual analytic practices and conventional terminology,[7] in what follows I attempt to steer a middle course, relying heavily on the sovereignty concept even while seeking to allow for its varying uses and meanings. More specifically, I seek to accommodate the conception of sovereignty both as an expression of the widespread need to achieve community and independence through the preservation and advancement of statehood and as a potential obstacle to cooperation across national boundaries which the processes of globalization require. In the former instance situations are approached and resolved in a "convenience-of-the-states" context, and in the latter they are addressed and handled in a "states-are-obliged-to-go-along" context.[8] Put differently, in the convenience-of-the-states context sovereignty remains inviolable, while in the states-are-obliged-to-go-along context its inviolability is relaxed and made subject to modification. Both attitudinal contexts, it should be stressed, presume the continued viability of states and their sovereignty, but they are differentiated by the degree to which sovereign prerogatives are considered predominant. In effect, they highlight the question of whether we are presently witnessing the emergence of a subtle but worldwide consensus in which habitual attachments to the convenience of states are giving way to new habits that allow states to accept or otherwise yield to the wishes of their international communities.

In short, sovereignty needs to be viewed as a continuous rather than as a dichotomous variable. From a strict legal perspective, to be sure, it is a dichotomous variable: states are either recognized to have a defined territory and population over which their governments exercise control, or they are not—either they have sovereignty, that is, or they do not—and if a state is so recognized, then humanitarian intervention by a community of states violates its sovereignty and established principles of international law. But if the relative rights of states and their international communities are conceived to have political as well as legal dimensions, then the continuum between sovereignty and nonsovereignty consists of numerous values rather than just two extreme points. These values can be viewed as deriving from four main determinants:

1. *Situational determinants:* To some degree the values are shaped by the severity of the conditions within the particular state that is evoking humanitarian concerns abroad. The conditions may be highly severe, quite severe, moderately severe, incipiently severe, and so on

across a wide range of values, depending on how the situation is defined in the interplay of the mass media, politicians, academic specialists, public interest groups, and the many other actors who participate in the processes whereby humanitarian issues are framed and contested.

2. *Domestic determinants:* The orientations of citizens and policy makers of the state in which the humanitarian situation is located also contribute, at least in part, to the range of values along the sovereignty-nonsovereignty continuum. These values can be maximally, moderately, mildly, or minimally—and so on across a wide range of intensities— opposed to outside intervention or receptive to it, depending on how effectively the state's authorities exercise control, how historically embedded and extensive its patterns of patriotism are, how coherent the opposition groups within the state are, and how amenable other aspects of the state's political processes are to outside intervention.

3. *International determinants:* In part, too, the values on the continuum are a product of the international milieu prevailing at the time the humanitarian situation arises. This milieu can vary across a range delineated by high, increasingly high, moderately high, somewhat high, and so on across various degrees of inclination to intervene, depending on the interest calculations of potential donor states, the clarity of emergent global norms, and the degree to which compassion or disaster fatigue is running strong in the currents of world opinion.

4. *Legal determinants:* And, of course, the location of the relative rights of states and international communities on the sovereignty continuum is partially shaped by the legal circumstances that define the prevailing state of international law. Depending on how prior situations, precedents, court cases, and other legal sources combine to produce a prevailing juridical setting, the definition of "rights" can vary across many degrees of specificity, from very precise, through somewhat exact, to highly ambiguous. The manner in which rights are conceived may favor states or international organizations.

Sovereignty, in short, is thoroughgoingly complex. It is pervaded by political considerations and, to repeat the initial point, is thus always in a process of becoming. The extent to which it enables states to husband their rights or enables international organizations to set aside those rights can vary as widely as the numerous permutations and combinations inherent in the foregoing determinants.

Not only does viewing sovereignty in this way serve to inhibit the tendency to regard the relative rights of states and their international communities as fixed, stable, or constant, but conceiving of it as a continuous variable determined by a multiplicity of sources also facilitates an appreciation of the dynamism of the processes in which sovereignty is embedded. Among other things, it suggests the possibility that each increment of diminished (or enhanced) sovereignty—of successful (or unsuccessful) humanitarian intervention that sets aside (or moves forward) the rights of states—may alter the global context and thereby pave the way for subsequent increments. Indeed, it may even be that the movement of the sovereignty concept through time amounts to a momentum that is both a source and a product of the transformations presently at work in world politics.

It is instructive to take note of another, somewhat different approach that treats sovereignty as a variable. In his cogent inquiry into how the postwar collapse of empires created a new form of sovereignty in the third world, Jackson draws a distinction between negative and positive sovereignty. He posits negative sovereignty as a "formal-legal" and "absolute condition" that protects weak and ineffective states in the developing world against outside intervention, whereas positive sovereignty is conceived as a set of rights that attaches to strong and effective states in the developed world.[9] Clarifying and useful as Jackson's distinction is, however, it is not the same as the conception of the sovereignty continuum developed here. My formulation locates both negative and positive sovereignty as subject to variation along the continuum. It argues, in effect, that the vast changes presently at work in world politics have altered international society's capacity to maintain the absolute condition under which states are protected from its intrusions. All states are seen as having become subject to movement along the sovereignty continuum. None is immune any longer to the dynamism that results from the shifting permutations and combinations of the determinants that locate it on the continuum.

Given the universality of its application, the sovereignty-as-a-continuous-variable perspective serves to highlight both the questions that need to be probed and the questions that may lead to dead ends if the relative rights of states and of their international communities are to be cogently assessed. If this conception of sovereignty as a dynamic process is sound, there is clearly little to be gained by phrasing the task as that of exploring whether international communities have the right to initiate humanitarian interventions in the domestic affairs of states. That is a normative question, the answer to which may serve as a justification for a course of action, but it is not a question that can provide any insight into sovereignty as a process that is susceptible to fluctuation and transformation. The problem, in other words, is to address an empirical question: is the relative balance between the sovereign rights of states and the rights of their international organizations presently undergoing transformation, and if so, at what pace is this transformation occurring, and toward which extreme of the sovereignty continuum? Posed in this way, our task is clearly one of searching for the dynamics that underlie, shape, and transform the legal principles that define the rights of international communities as they evolve through time.

To facilitate matters, let me anticipate my overall conclusion that the current era—say, from the 1950s into the early decades of the twenty-first century—is one in which the values that attach to sovereignty, insofar as outside humanitarian intervention is concerned, are being relocated away from the strict convenience-of-the-states extreme of the continuum and toward the states-are-obliged-to-go-along extreme. Put differently, I view the processes of globalization as more powerful than the processes pressing for territorial independence, even as it is also the case that both are operative simultaneously.

It must be stressed at the outset that this assessment is not founded on hard data. Given the foregoing conception of the analytic challenge, one cannot rely on specific legal codes or the formal documents of governments and international organizations for the full array of evidence that is needed. Such materials are not irrelevant, but neither are they sufficient. Far from it: they are a measure of only a minuscule aspect of the sovereignty phenomenon if the latter is conceived as deriving from the broad and complex set of sociopolitical determinants noted above. Since systematic studies of the values associated with these determinants that attach to sovereignty have not been undertaken (as far as I know), there is little choice but to fall back on other forms of evidence. In some sense, accordingly, the ensuing analysis is based on anecdotal data, on impressions of how isolated cases form an overall pattern.

This assessment and the impressions on which it rests do not stem simply from intuitive insights or value preferences, however. Rather, they are derived from a model of world politics I have developed which lends itself to a variety of applications, including the issues of concern here. I call the model a "turbulence" or "bifurcationist" theory of world politics, and what follows seeks to link its major premises to the several aforementioned determinants of where the balance of rights is located on the sovereignty continuum at a particular point in time.[10]

The turbulence model has the further advantage (as would any theory) of pointing the way to the kinds of empirical materials that are needed in order to extend the analysis beyond anecdotal cases. To note a lack of systematic evidence is not to suggest that there need be no concern about methodological rigor. Hard data may not be available, but that does not relieve us of being clear about how we know a shift along the sovereignty continuum when we come upon one. What sort of real-world situations are indicative of a shift? Should signs of a shift be sought in public attitudes, in the compliance or defiance of governments, in the policy statements of international organizations, in norms articulated by the mass media, in the patterns formed by sequences of events? And how much weight should be given to these forms of political data relative to political data expressive of the legal orientations and claims of governments, courts, and international organizations? What kinds of systematic data, in short, should be gathered if time and resources permitted?

In part, the foregoing listing of determinants that distribute values across the sovereignty continuum tell us where to begin to look for evidence bearing on these questions, and in turn, the turbulence model provides a basis for juxtaposing and contextualizing the data indicative of how the situational, domestic, international, and legal determinants operate and interact. Of course, every potential interventionary situation embraces particulars that significantly affect the kind of actions that are feasible and that thus have to be taken into account, but it places the value cart ahead of the analytic horse to focus on the particulars without first being cognizant of the more general circumstances in which horses are able to pull carts in desirable directions.

Some might question whether meaningful generalizations are possible, given the diversity of the myriad situations in which the question of collective intervention arises. It is absurd, they might argue, to seek an understanding that holds across all types of situations, from human rights violations to genocide, from chemical weapons production to widespread famine, from civil wars to the breakdown of environmental protection. Though the ensuing analysis does not dismiss the relevance of the path-dependent, historically specific orientations and institutions that are unique to every situation, the argument that generalization is unwise or impossible is considered far-fetched and erroneous. It is presumed, rather, that all interventionary situations, whatever their issue content, have common qualities. The world has become so interdependent, its communications links so extensive, its economy so globalized, that no state's sovereignty is immune from the centralizing and decentralizing dynamics that are fomenting authority crises and restructuring the foundations of legitimacy. Accordingly, it is reasonable to presume that, in one form or another, all the determi-

nants of values on the sovereignty continuum are operative in every interventionary situation.

The Fact-Value Problem

Although present circumstances offer no choice but to generate and
evaluate evidence in a less than systematic fashion, it is useful to note a
major risk inherent in this procedure, in the hope that through explication
the risk can be lessened. The risk involves a subtle process wherein one's
preferences with regard to the issue of international humanitarian intervention shape, color, or otherwise distort one's selection and interpretation
of the relevant facts. Whether we prefer to justify or constrain such interventions, we are endlessly confronted with tensions between the expertise
and the values we bring to the task. It is all too easy to allow, unknowingly,
the latter to exert a pull on the former. Humanitarian and statehood issues
are so fundamental to political life that one is constantly subject to subtle social and self-generated pressures to tailor the analysis so as to ensure com-
fortable conclusions and desired recommendations, irrespective of whether
the proposed course of action is appropriate to the social and political
milieu into which it is to be introduced. In assessing whether the situation
in Tibet warrants humanitarian intervention, for example, it may matter a
great deal whether one is a Western liberal or a third world skeptic. Strong
subconscious temptations can influence one to justify the conclusion that
circumstances either favor or do not favor a Tibetan intervention and then
to exaggerate the possibility that a successful intervention can actually be
accomplished.

Such temptations, moreover, are double-edged. They tug in opposite
directions and thus make it all the more difficult to maintain a balanced
analytic perspective. The values located at both ends of the sovereignty
continuum involve such deeply held convictions—in one case, convictions
about territorial community and the need to protect against unwanted
external intrusions; and at the other extreme, convictions about the dignity of individuals and their right to enjoy basic liberties and reasonable
standards of living—that the inclination to move to a polar position is
especially acute. Yet, as previously indicated, neither pole on the continuum is morally superior to the other. People are entitled to form their own
communities, to value their own territory, and to protect their own cultures by keeping out strangers and maintaining rigid criteria for inclusion
and exclusion; and they are entitled to pursue these goals through the

achievement and maintenance of statehood. Likewise, it is surely appropriate for people to worry about the plight of their fellow human beings and to
try to do something about those whose plights are shocking and beyond the
pale of minimally acceptable standards. Though these two sets of values
need not offset each other and can even be mutually reinforcing, they are
incompatible when juxtaposed in the context of the relative rights of states
and their international communities.

Moreover, being deeply buried in the human psyche, both sets of convictions are powerful magnets that can sweep aside all nuances, ignore all
proposals for compromise, and exert strong pressures for zero-sum solutions. To accord primacy to the rights of states, therefore, can be to down-
grade the right of humanitarian intervention, and vice versa. And to vary
these priorities from one situation to the next in the light of differing
severities is to become so entangled in inconsistencies as to foster a tendency to cling rigidly to one or the other extreme. In sum, adhering to a
detached perspective in assessing relative rights is no easy matter. Every-
thing militates against it. Every impulse favors one extreme or the other.

Perhaps the only sure way to cope with this fact-value dilemma is to
recognize its existence, to admit that we have strong beliefs that can distort
our observations, and thus to remain continuously aware of the dilemma as
we undertake the analytic task of tracing movement along the sovereignty
continuum. Acknowledging that our underlying preferences may be at work,
however, presents a huge challenge. We are confident of our expertise, and
we know that it can contribute to solutions, all of which makes us vulnerable to being blinded by the insidious ways in which we allow it to be
compromised by our commitments.

The Turbulence Model

Founded on the premise that such dramatic developments as the end of
the cold war, the collapse of the Soviet Union, and the ouster of Iraq from
Kuwait by a thirty-two nation coalition are but manifestations, outcomes
as it were, of deep transformations in international relations, the turbulence model digs beneath the level of current affairs. It treats current affairs
as consequences of more profound shifts in the underpinnings of world
politics which have been under way for several decades and which paved
the way for the spectacular series of events that began in Eastern Europe in
1989. Why make this distinction between outcomes and underpinnings?
Because to assess the possibility that new global norms relevant to human-

itarian interventions may be emerging—that movement on the sovereignty continuum may be occurring—we need to probe the deeper structures out of which behavior flows, and thereby frame the relative rights of states and their international communities in a larger perspective. Conceiving of these rights as outcomes rather than as underpinnings, we are impelled to extend our search for understanding beyond the norms and precedents of international law to the aforementioned attitudinal and behavioral sources from which the prevailing political balance derives. The relative rights of states and international organizations are thus to be found not in constitutional documents, court decisions, or any other formal assertions of national or global norms; rather, they stir in the minds and hearts of publics and officials—in their premises, orientations, perceptions, memories, habits, and belief systems—and also take root in the practices and institutions of collectivities. It is here, in deeper ideational and structural sources, that the world's normative premises relative to sovereignty may be undergoing a long-term process of slow but relentless erosion.

At the core of the long-term process of change is a new ideational construct that values autonomy over compliance and interdependence over independence. Autonomy can mean a variety of things, depending on the context in which it is assessed, but in all contexts it involves a readiness to contest authority whenever the alternative involves yielding to tradition and unthinkingly accepting unwanted directives issued by those higher in the pecking order. This underlying ideational predisposition applies to the individual in the group, the group in the province, the province in the state, and the international organization in relation to its member states. The scope of these contexts differ, but the same readiness to seek autonomy by challenging authority obtains for all of them.

To aspire to autonomy, however, is not necessarily to seek independence. Rather, achieving autonomy means being free to select the ways in which interdependence with other individuals, groups, provinces, states, and international organizations is established.[11] The world has become too complex and dynamic for independence to satisfy needs and wants. Instead, there is widespread recognition that needs and wants have to be sought through reciprocal arrangements with others, that it is not contradictory to maintain both autonomous and interdependent relationships in the global system. Thus, concerned individuals have spawned large and unwieldy social movements, ecological groups have formed regional consortia, republics in the former USSR have sought to fashion a new commonwealth, the states of Europe have pooled their efforts to establish a monetary union, the United States and Canada have reached out to Mexico in an effort to widen their free-trade agreement, and international organizations have redefined their ties to the domestic affairs of states.

If the dominant outcomes of the emergent global order derive from a stress on autonomy in the context of interdependence, as distinguished from the old order's emphasis upon compliance in the context of independence, and if this shift has provoked movement along the sovereignty continuum, what are the transformed underpinnings that have given rise to the changes? The turbulence model's answer focuses on the basic parameters of world politics. If the parameters of any system are conceived as the boundaries beyond which lie its environment (those recurrent patterns that may impact upon but are not a part of the system's functioning), and within which the variables of the system undergo their ceaseless processes of variation, then it follows that normally the parameters are fixed features of the system. They provide its continuities in the sense that they remain constant even as fluctuations occur in its variables. They are, in effect, the foundations of global order—those values, premises, resources, and enduring institutions that underlie and limit the nature of the international pecking order, that accord legitimacy to alliances, that underpin orientations toward war, that justify concern for human rights, that shape predispositions toward authority and authorities, and so on through all the sources that give rise to variation within the system.

The bifurcation model defines turbulence as the onset of such high degrees of systemic complexity and dynamism that the basic parameters of world politics undergo profound transformation. In effect, the parameters become for a time variables that shift sufficiently to undermine the bases of the prevailing global order and thereby foster the emergence of a new order. And that is exactly what has happened in recent decades. For the first time since the period that culminated in the settlement of Westphalia in 1648, turbulence has overwhelmed world politics and altered its basic parameters so extensively and rapidly that the underpinnings of a new world order have been laid.[12]

Elsewhere I have identified three parameters that are central to any prevailing global order: the overall structures of global politics (a macro parameter), the authority structures that link macro collectivities to citizens (a macro-micro parameter), and the skills of citizens (a micro parameter).[13] Each of these parameters is judged to have undergone transformation in the current era, and the relative simultaneity of the transformations is considered a major reason why signs of an emergent global order—of deep underpinnings fostering unexpected outcomes—took politicians, journalists, academics, and others so utterly by surprise when the collapse of communism rendered them unmistakably manifest late in 1989.

Table 2 summarizes the changes in the three parameters, but the order of their listing should not be interpreted as implying causal sequences in which the actions of individuals are conceived as preceding the behavior of collectivities. On the contrary, incisive insights into movement along the sovereignty continuum are crucially dependent on an appreciation of the profoundly interactive nature of the three parameters—on recognizing that even as individuals shape the actions and orientations of the collectivities to which they belong, so do the goals, policies, and laws of the latter shape the actions and orientations of individuals. Out of such interaction a network of causation is fashioned which is so thoroughly intermeshed as to render impossible the separation of causes from effects. Indeed, much of the rapidity of the transformations at work in world politics can be traced to the ways in which the changes in each parameter stimulate and reinforce the changes in the other two.

The Micro Parameter: A Skill Revolution

The transformation of the micro parameter is to be found in the shifting capabilities of citizens everywhere. Individuals have undergone what can properly be termed a skill revolution. For a variety of reasons ranging from the advance of communications technology to the greater intricacies of life in an ever more interdependent world, people have become increasingly more competent in assessing where they fit in international affairs and how their behavior can be aggregated into significant collective outcomes. Included among these newly refined skills, moreover, is an expanded capacity to focus emotion as well as to analyze the causal sequences that sustain the course of events. In the case of the Kurds today, for example, their ability to evaluate the protections offered by statehood as well as to assess any gains that may be realized through a violation of the sovereignty principle by international organizations have probably enlarged considerably.

Put differently, it is a grievous error to assume that citizenries are a constant in politics, that the world has rapidly changed and complexity greatly increased without consequences for the individuals who comprise the collectivities that interact on the global stage. As long as people were uninvolved in and apathetic about world affairs, it made sense to treat them as a constant parameter and to look to variabilities at the macro level for explanations of what happens in world politics. Today, however, the skill revolution has expanded individuals' learning capacity, enriched their

TABLE 2.
The Transformation of Three Global Parameters

Parameter	Previous Condition	New Condition
Micro parameter	Individuals less analytically skillful	Individuals more analytically skillful
Macro-micro parameter	Authority structures in place as people rely on traditional and/or constitutional sources of legitimacy to comply with directives emanating from appropriate macro institutions	Authority structures in crisis as people evolve performance criteria for legitimacy and compliance with the directives issued by macro officials
Macro parameter	Anarchic system of nation-states	Bifurcation of anarchic system into state-centric and multi-centric subsystems

cognitive maps, and elaborated the scenarios with which they anticipate the future. It is no accident that the squares of the world's cities have lately been filled with large crowds demanding change.

It is tempting to affirm the impact of the skill revolution by pointing to the many restless publics that have protested authoritarian rule and clamored for more democratic forms of governance. Although the worldwide thrust toward an expansion of political liberties and a diminution in the central control of economies is certainly linked to the existence of citizens and publics with greater appreciation of their circumstances and rights, there is nothing inherent in the skill revolution that leads people in more democratic directions. The change in the micro parameter is not so much one of new orientations as it is an evolution of new capacities for cogent analysis. The world's peoples are not so much converging around the same values as they are sharing a greater ability to recognize and articulate their values. Thus this parametric change is global in scope because it has enabled Islamic fundamentalists, Asian peasants, and Western sophisticates alike to serve their respective orientations more effectively. And thus, too, the commotion in public squares has not been confined to cities in any particular region of the world. From Seoul to Prague, from Soweto to Beijing, from Paris to the West Bank, from Belgrade to Rangoon, from Mongolia to Madagascar—to mention only a few of the places where collective demands have recently been voiced—the transformation of the micro parameter has been unmistakably evident.

Equally important, evidence of the skill revolution can be readily inferred from trend data for education, television viewing, computer usage, travel, and a host of other situations in which people are called upon to employ their analytic and emotional skills. And hardly less relevant, a number of local circumstances—from traffic jams to water shortages, from budget crises to racial conflicts, from flows of refugees to threats of terrorism—relentlessly confront people with social, economic, and political complexities that impel them to forgo their rudimentary premises and replace them with more elaborate conceptions of how to respond to the challenges of daily life.[14]

This is not to say that people everywhere are now equal in the skills they bring to bear upon world politics. Obviously, the analytically rich continue to be more skillful than the analytically poor. But though the gap between the two ends of the skill continuum may be no narrower than in the past, the advance in the competencies of those at every point on the continuum is sufficient to contribute to a major transformation in the conduct of world affairs. More important for present purposes, the emergent global order rests on increasingly relevant micro foundations—on individuals who cannot be easily deceived and who can be readily mobilized on behalf of goals they comprehend and means they approve. Since the new global order is thus more inclusive than its predecessors, it is reasonable to presume that issues pertaining to possible compromises of the sovereignty principle have moved beyond elite circles in many societies and are now being pondered and debated more widely among their citizenries.

The Macro-Micro Parameter: A Relocation of Authority

This parameter consists of the recurrent orientations, practices, and patterns through which citizens at the micro level are linked to their collectivities at the macro level. In effect, it encompasses the authority structures whereby large aggregations, private organizations as well as public agencies, achieve and sustain the cooperation and compliance of their memberships. Historically, these authority structures have been founded on traditional criteria of legitimacy derived from constitutional and legal sources. Under these circumstances individuals were habituated to compliance with the directives issued by higher authorities. They did what they were told to do because, well, because that is what one did. As a consequence, authority structures remained in place for decades, even centuries, as people unquestioningly yielded to the dictates of governments or the leadership of any other organizations with which they were affiliated. Yes, revolutions did occur in America, France, Russia, and China; and yes, mass upheavals spread briefly on the European continent in the mid-nineteenth century;[15] but important as such events were historically, none of them proved to be expressive of a parametric transformation. In every case, ensuing developments settled back into the traditional pattern whereby state sovereignty and governmental authority served as the primary basis for political order.

In the present era, however, most dislocations of authority have not reverted back to the traditional pattern. Instead, for a variety of reasons, including the expanded analytic skills of citizens as well as a number of other factors noted elsewhere,[16] the foundations of this parameter have undergone erosion. Throughout the world today, in both public and private settings, the sources of authority have shifted from traditional criteria of legitimacy to performance criteria. Where the structures of authority were once in place, in other words, now they are in crisis, with the readiness of individuals to comply with governing directives being very much a function of their assessment of the performances of the authorities. The more the performance record is considered appropriate—in terms of satisfying needs, moving toward goals, and providing stability—the more likely it becomes that individuals will cooperate and comply. The less they approve of the performance record, the more likely they are to withhold their compliance or otherwise complicate the efforts of macro authorities.

As a consequence of the pervasive authority crises, states and governments have become less effective in confronting challenges and implementing policies. They can still maintain public order through their police powers, but their ability to address substantive issues and solve substantive problems is declining as people find fault with their performances and thus question their authority, redefine the bases of their legitimacy, and withhold cooperation. Such a transformation has been playing out dramatically since 1989 in the former Soviet Union and within all the countries of Eastern Europe. But authority crises in the former Communist bloc are only the more obvious instances of this newly emergent pattern. It is equally evident in every other part of the world, albeit the crises take different forms in different countries and different types of private organizations. In Canada the authority crisis is rooted in linguistic, cultural, and constitutional issues as Quebec seeks to secede or otherwise redefine its relationship to the central government. In France the devolution of authority was legally sanctioned through legislation that privatized several governmental activities and relocated authority away from Paris and toward the provinces. In China the provinces enjoy a wider jurisdiction by, in effect, ignoring or defying Beijing. In Yugoslavia the crisis led to violence and civil war as some of the component republics sought autonomy and independence.

In the crisis-ridden countries of Latin America the challenge to traditional authority originates with insurgent movements or the drug trade. And in those parts of the world—such as the United States, Israel, Argentina, the Philippines, and South Korea—where the shift to performance criteria of legitimacy has not resulted in the relocation of authority, uneasy stalemates prevail in the policy-making process as governments have proven incapable of bridging societal divisions sufficiently to undertake the decisive actions necessary to address and resolve intractable problems.

Nor is the global authority crisis confined to states and governments. It is also manifest in subnational jurisdictions, international organizations, and nongovernmental transnational entities. Indeed, in some cases the crises unfold simultaneously at different levels: just as the issue of Quebec's place in Canada became paramount, for example, so did the Mohawks in Quebec press for their own autonomy. Similarly, just as Moldova recently rejected Moscow's authority, so too did several ethnic groups within Moldova seek to establish their own autonomy by rejecting Moldova's authority. Likewise, to cite but a few conspicuous examples of crises in international and transnational organizations, the United Nations Educational, Scientific, and Cultural Organization, the Palestine Liberation Organization, the Catholic Church, and the Mafia have all experienced decentralizing dynamics that are at least partly rooted in the replacement of traditional criteria of legitimacy with performance criteria.

The relocation of authority precipitated by the structural crises of states and governments at the national level occurs in several directions, depending in good part on the scope of the enterprises people perceive as more receptive to their concerns and thus more capable of meeting their increased preoccupation with the adequacy of performances. In many instances this has involved "downward" relocation of authority toward subnational groups— ethnic minorities, local governments, single-issue organizations, religious and linguistic groupings, political factions, trade unions, and the like. In some instances the relocating process has moved in the opposite direction, toward more encompassing collectivities that transcend national boundaries. The beneficiaries of this "upward" relocation of authority range from supranational organizations such as the European Union to intergovernmental organizations such as the International Committee of the Red Cross; from nongovernmental organizations such as Greenpeace to professional groups such as Médecins sans Frontières; and from multinational corporations such as IBM to inchoate social movements that join together environmentalists or women in different countries. Needless to say, these multiple directions in which authority is being relocated serve to reinforce the tensions between the centralizing and decentralizing dynamics that underlie the turbulence presently at work in world politics.

It follows that any idea founded on the existence of an ultimate arbiter whose decisions evoke unquestioned compliance is presently being undermined, and one such idea is sovereignty. The disciplined, unhesitating obedience that sustains organizations expressive of this idea is bound to dissipate once authority becomes associated with performance and other nontraditional criteria. Such a process is already evident in perhaps the most disciplined organization extant today, the Mafia,[17] and it can also be discerned in military establishments, many of which are encountering serious difficulties in recruiting, disciplining, and retaining their personnel.[18] Thus it is hardly surprising that the crises besetting the macro-micro parameter are, as will be seen, eroding the principle that under all circumstances states have the right to refuse to comply with the directives of external authorities or the demands for autonomy from internal authorities. Though states more often than not enjoy continued success in exercising their sovereign privileges, the idea that such a practice is questionable has been planted wherever the transformation of the macro-micro parameter has reached crisis proportions. Accordingly, even though challenges to state authority and efforts to redirect legitimacy sentiments toward supranational or subnational collectivities still fail in many situations, the apparent increased frequency of such challenges points to the interpretation (elaborated below) that both domestic and international determinants are inducing movement along the sovereignty continuum.

The Macro Parameter: A Bifurcation of Global Structures

For more than three centuries the overall structure of world politics has been founded on an anarchic system in which sovereign nation-states did not have to answer to any higher authority and thus managed their conflicts through accommodation or war. States were not the only actors on the world stage, but traditionally they were the dominant collectivities that set the rules by which the others had to live. The resulting state-centric world evolved its own hierarchy based on the way in which military, economic, and political power was distributed. Depending on how many states had the greatest concentration of power, at different historical moments the overall system was varyingly marked by hegemonic, bipolar, or multipolar structures.

Today, however, the state-centric world is no longer predominant. Owing to the skill revolution, the worldwide spread of authority crises, the global-

ization of national economies, and a variety of exogenous sources of turbulence elaborated elsewhere,[19] it has undergone bifurcation. A complex,
multi-centric world of diverse, relatively autonomous actors has emerged,
replete with structures, processes, and decision rules of its own. The sovereignty-free actors of the multi-centric world consist of multinational
corporations, ethnic minorities, subnational governments and bureaucracies, professional societies, political parties, transnational organizations,
broadly based social movements, and the like. Individually, and sometimes
jointly, they compete, conflict, cooperate, or otherwise interact with the
sovereignty-bound actors of the state-centric world.[20]

It follows that although the bifurcation of world politics has not pushed
states to the edge of the global stage, states are no longer the only key
actors. Now they are faced with the new task of coping with disparate
rivals from another world as well as with the challenges posed by counter-
parts in their own world. A major outcome of this transformation of macro
structures is, obviously, a further confounding of the hierarchical arrangements through which the new global order is sustained. Not only have
authority crises within states rendered the international pecking order
more fluid, but the advent of bifurcation and the autonomy of actors in the
multi-centric world have so swollen the population of entities that occupy
significant roles on the world stage that their hierarchical differences were
scrambled virtually beyond recognition well before the end of the cold war
intensified the struggle for international status.

The wide diffusion of power and authority in a bifurcated world has,
needless to say, further contributed to movement along the sovereignty
continuum. With transnational organizations and players in the global economy able to ignore traditional political jurisdictions and move freely beyond their scope, the idea that states have the right to make final decisions
has become increasingly problematic. The greater the extent to which
bifurcated structures become embedded in and underlie the practices of
organizations and the activities of producers and consumers, the less are
state authorities inclined to exercise, or even be aware of, their right to
withhold or apply ultimate sanctions. To be sure, states continue to maintain large bureaucracies designed to monitor transgressions of their traditional political jurisdictions, and transnational actors continue to adhere to
the rules and procedures required by national bureaucracies; but the existence of the monitoring activities and the obeisance paid them by organizations in the multi-centric world is not necessarily a measure of sovereignty's continued effectiveness. History is replete with bureaucracies that
survive even though their original purposes have been rendered obsolete by

transformations of their environments and functions. Put differently, this lag time stems from "rapid and continuing changes . . . which have eroded national boundaries and the powers of government but left the structure— and the rhetoric—of national politics in place."[21]

Sovereignty in a Turbulent World

Given a world with new parametric values represented by the skill revo- lution, the relocation of authority, and the bifurcation of global structures, what kinds of movement can be expected on the sovereignty continuum? How are these transformations likely to affect the ways in which sover- eignty's situational, domestic, international, and legal determinants im- pact on the relative rights of states and their international communities? Hints as to the answers to these questions have been noted in the process of outlining the turbulence model, but a more systematic response to them is now in order.

Situational Determinants

For a number of reasons, the advent of a turbulent, bifurcated world politics has tended to deepen the severity of the circumstances around which the question of possible external humanitarian intervention in the internal affairs of states arises. Of course, such situations have always been distressing and eye-catching, else collective intrusion would not have be- come an issue, much less a reality; but today those crisis conditions within societies which catch the world's eye and encourage international interven- tion are likely to seem far more severe and ominous than was the case in preturbulent times. This greater perceived severity can in part be traced to the breadth and depth of the global communications system that has evolved with the revolution in microelectronic technology. Now more people see and hear more about the desperate circumstances of their fellow humans than ever before, and the messages they receive are qualitatively as well as quantitatively different, as the details of close-up television pictures re- lentlessly tell stories on a scale of horrendousness not matched in earlier eras. Indeed, both the content and the horror of televised coverage can be so relentless and severe as to give rise to compassion fatigue, to the "crisis of crisis awareness,"[22] which in turn can add to the urgency of calls for ame- lioration through international intervention.

The severity of humanitarian crises has also been intensified by the continuing proliferation of global interdependencies. As the course of events in any part of the world becomes increasingly dependent on developments anywhere else, so can increasingly explosive humanitarian situations cascade their repercussions well beyond the locale in which they originated.[23] Put more succinctly, people flee starvation, violent repression, and civil war, and in the very act of fleeing they extend the scale and severity of the circumstances that may call for international intervention. The advent of mass migrations cascading across the fault lines of interdependence is illustrative in this regard. The dislocations unleashed by the spread of turbulent conditions have led huge numbers of people to seek economic and political surcease from calamity and, as a consequence, humanitarian situations seem bound to become ever more compelling and severe.

Since the gap between wealthy and poverty-stricken societies shows no signs of lessening in the decades ahead, it seems likely to add to the severity of the situations that draw attention to the possibility of international intervention. Not only is it a disparity that can be readily depicted in a variety of vivid ways, but its persistence is likely to penetrate ever more deeply into the humanitarian conscience of those on the wealthy side of the divide. And if in fact the disparity widens, as is likely in a number of cases, the plight of poor countries will loom as increasingly severe and will agitate the conscience of the rich all the more, thereby further reducing the protection that the sovereignty of the impoverished states provides against outside intervention.

There is, of course, a difference between those situational determinants that arise out of human conflict or neglect and those that have their roots in famines, earthquakes, and nature's many other ways of creating disaster. As indicated by the role played by the International Red Cross, the latter situations compel humanitarian intervention irrespective of their severity. It is only when situations are driven by human aggression, as is the case when genocide or mass migrations are at issue, that varying degrees of severity are likely to evoke correspondingly different shifts in the balance between the rights of states and those of their international communities. The United Nations–sponsored, United States–led intervention in Somalia is an archetypical instance of this likelihood.

It follows that situational determinants do not necessarily conduce to movement away from the convenience-of-the-states end of the sovereignty continuum. To the extent that governments can demonstrate their competence to maintain minimal living conditions and resist undertaking aggression against their own peoples, they will be less likely to attract television coverage and the propriety of their sovereign rights will seem more compelling. While this null hypothesis cannot be dismissed, it seems highly unlikely that the foreseeable future will be marked by movement in this direction. The null hypothesis allows for circumstances in which the rights of states may prevail over those of their international communities, but the prevalence of turbulence on a global scale suggests that situational determinants are often likely to heighten the legitimacy of humanitarian interventions.

The significance ascribed to situational determinants, in other words, does not derive simply from the analyst's bias in favor of a diminution of sovereignty's scope. Rather, their importance appears inherent in the present circumstances of world politics. The severity of humanitarian crises can lessen as well as increase, but it seems reasonable to anticipate that any movement along the sovereignty continuum in the current milieu is likely to be away from the convenience-of-the-states extreme and toward the states-are-obliged-to-go-along extreme.

Domestic Determinants

Let us be clear about the nature of domestic determinants. At any moment in time the balance between the rights of states and those of their international communities is partially shaped by the aggregate views of publics and policy makers around the world. As will be seen, there are numerous ways in which such a global sum of domestic orientations—world opinion, so to speak—is crucial to movement along the sovereignty continuum, but for analytic purposes the worldwide status of sovereign prerogatives is treated here as a dimension of international and legal determinants. At the same time, allowance needs to be made for the possibility that judgments of the propriety of humanitarian interventions vary depending on whether the action in question is directed toward other societies or one's own. It is one thing to support intrusions upon the sovereignty of other states, but it may be quite another to be receptive when such actions occur at home. The idea that one's own internal affairs justify outside intervention is likely to evoke far more powerful reactions than will any general principles about sovereignty to which one adheres. And it is this idea, along with the actions expressive of it, from which the concept of domestic determinants of movement along the sovereignty continuum derives. The willingness of people to accept intervention at home involves the nature and history of a society's patriotism, the ability of its officials to mobilize public resistance to intervention, the coherence of opposition groups, and the many other internal determinants of how societies respond to external pressures.

This is not to imply, however, that people necessarily oppose interventions within their own societies even as they may support them elsewhere. Not only are those who are oppressed or victimized by the circumstances that pose the issue of external intervention likely to welcome such actions, but the rally-around-the-flag phenomenon has been undermined by the parametric transformations that have brought on global turbulence. More precisely, the phenomenon has been both weakened and strengthened as the dynamics of turbulence stir up contradictory tendencies within societies with regard to their sovereign prerogatives vis-à-vis the rest of the world. On the one hand, the skill revolution has given citizens a greater appreciation of the way in which pervasive global interdependence and complexity make it increasingly difficult for states to cling unqualifiedly to the principle that their rights necessarily and invariably have priority over those of their international communities. On the other hand, the lessened effectiveness of states, the challenges to their authority, and the advent of more intensive subgroupism have fostered among publics a heightened sense of territoriality, a search for shared identity, and an inclination to press for exclusive jurisdiction over their internal affairs.

In some instances—as in the case of the republics that have emerged from the breakup of the Soviet Union and Yugoslavia—this pressure for exclusive jurisdiction takes the form of nationalism and the assertion of statehood's privileges. As the former president of Ukraine, Leonid M. Kravchuk, observed in comparing the interests of his country with those of the Commonwealth of Independent States, "Sovereignty is not something up for bargain or for sale. . . . Decisions interfering in internal policies are not accepted by us."24 But in the many instances in which the crises of authority are not sustained by issues of statehood and the integrity of national boundaries, the pressures to relocate authority take the form either of subgroupism (aspirations to greater autonomy and diminished control by national governments) or of an acceptance of external inroads into the affairs of the national community. In other words, in countries that have not been recently swept along by the rush to independence, the greater capacity to construct elaborate scenarios linking personal welfare to international processes seems to have led citizens to less rigid conceptions of national loyalty and to greater acceptance of movement away from the states' rights end of the sovereignty continuum. The experience of Matt Darcy, a thirty-one-year-old car salesman in Michigan, is illustrative in this regard: he got himself into trouble (and out of a job) by commenting in a nationally televised interview, "If America makes a good product, I buy it.

If they don't, I buy what's good for my money. I don't have to spend money [on a domestic car] because it's American."[25]

While one or the other of these contradictory tendencies may be predominant in a particular country, it would be a mistake to view them as unchallenged in their own locale. A more accurate picture is one in which both are at work everywhere, endlessly clashing and feeding on each other. The parametric transformations unfolding in world politics have roiled individual and group identities to the point where champions of values along the full breadth of the sovereignty continuum are bound both to encounter opposition and to find support in every corner of their societies. It might even be said that people long for a renewed sense of belonging even as they grasp that the authority of their states is questionable, that the symbols of sovereignty may not serve their psychic needs, and that their interests may be advanced by processes unfolding abroad. A poignant insight into this longing and the ambivalence it fosters was evident at the 1992 Winter Olympics in Albertville, France, where the athletes of the former Soviet Union competed as the Unified Team of the Commonwealth of Independent States: as Viktor Tikhonov, the coach of the Unified Team's victorious hockey team, observed, "I told the players, 'In Albertville, we are called a team without a flag, without an anthem and without a motherland. This is not so. Each of us has a home, a family and a motherland. Millions of our compatriots are watching us, and we cannot ruin their expectations.'"[26]

In short, to the extent that citizens are more analytically skillful and thus more resistant to being mobilized by vague symbols of sovereign authority, or to the extent that citizens' expanded skills induce confusion over the appropriateness of traditional state prerogatives, political leaders cannot rely on wholesale and unquestioned support for their opposition to humanitarian interventions that intrude upon their country's sovereign rights. Thus, it is no accident that everywhere appeals to sovereignty appear to be mouthed less and less often by public officials. Whereas once such appeals were central to the lexicon of politics, today they are conspicuous by their relative absence from the dialogues of world affairs. And where they are voiced, they do not necessarily silence those whose analytic skills have led them to assess whether benefits necessarily inhere in territorial and sovereign values. Yes, publics in Japan and the United States have begun to bash each other's cultures and trading practices with an intensity that implies a sense of violated sovereignty, but for every bashing there are leaders on both sides who publicly question the merits of such conduct.

While movement along the sovereignty continuum is halting, punctuated, and anything but a smooth trendline, it does appear to favor humanitarian interventions insofar as domestic determinants are concerned. Indeed, it seems likely that internal societal dynamics will continue to agitate such movement well into the future. The discrepancy between the simple symbols of national sovereignty and the realities of governmental and economic crises is so great that both publics and their leaders are likely to be increasingly disillusioned by the symbols as the realities worsen. The symbols do provide psychic satisfactions—"The fact of sitting around the table with the most important states in the world is a reaffirmation of sovereignty," said the foreign minister of San Marino on the occasion of the UN Security Council's approval of his twenty-four-square-mile country's admission to membership[27]—and they are also vague enough to allow diverse segments of a population to converge and cooperate:

> Before the beginning of 1991 nearly all [the former Soviet republics] were demanding "sovereignty." This was a capaciously ambiguous concept—it might mean anything from full independence to the right to run your own refuse collection; but it had the advantage of providing an issue on which intellectuals and the local apparatchiks could cooperate. For the former the word stood for their dreams of national self-determination and democracy; for the latter, it meant they would at last have real power.[28]

In Quebec, too, support for independence has been sought by infusing the sovereignty concept with a measure of ambiguity that allows for a diversity of meanings to be attached to it. One news account, for example, reported that the leader of the Parti Québecois, Jacques Parizeau, "muddied the waters . . . by telling Quebecers a 'sovereign Quebec' would continue to use the Canadian dollar and its citizens would keep their Canadian passports, regardless of whether Ottawa approved."[29]

To repeat, however, the psychic and consensus-building virtues that attach to the symbols of sovereignty are unlikely to sustain their appeal in the face of either projected or actual problems. In Quebec, for example, a projection that the economy would slump by as much as 15 percent if voters chose independence appeared to induce slippage in support for the proposal.[30] In Ukraine, second thoughts about sovereignty began to emerge as "many of those who voted for statehood . . . did so only because they thought they would be better off in an independent Ukraine and not out of strong nationalist feelings."[31] Similarly, Estonians have discovered that independence and the privileges of statehood offer no magic solutions to the problems of hunger, inflation, and ethnic conflict.[32] Such realities, on the contrary, can emerge as products of sovereignty, in which case the inclination to cling to the inviolability of territory and statehood may well erode, thereby inducing further movement away from the state's rights extreme of the continuum. The greater the harshness of the economic and political conditions that prevail, in short, the more likely it becomes that claims to exclusive jurisdiction will fall on deaf ears or become, in the words of Ivan Kapitanets, the deputy commander of the Black Sea fleet, expressions of the "childhood illness of sovereignty and state independence."[33]

Such a conclusion again implies the need to pose another null hypothesis and ask whether domestic determinants necessarily conduce to movement away from the convenience-of-the-states end of the sovereignty continuum. Clearly, a negative response is warranted. Present-day turbulence highlights the relocation of authority away from states and the acquisition of legitimacy by subgroups, but the conditions that produce these decentralizing tendencies may change and foster a reversal favoring the virtues of national sovereignty. At some distant point in time, for instance, more analytically skillful citizens may discern that their subgroups are no better at improving their circumstances than were their states, thus encouraging a swing in public moods that accords legitimacy to systemic rather than subsystemic authorities.[34] Conceivably, too, a global economic upturn may occur which enables states to regain some of their former clout and authority. None of these developments seems likely in the current period of parametric transformations, but they are theoretically possible if it is recalled that sovereignty is subject to variability in opposite directions across a broad continuum.

International Determinants

While situational and domestic determinants of the values that attach to sovereignty consist of deep-seated, slow-moving, and fluctuating societal processes that slowly cumulate to an increasing acceptance of external interventions, international determinants of those values tend to acquire momentum through specific acts in which interventionary efforts are initiated. As such, as the bases of successful or failed attempts to intervene in the domestic affairs of states, international determinants are readily discernible in trend-setting events that sustain an aggregative process. More precisely, each interventionary act, whatever its outcome, is so conspicuous, still so much a break with historic conventions, that it serves as an explicit stimulus to subsequent events of a comparable nature. Every time a national election is supervised by impartial observers brought in from abroad, for example, the norm that affirms such an intervention in domestic affairs is reinforced, making it harder subsequently for authoritarian regimes elsewhere to prevent such intrusions and easier for their opponents who fear repression to appeal successfully for outside supervision. Likewise, each occasion in which the United Nations is able to intrude peacekeeping forces into domestic conflicts serves to legitimate international concern and action with respect to such conflicts that arise elsewhere. In the same manner, as the International Monetary Fund (IMF) or the World Bank achieves, case by case, compliance with its demands that domestic adjustments be made in exchange for needed financial resources, it facilitates adherence to comparable policies in subsequent situations and thereby supplements the appropriateness of external involvement in domestic economies.

And this appears to be exactly what has occurred in this turbulent, post–cold war era. Calls for supervised elections, for international peacekeeping forces, and for IMF involvement seem to have acquired increasing degrees of legitimacy. Put differently, it is no accident that supervised elections, UN peacekeeping efforts, and IMF-induced adjustments tend to occur in rapid-fire succession. Each such event is part of an aggregative international process that undermines traditional interstate norms and sets precedents for future interventions. This momentum has been cogently documented with respect to the vulnerability of domestic economies to international management,[35] but it can also be at least impressionistically discerned as operative in the electoral and peacekeeping arenas. And it also appears to have spread from global to regional international organizations. While neither the recent intrusion of the Organization of American States into the domestic politics of Haiti nor the European Union's involvement in the internal affairs of Yugoslavia was immediately successful, their simultaneity highlights how quickly the momentum favoring external intervention can gather steam.[36]

Furthermore, with the bifurcation of the macro parameter and the advent of a multi-centric world capable of supporting challenges to the authority of states, the aggregative international processes that undermine traditional conceptions of national jurisdictions have come to be championed by active and innovative actors who need not pay heed to the responsibilities and constraints of sovereignty.[37] The human rights movement, the ecological movement, the women's movement, and the peace movement, whatever else they may be and whatever else they may accomplish, serve crucial roles as mobilizers and stimulators of change in this regard.[38] They make it possible for Amnesty International to claim that "[h]uman rights are now part of the working agenda of every government on earth—not by their *own* choice but because of the persistent pressure of the world's citizenry."[39] Indeed, in the United States leaders of Amnesty International and other human rights groups are now regularly consulted by public officials: "We see assistant secretaries and desk officers all the time. Even if we don't get what we want, we're in the mix now. The relationships are warm. They seek, we give. They call, we help."[40]

Supplemented by situational and domestic determinants, in short, the international milieu also appears to be contributing to movement toward the states-are-obliged-to-go-along extreme of the sovereignty continuum. It would seem to be only a matter of time before humanitarian interventions become caught up in this momentum, if they have not already. The wide and rapid success of the human rights movement highlights the way in which the international milieu—that amorphous complex of attitudes, sentiments, and predispositions which underlies how governments and publics approach specific situations in which the rights of states and those of their international communities are pitted against each other—can gather momentum and become an agent of change, perhaps even of change in the legal criteria used to justify international intrusions into the realm of national sovereignty.[41] Indeed, it has been cogently argued that in international law "the sovereign had finally been dethroned" when the United Nations in 1948 adopted the Universal Declaration of Human Rights,[42] and this deposition is empirically discernible in the fact that even those states most resistant to such intrusions have had to accept, or at least acknowledge, the legitimacy of outside interventions in their affairs. As a specialist in Latin American affairs put it, "It would be hard to find a country in this hemisphere in which raised consciousness of human rights has not had any effect. Even in the most extreme case of Cuba, Fidel Castro has had to deal with the United Nations Human Rights Commission, and he has had to respond to questions posed not by the United States or the Cuban-American community but by Latin Americans."[43]

Just as heads of states find it increasingly difficult to resist the momentum inherent in the changing international milieu, so is that momentum likely to embolden officials of international communities to allow themselves to move from a traditional convenience-of-the-states perspective to a perspective in which they are embued by the states-are-obliged-to-go-along orientation. Traces of this attitudinal shift can be detected in the conduct of top UN officials. Their shifts are nuanced and incremental rather than bold assertions, but they nonetheless appear to be patterned and, as such, significant. Their readiness to bring governance to Afghanistan by convening a conference of rival factions was prompted not only by circumstances in that troubled country, and the success of their plan was due not only to the war-weariness of the factions; rather, both the initiative and the world organization's success in the situation also stemmed from memories of—that is, the momentum created by—recent interventions successfully carried out by the United Nations which rendered moot the question of Afghanistan's sovereign prerogatives.[44] In a like manner the International Atomic Energy Agency recently approved a plan to conduct nuclear inspections in countries that have accepted the Nuclear Nonproliferation Treaty but that are suspected of developing nuclear weapons in secret. The IAEA has always had the right to intervene in this way, but only now is it planning to exercise the right.[45] Likewise, though the UN secretary-general is an employee of states and the chief spokesperson for the state-centric world, there are signs that the most recent appointee to the post, Boutros Boutros-Ghali, sees the organization as more than the sum of its parts and is thus willing to make decisions that can be construed as intruding upon the sovereignty of UN members.

However, taking note of an international milieu and momentum that are tipping the balance between states and their international communities in favor of the latter is not to imply a wholesale shift that will one day culminate in the obsolescence of the sovereignty principle. After all, the bifurcation of world politics posits a continued viability for the state-centric world. And the psychic needs that accord high value to community ties and territoriality are not about to attenuate. Accordingly, the shifting balance needs to be viewed as a limited one, a trendline favoring movement on the sovereignty continuum that takes the form of a gentle, if ragged, slope that differentiates among issue areas and allows for states to retain their rights on a wide range of issues involving substantive rather than symbolic interests. Put differently, though it seems excessively simplistic to argue that at present "there is no greater authority than the sovereign, egoistic nation-state,"[46] and though "no doubt one should resist the idea that [the nation state] is becoming dissolved," it is also the case that "the character of states, and their interrelations, are being quite dramatically influenced by factors operating both below and above the level of the nation state itself."[47]

Again, however, a null hypothesis needs to be framed: if the United Nations experiences a series of rebuffs, as it has lately in Yugoslavia and Cambodia, conceivably the momentum favoring modifications of the sovereignty principle will be brought to a halt and movement on the sovereignty continuum reversed. This is hard to imagine in a world composed of ever more analytically skillful citizens whose sensitivities and institutions place a high value on human rights, survival, and dignity; but given the uncertainties that attach to turbulent conditions, long pauses in the movement away from sovereign rights are not beyond the realm of possibility.

Legal Determinants

Given the common tendencies fostered by situational, domestic, and international determinants, what can one say in response to the question of whether international communities have the right to intervene in the affairs of member countries? The question is deceptive.[48] It addresses the murky space where law and politics converge, where legal precepts prevail which may no longer limit or guide behavior. Surely there is a large body of international law, bulwarked by the conventions of the interstate system, that points to the conclusion that international communities do not have the right to intervene, that sovereignty is inviolable and not open to qualification. At the same time, there is a welter of practice which suggests otherwise, and points to violations of sovereignty which are accepted without vigorous protest. Even Saddam Hussein, resistant as he is to the United Nations, does not return to the sovereignty theme, and it is probably significant that the one UN member with a long history of reliance on the theme, the People's Republic of China, voted to abstain in the Security Council when the United Nations intruded upon Iraq's sovereignty.

In short, the central thrust of the foregoing analysis is that, irrespective of the prevailing legal order, the odds are against international law's retaining its viability with respect to the prerogatives of statehood. As stated at the very outset, the dictates of the law provide no more than an intermittent pause in political relationships. The present pause has lasted some four hundred years, but that is not to say that it is beyond being undermined. All the indicators point to the contrary. They all suggest that the legal status of sovereignty rights is bound to be subverted by the transformative dynamics currently at work in world politics.

Some might argue with this conclusion on the grounds that there is a wide gap between a raised consciousness and a legal precept, that people may believe that humanitarian interventions are justified even as states effectively ward off interventionary actions by adhering to their legal rights. The record in the human rights area, however, belies this line of reasoning. The sensitivity to human rights concerns is not confined to publics and nongovernmental groups. So many governments have evidenced a readiness to adhere to minimal standards of human rights that the emergent norms in this area come close to having the clout and prestige of law.

Then there is the realist argument that the pattern wherein international communities intervene in the domestic affairs of their members is misleading, that such interventions occur not because states feel obliged to accept them, but because it is in states' interest to allow them to take place. In this view, the widespread acceptance of interventionary behavior derives from convenience rather than law, and thus the sovereignty of states is seen to remain intact because lately states have chosen not to exercise it. If push ever comes to shove, if a state ever was faced with an unwanted intervention, this reasoning concludes, it would surely protest that its sovereignty had been violated. But recent history does not support this conclusion: one could cite innumerable occasions when states might have been expected to register such protests but either did not do so or did so half-heartedly, without any real conviction.

Furthermore, the realist contention suffers from a flawed conception of law in relation to change. To view international law as continuing to favor states because the precedents underlying claims to sovereign privilege have not been specifically abrogated and thus continue to prevail even though states do not claim them is to cling to such a narrow, technical, and formal conception of the law as to render inquiries into the dynamics of social change virtually impossible. The test of change is to be found in behavior and not in legal sanctions. Eventually, enduring change does indeed find expression in legal arrangements, but many intervening steps expressive of change occur before change is codified or ratified at the international level.

Conceivably, of course, the realist contention may ultimately be borne out. Still another null hypothesis tells us that the International Court of Justice and other judicial bodies, not to mention foreign offices and multilateral bodies, may take actions that run counter to the prevailing momentum and reassert the unqualified nature of sovereignty. Again, however, such developments seem highly unlikely. In a "borderless" world of "global webs," "global factories," "off-shore banks," "de-nationalized inter-corporate alliances," and intersocietal "connections" that span national boundaries and evolve institutions such as the European Union, which is "neither a state nor an international organization,"[49] it is difficult to construct a scenario wherein the juridical authority of states is reaffirmed and sovereignty declared as the ultimate principle of world politics.

This is not to say that the failure of the null hypothesis means that we will witness a wholesale reversal of the historic foundations of international law. Even as profound transformations unfold, so do longstanding habits, bureaucratic inertia, and historic continuities persist. The foregoing discussion has dealt only with the question of whether sovereignty is likely to protect states from external intervention when humanitarian concerns are at issue. On a variety of other issues, clearly, the legal status of states is unlikely to be significantly jarred, and alterations are unlikely to be made in the sanctity states enjoy under treaties and the many other formal instruments of international communities.

Sovereignty's Future

Despite any pause induced by a systematic effort to subject the pattern of movement along the sovereignty continuum to the counterintuitive reasoning of null hypotheses, the expectation that ever-greater legitimacy will be attached to international humanitarian interventions in the domestic affairs of states remains intact. There are just too many diverse sources of change at every level of systemic activity to give much credence to the null hypotheses. Furthermore, and perhaps most telling of all, the dynamics of change are such that at some threshold the probabilities of a reversal of course drop to near zero. If it is assumed, as seems reasonable, that the parametric transformations sustaining turbulence in world politics are not transitory phenomena,[50] the continuing refinement of analytic skills, the persistent deepening of authority crises, and the unending processes of structural bifurcation seem destined to cumulate to a threshold point at which the relocation of values on the sovereignty continuum becomes irreversible for the foreseeable future.

The key to this transformation lies in the fragility of authority structures and the ways in which the crises enveloping them undermine the integrity and prerogatives of national institutions. Those who seek to lead and govern in public affairs have long been hampered by poverty, resource shortages, internal conflicts, and a host of other problems that make it difficult to develop coherent policies and sustain progress toward a better life. But now, with citizens ever more sensitive to their own well-being, with publics ever more capable of coming together quickly to press their demands in downtown squares, and with the lenses of global, regional, and local television cameras ever more ready to record leadership performances, the authority of officials is increasingly delicate and susceptible to disarray and relocation. And when the newly developed skills of citizens are trained on the restructuring of systemwide governance—on territoriality, political inclusion and exclusion, decision-making procedures, judicial rights, and all the other explosive issues that surface when sovereignty climbs high on political agendas—the authority that attaches to governmental institutions seems likely to become especially tenuous. For sovereignty highlights the extent to which people can exercise control over their own lives; and now that citizens have a growing capacity to connect the acts of leaders to their own situations, to the degree of freedom they can exercise on their own behalf, they are likely to be acutely sensitive to any movement toward the convenience-of-the-states extreme on the sovereignty continuum which jeopardizes their own well-being. That these sensitivities may lead to authority crises, to stalemated governments and paralyzed bureaucracies, is not seen as nearly so threatening as the pursuit of unwanted modifications of the people's sovereign rights. Thus have authority crises deepened, and thus do efforts to reassert the privileges and benefits of sovereignty seem destined to founder, caught up in the entangling networks of competence and agitation woven by newly empowered masses.

Even under the best of circumstances, in other words, sovereign authority rests on a precarious set of relationships in which those who worry about and lead whole systems have to evoke and sustain the compliance of the followers encompassed by the system. Effective sovereign authority can be traced to documentary evidence of international law, but such documents are only written expressions of relational patterns, of ideational premises and behavioral habits on the part of leaders and followers which are deep-seated and taken for granted as the legal foundations of the interstate system. As such, as deeply embedded premises and habits, the traditional authority structures of sovereign states have been sturdy and capable of withstanding severe challenges. But in a time of profound and global transformation, even the most sturdy authority relations are revealed as delicately balanced and susceptible to erosion. Indeed, as recent history demonstrates yet again, once entrenched authority comes into question, it can deteriorate with enormous speed as all concerned begin to experience the heady atmosphere that accompanies the recognition that challenge is no less an appropriate response to authority than is compliance.

The transformation of the macro-micro parameter, and especially the replacement of the older basis for relating to authorities—traditional compliance habits—with performance criteria of legitimacy, thus seems likely to serve as a continuing limitation on the appeal of the sovereignty principle. This is because the power of the appeal depends on the maintenance of appropriate habits of accepting and heeding the sovereign authorities, a requirement that is often highly problematic under fluid conditions wherein citizens are more impelled to question than to comply with authority. Habits of compliance are distinguished by their unthinking character, and people do not act or refrain from acting unthinkingly unless they have had repeated experiences that support their readiness not to give second thought to their own conduct. In the absence of repeated affirming experiences, the habits supportive of sovereign prerogatives can readily be undermined, even extinguished, by contrary events, by televised scenes of authority being challenged elsewhere in the world, by policy failures at home, and by a host of other intervening developments.

Put differently, since authority structures are founded on habitual modes of cooperation, they are much more difficult to sustain than they are to tear down once they come into question. Global orders may take centuries to evolve deep habitual structures, but we know now (as we always should have known) that such orders can unravel with startling speed.

The basic reason why deterioration unfolds so speedily is that the point of breakdown is marked by people's managing to step outside the ideational paradigm that kept the structures of sovereignty intact: viewed from their new perspective, the underpinnings of the structures no longer seem compelling. People see how the sovereignty of their states and the prohibitions against interventions by international communities may be hindering their welfare, how their compliance allows for official actions to which they are unable to subscribe once they have broken free of the paradigm on which their habits were founded. Whereas only a few such paradigm-freeing events may be necessary to initiate the breakdown of authority structures—those surrounding the failed coup in the former Soviet Union are an obvious case in point—numerous and repeated instances of satisfactory leadership performance and effective authority may be necessary to rebuild the habits of cooperation, toleration, and compliance on which the sovereignty principle has rested for centuries.

If anything, in sum, movement away from the convenience-of-the-states extreme on the sovereignty continuum is likely to accelerate in the years ahead. The threshold beyond which a reversal is possible may have already been passed.

This conclusion raises the question of what kind of movement along the sovereignty continuum may occur in the foreseeable future. Three alternative patterns are plausible. One involves movement that eventually culminates at the states-are-obliged-to-go-along extreme; the second depicts a pattern in which the movement comes to a halt and stabilizes at some point short of this extreme; and the third traces a continual fluctuation that neither culminates nor stabilizes. In short, is the present global turbulence likely to subside? And if it does, at what point on the continuum will a worldwide consensus form around a new set of values that fix the rights of states vis-à-vis their international communities?

Of the three alternative patterns, the first is the least likely. Culmination at the states-are-obliged-to-go-along extreme means that the sovereignty principle will have become obsolete and the authority of international communities to intervene in the domestic affairs of their members will have become established as central to the normative structure of world affairs. Such a postturbulence outcome seems improbable because, as already noted, the psychic needs for territoriality and independence are sufficiently powerful to enable states to retain their prerogatives in a variety of issue areas.

Nor do the prospects for the second alternative appear very great. It is not necessarily the case that parametric transformations come to an end just because they began. They may be more enduring than transitional. The world, its publics and their leaders, may become weary of the pervasive turbulence and search for ways to move beyond it; but there can be no assurances that the efforts will be rewarded. Exhaustion with continual commotion may conduce to a greater readiness to ameliorate conflict; but clearly it is hardly the basis for evolving a new set of parametric values which fixes the nature of sovereignty for an extended period. Time is needed for experimentation, for trial and error, for sorting out alternatives, for actors with different learning curves to arrive at the same plateau on which new relationships in a postturbulence era can flourish. At best, therefore, it will surely require a long stretch of time, extending across decades, before the outlines of a new global order that establishes the relative rights of states and their international communities come fully into focus.

By a process of elimination, therefore, the third pattern, in which world politics is marked by continued turbulence, appears the most likely. Why? Because all three parametric transformations are in the direction of enduring commotion rather than stable patterns. They do not point to the emergence of new political entities that can supplant the state as effective means of achieving societal cohesion and progress. They do not hint at the development of global structures that can accommodate both the decentralizing dynamics operative within the state-centric world and the centralizing dynamics at work in the multi-centric world. They do not suggest that more analytically skillful citizens and publics are likely to be impressed with the intractability of most of the issues on the global agenda and thus be accepting of leaders whose performances are bound to fall short of their expectations. Rather, the central tendency in the case of each parameter involves movement toward end points that are inherently and profoundly pervaded with uncertainty and dynamism, with impulses to sustain change rather than settle for new equilibria, with a potential for restless dissatisfaction with power balances, and continuing resistance to whatever pecking order may seem to prevail.

In short, the most powerful forces underlying the emergence of a new global order are all conducive to persistent, long-term tensions between the need for more centralized international institutions and the equally compelling need to develop more decentralized domestic institutions. That being the case, at no time in the foreseeable future is movement on the sovereignty continuum likely to settle around a new set of values that become fixed and effective.

Chapter Ten

Sovereignty and Intervention

STEPHEN D. KRASNER

In the past, even the recent past, the principle of nonintervention was deemed to be sacrosanct. Third world states emphasized the inviolability of sovereignty and the primacy of the norm that states should be immune from interference in their internal affairs. When the great powers did intervene, as in the Soviet invasion of Czechoslovakia in 1968 or the American involvement in the Vietnamese civil war, they took care to provide a covering rationale by arguing that they had been invited by some legitimate national authority. With the collapse of the Soviet Union, however, diplomats have more frequently equivocated. In lieu of unqualified condemnation of intervention, more attention has been given to the conditions under which intervention should be considered legitimate.

How should this shift in rhetoric and policy be understood? There are two prevailing theoretical perspectives in the study of international relations, neither of which offers a fully satisfactory explanation for the phenomenon of intervention. The first is liberal interdependence. The second is realism. Advocates of a liberal interdependence perspective suggest that the fundamental nature of the international system is changing: actors, attitudes, and interests have been transformed by technological change. Advocates of realism contend that while the distribution of power has altered, the basic nature of the system has remained the same: the most important determinant of behavior and outcomes is the distribution of power among states.

Advocates of liberalism have presented a forceful discussion of how and why the international system may be in the midst of fundamental transformation, but liberalism does not offer a satisfactory empirical explanation for the pattern of intervention, because intervention is an old occurrence, not a new one. Efforts to change the domestic political regimes of other states have been an endemic characteristic of the state system. Liberalism, which emphasizes the transformation of the international system as a result of changes in technology, actors, and values, cannot explain the absence of change in the frequency of intervention. Over time, there has been no consistent relationship between technological change and intervention.

Liberal analyses might, however, provide insight into the motivation for intervention in the contemporary world. At least some variants of liberalism emphasize the transformation of values at the global level, a transformation that has been facilitated by the ease with which ideas and knowledge are transferred across international boundaries. More specifically, a liberal perspective would suggest that the growing consensus on human rights and democracy provides the motivation for recent interventions.

Realism, however, also fails to provide an adequate explanation for intervention, because intervention in the internal affairs of another state violates one of the basic analytic assumptions of realism: namely, the assumption that all states are capable of autonomously determining their own policies. A state whose political regime—the nature of its government, the relationship between rulers and ruled, and the individuals who hold public office—is influenced or determined by external actors is not autonomous.

Realism's emphasis on the central importance of the distribution of power among states does, however, provide a powerful explanation for the pattern, if not the specific motivations, for intervention. Interventions have occurred when there is an asymmetry of power. More powerful states intervene in the internal affairs of less powerful states. In an anarchical world there is nothing to prevent a state from exploring all possible foreign policy options, including the option of intervening in the internal affairs of other states.

If, as realism asserts, the international system is anarchical—which implies that states have the right of self help, that they are not subject to any external authority—then the integrity of weaker states may be compromised by the actions of stronger ones. When self-help clashes with nonintervention, self-help prevails. The changing distribution of power in the international system is the best explanation for the pattern of intervention, but realists must acknowledge that the very existence of successful intervention violates the ontological assumption that all states are autonomous actors.

Liberal Interdependence

What unites the wide variety of arguments that can be classified as expressing a liberal interdependence perspective is the claim that technological developments, especially the dramatic increase in communications flows, and the reduction in the costs of transportation, have made the world more interdependent, enhanced the power and legitimacy of actors other than national states, altered the way in which individuals understand and pursue their interests, and even transformed underlying preferences. Examples of such arguments abound.[1]

Advocates of a liberal interdependence perspective have pointed out that the well-being of individual states is more bound up with global transactions than it has been at any point in the past. Trade ratios have increased. The ability to conduct national monetary policy has been constrained by international capital flows.[2] Multinational firms can source, produce, and sell their products in many different countries. Environmental quality can be affected by the flow of pollutants across international borders (as in the case of acid rain), or by general environmental degradation caused by the depletion of the ozone layer, or by global warming.

Even the nature of international security has been dramatically altered. Nuclear weapons and ballistic missiles have made it impossible for even the most powerful states to defend against attacks, though they may still deter attacks. The diffusion of technology has enabled even relatively weak and backward states to procure, or at least attempt to procure, weapons of mass destruction. Civil conflicts, economic privation, or political repression can touch off population movements that change domestic attitudes and threaten political stability in other countries.

Some analysts working from a liberal interdependence perspective have suggested that interests and even underlying preferences have been transformed. The value of individual human rights is becoming universally accepted. Political systems based on ethnic cleavages are reviled. Democracy is viewed as the only legitimate form of government.[3] The Cable News Network (CNN) is not just a purveyor of information but a setter of political agendas. The fate of the Kurds in Iraq cannot be ignored by governments in Europe and the United States because television vividly displays the repression of the Kurdish minority to mass audiences in the West who are committed to democracy and the dignity of the individual.

The implication of an interdependence perspective is that intervention will become both more common and more legitimate in the new world order. The distinction between domestic and international politics has been eroded. The United States and France can criticize Germany for not reducing its fiscal deficit. The European Bank for Reconstruction and Development can make its lending contingent not just on macroeconomic management but also on progress toward marketization and democracy. Industrialized countries can prod poor states with large tropical rainforests to modify their land use policies. The broad consensus on political norms and values can legitimize pressure to alter the basic nature of the polity of other states. In sum, an analysis based on a liberal interdependence perspective concludes that the nature of the international system has been transformed in ways that make interventions more frequent and more legitimate.

Realism

Realism regards the international system as anarchical. States are the constituent elements of the system. Each state has the capacity to independently formulate its own foreign and domestic policies. The degree of stability in the system, both the disposition for peaceful dispute resolution and the robustness of international regimes, is a function of the distribution of power among states. Change occurs because of alterations in the distribution of power.

Intervention poses a serious logical problem for realism as a theory of international politics. Realism is completely consistent with a situation in which the behavior of any given state is constrained by the capabilities and policies of other states that it confronts in the external environment. In fact, this constraint is the very essence of a sovereign state system. It is what distinguishes such a system from an imperial order, in which there is only one authoritative center, which must be concerned not with international war (because there are no other autonomous actors) but rather with the danger of internal revolt.

Realism cannot, however, so easily accommodate a situation in which the behavior of one state is constrained not by the external environment but by developments within its own borders which have been directly affected by the intervention of other states. Intervention violates the analytic framework of realism because intervention inevitably compromises the independent decision-making ability of the target state. The component parts of the Soviet Empire had little independent decision-making capability; for instance, for a period after World War II, the minister of defense in Poland was a Soviet general. No Soviet satellite could decide that its security would best be guaranteed by joining the North Atlantic Treaty Organization. Any political actor in the Western Hemisphere contemplating adopting a communist form of government during the cold war was confronted with the fact that it was likely to face either covert or overt intervention by the United States even if it made no effort to change its international behavior. Hence, intervention in the internal affairs of a state implies that the autonomy of the decision-making unit of that state can be compromised by internal pressures, not just external constraints—a violation of realism's assumption that all states can be treated as autonomous actors.

Self-help and nonintervention are logically contradictory. Anarchy necessarily implies self-help. There is no universal political authority. Each state decides its own policy, and there is no constraint on the options that can be considered, including intervention in the internal affairs of another state. Nonintervention, or the principle that no state should be subject to interference in its internal affairs, follows directly from the assumption that each state is a sovereign actor capable of deciding on its own policies. Self-help implies that each state can do anything it chooses; noninterference implies that there are some things that a state should not do.[4]

In sum, there is a profound inconsistency at the core of realism. On the one hand, realism is based on an ontological assumption that sovereign states are the constituent parts of the international system and that these states function in a self-help system in which there are no external constraints on the policies that they might pursue. On the other hand, the assumption that states are autonomous implies that intervention in the internal affairs of other states does not occur, for if it did such states would not be autonomous actors. If external powers could bribe officials of a weaker country, remove and install government officials, or even dictate the basic constitutive rules of the polity, then the targets of these activities would not be capable of engaging in self-help. Their policies would be constrained not by external threats and opportunities, the constraint that always exists for a realist analysis, but rather by the absence of an independent decision-making authority within the state.

Realist analysis has been able to slide past this contradiction between self-help and the assumption of autonomy because it has usually focused on major powers and issues of security. It is impossible to avoid confronting this inconsistency when dealing with questions of intervention.

The following cases suggest that when there is a contradiction between self-help and noninterference, self-help prevails. Intervention in the internal affairs of other states has been a pervasive characteristic of the sovereign state system from its very beginnings. The extent to which such intervention has compromised the autonomy of particular states depends on the distribution of power in the international system. When the distribution of capabilities is highly asymmetrical, the powerful can not only constrain the external options of the weak but may also be able to shape their internal character as well. Intervention is most likely to occur when power disparities among states are high. In a multipolar system, intervention is less likely unless all of the major powers are in agreement. The specific motivations of powerful states, however, are not necessarily related to systemic factors; that is, they are not necessarily a reflection of efforts to create or maintain equilibrium within the international system. Rather, the strong may be moved by a variety of considerations, some of which (e.g., ethical commitments to specific political agendas) may have nothing whatsoever to do with the balance of power. Asymmetrical capabilities are a necessary condition for intervention, but not a sufficient one.

Illustrative Cases: Rulers and Ruled

The relationship between rulers and ruled is a central question for any polity. How do political authorities treat individuals or groups? What kind of control do the ruled have over their rulers? Contemporary discussions have focused on liberal concerns associated with individuals, such as free speech or the right to a fair trial. In earlier periods the collective prerogatives of religious and ethnic groups, such as the right to engage in particular spiritual practices or to be educated in a certain language, drew more attention. Issues related to the relationship between rulers and ruled have an international dimension when the way in which one state treats persons (either individuals or groups) within its territorial boundaries is challenged by other states.

External interference in the relationship between ruler and ruled has been an enduring and pervasive characteristic of the sovereign state system since its very inception. There have been two dominant motivations for such intervention. The first is that states have intervened in the internal affairs of their neighbors because they feared that domestic developments elsewhere could undermine their own security, either by increasing the chance of interstate conflict or by undermining the legitimacy of their own regimes. The second is that values related only loosely to material or security interests have prompted states to pressure others to change the way in which they treat their own subjects or citizens.

Religious Practices and the Peace of Westphalia

The practice of religion was a central question involving rulers and ruled throughout the early modern period in Europe. Once the Reformation had demolished any illusions of Christian unity, the treatment of different religious sects became a cardinal concern of secular rulers because religion impinged on both the internal legitimacy of particular states and the external stability of the European state system. Failure to resolve religious questions contributed to devastating domestic and international wars in the sixteenth and seventeenth centuries.

The first European effort to settle the issue of religious dissent, a resolution that seemed to confirm the absolute rights of sovereignty and nonintervention, was the Peace of Augsburg of 1555. The Peace recognized the division of Germany between Catholic and Lutheran areas and placed decisions about religion in the hands of each prince, although, hinting at future efforts at religious toleration, it also guaranteed freedom of worship for both Lutherans and Catholics living in eight imperial cities that had mixed populations.[5]

The Augsburg solution, which gave the ruler the right to choose the religion of his territory, was not stable. Individual Christians were often more concerned about the salvation of their souls than about the penalties imposed by the state, and religious disputes continued to fuel intense military and political conflict in Europe.

In France, the Huguenot revolt of the 1570s caused widespread death and destruction and threatened the monarchy. In England, religious disagreement undermined the mutual expectations that had undergirded the British political system and led to the brutal British civil wars of the seventeenth century, the end of the Stuart line, and the removal of two monarchs.

The greatest strife and disorder occurred in Germany, the center of the Reformation. Germany had the most fragmented political order in Europe. The Holy Roman Empire of the German People was the supposed successor to the Roman Empire. The emperor, who after 1450 was almost always the Habsburg ruler of Austria, was elected by a small group of religious prelates and major secular rulers (the Electors). The Imperial Diet had three separate councils comprising, respectively, the Electors, the principalities, and the cities. There were also two imperial courts, some fifty imperial cities, about one hundred principalities, several thousand imperial knights living on small estates in the south and the west, and a number of ecclesiastical states.[6] The relative power of the emperor and the princes, and the authority of the Diet and the courts, was ambiguous and changed over time.

The Thirty Years' War was precipitated by Habsburg attempts to turn back the Reformation in Bohemia. Germany was devastated by the war. The armies were undisciplined. Many cities and towns along the Rhine were pillaged many times. Starvation and disease were widespread. The rural population might have decreased by 40 percent, the urban population by 33 percent.[7] France and Sweden emerged as the military victors, but the devastation of the war convinced many of the combatants that some formula needed to be found which could limit religious strife.

In the Peace of Westphalia, which brought the Thirty Years' War to an end, nonintervention was ignored in the provisions that dealt with religious questions. The Peace, which consisted of the Treaty of Osnabrück and the Treaty of Münster, sought to restore order by establishing rules that defined the control that rulers could legitimately exercise over religious matters. Though the principle of Augsburg was rhetorically endorsed, the Peace of Westphalia limited the ability of rulers within Germany to arbitrarily dictate the religion of their subjects. The regulations and laws that had governed religion on January 1, 1624, were to be restored. Where there was agreement between ruler and subject on religious practices as of that date, these practices were to continue unless they were changed by mutual consent.[8] Dissenters (Catholic or Lutheran) who did not have any rights in 1624 and who wanted to move or were ordered to do so were given five years to sell their goods.[9] The rights given to Lutherans were also given to Calvinists but not to members of other Protestant sects.

Those Catholics who lived in Lutheran states or Lutherans who lived in Catholic states were given the right to practice their religion in the privacy of their homes, and to educate their children at home or to send them to foreign schools. Subjects were not to be excluded from the "Community of Merchants, Artizans or Companies, nor depriv'd of Successions, Legacies, Hospitals, Lazar-Houses, or Alms-Houses, and other Privileges or Rights" because of their religion. Nor were they to be denied the right of burial or charged an amount for burial different from that levied on those belonging to the religion of the state.[10]

Cities with mixed Lutheran and Catholic populations (Augsburg, Dunckelspiel, Biberach, Ravensburg, Kauffbeur) were to have freedom of religious practices for Catholics and Lutherans.[11] In the first four of these cities, public offices were to be divided equally between adherents of the two sects.[12]

The Peace of Westphalia provided that Catholics and Lutherans should be equally represented in the assemblies of the empire. Religious issues were to be decided by consensus.[13] Representatives to the imperial courts were to include members of both religious groups.

The norm of nonintervention was not reflected at all in the Peace of Westphalia, which attempted to mitigate religious strife by revising the constitution of the Holy Roman Empire along corporatist lines. Important decisions in the Diet and the imperial courts could not be taken without the approval of both Catholic and Protestant representatives. Weaker German princes were obligated to offer some degree of toleration, at a minimum giving dissenting subjects five years to sell their property.

The stronger Catholic powers, France and Austria, made no commitments to toleration within their own territories. The king of France was obligated to "abolish all Innovations crept in during the War" in those territories that were ceded to France by the Treaties of Münster and Osnabrück.[14] In Catholic Austria, the Habsburg rulers supported the Counter Reformation.

Power, not consistency of principle, is the best explanation for the religious provisions of the Peace of Westphalia. The strong imposed constraints on the weak because they feared religious disorder in the center of Europe. The strong did not, however, apply the same principles to themselves.

The Protection of Minorities

Minority protection, now so prominent because of developments in Central Europe and the former Soviet Union, has been a concern of the international community since at least the nineteenth century, and since a much earlier time if Western European attention to the fate of Christians in the Ottoman Empire is considered. Like religious conflicts, ethnic conflicts within states attract the attention of external powers because such conflicts can increase instability in the international system and can impinge on the legitimacy of other regimes.

In the later nineteenth and early twentieth centuries, systematic efforts were made to create an international regime that would protect the rights of national minorities, especially in Central and Eastern Europe. Provisions for the protection of such rights were included in a number of treaties in the nineteenth century that were guaranteed by the great powers, most notably the Berlin Treaty of 1878. After World War I, extensive minority rights provisions were written into a number of peace treaties, and a monitoring and enforcement mechanism was established within the League of Nations.

These efforts failed. National governments disregarded their obligation to protect the rights of minorities within their own borders. Neither the major powers nor the League of Nations acted to enforce the regime. After

World War II, the effort to guarantee the rights of national minorities was virtually abandoned, replaced by a liberal emphasis on purely individual human rights.

During the nineteenth century minorities were defined primarily, although not exclusively, by religion. European attention was focused on the collapsing, multireligious and multiethnic Ottoman Empire. Efforts to protect Christians within the Ottoman Empire can be traced back as far as unilateral commitments by European monarchs in the thirteenth century and explicit treaty agreements between the Porte and France, Austria, and Russia in the seventeenth and eighteenth centuries.[15]

As the Ottoman Empire fell apart during the nineteenth century, the major European powers intervened more actively. Clauses for the protection of religious minorities were included in the treaties granting independence to the states that were formed out of the empire. For instance, the protocol signed by Great Britain, France, and Russia in 1830, which guaranteed the independence of Greece, stated that to preserve Greece from "the calamities which the rivalries of the religions therein professed might excite, . . . all the subjects of the new State, whatever their religion may be, shall be admissible to all public employments, functions and honours, and be treated on a footing of perfect equality, without regard to difference of creed, in their relations, religious, civil or political." When Moldavia and Wallachia secured their independence in 1856 the western powers sought to guarantee equal treatment for adherents of all creeds, including Jews.[16]

Nineteenth-century efforts to guarantee minority rights reached their climax at the Congress of Berlin of 1878. At the congress, convened to deal with the consequences of the Balkan wars of the 1870s, the representatives of the great powers agreed that religious toleration would be one of the conditions for the recognition of new states. Such stipulations were included in the treaties regarding Romania, Serbia, Montenegro, and Bulgaria. The treaty signed with the Ottoman Empire provided that the Porte would protect the rights not only of religious minorities but also of a number of ethnic minorities, including the Armenians.[17] These measures were ineffectual. The Ottoman government supported a number of massacres against the Armenians, the first of which occurred in 1894. Others followed, despite protests from the western powers. Article 44 of the Treaty of Berlin of 1879 prohibited Romania from engaging in religious discrimination against Jews of Romanian citizenship, but Romania evaded this obligation by declaring that no Jew could be a citizen. The major Western European powers did little or nothing to enforce the minority rights provisions of the treaties that were signed as a result of the Congress of Berlin.[18]

Despite the failure of the nineteenth-century system, efforts to establish and protect minority rights were vigorously renewed at the end of World War I. Guarantees took several forms. Austria, Hungary, Bulgaria, and Turkey were defeated states, and protections were written into their peace treaties. Poland, Czechoslovakia, Yugoslavia, Romania, and Greece were new or enlarged states. They signed minority rights treaties with the Allied and Associated Powers. Albania, Lithuania, Latvia, Estonia, and Iraq, as a result of pressure that was brought upon them when they applied to join the League of Nations, made declarations granting minority rights that were similar to the rights in the minority treaties. Germany assumed obligations for minority rights in the Geneva Convention, a bilateral treaty signed with Poland which established an elaborate minority rights system for Upper Silesia and gave an important role to the League.[19]

The rationale for the protection of minority rights was that stable domestic orders were necessary for international peace, an obvious conclusion that could be drawn from the experience of World War I, which had been precipitated by the assassination of the Archduke Ferdinand by a Serbian nationalist. Collective security, the Wilsonian vision that informed the effort to create a peaceful international order, could only work if most states were democratic. The relationship between minority rights and collective security was more important than any effort to guarantee the rights of minorities for their own sake. The treaties sought to resolve the minority problem by making minorities loyal citizens of the states in which they lived.[20]

The protections offered to minorities were elaborate. For instance, the Polish Minority Treaty provided that "Poland undertakes to assure full and complete protection of life and liberty to all inhabitants of Poland without distinction of birth, nationality, language, race or religion" (Article 2). Religious differences were not to affect public or professional employment (Article 7). Where there were a considerable number of non–Polish speakers, they would be educated in their own language in primary school, although the state could mandate the teaching of Polish (Article 8). Jews would not be obligated to perform any act that violated the Jewish sabbath; for this reason Poland agreed not to hold elections on Saturday (Article 11). The treaty was made part of the fundamental law of Poland.[21]

Monitoring and enforcement of the post–World War I minority treaties was much more institutionally elaborated than had been the case for the nineteenth-century treaties, which left enforcement entirely in the hands of the great powers. The various treaties and other declarations designated the Council of the League of Nations to assume the responsibility for supervision and implementation. The Permanent Court of International Justice was given the right to make binding decisions. Any member of the Council of the League could submit a case to the court.[22]

The minorities regime established after World War I was a clear violation of the norm of noninterference. As a condition of full participation in the international community, the smaller states of Central and Eastern Europe were compelled to accept limitations on their internal sovereignty which extended to details as small as the days of the week on which elections could be held. Clemenceau, in a covering letter conveying the Polish Minorities Treaty, argued that the provisions of the treaty were consistent with diplomatic precedent. He stated:

> This Treaty does not constitute any fresh departure. It has for long been the established procedure of the public law of Europe that when a State is created, or even when large accessions of territory are made to an established State, the joint and formal recognition of the Great Powers should be accompanied by the requirement that such States should, in the form of a binding international Convention, undertake to comply with certain principles of Government.[23]

The provisions for minority rights were imposed on the weaker states of Central and Eastern Europe by the victorious allied powers. The importance given to minority rights after World War I reflected the configuration of power at that historical moment. Three of the multinational empires— Germany, Austria-Hungary, and the Ottoman Empire—had been destroyed entirely by the war. The fourth, Russia, was in the hands of a new revolutionary regime. The peace was dictated by the liberal states of Western Europe, and by the United States.[24]

The victors did not accept any restrictions on their own sovereignty. Britain refused to allow any issues related to Wales or Ireland to become a matter of concern to the League. Italy refused to accept any provisions regarding minorities, despite the fact that the peace settlement placed a large number of German speakers in the area of the Brenner Pass, within Italy's new borders. Questions related to the treatment of African Americans and Asians in the United States were completely off the agenda.[25]

The regime for the protection of minorities established within the League failed as badly as its nineteenth-century precursor. States that were subject to minorities provisions viewed the regime as an infringement on their internal sovereignty. Their leaders maintained that the failure to impose similar obligations on all states violated the principle of the sovereign equality of states. They pointed out that Germany and Italy were not subject to the same constraints.[26] By the time Poland formally renounced its obligations toward minorities in September 1934, when its representative declared that without a uniform and general system Poland would no longer cooperate with international bodies, the minorities regime was already a dead letter.[27]

The Abolition of the Slave Trade

Religious toleration, reflected in some of the provisions of the Peace of Westphalia, was ultimately adopted by all of the states of the west, although this was a long process driven more by different domestic pressures than by external intervention. Efforts to protect the rights of religious and ethnic minorities in Central and Eastern Europe in the nineteenth and early twentieth centuries were an abject failure. In contrast, the British crusade to end the slave trade, another issue involving relations between rulers and ruled, was a triumphant success.

The abolition of the slave trade across the Atlantic was a result of principles and norms that were supported by the most powerful states in the international system, especially the dominant maritime power, Great Britain. Britain coerced, badgered, cajoled, and threatened other countries, notably Portugal and Brazil, into accepting an end to the slave trade, and played the major role in enforcing and monitoring the international regime that it had itself created through a series of international treaties.

Britain outlawed slavery for vessels sailing under its own flag in 1807.[28] During the Napoleonic Wars, Britain used its navy to capture slave ships from enemy states, France, and the Netherlands, justifying such action in terms of its rights as a belligerent. The slaves on these ships were set free, usually in Sierra Leone.[29] By 1815 Britain, Russia, Austria, Prussia, France, the Netherlands, Sweden, and the United States had agreed to prohibit the transatlantic slave trade. In 1817 Spain also agreed to abolish the slave trade north of the equator and in 1820 agreed to abolish it completely.[30]

Despite these commitments, the slave trade was so lucrative that large numbers of Africans continued to be transported across the Atlantic. The major effort to enforce the ban on slaving was undertaken by Britain. Between 1818 and 1820, Britain signed treaties with a number of European countries which gave British warships the right to search and seize vessels suspected of engaging in the slave trade.[31]

Brazil and Portugal were the most recalcitrant slave-trading countries. Brazilian agriculture was heavily dependent on slave labor. Immediately after abolishing the slave trade for British shipping in 1807, Britain began to put pressure on Portugal, whose colonies in Africa and South America were both a major source and a target of the slave trade. Portugal at first totally rejected British initiatives. However, when France invaded Portugal in late 1807, the Portuguese royal family was forced to flee to Brazil under British protection. In 1810 Portugal signed a commercial treaty with Britain which provided in part that Portugal would cooperate with Britain in bringing about the gradual abolition of the slave trade. Britain conceded to Portugal the right to continue slave trading within its African territories. In 1815 Portugal signed an agreement with Britain agreeing to abolish the slave trade north of the equator, a commitment of limited consequence since most of Portugal's trade between Africa and Brazil was south of the equator.

In 1839 Britain unilaterally authorized its navy to board and seize suspected slavers that were flying the Portuguese flag. This came after long and unsuccessful efforts to sign a bilateral treaty with Portugal authorizing such seizures. The slaves were to be released in the nearest British port, and the disposition of the ships was to be decided by British admiralty courts; the crews of such ships, however, were to be returned to their own countries for trial.[32]

Britain focused its attention on Brazil after that country's independence in 1822. In exchange for recognition by Britain in 1826, Brazil agreed to abolish the slave trade by 1830, despite strong opposition from many members of its parliament. The treaty stipulated that the slave trade would be treated as piracy after that date, providing Britain with legal grounds for seizing slave-trading ships on the high seas.[33] Despite the agreement, slave trading continued between Brazil and Africa, even increasing in the 1830s beyond what it had been before the treaty was signed.[34]

Confronted with the continuation of the slave trade some twenty years after it should have been abolished under the 1826 treaty, Britain acted unilaterally. Slaving had already been declared piracy, and this gave British ships the right to board and seize suspected slavers on the high seas. In 1850, British warships entered Brazilian ports and seized and burned a number of vessels that were suspected of engaging in the transport of slaves. During these operations the British were frequently fired upon from Brazilian forts. It is difficult to imagine a less ambiguous violation of nonintervention.[35]

These pressures were effective. Confronted with British naval power and the antipathy of other advanced states, Brazil passed and enforced legislation designed to end the slave trade. One Brazilian leader speaking to the Brazilian Chamber of Deputies in 1850 recognized that Brazil was the only country actively resisting the antislavery regime and stated, "With the whole of the civilised world now opposed to the slave trade, and with a powerful nation like Britain intent on ending it once and for all, Can we resist the torrent? I think not."[36]

Thus, the abolition of the slave trade was a triumph for human rights and freedom made possible in large measure by the commitment and power of Great Britain. Self-help, Britain's commitment to ending international commerce in human beings, triumphed over nonintervention.

Unlike issues related to religious toleration or the treatment of minorities, Britain's behavior cannot be explained in terms of specific economic, political, or security interests. The economic consequences of the abolition of slavery for Britain and its colonies were ambivalent at best because British plantations in the Caribbean were heavily dependent on slave labor. Rather, Britain's action was strongly motivated by the values and commitments of important parts of its domestic population. The British government was pressured by antislavery groups that based their opposition on religious doctrine, not economic self-interest or national security.

Interventions and Domestic Regimes

Religious toleration, the protection of minorities, and the abolition of the slave trade are all examples of external intervention in the internal affairs of other states. The focus of these interventions was the relationship between the ruler and some set of subjects or citizens—dissenting religious groups, ethnic and religious minorities, and slaves. Interventions have not, however, been limited to human rights issues. External actors have also tried to change or influence the very nature of the polity, the basic principles and institutional arrangements, of other states. As in the case of human rights, the necessary condition for intervention was power asymmetry between the intervener and the target. The primary motivation for interventions has been the fear that internal developments in weaker countries would undermine the stability of the international system in general or adversely effect political stability in other states.

The Holy Alliance formed after the Napoleonic Wars by Austria, Prussia, and Russia asserted that stability in Europe could only be preserved if republicanism was repressed. World War I was precipitated in part by Austro-Hungarian interventions in the Balkans which were motivated by the fear that domestic developments in Serbia and elsewhere would undermine the political stability of the Habsburg's multiethnic empire. After World War I, the major western powers intervened in Russia to try to prevent the consolidation of the Bolshevik regime. After World War II, the Soviet Union intervened to establish communist regimes in Eastern Europe. Despite the norm of nonintervention, efforts to change the basic nature of the political system have been a pervasive characteristic of the sovereign state system: sovereignty has given the strong the ability to engage in self-help; it has not guaranteed that the weak would be insulated from even the most pervasive and dramatic forms of intervention in their internal affairs.

The Holy Alliance and the Concert of Europe

If religion was the primary issue around which political legitimacy revolved in the sixteenth and seventeenth centuries, the fulcrum of debate from the late eighteenth century to the early twentieth century was the extent to which political authority rested on the consent of the governed. The French Revolution and the systemwide wars that followed were, for the conservative monarchies of Europe, a dramatic illustration of the way in which changes in domestic regimes could threaten international political stability. In contrast, British statesmen focused more on the balance of power among states and the preservation of territorial boundaries. After the Napoleonic Wars, interventions to alter the domestic regimes of weaker states were a frequent occurrence in Europe. The constraint on intervention was not commitment to principle; rather, it was the extent to which the major powers could agree on a common course of action.

The Treaty of Chaumont, concluded in 1814, established the Congress system in which the great powers would periodically meet to consider the affairs of Europe as a whole. France was admitted at the Congress of Aix-la-Chapelle in 1818. The central issue was whether the European powers would attempt to influence the domestic regimes of states within Europe or whether they would simply attempt to maintain the balance of power and the Napoleonic border settlements. The conservative monarchical regimes—Russia, Austria, and Prussia—favored the former course; Britain the latter.

The explicit objective of the Holy Alliance established by Prussia, Austria, and Russia in 1815 was to prevent the rise of republican governments. The members of the alliance maintained that republican governments were a threat to the peace and security of Europe and therefore that they had the right to intervene to prevent such developments. A protocol signed at the Conference of Troppau in 1820 stated:

> States which have undergone a change of government due to revolution, the results of which threaten other states, ipso facto cease to be members

of the European Alliance, and remain excluded from it until their situation gives guarantees for legal order and stability. If, owing to such alterations, immediate danger threatens other states, the parties bind themselves, by peaceful means, or if need be by arms, to bring back the guilty state into the bosom of the Great Alliance.[37]

Britain, under the leadership of Castlereagh, objected to the assertion by Prussia, Russia, and Austria that the Congress system could be used to repress the development of nonmonarchical regimes. Castlereagh argued that intervention was only justified if one state threatened the territorial integrity of another, and he feared that intervention would destabilize the international system.[38]

The differences between Britain, on the one hand, and Russia, Prussia, and Austria, on the other, led to a number of clashes between 1815 and 1825. At the Congress of Troppau, held in 1820, Russia, Prussia, and Austria declared their intention to intervene in Naples, Portugal, and Piedmont after revolutions had led to the promulgation of democratic constitutions. Castlereagh, the British foreign minister, objected to the Troppau declaration and opposed any general right of intervention.[39] At the Congress of Laibach in 1821, Metternich was authorized to send Austrian troops into Naples and Piedmont to reestablish absolutist regimes. At the Congress of Verona, France secured Russian, Prussian, and Austrian support to invade Spain and to restore the absolutist position of the king. Britain opposed these decisions.[40]

Britain was not, however, consistent in opposing intervention in the internal affairs of other states; realpolitik, not commitment to principle, best explains British policy. The British strongly objected to Metternich's advocacy of intervention in Spain in 1820 but did countenance Austrian efforts to repress republican developments in the German states (reflected in the Carlsbad decrees) and in Naples. The British did not want Russian and Austrian intervention in Portugal because it would weaken British influence on the Iberian Peninsula.

The Holy Alliance disintegrated in 1825 because of disagreement among France, Austria, Prussia, and Russia over whether or not they should aid the Greek revolt against the Ottoman Empire. The Russians, anxious to increase their strength in the disintegrating Ottoman Empire, and claiming the mantle of protection of Orthodox minorities, supported intervention even though the rebels were republican. The Austrians resisted any assistance for those attacking traditional authority. The British initially opposed intervention because they wanted a strong Ottoman Empire that could frustrate Russian expansion into the Mediterranean. As Russian pres-

sure continued, however, Britain, along with France, came to actively support the rebellion. A joint British, Russian, and French fleet destroyed
Ottoman naval forces at the Battle of Navarino in 1828, and in 1832 Greece
became an independent country, ruled by a Bavarian prince appointed by
the major powers.[41]

Even though the Holy Alliance collapsed in the mid-1820s, intervention
to repress republican movements continued. Republicanism threatened domestic political stability within the monarchical regimes of Europe and
could upset the balance of power. British attitudes toward domestic political changes were contingent on the consequences these changes would
have for the balance of power. Palmerston did not oppose Russia's quelling
of the Polish rebellion in the early 1830s because he was preoccupied with
developments in Belgium. Britain, along with Russia, supported Austrian
repression of the Hungarian uprising of 1849 because Britain wanted a
strong Austria in the European balance of power. Palmerston did not protest Austrian repression of republican movements in Palma and Modena in
1831 because he was worried about a clash between Austria and France. In
the 1830s Britain itself intervened with naval forces in civil clashes in Portugal and Spain to prevent any possible increase in the influence of Austria
and Russia on the Iberian Peninsula.[42]

In sum, interventions were frequent during the first part of the nineteenth
century. European politics were dominated by the five major powers—
Britain, France, Austria, Russia, and Prussia. The long, drawn-out collapse of
the Ottoman Empire destabilized Central Europe. The French Revolution
challenged traditional forms of domestic political authority. The constraint
on intervention was not some commitment to the principle of nonintervention but rather the balance of interests among the major powers. Britain was
the major check on the more conservative states, in part because British domestic political stability was not challenged by republican developments in
other countries, but also because Britain was anxious to frustrate the expansion of Russian and French influence on the Balkan and Iberian Peninsulas.

The Prevalence of Interventions

The interventions that occurred during the first half of the nineteenth
century were not exceptional. J. H. Leurdijk has attempted to compile a
complete listing of military interventions in the internal affairs of other
states for the period 1815–1975. He has identified forty-five cases in which
there was a formal military intervention targeted at the nature of the domestic political regime of another country. There were sixteen interven-

tions that began between 1815 and 1850. Fourteen of these sixteen were prompted by republican regime changes in the weaker states of Europe— Italy, Spain, and Germany.[43]

Between 1850 and 1900, there was only one intervention, that of France in Mexico. Between 1900 and 1917 there were nine interventions, all involving the United States in Central America and the Caribbean, a result of the collapse of what was left of the Spanish Empire, coupled with the consolidation of American power on the North American continent. Between 1918 and World War II there were seven interventions, the two largest of which involved civil wars in the Soviet Union and Spain. American intervention in Central America and the Caribbean continued. Between the conclusion of World War II and 1975 there were eleven interventions. Most, such as the interventions in Hungary, Laos, South Vietnam, and Czechoslovakia, were associated with the bipolar conflict between the Soviet Union and the United States.

Since 1975 there have been a number of additional interventions aimed at influencing domestic regimes. These include the American interventions in Grenada and Panama, the Soviet intervention in Afghanistan, the Israeli intervention in Lebanon, the Vietnamese intervention in Cambodia, the Tanzanian intervention in Uganda, and the intervention by the United Nations alliance in northern Iraq. Though the specific motivations for action have changed, intervention itself is hardly an unusual phenomenon. If instruments of statecraft other than the overt use of military force were listed (e.g., military assistance or advisers and economic aid), the number of cases of intervention would be far higher than the forty-five identified by Leurdijk.

Conclusions

Interventions have always been a feature of the international system. The pervasiveness of intervention poses problems for both liberal and realist perspectives. For realism, interventions are consistent with an understanding of international politics that emphasizes anarchy and the primacy of state power. States do what they please. The omnipresence of intervention in the internal affairs of other states supports Thucydides' account of the Athenians' statement to the Melians: "[I]n fact the strong do what they have the power to do and the weak accept what they have to accept."[44]

Intervention in the internal affairs of other states also, however, poses two serious problems for realist analysis. The first is that intervention violates the ontological assumption that states are independent actors.

Realism asserts that although the options of a state may be sharply curtailed by external constraints, state officials are still free to determine their own best course of action, limited and unattractive though it may be. Intervention implies that some states are not autonomous actors. On the contrary, the very nature of their polities may be determined by the actions of other states. Leaders or governments in some countries may be heavily dependent on the support of other states. In the many conflicts between self-help and nonintervention, between compromising the autonomy of another state and accepting limitations on self-help (i.e., on the range of policies that can be pursued), self-help prevails.

Second, as John Ruggie among others has pointed out, simply asserting that the strong will do what they choose does not explain what objectives they will pursue.[45] Intervention, both to alter relations between subjects and citizens and to change the nature of domestic regimes, has been motivated by a wide variety of factors. Most interventions have been prompted by core realist concerns: the stability of the international system or of the interveners' own regimes. The extent, however, to which domestic stability in the stronger state is threatened by developments in other countries is a function of internal, not systemic, factors. Developments that menaced Russia and Austria in the decades after the Napoleonic Wars were a matter of indifference to Britain, which was both more politically liberal and more geographically isolated. The sectarian conflicts of the seventeenth century were so threatening because the domestic political legitimacy of all of the major European states was deeply tied to religious authority, a problem that disappeared as a result of the spread of religious toleration. Sectarian issues that remain central for much of the Islamic world are irrelevant for Europe, and North America.

In some cases there is little or no relationship between intervention and the preservation of the territorial or political integrity of the intervening state. The most dramatic example offered in this chapter, perhaps the most dramatic historical example of all, is Britain's commitment to the abolition of the slave trade. The slave trade did not in any direct way threaten the political or territorial integrity of Britain, yet British governments committed treasure, arms, and lives to secure its total abolition. The various American interventions in Central America and the Caribbean, not to speak of Korea and Vietnam, were only remotely related to the security of the United States or to the integrity of the American polity. Overweening power was a prerequisite for such interventions but does not explain why America intervened in the way in which it did.

Hence, structural realism, with its assumption of homogeneity of objectives and its focus on the distribution of power among states, must be supplemented by some analysis of the motivations of the most powerful actors in the system. Power asymmetry is the necessary condition for intervention but does not explain the specific ways in which some states have attempted to change the domestic political characteristics of others.

The historical pattern of interventions also challenges liberal interpretations of the international system. Liberalism asserts that the world has fundamentally changed: Improvements in technology have dramatically increased knowledge and reduced the cost of communication and transportation. Greater interdependence has increased the benefits of mutual cooperation. Democratic liberal values have become more widely accepted. This consensus on values, coupled with greater global involvement, suggests that interventions could become both more frequent and more consensual.

Interventions, however, are not a new phenomenon. In the past they have been associated with power asymmetries, not with consensus regarding values. Interventions have taken place for reasons that the modern world would consider admirable (religious toleration and the abolition of the slave trade) as well as for reasons that would now be considered reprehensible (the support of monarchical regimes). They have involved the coordinated action of the major powers, as occurred, for example between 1815 and 1850, as well as unilateral action by a single state.

The prevalence of interventions in the past is not evidence that liberal interpretations of the contemporary order are wrong. Perhaps the increased capacity of individuals, the collapse of the Soviet Union, the triumph of democracy and capitalism, the integration of international capital markets, the growth of world trade, and the ease of transportation and communication have created a general consensus about political and economic values that will sustain more frequent interventions designed to enhance liberal freedoms and economic openness. There is some evidence to support this perspective, most notably the persistent pressure to end apartheid in South Africa.

On the other hand, gross violations of human rights and democracy have been routinely ignored by the international community. Little attention was paid to the killing fields of Cambodia. The fact that the suffering of tens of thousands in what was Yugoslavia has been graphically presented on television has not moved other states to effective action. The political disorder that has produced mass starvation in several African states has not precipitated any broad-scale intervention. Widely shared values, if they even exist, have not moved states to interventionist actions that would involve real costs in terms of blood and treasure.

Liberalism is a prospective theory. Perhaps its time has not yet come. The available evidence, however, does not suggest that the present is fundamentally different from the past. The most powerful explanation for intervention in the international system continues to be state power. The frequency of interventions has increased when power asymmetries were high—as shown by the interventions by the conservative powers of Europe in the middle of the nineteenth century; the interventions by the United States in Latin America at the end of the nineteenth century and the beginning of the twentieth; and the interventions by the Soviet Union in Eastern Europe after World War II.

Moreover, there is not yet any compelling evidence that the polities of the major powers are infused with a full commitment to democracy and liberalism. The United States and Japan do not share the same social purpose. Much of the Islamic world utterly rejects the West. The political trajectory of Russia and the other republics that were part of the Soviet Union is uncertain. Liberalism's optimistic assertions that shared values and interdependence will generate a consensus for constructive interventions are not supported by the available evidence.

Chapter Eleven

State Sovereignty and International Intervention:

Reflections on the Present and Prospects for the Future

GENE M. LYONS AND MICHAEL MASTANDUNO

Our introduction ended with a methodological problem: what kind of evidence is needed to determine whether the international system is moving, in effect, beyond Westphalia? Is political authority effectively shifting from individual sovereign states to an international community? We suggested two kinds of tests: first, the investigation of "critical" cases, particularly those involving major states, where the presumption is that authority will rest squarely with the states but where the evidence proves otherwise; and, second, the tracing of the cumulative effect of a series of incremental changes over time, on the assumption that the combined effects of structural developments, shifts in perception, and instances of intervention, none of which appears to be decisive on its own, produce a qualitative shift in the relationship between states and the international community.

"Critical" case evidence that would point decisively to movement beyond Westphalia is clearly not provided in the chapters above. In none of the issue areas examined could a strong case be made that major powers have deferred to the international community and have accepted significant constraints on their sovereign authority.[1] In fact, some of the evidence demonstrates the opposite—instances in which major powers have defined international community values in terms of their own interests and exempted themselves from the constraints on sovereignty they seek to impose on others. Janne Nolan makes this point explicitly; nonproliferation efforts generally involve attempts by stronger powers to restrict the access of weaker states to technology and weapons that the stronger powers already possess and reserve the right to retain. In the specific case of chemical weapons, the United States "discovered the limits on its own willingness to sacrifice sovereignty on behalf of a collective security goal"; it backed away from its earlier insistence on "anytime, anywhere" inspections for fear of compromising the security of its own weapons development activities. Ken Conca's chapter makes similar points: the developed world has defined the international environmental protection agenda and appears more interested in constraining the activities of developing states than in constraining its own activities. In negotiations to create a global forestry regime, for example, U.S. officials opposed broadening the scope to include temperate-zone forests along with rainforests.[2]

The absence of critical case evidence obviously cannot be taken to mean that major powers do not face any constraints on or challenges to their sovereignty. Indeed, many of the chapters above demonstrate that even for the major powers, sovereignty never has been absolute, and that the challenges to sovereignty have multiplied in an interdependent world. It does suggest, however, that a significant transfer of political authority from states to the international community has *not* taken place. This is not surprising; as we argued in the introduction, the processes for international decision making tend to be dominated by the major powers, which have been careful to limit the extent to which their own sovereign authority is constrained by international rules and obligations.

What about "cumulative" effects? Here the test is more ambiguous, and the evidence presented in the cases is more mixed. Nonetheless, the evidence does not suggest a decisive shift in the relationship between states and the international community at the present time. Whether or not the evidence suggests that we are in the early stages of a process of moving beyond Westphalia is a more difficult question, and one upon which the contributors to this volume obviously disagree. That question, unfortunately, can only be resolved decisively with the passage of time.

Of the four chapters in this volume which provide case studies, that by Thomas G. Weiss and Jarat Chopra reaches farthest in claiming that we are entering a period of fundamental change. Weiss and Chopra assert that the world has "outgrown" sovereignty, and they speak of the development of a "global humanitarian space" that is eroding any meaningful distinction between internal and external political authority. Nevertheless, they do concede there is "as yet no pattern of human values overriding domestic jurisdiction," and in their chapter they spend considerable time proposing ways to alleviate the widespread concern among weaker states that humanitarian intervention in the name of the international community is a subterfuge for the imposition of the political preferences of the stronger powers.

The chapters by Jack Donnelly, Janne Nolan, and Ken Conca are even more cautious. In the area of human rights, Donnelly does see movement from a pure statist model (which characterized relations between states and the international community prior to World War II), to a "relatively weak" internationalist model (within which states have come to accept "modest" constraints on their sovereignty). His principal finding, however, is that sovereignty remains the norm in this issue area, and is likely to remain so throughout the 1990s. Nolan observes an increasing interest on the part of the international community in the use of coercive and intrusive measures to implement nonproliferation objectives. Yet, instead of reflecting the true values of a global community, she finds that these measures reflect the interest of the strong in constraining the sovereignty of the weak. This is the central dilemma of the nonproliferation regime, and, she argues, it impedes the effectiveness of that regime. Conca's analysis, and his insight that environmental agreements are negotiated in an unequal world, reinforces further the critical importance of the "North-South" divide in understanding the current relationship between sovereignty and intervention. He speaks of the emergence of global norms for the protection of the environment, but emphasizes that the issues and debates are still framed in terms of sovereignty, or the rights and duties of individual states. The emergence of global environmental norms may constrain states in some ways but is also likely to strengthen sovereignty, to the extent that environmental management remains the responsibility of the state.

Neither critical nor cumulative evidence, then, points us beyond Westphalia. The contributions to this volume, however, yield important insights that bear on the present and future relationship between sovereignty and intervention. In our view the following four observations, drawn from the chapters, merit special emphasis.

First, constraints on state sovereignty not only have a long history, as demonstrated by Friedrich Kratochwil (in chapter 2) and Nicholas Onuf (in chapter 3), *but have been increasing significantly in recent years as a consequence of both growing interdependence and the end of the cold war.* For example, as chapter 6, by Donnelly, develops, until World War II human rights practices were generally considered to be a matter of internal politics; with the notable exception of slavery, states did not intervene to protect individual citizens from their own governments. The experience of the Holocaust put human rights in the international domain, especially since it was followed by the Nuremberg trials, which stipulated, through an internationally organized tribunal, that individuals could not hide behind their obligations as state functionaries when charged with responsibility for crimes against other human beings. The Holocaust led to the drafting of the Universal Declaration of Human Rights, which, in turn, inspired a series of human rights treaties, most importantly the Covenant on Civil and Political Rights and the Covenant on Economic, Social, and Cultural Rights. The treaties and covenants go beyond articulating the responsibilities of states and establish mechanisms of oversight and investigation to induce compliance. The overall result of these postwar developments is that human rights are no longer exclusively a subject of domestic jurisdiction, as (in Donnelly's words) "[s]tates now operate in an environment of formal and informal legal and political constraints on their human rights practices."

An important underlying reason for these developments is what Donnelly terms "moral interdependence"—the sense of satisfaction or repulsion the people of one state derive from observing the internal practices of the government of another state. Moral interdependence helps to explain both the incentives for international cooperation with respect to human rights, and, importantly, the limits to that cooperation. Because the costs and benefits of moral interdependence are less tangible than the costs and benefits of "material" interdependence, powerful states have been less inclined to undertake coercive intervention (or even to make attempts at coercive influence) in order to uphold human rights. The struggle against apartheid represents a significant exception, as a result of the extremely powerful feeling of revulsion that institutionalized racial discrimination generated among peoples in both the developed and the developing worlds. In general, however, and despite the steady development of international norms, Donnelly concludes that human rights practices "have not been, and are not likely to become, a standard subject for coercive intervention."

Humanitarian assistance, by contrast, has become and is likely to remain a standard subject for coercive intervention. Weiss and Chopra remind us that here, too, constraints on sovereignty and an interest in international intervention have a long history, going back more than a century to the universal outcry against human suffering during the Crimean War and to the founding of the International Committee of the Red Cross. Yet in the past several years, the intensity of international interest and activity in this area has been profound, as indicated by the willingness of the Security Council to use its powers under Chapter VII of the Charter to provide assistance to the Kurdish minority in Iraq without the agreement of the Iraqi government, and to authorize UN peacekeepers in Somalia and the former Yugoslavia to protect the delivery of humanitarian aid.[3] Moral interdependence helps to account for the propensity toward international intervention; like apartheid, mass starvation evokes an especially intense revulsion, particularly when, with the revolution in communications technologies, that starvation is witnessed daily by individuals all over the world. The end of the cold war is also a significant part of the explanation. It has provided the opportunity for the Security Council to act more decisively, and it has permitted the great powers, in particular the United States, to focus attention on humanitarian concerns without the constraint of a global geopolitical struggle.

Interestingly, Nolan's chapter on weapons of mass destruction (chapter 8), matches the time frame that Weiss and Chopra adopt in their discussion of humanitarian assistance. On reflection, the convergence stands to reason. The late nineteenth century witnessed a rapid acceleration of military developments that produced weapons of increasingly lethal capacity and cruelty. By the time of World War I, the machine gun, armored weapons carriers, the submarine, and debilitating gases had changed the nature of warfare. As Nolan points out, the introduction of these weapons had by the turn of the century already led to efforts, at the Hague conferences, to control their use (especially the use of gases). Similarly, it was the early effects of weapons of mass destruction that, as Weiss and Chopra demonstrate, led to the growth of humanitarian laws of war and to the founding of the Red Cross to alleviate human suffering from those weapons' devastating force.

Nolan shows that recent efforts to control the development of nuclear, chemical, and biological weapons have their origins in this early recognition that weapons of mass destruction were both destabilizing and immoral. One might trace a line from the Geneva Protocol of 1925, banning the use of chemical weapons, to the most recent chemical weapons convention banning their production and stockpiling; to the Nonproliferation Treaty (NPT) banning the development of nuclear weapons; to the convention forbidding the production of biological weapons; and to the Missile Technology Control Regime, which extended the control movement from weapons to delivery systems.

The postwar development of these regimes is rooted in both moral and material interdependence. Recognition of the capacity of biological, chemical, and nuclear weapons to inflict horrible damage on civilians as well as combatants is one incentive for control; the sense of vulnerability that comes with the inability to devise effective defenses is another. Yet as Nolan points out, these arms control regimes have been burdened by a critical weakness: they possess only a rudimentary capacity to monitor, evaluate, and especially enforce compliance. Participating states have accepted constraints on their weapons development within an essentially "laissez-faire" system of arms control. Since the Persian Gulf War, however, an ambitious effort has been under way to strengthen these regimes, and in particular to enable the international community to enforce the compliance of potential proliferaters through the use of intrusive and coercive instruments. These efforts necessarily involve more formidable constraints on sovereignty than did the earlier, more laissez-faire regulations.

This recent expansion of interest and effort can be traced directly to the end of the cold war. During the cold war, the nuclear arsenals of the United States and the Soviet Union were the primary arms control concern; nonproliferation efforts tended to be more sporadic and to be subordinated to other foreign policy objectives. As concern over "vertical" proliferation has abated, concern over "horizontal" proliferation has intensified, with the Iraqi case serving as the principal catalyst. The ability of Iraq to develop weapons of mass destruction and initiate the Gulf War dramatized both the "new" security threat of proliferation in a post–cold war world and the need to bolster existing regimes.

Finally, international norms for protecting the global environment have a more recent history than do humanitarian concerns, human rights, and arms control. Although the threat to the global environment actually originated in the growth and spread of industrialization during the nineteenth century, the mobilization of the international community only dates to the UN Conference on the Human Environment convened in Stockholm in 1972. Conca (in chapter 7) traces the process of norm creation from Stockholm to the second UN conference on the environment, convened in Rio de Janeiro in 1992. He documents a rapidly growing environmental awareness on the part of the international community and finds that between the two conferences there was a shift in the dominant paradigm of environmental discourse, from a concern over "limits to growth" to a concept of "global change" which focuses on the collective management of global-scale natural systems.

An important source of the global environmental movement is interdependence. As Conca notes, "modern states are ecologically interdependent, and agreements that recognize this fact can and do limit the autonomy of action of individual governments." As awareness of ecological interdependence has increased, so too have efforts by representatives of the international community to constrain sovereignty in order to achieve environmental objectives. In the case Conca examines, that of deforestation in the Brazilian Amazon, the complexity of the relationship between sovereign states and the international community is played out fully. It is obvious that the government of Brazil was subject to intense pressure to conform to global environmental norms; at the same time, government officials sought to use that pressure to heighten the presence of the state in environmental policy.[4]

Our second observation is that *while constraints on state sovereignty traditionally were largely constraints on states' behavior with regard to other states, in recent decades constraints on sovereignty have increasingly involved the internal affairs of states, or how governments relate to their own citizens, economies, and territories.* As discussed elsewhere in this volume, the international system that emerged out of the settlement of Westphalia was initially centered in Europe, and premised on the idea that viable governments possessed both the obligation and the authority to maintain domestic order within their borders and to conduct effective relations with other sovereign units. The state was sovereign internally— and externally as well. As international society developed, so too did constraints on external sovereignty. European states were expected to engage in diplomatic relations, uphold the balance of power, avoid intervention in the affairs of other sovereign states, and conduct armed conflict according to the humanitarian and other laws of war. Subsequently, the League of Nations and the United Nations broadened the membership of international society beyond the states of Europe, and sought to institutionalize and codify the constraints on external sovereignty.

While constraints on external sovereignty remain, the contributions to this volume highlight the growing importance of constraints on internal sovereignty. To be sure, constraints on internal sovereignty are not new; as Krasner argues in chapter 10, "external interference in the relationship between ruler and ruled has been an enduring and pervasive characteristic of the sovereign state system since its very inception." Nonetheless, in recent decades a wider and wider range of issues and activities that were traditionally considered domestic and beyond the reach of international society have become the subjects of international scrutiny, attempts at influence, and in some instances intervention. This trend is evident across the four issue areas examined above and in others as well, such as in the relationship between the international and domestic economies. Trade negotiations among sovereign states used to concern border restrictions such as tariffs. Today, the negotiating agenda is dominated by subjects that traditionally were squarely in the realm of domestic politics, such as health and

safety practices, environmental standards, labor policies, and the management of national monetary and fiscal policies.

Whether or not the expanding constraints on internal sovereignty will
lead ultimately to a fundamental transformation of the Westphalian system depends, first, on the extent to which recent, prominent cases of international intervention represent the beginnings of a trend or are single occurrences in exceptional circumstances. That question, debated without
resolution in the chapters above, is relevant to a number of recent international interventions, for example, the intervention to provide humanitarian assistance to the Kurds in Iraq; the intervention to assure the dismantling of Iraqi weapons capabilities; the intervention to facilitate the return
to democracy in Haiti; the intervention to conduct on-site monitoring of
human rights practices in El Salvador; and the interventions to provide
humanitarian assistance to the peoples of Somalia and the former Yugoslavia. Second, for there to be fundamental change, these and similar interventions must represent more than constraints or infringements on the
sovereign authority of states, since constraints and infringements on sovereignty—both external and internal—have been an enduring feature of the
Westphalian system. They must also represent a legitimate transfer of
authority to a credible and viable international community. It is thus the
question of the credibility and viability of the international community
that is the subject of the following observation.

Our third observation is that *the international community has developed a formidable institutional presence, yet clearly lacks the resources
and organizational capacity to serve as a viable alternative to the society
of sovereign states.* As Jackson indicates in chapter 4, the international
community has been progressively institutionalized beginning with the
Concert of Europe in the nineteenth century, and there now exists a diffuse
but well-established mix of institutional arrangements through which states
conduct a considerable amount of their business. Nevertheless, it is also
apparent that states have been unwilling to encourage the development of
the organizational and administrative capacity and provide the resources
that are necessary for the international community to carry out effectively
the myriad tasks that have been assigned to it. Put differently, over the past
half-century an impressive array of institutions and norms have developed,
pointing in the direction of a more active international community, but the
policies and procedures for implementing those norms and strengthening
those institutions remain underdeveloped.

Nolan's discussion of arms control is instructive. On the one hand, a
plethora of regimes, institutions, and treaties have emerged for the purpose

of retarding the development and proliferation of weapons of mass destruction. On the other hand, the regimes "all have one thing in common: they lack clout, money, authority, and sufficient international support." One could add, as Nolan does, that they lack early warning and detection capability, enforcement authority, and the ability to stop determined violators. These weaknesses have become more apparent as the institutions have been called upon to do more to stop proliferation and have been blamed, quite unfairly, when proliferation has occurred. The International Atomic Energy Agency (IAEA) is an obvious example: traditionally it has been granted sparse resources and modest powers, yet it took a considerable share of the blame when the full extent of Iraqi nuclear activities was revealed. Both the Security Council and the major Western powers are now calling upon the IAEA to do a great deal more than carry out perfunctory inspections of declared sites; whether it will be granted the requisite resources or authority remains to be seen. The IAEA currently relies heavily on the United States for intelligence, and for assistance in carrying out negotiations with renegade states such as North Korea. It is also unclear whether the agency has the authority to carry out the challenge inspections now proposed, or whether an amendment of the NPT is required.

Donnelly's chapter tells a similar story. Human rights norms have been thoroughly internationalized, and an extensive array of global and regional regimes have emerged, but procedures for implementing and enforcing those norms remain extremely weak. For example, the so-called 1503 procedure of the UN Commission on Human Rights is slow and cumbersome, and the commission's ultimate enforcement authority is limited to publicizing the evidence it collects and its assessment of that evidence. Although efforts are ongoing to strengthen this and other entities for the protection of human rights, Donnelly is forced to conclude that at the present time "[m]ultilateral procedures for coercive intervention to enforce international human rights obligations simply do not exist."[5]

The gap between obligations and resources may be most profound in the area of international peacekeeping. The peacekeeping obligations taken on by the United Nations have expanded tremendously. At the beginning of 1992, there were roughly eleven thousand peacekeepers deployed under UN auspices; at the beginning of 1994, there were more than seventy-five thousand, spread over some twenty countries, with the demand increasing.[6] These units are being assigned tasks beyond traditional peacekeeping. These tasks include the disarming of rival factions (in Somalia and El Salvador), the care and feeding of war victims (in Bosnia), the facilitation of political reconciliation (in Mozambique), and the running of elections (in

Namibia and Cambodia). In many cases, however, member states have been reluctant to provide financial resources or to ensure that there are sufficient personnel and adequate equipment to carry out UN missions in a timely fashion. The United Nations lacks a standing army or designated standby units, and when Secretary-General Boutros-Ghali floated the idea of creating this capacity, the response was not encouraging. This leaves the United Nations with no choice but to rely on the goodwill and cooperation of member countries—some of which are growing reluctant to contribute peacekeepers if the threat of casualties is high, if vital national interests are not engaged, if burdens are not shared equitably, or if the United Nations seems unlikely to be able to compensate them financially.[7]

Our fourth observation is related to the third: *the legitimacy of the international community will continue to be questionable as long as there are fundamental differences between North and South with regard to whose values and interests the international community represents.* The chapters above suggest that the international community not only lacks resources and capacity but also suffers from a significant credibility problem. Many developing countries view any approach that calls for an activist or strengthened international community with suspicion and skepticism. They view international intervention not as the necessary counterpart to the pursuit of community values but rather as the coercive expression of the interests of the dominant states, and in some cases of former colonial powers. If the major powers claim to be acting, through the exercise of their international decision-making authority, as the guardians of the common good, less powerful states seem to want to know, who is guarding the guardians? To the extent that these attitudes are persistent and pervasive, they call into question both the existence of a genuine international community and claims that the international system is in the process of moving beyond Westphalia.

Evidence of this North-South divide, and its detrimental impact on the development of international community and the effectiveness of international intervention, can be found across the issue areas. Weiss and Chopra, discussing obstacles to the acceptance of international intervention for humanitarian purposes, point explicitly to fear among developing states that humanitarian interventions will be abused by powerful states for self-interested motives. They also remind us that although the Western powers supported the potentially precedent-setting Resolution 688 in the Security Council, Cuba, Yemen, and Zimbabwe voted against it, and China and India abstained. Nolan views the NPT as "unabashedly designed to protect a hierarchical international system," and argues that the future effectiveness of nonproliferation regimes depends on the extent to which the political and security concerns of developing states (the would-be proliferaters) are taken into account. Conca finds that the North sets the environmental protection agenda, and that "the global environmental debate tends to re-create the basic disputes over political economy and global governance that divide North and South."

The widely divergent perspectives of North and South obviously pose a major problem. If developing countries, which constitute a majority of the members of the international community, view international intervention as an expression of the political will of the minority and resist it wherever possible, it is difficult to anticipate a legitimate transfer of authority from states to the international community. One obvious but difficult solution is to enlarge international decision-making procedures to accommodate less powerful states. (The most probable change in the Security Council, the addition of Japan and Germany as permanent members, addresses some problems of participation but not this particular one.) In the absence of institutional or attitudinal changes, it will be a challenge for the international community to prevent international intervention from being the divisive North-South issue of the 1990s, as debt was during the 1980s and demands for a new international economic order were during the 1970s.

In the remainder of this chapter we return to the difficult question of whether we are witnessing the early stages of a *process* of movement beyond Westphalia.[8] Is Rosenau on the right road, or is Krasner? Although a definitive answer must await the accumulation—and interpretation—of additional evidence, we propose here a way to track the continued evolution of the balance between the authority of sovereign states and the authority of the international community. Our idea is built on the critical concept of legitimacy. Because intervention clashes with the established norm of sovereignty, it is imperative for interveners to legitimate or justify their action. What is accepted by states as legitimate grounds for intervention, in turn, reveals a great deal about the nature of the international system. Legitimate justifications for intervention in a purely realist world differ significantly from what would be accepted as legitimate justifications in a purely globalist world.

On what grounds can intervention be justified as legitimate? The seven justifications shown in table 3 and described below represent a continuous sequence, from a purely realist world, through international society, to a purely cosmopolitan or global world. By locating past and current international practice along this continuum, we might gain insights into the bal-

TABLE 3.
Justifications for International Intervention

Pure Realism		Contemporary International Society				Pure Globalism
(1) Might makes right	(2) Self preser- vation	(3) Consent of subject government	(4) Collapse of governing authority in subject country	(5) Consensus in the international community	(6) Universal values or principles	(7) Global governing authority

ance between state sovereignty and collective authority, and how it has changed over time.

At one extreme is the pure realist justification captured by the classic Melian dialogue as described by Thucydides. Athenians, in anticipation of destroying Melos, justified their action by arguing that the "strong do what they have the power to do, and the weak accept what they have to accept."[9] Intervention is legitimized by power, without qualification. Although states still sometimes behave according to this logic, the justification is at odds with the norms of contemporary international society, according to which sovereign states are recognized as equals under international law regardless of disparities in power, size, or type of government.

A second justification qualifies the Athenian argument by claiming that intervention can be legitimized if the states that carry it out are acting in the interest of self-preservation. Edward Luttwak, for example, considers such a justification morally and legally feasible in the case of a cutoff of vital raw materials, such as oil.[10] In the Gulf War, the calculations of at least some states that participated in the United Nations–sanctioned coalition were undoubtedly influenced by the need to preserve the flow of oil and, in this sense, their motive was arguably self-preservation. In general, however, the concept of "self-preservation" also moves beyond what is currently recognized as justifiable or legitimate, since it could obviously be used to defend a wide variety of interventions in cases where there was no threat to the lifeblood of a national economy.

A third justification moves us closer to what has come to be accepted practice in contemporary international society: intervention is legitimate if carried out with the consent of the subject government. This justification provides room for intervention while upholding the norm of sovereignty by leaving the state with the discretion to determine whether intervention will take place on its territory. Until very recently, international intervention by the United Nations was generally conducted in this manner. For example, the rules of UN peacekeeping that were first formulated during the Middle East crisis in 1956 specified that peacekeeping forces could not be deployed without the consent of the government on whose territory they were to serve. Even great powers, intervening unilaterally, deem it necessary to provide this justification; more often than not, they claim rightly or wrongly to have been "invited in" by the governments of weaker states against whom they intervene. Strong powers may intervene without accountability, but they risk losing credibility in the eyes of the larger community to which they may subsequently wish to turn for support, and generating controversy among political groups in their own country.

The fourth justification is one that is increasingly likely to be recognized as legitimate in international society: the existence of civil war or other circumstances in which central authority collapses and governments can no longer carry out the functions normally associated with sovereignty, such as providing security or ensuring sustenance to the population or significant parts of it. The cases of the former Yugoslavia and of Somalia and Rwanda are illustrative. This justification is compatible with the sovereignty norm, on the underlying assumption that sovereignty brings with it certain responsibilities or presupposes some minimal level of governing capacity. Nevertheless, to the extent that international intervention under these conditions becomes routine, it would suggest some shift in the balance between the sovereign authority of states and the authority of the collective.

The fifth justification for intervention has gained some acceptance in international society: the existence of a pro-intervention consensus among the members of the international community *defined as states*. Resolutions of the UN Security Council, providing a mandate for intervention under Chapter VII of the Charter, may be taken as a legitimate expression of the voice of the international community. As noted in the introduction, international intervention is generally recognized as more legitimate than unilateral intervention for precisely this reason, and this helps to explain why there has been such an increase in Security Council activity since the end of the cold war. As already suggested, however, it is fair to question, as many in developing countries do, whether the council, as currently structured, is representative of the broader international community or is simply a vehicle for expressing and authorizing the collective intent of the major powers. The criticism is valid even though decisions of the council require four votes in addition to the votes of the five permanent members, for a total of nine out of the fifteen votes, and even though nonpermanent members often vote not only in their own right but as representatives of larger clusters of countries.

The sixth justification for intervention is the claim that the intervention is legitimized by universal values or principles beyond the particular interests of states. Examples might include good governance, human rights, the sanctity of the environment, and democracy as a form of government. Here we may be standing between the community of states and the community of humankind, at the center of the dilemma between the "right" of the international community to intervene in the name of universal values and the danger of weakening the principle of nonintervention until the weak have no defense against the strong. In any event, even globalists might question whether international society today is truly at the point at which any of the universal norms has such widespread support that it could easily justify intervention against a sovereign state. In human rights, an area in which considerable progress has been made over time in establishing and nurturing a set of international principles, the consensus that unites governments remains a fragile one. In other areas, such as the environment or arms control, an international consensus may be in the very early stages of a process of emerging but clearly has not yet reached a point where intervention can be routinely expected. Much will depend on the international community's future experiences with new environmental and arms control treaties, on how monitoring systems are organized, and on the degree to which governments recognize that their own interests are compatible with the "common good" in a world of growing interdependence.

The seventh, and final, justification is that one might operate in a world beyond the nation-state, in which the authority to intervene coercively in the affairs of component political units would be concentrated in a central international authority, such as, perhaps, a greatly strengthened United Nations. Alternatively, the legitimate right to intervene could be dispersed to several regional governing authorities.[11] International society clearly has not moved to this outer limit of the balance between the sovereignty of the unit and the authority of the international community.

If one adopts a long historical perspective, a gradual movement from the extreme of pure realism to the justifications found near the center of the spectrum becomes apparent. To find an era of "might makes right" (justification 1), one need look back no further than the nineteenth and early twentieth centuries, when powerful states applied a double standard: the principle of nonintervention generally applied in relations among the "civilized" states of Europe, but in Europe's relations with weaker and less developed states such as China, Persia, Egypt, Turkey, and the countries of

Latin America, intervention was routine and was considered legitimate.[12] This double standard became problematic after World War II, and members of an expanded international society came to accept intervention as legitimate when carried out with the consent of the subject government (justification 3). At the present time, intervention is increasingly perceived as legitimate in cases of civil war or other circumstances characterized by the collapse of central governing authority (justification 4), and on the basis of an articulated consensus among members of the international community defined as states (justification 5). Granted the problematic status of the international community, it is reasonable to conclude that in contemporary international society, widely recognized justifications for intervention fall in the middle of the spectrum from a purely realist to a purely globalist world.

As we approach the twenty-first century, movement away from the center and toward either end of the spectrum would signal an unambiguous shift in the balance between state sovereignty and international authority. For example, if intervention on the basis of "might makes right" (justification 1), or on the basis of self-preservation broadly defined (justification 2) again came to be recognized as legitimate, it would indicate a shift in the balance in favor of the sovereign authority of states. Movement toward this purely realist world is unlikely, owing to the growth of interdependence and the expansion of international society. Alternatively, if international intervention came to be legitimized on the basis of universal values or principles (justification 6), or as the result of the creation of new global governing structures (justification 7), it would reflect a clear shift in the direction of international authority beyond the Westphalian principles. Thus far, there is no evidence to suggest that the balance has shifted to this extent. It would require, among other things, the emergence of a fully legitimate and capable international community; agreement among the members on the definition of universal principles; a willingness on the part of powerful states to intervene when called upon by the international community and to be the subjects of intervention; and a willingness on the part of weaker states to abandon their tenacious defense of the sovereignty principle in deference to universal principles.

In the short term, we are likely to witness continued attempts by the international community to "chip away" at the sovereign autonomy of states by working within the bounds of the fourth and fifth justifications for intervention. For example, the permanent membership of the Security Council might be expanded to give expression to the views of a more representative group of member states, including those from Africa, Asia, and Latin America, thereby enhancing the already recognized legitimacy of international interventions authorized by the Security Council, and perhaps even preparing the groundwork for the regular use of international intervention. The authority of the Security Council to order intervention might be enhanced even further, to the extent that the concept of "threats to international peace and security," already an accepted justification for international action, would be broadened to include such behavior as upsetting the regional balance of power, mistreating minorities, continually violating human rights, or even perhaps abusing the environment. Finally, the very act of intervention in cases where central authority has collapsed, as it has in Somalia and the former Yugoslavia, helps to set precedents and might legitimate subsequent interventions in similar circumstances.

In sum, we may be entering the very beginning of a period in which the balance between state sovereignty and international authority shifts decisively. It is difficult to ignore the increasing resort to international intervention with or without government consent, or the structural changes that appear to be eroding the traditional authority of the sovereign state. Nevertheless, it is undoubtedly premature to declare that international society has moved beyond Westphalia and has overcome the idea of state sovereignty. The idea of state sovereignty is alive and well among both the more powerful and less powerful members of contemporary international society. Even if states increasingly share authority with intergovernmental and nongovernmental organizations, the state system endures.

Notes

Chapter One Introduction

An earlier version of this chapter appeared in *International Social Science Journal* 138 (Nov. 1993): 517–32. The authors wish to thank Oran Young, George Demko, and the contributors to this volume for their comments and suggestions.

1. For background on the conflicts in Somalia, Yugoslavia, and Haiti, see Jeffrey Clark, "Debacle in Somalia: Failure of the Collective Response," in Lori Fisler Damrosch, ed., *Enforcing Restraint: Collective Intervention in Internal Conflicts* (New York: Council on Foreign Relations Press, 1993); James B. Steinberg, "International Intervention in the Yugoslavia Conflict" in ibid.; and Domingo E. Acevedo, "The Haitian Crisis and the OAS Response: A Test of Effectiveness in Protecting Democracy," in ibid.

2. U.N. Press Release SG/SM/4560, Apr. 24, 1991.

3. Boutros Boutros-Ghali, *An Agenda for Peace*, UN Doc. no. S/24111, June 14, 1992, 5.

4. Inis Claude, *Swords into Plowshares*, 4th ed. (New York: Random House, 1974), 183–84.

5. Damrosch, ed., *Enforcing Restraint*, 364. For other recent discussions of this question, see Gidon Gottlieb, *Nation against State: A New Approach to Ethnic Conflicts and the Decline of Sovereignty* (New York: Council on Foreign Relations, 1993); Laura W. Reed and Carl Kaysen, eds., *Emerging Norms of Justified Intervention* (Cambridge, Mass.: American Academy of Arts and Sciences, 1993); Thomas G. Weiss, ed., *Collective Security in a Changing World* (Boulder, Colo.: Rienner, 1993); Louis Henkin et al., *Right vs. Might: International Law and the Use of Force*, 2d ed. (New York: Council on Foreign Relations, 1991); and Lori Fisler Damrosch and David J. Scheffer, eds., *Law and Force in the New International Order* (Boulder, Colo.: Westview, 1991).

6. "Everybody's Business," *Wall Street Journal*, Aug. 24, 1992, A8.

7. "New Ways to Run the World," *Economist*, Nov. 5, 1991, 11.

8. See Gil Loescher, *Beyond Charity* (New York: Oxford University Press, 1993).

9. See David Sanger, "US—North Korean Atom Accord Expected to Yield Dubious Results," *New York Times*, Jan. 9, 1994, 1.

10. The draft treaty, expected to enter into force in early 1995, outlines an ambitious set of inspection procedures, including a provision that any party to the treaty may request "challenge" inspections of another party's suspicious facilities. See

"Chemical Industry Braces for Impact of CW Treaty," *Export Control News* 7, no. 2 (Feb. 1993): 4–5.

11. Adam Watson, "European International Society and Its Expansion," in Hedley Bull and Adam Watson, eds., *The Expansion of International Society* (New York: Clarendon, 1984), 23–25.

12. For the classic discussion of the concept of international society, see Hedley Bull, *The Anarchical Society* (New York: Oxford University Press, 1977).

13. Watson, "European International Society and Its Expansion," 27.

14. There is, of course, the potential for conflict among the permanent five as well, as suggested by U.S. and Russian differences over Serbia, and U.S. and Chinese differences over whether and how to pressure North Korea. For a skeptical view of the ability of the permanent five to act in concert, see Charles William Maynes, "Containing Ethnic Conflict," *Foreign Policy*, no. 90 (spring 1993): 7–8.

15. Good recent discussions include Marc Trachtenberg, "Intervention in Historical Perspective," in Reed and Kaysen, eds., *Emerging Norms of Justified Intervention*, 15–36; and Ernst B. Haas, "Beware the Slippery Slope: Notes toward the Definition of Justifiable Intervention," in ibid., 63–87.

16. On the latter point, see Stanley Hoffman, "The Problem of Intervention," in Hedley Bull, ed., *Intervention in World Politics* (New York: Oxford University Press, 1984), 7–28.

17. There are also many instances, of course, of "covert" intervention, which may or may not involve the physical crossing of borders.

18. See Gerhard von Glahn, *Law among Nations*, 4th ed. (New York: Macmillan, 1981), 249–51.

19. See Virginia Gamba, "Justified Intervention? A View from the South," in Reed and Kaysen, eds., *Emerging Norms of Justified Intervention*, 115–25.

20. See Evan Luard, "Collective Intervention," in Bull, ed., *Intervention in World Politics*, 157–58. On the role of legitimacy in enhancing compliance with international law, see Thomas M. Franck, *The Power of Legitimacy among Nations* (New York: Oxford University Press, 1990).

21. Hedley Bull, "Conclusion," in Bull, ed., *Intervention in World Politics*, 195. The pressure for international "blessing" also applies increasingly to attempts at political influence and isolation, as states seek to develop a broad international constituency to support their policies, and try to avoid being chastised for unilateral actions.

22. This is a crucial insight in E. H. Carr's classic, *The Twenty Year's Crisis* (London: Macmillan, 1939).

23. Bull, "Introduction," in Bull, ed., *Intervention in World Politics*, 2.

24. See Damrosch, ed., *Enforcing Restraint*, 375.

25. U.S. officials at the time characterized the Liberian situation as an "African problem" requiring an "African solution." The Security Council's failure to act more decisively was due in part to U.S. reluctance. Even at the regional level, one could question whether intervention reflected common values or the particular interests of the most powerful state in ECOWAS, Nigeria. For discussion see David Wippman, "Enforcing the Peace: ECOWAS and the Liberian Civil War," in Damrosch, ed., *Enforcing Restraint*, 157–204.

26. For another inquiry into the "Westphalian" issue, see Mark Zacher, "The

Decaying Pillars of the Westphalian Temple," in James N. Rosenau, ed., *Governance without Government* (New York: Cambridge University Press, 1992), 58–101.

27. For an overall view of Rosenau's position, see his *Turbulence in World Politics* (Princeton: Princeton University Press, 1990).

28. In general, see Harry Eckstein, "Case Study and Theory in Political Science," in Fred Greenstein and Nelson Polsby, eds., *Strategies of Inquiry*, vol. 7 of *Handbook of Political Science* (Reading, Mass.: Addison-Wesley, 1975).

Chapter Two Sovereignty as *Dominium*

1. On the issue of the contestability see William Connolly, *The Terms of Political Discourse*, 2d ed. (Princeton: Princeton University Press, 1983), especially chap. 1.

2. See Bruce Ackerman, *Private Property and the Constitution* (New Haven: Yale University Press, 1977), 116.

3. For a general discussion, see Walter Ullmann, "The Medieval Idea of Sovereignty," *English Historical Review* 250 (1949); Michael Wiks, *The Problem of Sovereignty in the Later Middle Ages* (Cambridge: Cambridge University Press, 1963); F. H. Hinsley, *Sovereignty* (London: Watts, 1966).

4. Jean Bodin, *Six livres de la république* (Paris, 1577), bk. 1, chap. 8.

5. See Grotius, *De Jure Belli Ac Pacis Libri Tres* (Oxford: Clarendon, 1925), bk. 1, chap. 3, sec. 7.

6. Harold Laski, *A Grammar of Politics* (New Haven: Yale University Press, 1929), 52.

7. Stephen Krasner, *Defending the National Interest: Raw Materials Investment and U.S. Foreign Policy* (Princeton: Princeton University Press, 1978).

8. See on this point the critique by Timothy Mitchell, "The Limits of the State: Beyond Statist Approaches and Their Critics," *American Political Science Review* 85, no. 1 (1991): 77–96.

9. See the discussion of Fritz Schulz, *Classical Roman Law* (Oxford: Clarendon, 1951), 386–90. See also J. A. Crook, *Law and Life of Rome* (Ithaca: Cornell University Press, 1984), chap. 5. One consequence of this tight bundling of rights was that landlord-tenant relations were not part of the law of property but were part of the law of obligation, and that there was a very restricted possibility of conveyance of use rights.

10. It is important to emphasize here the *spatial* exclusion as part and parcel of property right. To that extent the argument that a shift from use right to exclusive rights is characteristic of the Westphalian system is not wrong but imprecise. There are several exclusionary rights that do not have the implications that spatial exclusion provided. Thus, certain rights and privileges that are conferred on the holder of a Ph.D. degree are exclusively his, but they are inalienable—they can be neither traded nor given away (although "licenses" such as a plumbing license can be sold after conferral in certain jurisdictions). For a further conceptual analysis see Frank Snare, "The Concept of Property," *American Philosophical Quarterly* 9 (Apr. 1972): 200–206.

11. Similarly, landlord-tenant relations that are part of "property" in common law did not belong to "property" in Roman law.

12. See, e.g., the fully developed distinction in Jean Jacques Rousseau, *The Social*

Contract, trans. G.D.H. Cole (New York: Dutton, 1950), bk. 1, chap. 4, pp. 10–11, which deals (among other things) with the "loss" of title through war: "War then is a relation not between man and man, but between State and State, and individuals are enemies only by accident, not as men, nor even as citizens, but as soldiers. . . . The foreigner, whether king, individual, or people, who robs, kills, or detains subjects without declaring war on the prince, is not an enemy but a brigand. Even in real war, a just prince, while he rightly takes possession *of all that belongs to the public in an enemy's country,* respects the lives and goods of individuals; he respects the rights on which his own are founded."

13. See, e.g., Grotius, "the right to use things that have become the property of another" (Grotius, *De Jure Belli ac Pacis,* bk. 2, chap. 2, pp. vi-xvii); Samuel Pufendorf, *De Jure Naturae et Gentium* (Oxford: Clarendon, 1934), bk. 2, chap. 6, sec. 5.

14. Collective ownership of property is characterized by a rule of allocation that stipulates that the "use of material resources in particular cases is to be determined by reference to the collective interests of the society as a whole." Jeremy Waldron, *The Right to Private Property* (Oxford: Clarendon, 1988), 40.

15. Grotius, *De Jure Praedae Commentarius,* trans. G. L. Williams, with W. H. Zeydel (Oxford: Clarendon, 1950), 228.

16. Harold Demsetz, "Toward a Theory of Property Rights," in Erik G. Furubotn and Svetozar Pejovich, eds., *The Economics of Property Rights* (Cambridge, Mass.: Ballinger, 1974), 31–42, quotation on 34. See also the grander-scale "history" by Douglas North and Robert Paul Thomas, *The Rise of the Western World* (Cambridge: Cambridge University Press, 1974).

17. For a good, brief discussion of the ideological nature of such constructs, and a devastating critique of the economic theory of property rights and the economic analysis of law in general, see Alan Ryan, *Property* (Minneapolis: University of Minnesota Press, 1987), chap. 9. In addition to the minor problem that the empirical specification of transaction costs is usually not even contemplated, Ryan points out that Coase's argument does not establish the superiority of private property in counteracting the incentives that lead to the well-known tragedy of the commons. All it shows is the need of finding an arrangement by which the participants in a regime pay the full social costs of their activity. Thus, not only is a "public" solution logically equally possible, but it can be shown that many problems similar to the tragedy of the commons cannot be averted by the extension of private property rights. Furthermore, given the economic agnosticism as to what constitutes a "productive," as distinct from an "unproductive," transfer, privatization is likely to produce strategic behavior in people that encourages blackmail. Although hold-ups and blackmail are—of course—Pareto efficient, it is hard to claim that social welfare is thereby enhanced.

For an excellent discussion of the effective use of norms in private ordering, see Robert Ellickson, *Order without Law* (Cambridge: Harvard University Press, 1991). Ellickson shows in his study of dispute settlement among neighbors in Shasta County, California, that indeed private ordering (i.e., agreeing on specific rules and norms without governmental interference or legislation) is possible and effective, but that it does not follow the logic of Coase's analysis as outlined in his "Problem of Social Cost." Actually, according to this analysis, the reasons work exactly in the opposite way. The neighbors resort to private settlement and achieve efficient outcomes because of high transaction costs, not in spite of them. They also reach cooperative solutions not through bargains struck on the basis of established entitlements but by developing more diffuse and adaptive norms that *trump* formal entitlements.

18. Waldron, *Right to Private Property,* 31.

19. Honore prefers a different and rather arcane-looking classification and opposes the use of "bundles of rights" sticking with "things." For the classification, see Tony Honore, "Ownership," in *Making Law Bind* (New York: Oxford, 1987), 132, and for the argument concerning "things," see 134.

20. See Philip Allott, "Power Sharing in the Law of the Sea," *American Journal of International Law* 77 (Jan. 1983): 1–30.

21. See Leo Gross, "The Peace of Westphalia, 1648–1948," *American Journal of International Law* 42, no. 20 (1948): 47 f.

22. See in this context my "Of Systems, Boundaries, and Territoriality: An Inquiry into the Formation of the State System," *World Politics* 39 (Oct. 1986): 27–52.

23. See Charles Tilly, ed., *The Formation of the National States in Western Europe* (Princeton: Princeton University Press, 1975).

24. See Henry Kissinger, *A World Restored* (New York: Grosset and Dunlap, 1964).

25. For a discussion of these issues see Ti-Chiang Chen, *The International Law of Recognition* (London: Stevens, 1951).

26. See, e.g., John Locke's usage of "the people" in this sense in his *Second Treatise.*

27. See Robert Jackson, *Quasi-States: Sovereignty, International Relations, and the Third World* (Cambridge: Cambridge University Press, 1991).

28. See, e.g., the attempts of Myres McDougal and the "New Haven School" to create such a framework; for a brief outline of this framework see Myres McDougal, "Some Basic Concepts about International Law: A Policy-Oriented Framework," in Richard Falk and Saul Mendlovitz, eds., *The Strategy of World Order,* vol. 2, *International Law* (New York: World Law Fund, 1966); Myres McDougal and Harold Lasswell, "The Identification and Appraisal of Diverse Systems of Public Order," in ibid.; Myres McDougal and Lung-chu Chen, "The Protection of Aliens from Discrimination and World Public Order: Responsibility of States Conjoined with Human Rights," *American Journal of International Law* 70 (1976): 432–69.

29. See Rousseau, *Social Contract,* bk. 1, chap. 4.

30. *Curtiss Wright,* as quoted in William Bishop, *International Law, Cases, and Materials* (Boston: Little, Brown, 1962), 89.

31. Michael Levitin, "The Law of Force and the Force of Law: Grenada, the Falklands, and Humanitarian Intervention," *Harvard International Law Journal* 27 (spring 1986): 621–57, quotation on 654.

32. See *Great Britain v. Albania,* ICJ Reports 1949. In this case Great Britain had ordered its minesweepers into Albania's waters after mines had killed forty-four British sailors on a British ship that was utilizing the channel for transit passage. The British did not claim self-defense as a basis for their action but used the minesweeping as "a self-help measure to obtain evidence to support the British claim for damages and therefore as an aid in administering justice." Oscar Schachter, *International Law in Theory and Practice* (Dordrecht: Nijhoff, 1985); see also the extensive

discussion in James L. Brierly, *The Law of Nations*, 6th ed. (New York: Oxford University Press, 1963), chap. 9.

33. See *Military and Para-Military Activities in and against Nicaragua* (Nicaragua vs. US), 1985 ICJ 169.

34. This argument was advanced by Myres S. McDougal and Florentino P. Feliciano, "Legal Regulation of Resort to International Coercion: Aggression and Self-Defense in Policy Perspective," *Yale Law Journal* 68 (1959): 1057.

35. Not only does the Security Council have ample enforcement powers under Chapter VII, but antecedent to any peace-keeping measure the council's determination of what constitutes an abridgment of "territorial integrity" is authoritative. On the latter point see Rosalyn Higgins, "The Place of International Law in the Settlement of Disputes by the Security Council," *American Journal of International Law* 64 (1970); see also Ian Brownlie, *Principles of Public International Law*, 3d ed. (Oxford: Clarendon, 1979), 696 f.

36. See C.M.H. Waldock, "The Regulation of the Use of Force by Individual States in International Law," *Recueil des Cours* 81, no. 2 (1952): 451–517.

37. See David Luban, "Just War and Human Rights," *Philosophy and Public Affairs* 9 (winter 1990): 160–81.

38. W. Michael Reisman, "Coercion and Self-Determination: Construing Charter Art. 4(4)," *American Journal of International Law* 78 (July 1984): 642–45, quotation on 643.

39. See Luban's own interpretation in his "The Romance of the Nation State," 392.

40. For a general discussion of this point see chap. 6 of my *Rules, Norms, and Decisions* (Cambridge, 1989).

41. Luban, "Romance," 392, 397.

42. Reisman, "Coercion and Self-Determination," 644.

43. Ibid., 644.

44. Ibid., 643.

45. See, e.g., the debate about the quasi-authoritative status of General Assembly resolutions in international law and the arguments about "soft law." See Rosalyn Higgins, *The Development of International Law through the Political Organs of the United Nations* (New York: Oxford University Press, 1963); Jorge Castaneda, *Legal Effects of United Nations Resolutions* (New York: Columbia University Press, 1969); G. Arangio-Ruiz, "The Normative Role of the General Assembly of the United Nations and the Declaration of Principles of Friendly Relations," *Recueil des Cours* 137, pt. 3 (1972): 419–742. For a discussion of "soft law," see Joseph Gold, "Strengthening the Soft International Law of Exchange Arrangements," *American Journal of International Law* 77 (July 1983): 443–89; Ignaz Seidl-Hohenveldern, "International Economic Soft Law," *Recueil des Cours* 163, pt. 2 (1979): 165 ff; see also a critical argument against "soft law" by Prosper Weil, "Towards Relative Normativity in International Law?" *American Journal of International Law* 77 (July 1983): 413–42; Oscar Schachter, "The Twilight Existence of Non-binding International Agreements," *American Journal of International Law* 71 (1977): 296–304. For a fundamental discussion of the issues of obligation and legitimacy see Thomas Franck, "Legitimacy in the International System," *American Journal of International Law* 82 (Oct. 1988): 705–59.

46. This point is eloquently made by R. S. Summers, "Naive Instrumentalism and the Law," in P.M.S. Hacker and J. Raz, eds., *Law, Morality, and Society* (Oxford: Clarendon, 1977), chap. 6. See also Gordon Gottlieb, "The Nature of International Law: Toward a Second Concept of Law," in Cyril Black and Richard Falk, eds., *The Future of the International Legal Order,* vol. 4 (Princeton: Princeton University Press, 1972), chap. 9.

47. See, e.g., the argument by Fernando Téson, *Humanitarian Intervention: An Inquiry into Law and Morality* (Dobbs Ferry, N.Y.: Transnational, 1988), chap. 7.

48. See also Ian Brownlie's assessment of state practice of the League and of postwar state practice in his "Humanitarian Intervention," in John Norton Moore, ed., *Law and Civil War in the Modern World* (Baltimore: Johns Hopkins University Press, 1974), chap. 10.

49. See Michael Akehurst, "Humanitarian Intervention," in Hedley Bull, ed., *Intervention in World Politics* (Oxford: Clarendon, 1984), chap. 7, quotation on 97.

50. This is the standard enunciated in the *Caroline* case.

51. See, e.g., the discussion of Manoucher Ganji, *International Protection of Human Rights* (Geneva: Libraire Droz, 1962), chap. 1. See also the work of Richard Lillich, who relies heavily on Ganji's argument of a customary right to humanitarian intervention in his reply to Brownlie in Richard Lillich, "Humanitarian Intervention: A Reply to Ian Brownlie and a Plea for Constructive Alternatives," in Moore, ed., *Law and Civil War in the Modern World,* chap. 10.

52. He warns: "Collective irresponsibility in the use of force is not out of the question, nor is collective timidity and indecisiveness. . . . Collective gun-shyness is perhaps as likely to be encountered as unilateral trigger-happiness and is not necessarily more conducive to world order." Inis L. Claude, "The Vogue of Collectivism in International Relations," in *States and the Global System* (New York: St. Martin's, 1988), chap. 10, quotation on 142.

CHAPTER THREE INTERVENTION FOR THE COMMON GOOD

1. According to R.B.J. Walker, sovereignty "is the constitutive *principle* of modern political life"; and to Robert H. Jackson, "sovereign statehood [is] the constitutive principle of international society." R.B.J. Walker, "Sovereignty, Identity, Community: Reflections on the Horizons of Contemporary Political Practice," in R.B.J. Walker and Saul H. Mendlovitz, eds., *Contending Sovereignties: Redefining Political Community* (Boulder, Colo.: Rienner, 1990), 159, Walker's emphasis; Robert H. Jackson, "Quasi-States, Dual Regimes, and Neoclassical Theory: International Jurisprudence and the Third World," *International Organization* 41 (1987): 519. See also Nicholas Greenwood Onuf, "Sovereignty: Outline of a Conceptual History," *Alternatives* 16 (1991): 425–46.

2. "A rational being belongs to the realm of ends as a member when he gives universal laws in it while also himself subject to these laws. He belongs to it as sovereign *[oberhaupt]* when he . . . is subject to the will of no other." Immanuel Kant, *Foundations of the Metaphysics of Morals,* trans. Lewis White Beck (New York: Liberal Arts, 1959), 52.

3. Richard K. Ashley, "Living on Border Lines: Man, Poststructuralism, and War," in James Der Derian and Michael J. Shapiro, eds., *International/Intertextual Read-*

ings: Postmodern Readings of World Politics (Lexington, Mass.: Lexington Books, 1989), 264–71; and Richard K. Ashley, "Imposing International Purpose: Notes on a Problematic of Governance," in Ernst-Otto Czempiel and James N. Rosenau, eds., *Global Changes and Theoretical Challenges: Approaches to World Politics for the 1990s* (Lexington, Mass.: Lexington Books, 1989), 264–69.

4. Emmerich de Vattel, *The Law of Nations or the Principles of Natural Law Applied to the Conduct and to the Affairs of Nations and of Sovereigns*, trans. Charles G. Fenwick (Washington, D.C.: Carnegie Institution, 1916), Introduction, sec. 15, p. 6. Though Vattel usually gets credit for announcing the principle of nonintervention, his more precise formulation of nations' rights and duties in this respect follows Christian Wolff's. Vattel, *Law of Nations*, pt. 2, chap. 4, sec. 54, p. 131; Christian Wolff, *Jus gentium methodo scientifica pertractatum*, trans. Joseph H. Drake (Oxford: Clarendon, 1934), sec. 269, p. 137.

5. Vattel, *Law of Nations*, Introduction, sec. 13, p. 6.

6. John Stuart Mill, *Principles of Political Economy with Some of Their Applications to Social Philosophy*, ed. W. J. Ashley (London: Longmans, Green, 1929), chap. 11. Mill defined "intervention" as the "extension of governmental agency" at cost to "individual agency" (p. 948).

7. On the concept and practice of international intervention, see, for example, "Intervention and World Politics" (special issue), *Journal of International Affairs* 22 (1968): 165–246; R. J. Vincent, *Nonintervention and International Order* (Princeton: Princeton University Press, 1974); Hedley Bull, ed., *Intervention in World Politics* (Oxford: Oxford University Press, 1984). On the admissibility of intervention as a legal question, see Ellery C. Stowell, *Intervention in International Law* (Washington, D.C.: Byrnes, 1921); Fernando R. Téson, *Humanitarian Intervention: An Inquiry into Law and Morality* (Dobbs Ferry, N.Y.: Transnational, 1988); Lori Fisler Damrosch and David J. Scheffer, eds., *Law and Force in the New International Order* (Boulder, Colo.: Westview, 1991), 111–243. Téson's book has an extensive bibliography (Téson, *Humanitarian Intervention*, 251–63).

8. Thus Stowell devoted the greater part of his classic monograph *Intervention in International Law* to "humanitarian intervention," with subheadings for persecution, oppression, uncivilized warfare, injustice, suppression of the slave trade, humanitarian asylum, and foreign commerce (pp. 51–277).

9. Nicholas Greenwood Onuf, *World of Our Making: Rules and Rule in Social Theory and International Relations* (Columbia: University of South Carolina Press, 1989), chap. 1.

10. On "constructivism" used pejoratively to describe deliberate and sustained efforts to make over society, see F. A. Hayek, *Law, Legislation, and Liberty: A New Statement of the Liberal Principles of Justice and Political Economy, I: Rules and Order* (Chicago: University of Chicago Press, 1973), 8–34. I would use the term *constitutivism* for my position but for the difficulty I have in saying it.

11. I have adapted this definition from Max Black, *Models and Metaphors* (Ithaca: Cornell University Press, 1962), 208. See further Onuf, *World of Our Making*, 78–81.

12. See Anthony Giddens, *New Rules of Sociological Method: A Positive Critique of Interpretative Sociology* (New York: Basic Books, 1976); idem, *Central Problems in Social Theory: Action, Structure, and Contradiction in Social Analysis* (Berkeley and Los Angeles: University of California Press, 1979); idem, *The Consti-*

tution of Society: Outline of the Theory of Structuration (Berkeley and Los Angeles: University of California Press, 1984); and David Held and John B. Thompson, eds., *Social Theory of Modern Societies: Anthony Giddens and His Critics* (Cambridge: Cambridge University Press, 1989), which includes Giddens's reply to his critics (pp. 249–301). See also Onuf, *World of Our Making*, 55–65.

13. Giddens, *Constitution of Society*, 17.

14. Ibid. To similar effect: "Structure, as recursively organized sets of rules and resources, is out of time and space, save in its instantiations and co-ordination as memory traces" (p. 25).

15. Giddens, *Central Problems in Social Theory*, 66; idem, *Constitution of Society*, 25.

16. Giddens, *Central Problems in Social Theory*, 66–68; idem, *Constitution of Society*, 21–23. Noting Giddens's "vacillation between rules as analytical constituents of *praxis*, and rules as concrete practices in themselves," Ira J. Cohen concluded that Giddens tended "to conceive rules from an analytic standpoint." Ira J. Cohen, *Structuration Theory: Anthony Giddens and the Constitution of Social Life* (New York: St. Martin's, 1989), 237.

17. Onuf, *World of Our Making*, 81–94.

18. Ibid., 110–19.

19. Ibid., 67–78, 128–44.

20. See further Nicholas Onuf, "The Constitution of International Society," *European Journal of International Law*, forthcoming.

21. Giddens, *New Rules of Sociological Method*, 75, there underscored, and repeated in idem, *Central Problems in Social Theory*, 55. Further: "The concept of agency as I advocate it here, involving 'intervention' in a potentially malleable object world, relates directly to the more generalised notion of *Praxis*" (pp. 55–56). Cf. Roy Bhaskar, *The Possibility of Naturalism: A Philosophical Critique of Contemporary Human Sciences* (Atlantic Highlands, N.J.: Humanities, 1979), 104:

> Now *praxis*, doing or acting, typically consists in causally intervening in the natural (material) world, subject to the possibility of a reflexive monitoring of that intervention. . . . Now human activity is in fact a more or less continuous stream in time of such (more or less deliberate, more or less routine) causal intervenings in the world, subject to the continuing possibility of reflexive self-awareness, but only analytically separable into *episodes*.

22. Walker, "Sovereignty, Identity, Community," 159. On the drafting and adoption of the U.S. Constitution (1787–88) as an oblique challenge to the concept of state sovereignty, see Peter Onuf and Nicholas Onuf, *Federal Union, Modern World: The Law of Nations in an Age of Revolutions, 1776–1814* (Madison, Wisc.: Madison House, 1993), chaps. 2, 5.

23. See F. H. Hinsley, *Sovereignty*, 2d ed. (Cambridge: Cambridge University Press, 1986), for a conventional history. The sketch presented here follows Onuf, "Sovereignty," though with greater attention to effects of conceptual change on rules.

24. Kratochwil's contribution to this volume centers on the development of territoriality as a legal property of statehood, and thus "the sovereignty game" that states play as international actors.

25. Indeed the act of withdrawing concessions or assistance against the wishes of its recipient is often castigated as interventionary. See Lori Fisler Damrosch, "Politics across Borders: Nonintervention and Nonforcible Influence over Domestic Affairs," *American Journal of International Law* 83 (1989): 31–34. The classic analysis of policies to create manipulable dependencies by conferring advantages subject to withdrawal is Albert O. Hirschman's *National Power and the Structure of Foreign Trade,* expanded ed. (Berkeley and Los Angeles: University of California Press, 1980).

26. On "territorial integrity and political independence," see Anthony D'Amato, *International Law: Process and Prospect* (Dobbs Ferry, N.Y.: Transnational, 1987), 57–74.

27. Nicholas Greenwood Onuf, "The Principle of Nonintervention, the United Nations, and the International System," *International Organization* 25 (1971): 214–15.

28. "Declaration on the Inadmissibility of Intervention in the Domestic Affairs of States and the Protection of their Independence and Sovereignty," Resolution 20/2131, Dec. 21, 1965, adopted by a vote of 109–0–1 (109 for, 0 against, 1 abstaining), and summarized in Onuf, "Principle of Nonintervention," 216–19.

29. "Declaration on the Principles of Friendly Relations and Cooperation among States," Resolution 25/2625, Oct. 24, 1970, adopted without vote. This declaration is widely described as "an authoritative interpretation of the UN Charter." Damrosch, "Politics across Borders," 9.

30. "Declaration on the Inadmissibility of Intervention and Interference in the Internal Affairs of States," Resolution 36/103, Dec. 9, 1981, adopted by a vote of 120–2–6. Among the declaration's more tendentious provisions (II[1]), is the stipulation that states must "refrain from the exploitation and the distortion of human rights issues as a means of interference in the internal affairs of States, of exerting pressure on other States or creating distrust and disorder within or among States or groups of States."

31. Consider subversion, which Resolutions 20/2131 and 25/2625 list as an inadmissible form of intervention. Loch K. Johnson has identified forty-two "options" available to agents engaging in "covert operations" and ranked them in order of intrusiveness. He asked, "where should one draw a bright line against excessive covert operations?" His answer:

> Each important covert operation warrants inspection on a case-by-case basis, drawing on the substantive knowledge and ethical wisdom [?] of a small number of well-informed individuals: elected officials in the executive and legislative branches (and their top aides) who understand the theory and practice of strategic intelligence, who have studied the conditions in the target nation and its region, and, most important in a democracy, who are sensitive to the likely attitudes of the . . . public toward the proposed secret intervention.

To assist these individuals, Johnson proposed "a checklist of eleven guidelines"; there is no "bright line." "On Drawing a Bright Line for Covert Operations," *American Journal of International Law* 86 (1992): 286, 299, 305.

32. Leo Gross, "Expenses of the United Nations for Peacekeeping Operations: The Advisory Opinion of the International Court of Justice," *International Organization* 17 (1963): 26–35; Rahmatullah Khan, *Implied Powers of the United Nations* (Delhi: Vikas, 1970), 17–73.

33. See, in addition, Nicholas Greenwood Onuf, *Reprisals: Rituals, Rules, Ratio-*

nales, Center of International Studies, Princeton University, Research Monograph no. 42 (1974), 53–55. Note, however, that an emphasis on purposes may also lead to a concern with "original intent" and a restrictive interpretation of the powers available to the organization or to members' governments acting on its behalf. Tom J. Farer, "An Inquiry into the Legitimacy of Humanitarian Intervention," in Damrosch and Scheffer, eds., *Law and Force in the New International Order,* 190–92.

34. Thomas Franck and Edward Weisband, *Word Politics* (New York: Oxford University Press, 1971); Onuf, *World of Our Making,* 219–27.

35. Cf. W. Michael Reisman, "Sovereignty and Human Rights in Contemporary International Law," *American Journal of International Law* 84 (1990): 866–76.

36. For more on self-determination, see W. Ofuatey-Kodjoe, *The Principle of Self-Determination in International Law* (New York: Nellen, 1977); Hurst Hannum, *Autonomy, Sovereignty, and Self-Determination: The Accommodation of Conflicting Rights* (Philadelphia: University of Pennsylvania Press, 1990).

37. Nevertheless, when civil strife reached a level that seriously affected other states, their governments were free under traditional international law to recognize both sides as belligerents, thereby bringing neutral rights and duties into play. Such an act was significantly interventionary from the embattled government's perspective, but not necessarily unwelcome, given the content of neutral states' rights and duties. The American Civil War is a well-known case in point. See Quincy Wright, "The American Civil War, 1861–1865," in Richard A. Falk, ed., *The International Law of Civil War* (Baltimore: Johns Hopkins Press, 1971), 30–109.

38. Conversely, "international law issues no general license to any volunteer intervenor—whether well-intentioned or self-serving—to move in unilaterally with armed force." John Lawrence Hargrove, "Intervention by Invitation and the Politics of the New World Order," in Damrosch and Scheffer, eds., *Law and Force in the New International Order,* 124.

39. Resolution 678, Nov. 29, 1990, adopted 12–2–1. At least two resolutions adopted in the aftermath of hostilities conspicuously intervene in Iraqi affairs. In Resolution 687, Apr. 3, 1991, adopted 12–1–2, the Security Council decided that "Iraq shall unconditionally accept" the elimination of chemical and biological weapons and of the means of producing and using nuclear weapons. In Resolution 688, Apr. 5, 1991, adopted 10–3–2, the Security Council condemned Iraq for repressing its civilian population and demanded that it stop immediately.

40. See, for example, Oscar Schachter, "United Nations Law in the Gulf Conflict," *American Journal of International Law* 85 (1991): 456–61; and Burns H. Weston, "Security Council Resolution 678 and Persian Gulf Decision Making: Precarious Diplomacy," ibid. 85 (1991): 518–22.

41. As to intervention in the instance of human rights abuses, there is a large and vital literature, including Weiss and Chopra's contribution to this volume. As to intervention enabling regime change through electoral process, see Damrosch, "Politics across Borders," 13–28; and Thomas M. Franck, "The Emerging Right to Democratic Governance," *American Journal of International Law* 86 (1992): 63–77.

The General Assembly's ambivalence with respect to the latter of these developments is nicely illustrated by its Resolutions 46/130 and 137, adopted December 17, 1991, by votes of 102–40–13 and 134–4–13, respectively, and entitled "Respect for the Principle of National Sovereignty and Non-Interference in the Internal Affairs of

States in Their Electoral Processes," and "Enhancing the Effectiveness of the Principle of Periodic and Genuine Elections." The General Assembly reiterated these principles a year later (Resolutions 47/130 and 138) by comparable votes.

42. Michel Foucault, *Power/Knowledge: Selected Interviews and Other Writings, 1972–1977*, ed. Colin Gordon, several translators (New York: Pantheon, 1980), 131. Most of Foucault's work deals with this phenomenon and its interventionary consequences. With particular reference to sovereignty, see Foucault, *Power/Knowledge*, 92–108; Michel Foucault, *History of Sexuality*, vol. 1, *An Introduction* (New York: Vintage Books, 1980), 135–50.

43. Robert D. Putnam and Nicholas Bayne, *Hanging Together: Cooperation and Conflict in Seven-Power Summits* (Cambridge: Harvard University Press, 1987); Wendy Dobson, *Economic Policy Coordination: Requiem or Prologue?* (Washington, D.C.: Institute for International Economics, 1991).

44. Dobson, *Economic Policy Coordination*, 2, footnote deleted.

45. Ibid., 119.

46. On surveillance (a term of particular import for Foucault), see ibid., 47–62.

47. Leonard W. Doob, *Intervention: Guides and Perils* (New Haven: Yale University Press, 1993), 1.

48. Ibid., 165, emphasis deleted.

49. Ibid., 27.

50. Michel Foucault, *Birth of the Clinic* (New York: Pantheon, 1973).

51. Doob, *Intervention*, 177. One of Johnson's recommendations in "A Bright Line for Covert Operations," 304, suggests the reach of the clinical model: "Like the physician, the managers of strategic intelligence should employ the least interventionist means possible to cure the illness, inflicting the least amount of violence on the patient." Similarly, interventions in foreign exchange markets are either "sterilized"—"official purchases or sales are offset by domestic transactions"—or not. Dobson, *Economic Policy Coordination*, 102.

52. See generally John Williamson, ed., *IMF Conditionality* (Washington, D.C.: Institute for International Economics, 1983); Thomas J. Biersteker, ed., *International Financial Negotiations* (Boulder, Colo.: Westview, 1992).

CHAPTER FOUR INTERNATIONAL COMMUNITY BEYOND THE COLD WAR

I am grateful to Daniel Deudney, Nicholas Onuf, and especially Gene Lyons for helpful comments on an earlier version of this chapter. I also wish to thank the Social Sciences and Humanities Research Council of Canada for funding the research upon which it is based.

1. See S. M. Lynn-Jones and S. E. Miller, eds., *The Cold War and After* (Cambridge: MIT Press, 1993); and R. O. Keohane, J. S. Nye, and S. Hoffmann, eds., *After the Cold War* (Cambridge: Harvard University Press, 1993).

2. See, for example, M. Wight, *International Theory: The Three Traditions* (Leicester: Leicester University Press, 1991), chap. 1; and Hedley Bull, *The Anarchical Society* (London: Macmillan, 1977), chap. 2. For a superb historical reconstruction of this perspective see David Armstrong, *Revolution and World Order* (Oxford: Clarendon, 1993), chap. 1.

3. F. W. Maitland, "Moral Personality and Legal Personality," in D. Nichols, ed., *The Pluralist State* (London: Macmillan, 1975), 159–66.

4. I elaborate on this point in "Can International Society be Green?" in R. Fawn, J. Larkins, and R. Newman, eds., *Beyond International Society,* forthcoming.

5. See, for example, Richard Falk, "A New Paradigm for International Legal Studies: Prospects and Proposals," in R. Falk, F. Kratochwil, and S. H. Mendlovitz, eds., *International Law: A Contemporary Perspective* (Boulder, Colo.: Westview, 1985), 651–702.

6. Alan James, *Sovereign Statehood: The Basis of International Society* (London: Allen & Unwin, 1986), 25.

7. This feature of sovereignty was commented on in 1826 by James Kent, a Federalist, in the following terms: "When the United States ceased to be a part of the British empire, and assumed the character of an independent nation, they became subject to the system of rules which reason, morality, and custom had established among the civilized nations of Europe, as their public law." Quoted by Daniel Patrick Moynihan in *On the Law of Nations* (Cambridge: Harvard University Press, 1990), 15.

8. See Martin Wight, "De systematibus civitatum," in Hedley Bull, ed., *Systems of States* (London: Leicester University Press, 1977), 21–45.

9. In international law, according to Antonio Cassese, human beings were considered to be "under the exclusive control of States" from 1648 until 1918. See his *International Law in a Divided World* (Oxford: Clarendon, 1988), 99–103.

10. T. Hobbes, *Leviathan* (Oxford: Blackwell, 1946), chap. 13.

11. See Evan Luard, *International Agencies* (London: Macmillan, 1977), 320–21.

12. In the twentieth century, international legal subjects other than states have been recognized, including individuals, peoples under colonial rule, and international organizations. NGOs may be emerging as international legal subjects, although their independence of sovereign states is far from certain. See Cassese, *International Law in a Divided World*, chap. 4.

13. For further discussion of this point see Robert H. Jackson and Alan James, eds., *States in a Changing World* (Oxford: Clarendon, 1993), chap. 1

14. I explore this distinction at length in Robert H. Jackson, *Quasi-States: Sovereignty, International Relations, and the Third World* (Cambridge: Cambridge University Press, 1990).

15. For further analysis of this episode see Jackson, *Quasi-States*, chaps. 3, 4.

16. The Spanish Dominican Francisco de Vitoria argued in defense of the natural rights of the Indians in the Spanish conquests and colonizations of the new world. See M. Donelan, "Spain and the Indies," in H. Bull and A. Watson, eds., *The Expansion of International Society* (Oxford: Clarendon, 1984), chap. 5.

17. For a recent statement see R. Connaughton, *Military Intervention in the 1990s: A New Logic of War* (New York: Routledge, 1992).

18. For a recent legal analysis, see A. Tanca, *Foreign Armed Intervention in Internal Conflict* (Boston: Nijhoff, 1993).

19. The Soviet Union, Cuba, and China engaged in imposed interventions in sub-Saharan Africa in the 1960s and 1970s against colonial governments, mainly Portuguese colonies and Rhodesia. But by that time colonialism was illegitimate, and increasingly even unlawful, which made such actions not fundamentally objectionable to the international community.

20. I explore this question at greater length in "Armed Humanitarianism," *International Journal* 48 (autumn 1993).

21. See the definitive essay on the subject by J. S. Mill, "A Few Words on Non-Intervention," in G. Himmelfarb, ed., *Essays on Politics and Culture: John Stuart Mill* (Garden City, N.Y.: Anchor Books, 1963), chap. 10. Also see M. Walzer, *Just and Unjust Wars*, 2d ed. (New York: Basic Books, 1992), chap. 6.

22. Samuel P. Huntington, "The Clash of Civilizations," *Foreign Affairs* 72 (summer 1993): 22–49.

23. M. Doyle, "Kant, Liberal Legacies, and Foreign Affairs," *Philosophy and Public Affairs* 12 (summer–fall 1983): 205–35, 325–53.

24. Hobbes, *Leviathan*, chap. 13.

25. See G. Loescher and L. Monahan, eds., *Refugees and International Relations* (Oxford: Clarendon, 1990); A. Dowty, *Closed Borders* (New Haven: Yale University Press, 1987); and L. Gordenker, *Refugees in International Politics* (London: Croom Helm, 1987).

26. N. Van Hear, "Forced Migration and the Gulf Conflict, 1990–1991," *Oxford International Review* 3, no. 1 (1991): 20–21.

27. That is the problem of the revolutionary state in international society. See Armstrong, *Revolution and World Order*, chaps. 2–5.

CHAPTER FIVE   SOVEREIGNTY UNDER SIEGE

Parts of this chapter first appeared in "Sovereignty Is No Longer Sacrosanct," *Ethics and International Affairs* 6 (1992): 95–117, reprinted with permission.

1. For an early discussion, see Thomas G. Weiss and Kurt M. Campbell, "Military Humanitarianism," *Survival* 33, no. 5 (1991): 451–64. See also "Humanitarian Intervention: Caught in the Cross Fire," *Harvard International Review* 16, no. 1 (1993): 8–30; and Adam Roberts, "Humanitarian War: Military Intervention and Human Rights," *International Affairs* 69, no. 3 (1993): 429–49.

2. See also Thomas G. Weiss, "Intervention: Whither the United Nations?" *Washington Quarterly* 17, no. 1 (1993): 109–28.

3. For a discussion of possible reforms, see Erskine Childers and Brian Urquhart, "Strengthening International Response to Humanitarian Emergencies," unpublished document, dated Oct. 1991, from the Dag Hammarskjöld and Ford Foundations; and the main UN background document, "Strengthening of the Coordination of Humanitarian Emergency Assistance of the United Nations," UN Doc. no. A/46/568, Oct. 10, 1991.

4. "Note by the President of the Security Council," UN Doc. no. S/23500, Jan. 31, 1992, 3.

5. See James N. Rosenau, *The United Nations in a Turbulent World* (Boulder, Colo.: Rienner, 1992).

6. See also Jarat Chopra, "The Obsolescence of Intervention under International Law," in *Subduing Sovereignty* (Miami: Florida International University Press, forthcoming).

7. See further, on the debate behind Resolution 688, "Security Council Demands Iraq End Repression of Kurds, Other Groups; Calls Civilian's Plight 'Threat to Peace and Security,'" UNDPI Press Release, SC/5268, Apr. 5, 1991.

8. See R. J. Vincent, *Human Rights and International Relations* (Cambridge: Cambridge University Press, 1986).

9. See, for example, Donella H. Meadows et al., *The Limits to Growth* (New York: New American Library, 1972); Richard J. Barnet and Ronald E. Muller, *Global Reach* (New York: Simon and Schuster, 1974).

10. Roland Dahnreuther, *The Gulf Conflict: A Political and Strategic Analysis*, Adelphi Papers, no. 264 (London: International Institute for Strategic Studies, 1992), 74.

11. UN Doc. no. A/46/1, Sept. 6, 1991, 10–11. This theme was also prominent in an earlier and much-publicized speech, "Secretary-General's Address at the University of Bordeaux," UNDPI Press Release SG/SM/4560, Apr. 24, 1991.

12. For a discussion of this decision making with an emphasis on American policy, see Andrew Natsios, "Food through Force: Humanitarian Intervention and U.S. Policy," *Washington Quarterly* 17, no. 1 (1994): 129–44.

13. Gerald B. Helman and Steven R. Ratner, "Saving Failed States," *Foreign Policy*, no. 89 (winter 1992–93): 3–20.

14. See, for instance, Richard B. Lillich, ed., *Humanitarian Intervention and the United Nations* (Charlottesville: University Press of Virginia, 1973); idem, "Forcible Self-Help by States to Protect Human Rights," *Iowa Law Review* 53 (1967): 325; J.P.L. Fonteyne, "The Customary International Law Doctrine of Humanitarian Intervention," *California Western International Law Journal* 4 (1974): 203; Bruce Chilstrom, "Humanitarian Intervention under Contemporary International Law," *Yale Studies in World Public Order* (1974): 93; and H. Scott-Farley, "State Actor, Humanitarian Intervention, and International Law: Reopening Pandora's Box," *Georgia Journal of International and Comparative Law* 10, no. 1 (1981): 29–63.

15. For conflicting views on whether the pact outlawed formally declared "war" or uses of force short of a formal state of war, see D. W. Bowett, *Self-Defence in International Law* (Manchester: Manchester University Press, 1958), 132–38; and Ian Brownlie, *International Law and the Use of Force by States* (Oxford: Clarendon Press, 1963), 80–92.

16. See also Leland M. Goodrich and Edvard Hambro, *Charter of the United Nations: Commentary and Documents*, 2d ed. (Boston: World Peace Foundation, 1949), 262–66.

17. See, for instance, Robert Taber, *The War of the Flea: Guerrilla Warfare Theory and Practice* (London: Paladin, 1970).

18. James N. Rosenau, *Turbulence in World Politics: A Theory of Change and Continuity* (Princeton: Princeton University Press, 1990); Augustus Richard Norton, "The Security Legacy of the 1980s in the Third World," in Thomas G. Weiss and Meryl A. Kessler, eds., *Third World Security in the Post–Cold War Era* (Boulder, Colo.: Rienner 1991), 19–34; Lawrence Freedman, "Order and Disorder in the New World," *Foreign Affairs* 71, no. 1 (1991–92): 20–37; James N. Rosenau, "Normative Challenges in a Turbulent World," *Ethics and International Affairs* 6 (1992); Charles W. Kegley Jr., "The New Global Order: The Power Principle in a Pluralistic World," ibid., 6 (1992): 1–40; Daniel Patrick Moynihan, *Pandemonium: Ethnicity in International Politics* (New York: Oxford University Press, 1993); Joel Kotkin, *Tribes: How Race, Religion, and Identity Determine Success in the New Global Economy* (New York: Random House, 1993); "Ethnic Conflict and International Security" (special issue), *Survival* 35, no. 1 (1993); and "Reconstructing Nations and States" (special issue), *Daedalus* 122, no. 3 (1993).

19. For a general discussion, see Weiss and Kessler, eds., *Third World Security.* For specific case studies, see Thomas G. Weiss and James G. Blight, eds., *The Suffering Grass: Superpowers and Regional Conflict in Southern Africa and the Caribbean* (Boulder, Colo.: Rienner, 1992).

20. See Thomas M. Franck and Nigel S. Rodley, "After Bangladesh: The Law of Humanitarian Intervention by Military Force," *American Journal of International Law* 67 (1973): 275; Brownlie, *International Law and the Use of Force by States,* 338–42; Ian Brownlie, "Thoughts on Kind-Hearted Gunmen," in Lillich, ed., *Humanitarian Intervention,* 139–48; Tom J. Farer, "Humanitarian Intervention: The View from Charlottesville," in ibid., 149–64; and Jack Donnelly, "Humanitarian Intervention and American Foreign Policy: Law, Morality and Politics," *Journal of International Affairs* 37 (1984): 311–28.

21. See for instance, Lillich, "Forcible Self-Help," 325–51; John Norton Moore, "The Control of Foreign Intervention in Internal Conflict," *Virginia Journal of International Law* 9 (1969): 261–64; Myres McDougal and Michael Reisman, "Response by Professors McDougal and Reisman," *International Lawyer* 3 (1969): 444; H. Lauterpacht, *International Law and Human Rights* (London: Stevens, 1950), 120–21; L. Oppenheim, *International Law: A Treatise,* (ed., H. Lauterpacht) 8th ed. (London: Longmans, 1955), 667–72.

22. Louis René Beres, "International Law, Personhood, and the Prevention of Genocide," *Loyola of Los Angeles International and Comparative Law Journal* 11 (1989): 25–65, cited in Thomas R. Gillespie, "International Law and Human Rights: Continuing the Search for Acceptable Standards for Invoking Humanitarian Intervention" (paper presented at the International Studies Association Annual Meeting, Vancouver, B.C., Mar. 20–23, 1991).

23. See Larry Minear et al., *Humanitarianism under Siege* (Trenton, N.J.: Red Sea, 1990). This was one of the themes in Thomas G. Weiss and Larry Minear, "Do International Ethics Matter? Humanitarian Politics in the Sudan," *Ethics and International Affairs* 5 (1991): 197–214.

24. See Cyril E. Black, "Challenges to an Evolving Legal Order," in Cyril E. Black and Richard A. Falk, eds., *The Future of the International Legal Order* (Princeton: Princeton University Press, 1969), 1:23–36; Richard A. Falk, "The Interplay of Westphalia and Charter Conceptions of International Legal Order," in ibid.; idem, *Legal Order in a Violent World* (Princeton: Princeton University Press, 1968); Wolfgang Friedmann, *The Changing Structure of International Law* (New York: Columbia University Press, 1964); and Philip C. Jessup, *A Modern Law of Nations* (New York: Macmillan, 1951).

25. See Jack Donnelly, *Universal Human Rights in Theory and Practice* (Ithaca: Cornell University Press, 1989); David P. Forsythe, *The Internationalization of Human Rights* (Lexington, Mass.: Lexington Books, 1991); Terry Nardin and David R. Mopel, eds., *Traditions of International Ethics* (Cambridge: Cambridge University Press, 1992); United Nations Educational, Scientific, and Cultural Organization, *International Dimensions of Humanitarian Law* (Dordrecht: Nijhoff, 1988); and Marcel A. Boisard, *L'humanisme de l'Islam* (Paris: Michel, 1979).

26. See David P. Forsythe, "Human Rights in the Post Cold War World," *Fletcher Forum of World Affairs* 15, no. 2 (1991): 55–70.

27. For a discussion of the significance of these resolutions, see Mario Bettati,

"Un droit d'ingérence?" *Revue Générale de Droit International Public*, no. 3 (July–Sept. 1991): 639–70.

28. See also John Mackinlay and Jarat Chopra, "Second Generation Multinational Operations," *Washington Quarterly* 15, no. 3 (1992): 113–30; and idem, *A Draft Concept of Second Generation Multinational Operations, 1993* (Providence, R.I.: Thomas J. Watson Jr. Institute for International Studies, 1993).

29. United Nations Charter, Article 2(4); "Declaration on the Inadmissability of Intervention in the Domestic Affairs of States," General Assembly Resolution 20/2131, Dec. 21, 1965; "Declaration on Principles of International Law Concerning Friendly Relations and Co-operation among States," General Assembly Resolution 25/2625 Oct. 24, 1970.

30. Louis Henkin, "Law and Politics in International Relations: State and Human Values," *Journal of International Affairs*, spring–summer 1990, 183–208.

31. *Nationality Decrees Issued in Tunis and Morocco Case*, PCIJ, ser. B, no. 4, 1923, p. 143.

32. Hedley Bull, *The Anarchical Society* (New York: Columbia University Press, 1977).

33. See also Philip Allott, *Eunomia: New Order for a New World* (Oxford: Oxford University Press, 1990), chap. 3.

34. See *The Geneva Conventions of August 12, 1949, and Protocols Additional to the Geneva Conventions of August 12, 1949* (Geneva: International Committee of the Red Cross, 1989).

35. F. H. Hinsley, *Sovereignty*, 2d ed. (Cambridge: Cambridge University Press, 1986), chap. 1. This historical discussion is from chap. 2. See also Allott, *Eunomia*, par. 16.15 et seq.

36. The distinguishing feature of a new order established by the Treaty of Westphalia, state sovereignty obscured the humanitarian intentions of earlier founders of international law. See Theodor Meron, "Common Rights of Mankind in Gentili, Grotius, and Suárez," *American Journal of International Law* 85, no. 99 (1991): 110–16.

37. See R. J. Vincent, *Nonintervention and International Order* (Princeton: Princeton University Press, 1974).

38. See particularly, R. P. Anand, "Sovereign Equality of States in International Law," *Receuil des Cours*, 1986, pt. 2, pp. 11–228; and C. W. Jenks, *A New World of Law?* (London: Longmans, 1969), 133.

39. See Peter I. Hajnal, ed., *The Seven Power Summit: Documents from the Summits of Industrialized Countries, 1975–1989* (Millwood, N.Y.: Kraus, 1989).

40. Antonio Cassese, *International Law in a Divided World* (Oxford: Clarendon, 1986), 391. On the concept of "the common heritage of mankind" generally, see chap. 14.

41. Allott, *Eunomia*, par. 16.65.

42. See Jarat Chopra, "The New Subjects of International Law," *Brown Foreign Affairs Journal*, spring 1991, 27–30.

43. Article 6, *Judgement of the Nuremberg International Military Tribunal, 1946, American Journal of International Law* 41 (1947): 172; Article IV, "Convention on the Prevention and Punishment of the Crime of Genocide 1948," *United Nations Treaty Series*, vol. 78, p. 277.

44. D. W. Bowett, *The Law of International Institutions* (London: Stevens and Sons, 1975), 354. Also, see generally chap. 12.

45. *Reparations for Injuries Suffered in the Service of the United Nations, ICJ Reports*, 1949, p. 174; the legal capacity of the United Nations, including privileges and immunities, is provided for in Articles 104 and 105 of the UN Charter; Article 6 of the 1986 Vienna Convention on the Law of Treaties between International Organizations or between States and International Organizations refers to "the capacity of an international organization to conclude treaties"; *Re The European Road Transport Agreement* (Case 22/70), Court of Justice of the European Communities, [1971] *Common Market Law Reports*, p. 335; *Maclaine Watson v Department of Trade and Industry*, Court of Appeal, [1988] 3 *All England Law Reports*.

46. *Texaco Overseas Petroleum Company v The Libyan Arab Republic* (1977) 53 *International Law Reports*, p. 389; *Texaco v Libya* and *BP v Libya* (1974) 53 *International Law Reports*, p. 329.

47. See Werner J. Feld and Robert S. Jordan, *International Organizations: A Comparative Approach* (New York: Praeger, 1988); and Harold K. Jacobson, *Networks of Interdependence* (New York: Knopf, 1984).

48. J. Crawford, "The Criteria for Statehood in International Law," *British Yearbook of International Law* 48 (1976–77): 93–182.

49. *Treatment of Polish Nationals in Danzig*, PCIJ., ser. A/B, no. 44, p. 24; *Reparations for Injuries, ICJ Reports*, 1949, p. 180. Article 27 of the 1969 Vienna Convention on the Law of Treaties codified this principle with regard to treaties.

50. Allott, *Eunomia*, par. 11.28.

51. See W. Michael Reisman, "Sovereignty and Human Rights in Contemporary International Law," *American Journal of International Law* 84 (1990): 866–76.

52. See Heather A. Wilson, *International Law and the Use of Force by National Liberation Movements* (Oxford: Clarendon, 1988), chap. 7.

53. On human rights as an international concern beyond the domestic jurisdiction of states, see Martin Dixon and Robert McCorquodale, *Cases and Materials on International Law* (London: Blackstone, 1991), 165; M. N. Shaw, *International Law*, 3d ed. (Cambridge: Grotius, 1991), 196.

54. Ali A. Mazrui, *Cultural Forces in World Politics* (London: Currey, 1990), 22. Mazrui also distinguishes between peace and justice on religious grounds: by adopting peace over justice, the UN Charter allied itself with the Christian god of love, whose son was regarded as a prince of peace, whereas the god of Islam and that of Judaism have been gods of justice.

55. Articles 1–3, 28–30, Universal Declaration of Human Rights (1948); Articles 2–22, 26, 27, International Covenant on Civil and Political Rights (1966); Articles 1–18 and Protocols 1 and 6, European Convention for the Protection of Human Rights and Fundamental Freedoms (1950); Part I and Part II, Article 1, European Social Charter (1961); Part VII, Helsinki Final Act (Final Act of the Conference on Security and Cooperation in Europe [1975]); American Convention on Human Rights (1969); Preamble and Articles 1, 2, 17–22, 24, 26–30, 56, African Charter on Human Rights and Peoples' Rights (1981).

56. John Tessitore and Susan Woolfson, eds., *Issues before the Forty-fifth General Assembly of the United Nations* (Lexington, Mass.: UNA-USA/Lexington Books, 1991), 119–20.

57. On the artificiality of the origins of positivism, see Roberto Ago, "Positive Law and International Law," *American Journal of International Law* 51 (1957): 691.

58. For instance, John Finnis identifies the following: life, knowledge, play, aesthetic experience, sociability (friendship), practical reasonableness, "religion" in *Natural Law and Natural Rights* (Oxford: Clarendon, 1980), chap. 4. On the generic principles of a constitution, see Allott, *Eunomia*, par. 11.5.

59. See also René David and John E. C. Briefly, *Major Legal Systems in the World Today* (London: Stevens and Sons, 1985).

60. Finnis, *Natural Law*, 403.

61. Allott, *Eunomia*, xvii.

62. See, for instance, comments by Olara Otunnu, Eqbal Ahmad, and Jagat Mehta in "After the Cold War: The North/South Divide," *Boston Review* 18 (June–Aug. 1993): 1–10.

63. For a recent thorough examination of one region, see Thomas Pakenham, *The Scramble for Africa* (New York: Random House, 1991).

64. Mohammed Ayoob, "The Security Predicament of the Third World State: Reflections on State Making in a Comparative Perspective," in Brian Job, ed., *The Insecurity Dilemma: National Security of Third World States* (Boulder, Colo.: Rienner, 1992), 79.

65. For a definition of a threshold below which humanitarian intervention might be triggered, see Theodor Meron and Allan Rosas, "A Declaration of Minimum Humanitarian Standards," *American Journal of International Law* 85 (1991): 375–81.

66. Lillich, "Forcible Self-Help," 347–51.

67. Moore, "Control of Foreign Intervention," 264.

68. Larry Minear, "A Strengthened Humanitarian System for the Post–Cold War Era," testimony before the Select Committee on Hunger of the U.S. House of Representatives at a hearing entitled *The Decade of Disasters: The United Nations' Response*, reprinted in Larry Minear, Thomas G. Weiss, and Kurt M. Campbell, *Humanitarianism and War: Learning the Lessons from Recent Armed Conflicts*, Occasional Paper no. 8 (Providence, R.I.: Thomas J. Watson Jr. Institute for International Studies, 1991), 36–42.

69. Hugh Smith, "Humanitarian Intervention: Morally Right, Legally Wrong?" *Current Affairs* 68, no. 4 (1991): 7.

70. Oscar Schachter, "United Nations Law in the Gulf Conflict," *American Journal of International Law* (1991): 469.

71. See further Neil S. MacFarlane and Thomas G. Weiss, "Regional Organizations and Regional Security," *Security Studies* 2, no. 3 (1992): 6–37.

72. For a discussion of the need to develop specific criteria within the context of UN and non-UN humanitarian interventions, see David J. Scheffer, "Toward a Modern Doctrine of Humanitarian Intervention," *University of Toledo Law Review* 23, no. 2 (1992): 253–93.

73. "The UN Contribution to Future International Security" (lecture at U.S. Naval War College, Newport, R.I., Feb. 19, 1992), 10.

74. See "Human Rights and State Sovereignty" (report of a meting in Montreal organized by International Centre for Human Rights and Democratic Development, Oct. 1990).

75. See also Thomas G. Weiss and Larry Minear, eds., *Humanitarianism across Borders: Sustaining Civilians in Times of War* (Boulder, Colo.: Rienner 1993).

76. See, for instance, Inis Claude, *Swords into Plowshares* (New York: Random House, 1964), chap. 12.

77. See the reflections by Stephen Lewis, Clovis Maksoud, and Robert C. Johansen, "The United Nations after the Gulf War," *World Policy Journal* 8, no. 3 (1991): 537–74; and Brian Urquhart, "Learning from the Gulf War," *New York Review of Books* 38 (Mar. 7, 1991): 34–37.

78. Hans Kelsen, *The Law of the United Nations: A Critical Analysis of Its Fundamental Problems* (London: Stevens and Sons, 1950), 138. See also discussion of issues that follows, as well as pp. 149 et seq. on states and individuals as UN "organs."

79. For a more detailed analysis of these issues, see Thomas G. Weiss and Jarat Chopra, *United Nations Peacekeeping: An ACUNS Teaching Text* (Hanover, N.H.: Academic Council on the United Nations System, 1992), pt. 2, sec. E.

80. In addition to earlier citations, see also William J. Durch, ed., *The Evolution of UN Peacekeeping: Case Studies and Comparative Analysis* (New York: St. Martin's, 1993); Adam Roberts, "The United Nations and International Security," *Survival* 35, no. 2 (1993); Marrack Goulding, "The Evolution of United Nations Peacekeeping," *International Affairs* 69, no. 3 (1993): 451–64; Mats R. Berdal, *Whither UN Peacekeeping?* Adelphi Paper 281 (London: International Institute for Strategic Studies, 1993); William J. Durch, *The United Nations and Collective Security in the Twenty-first Century* (Carlisle, Pa.: U.S. Army War College, 1993); and *The Professionalization of Peacekeeping: A Study Group Report* (Washington, D.C.: U.S. Institute of Peace, 1993).

81. See Larry Minear et al., *United Nations Coordination of the Humanitarian Response to the Gulf Crisis, 1900–1992*, Occasional Paper no. 13 (Providence, R.I.: Thomas J. Watson Jr. Institute for International Studies, 1992).

82. This does not imply that better assistance (i.e., assistance that ultimately contributes to development, rather than simply emergency aid) or improved institutions would not also be necessary. On these issues, see Mary Anderson and Peter Woodrow, *Rising from the Ashes: Disaster Response towards Development* (Boulder, Colo.: Westview, 1989); and Randolph C. Kent, *Anatomy of Disaster Relief: The International Network in Action* (London: Pinter, 1987). For a detailed discussion with reference to refugees, see Leon Gordenker, *Refugees in International Politics* (London: Croom Helm, 1987). An effort has been made to develop some generic procedural guidelines; see United Nations Institute for Training and Research, *Model Rules for Disaster Relief Operations*, Policy and Efficacy Studies No. 8 (New York: UNITAR, 1982).

83. UN Doc. no. A/46/1, p. 10.

84. See Thomas G. Weiss, ed., *Collective Security in a Changing World* (Boulder, Colo.: Rienner, 1993).

85. Francis M. Deng, *Protecting the Dispossessed* (Washington, D.C.: Brookings, 1993).

86. See Benedict Anderson, *Imagined Communities: Reflections on the Origin and Spread of Nationalism* (London: Verso, 1991); and Allott, *Eunomia*.

87. See George Steiner, *Real Presences* (Chicago: University of Chicago Press, 1989), pt. 3.

88. See particularly Charles Taylor, *Sources of the Self: The Making of the Modern Identity* (Cambridge: Harvard University Press, 1989).

89. See, for example, Barbara Hendrie, "Cross-Border Relief Operations in Eritrea and Tigray," *Disasters* 13, no. 4 (1989): 351–60.

90. This debate was originally launched in Mario Bettati and Bernard Kouchner, *Le devoir d'ingérence* (Paris: De Noël, 1987), and continued in Bernard Kouchner, *Le malheur des autres* (Paris: Odile Jacob, 1991). For the ICRC view, see two recent speeches by President Cornelio Sommaruga, "Respect for International Humanitarian Law" (Dec. 10, 1991), and "La neutralité suisse et la neutralité du CICR" (Jan. 21, 1992), distributed by the ICRC, Geneva.

91. As France formerly had the only "ministry" in the Western world dedicated to humanitarian matters, its very visible minister, Bernard Kouchner, unleashed a wave of criticism about humanitarian politics and publicity. See Xavier Emmanuelli, *Les prédateurs de l'action humanitaire* (Paris: Michel, 1991); and Rony Brauman, "Morale et politique: Le baiser du vampire," *Politique Internationale,* no. 50 (winter 1990–91): 1–9.

92. See Natalino Ronzitti, *Rescuing Nationals Abroad through Military Coercion and Intervention on Grounds of Humanity* (Dordrecht: Nijhoff, 1985).

93. This simile comes from Smith, "Humanitarian Intervention," 10.

CHAPTER SIX   STATE SOVEREIGNTY AND
INTERNATIONAL INTERVENTION

1. The boundaries are not always entirely clear. For example, disappearances, which became an important form of human rights abuse in the 1970s, were in part an effort to try to obscure the picture by operating at the boundary between private violence (murder) and state terrorism. Nonetheless, the distinction is part of our ordinary language and in most cases is sufficiently clear.

2. *Oxford English Dictionary* (Oxford: Oxford University Press, 1971), 1469.

3. For an extended discussion of humanitarian intervention, see Jack Donnelly, "Human Rights, Humanitarian Crisis, and Humanitarian Intervention," *International Journal* 49 (autumn 1993): 607–40, and the sources cited there.

4. My own preference is to restrict the use of the term *intervention* to this strong sense of coercive interference. Not only does it identify a relatively precise and narrow range of activities, it preserves the essential conceptual relationship between sovereignty and nonintervention. In the interest of consistency with the other contributors to this volume, however, I will not object to using *intervention* to include noncoercive interference. I will, however, usually speak of "noncoercive interference" and "coercive intervention," in order to draw what I see as a crucial conceptual distinction while remaining within the linguistic conventions of this volume.

5. It is not clear that such actions involve intervention. Intervention is ordinarily understood to be an unusual or irregular event, an external interference in a realm of activity ordinarily governed by the rules of sovereignty. (Compare Marc Trachtenberg, "Intervention in Historical Perspective," in Laura W. Reed and Carl Kaysen, eds., *Emerging Norms of Justified Intervention* (Cambridge, Mass.: American Academy of Arts and Sciences, 1993). When there has been a transfer of authority, how-

ever, especially if it is permanent, the issue is no longer regulated by state sovereignty, and thus the interference is no longer intervention in a strict sense of that term. For the purposes of this volume, however, this conceptual distinction is of little importance.

6. Chapter 10 in this volume, by Stephen Krasner, falls into this category. For particular human rights applications, see George Kennan, *The Cloud of Danger: Current Realities of American Foreign Policy* (Boston: Little, Brown, 1977), 45, 214–15; and Hans Morgenthau, *Human Rights and Foreign Policy* (New York: Council on Religion and International Affairs, 1979).

7. Chapter 9 in this volume, by James Rosenau, comes close to reflecting such a position. In the field of human rights, see Richard Falk, *Human Rights and State Sovereignty* (New York: Holmes and Meier, 1981); and Charles R. Beitz, "Human Rights and Social Justice," in Peter G. Brown and Douglas MacLean, eds., *Human Rights and U.S. Foreign Policy: Principles and Applications* (Lexington, Mass.: Lexington Books, 1980). For broader statements of such a perspective, see Robert Johansen, *The National Interest and the Human Interest* (Princeton: Princeton University Press, 1980); and Charles R. Beitz, *Political Theory and International Relations* (Princeton: Princeton University Press, 1979).

8. See Hedley Bull, *The Anarchical Society* (New York: Columbia University Press, 1977).

9. The Wilsonian principle of self-determination, even had it been applied consistently in the Versailles settlement, was not a real exception. It applied principally to the peoples of Europe and was never intended to apply to colonized peoples in Africa or Asia. Self-determination was seen less as a human right than as a right of unusually "civilized" peoples.

10. J. Herman Burgers ("The Road to San Francisco: The Revival of Human Rights Ideas in the Twentieth Century," *Human Rights Quarterly* 14 [Nov. 1992]: 447–77) argues that efforts by H. G. Wells in the 1930s, which led to the drafting of an international declaration of human rights, helped to prepare the ground for the inclusion of human rights in the UN Charter and for the early efforts of the UN Commission on Human Rights. Burgers also draws attention to a 1929 declaration of the International Law Institute and a proposal in 1933 by Antoine Frangulis. These and other precursors (such as the activities of the Fédération des Droits de l'Homme in Paris in the 1920s and 1930s) should not be overlooked. Nonetheless, as Burgers readily allows, the Holocaust moved such proposals from the margins to the center of international relations.

11. Although there were no negative votes, the Soviet Union and its allies, which from the outset were unenthusiastic about the idea of an international human rights instrument, abstained on the grounds of an insufficient emphasis on economic and social rights. In addition, South Africa abstained because of the provisions on racial discrimination, and Saudi Arabia abstained because of the provisions on gender equality.

12. In deference to the lingering cold war—particularly the desires of the United States—the single treaty envisioned in 1948 was broken into two, the International Covenant on Economic, Social, and Cultural Rights and the International Covenant on Civil and Political Rights.

13. Similar procedures exist under the 1965 International Convention on the

Elimination of All Forms of Racial Discrimination, which entered into force in 1969; the 1979 Convention on the Elimination of Discrimination against Women, which entered into force in 1981; and the 1984 Convention against Torture and Other Cruel, Inhuman, and Degrading Treatment or Punishment, which entered into force in 1987. The Committee on Economic, Social, and Cultural Rights provides a similar review of reports submitted under the International Covenant on Economic, Social, and Cultural Rights. For a more detailed discussion of the machinery discussed in this and the following paragraphs, see Jack Donnelly, *International Human Rights* (Boulder, Colo.: Westview, 1993), chap. 4.

14. Even severe violators, however, may make symbolic gestures, such as the release of political prisoners or improvements in the treatment of such prisoners, in response to such international pressures. In addition, there may be subtle and indirect impacts on both the target state and foreign governments if the pressure persists for an extended period.

15. In recent years, the commission has received roughly four thousand communications a year. About four-fifths of these inquiries, though, are dropped by the individual after an initial exchange of letters, and most of the rest are clearly inadmissible. The fact that the commission has in the end registered only about forty new cases annually therefore is largely a testament to relatively good regional human rights records.

16. All of these procedures apply only to the civil and political rights recognized in the 1950 European Convention on Human Rights and Fundamental Freedoms, and its protocols. Economic and social rights are specified in the European Social Charter and are supervised through somewhat weaker procedures.

17. For an extended discussion of the OAS response, see Cecilia Medina Quiroga, *The Battle of Human Rights: Gross, Systematic Violations and the Inter-American System* (Dordrecht: Nijhoff, 1988).

18. For a detailed account of Argentina's efforts in the United Nations, see Ian Guest, *Behind the Disappearances* (Philadelphia: University of Pennsylvania Press, 1990), pt. 2.

19. Robert A. Pastor, *Condemned to Repetition: The United States and Nicaragua* (Princeton: Princeton University Press, 1987), 149–51.

20. Unfortunately, the Tunisian League, perhaps the most respected human rights NGO in the Arab world, was forced to close down in the spring of 1992. More generally as well, both relatively liberal and relatively repressive regimes in the Middle East have recently become even less tolerant of NGO activities as a result of the rise of politically active Muslim fundamentalist groups.

21. Helsinki Watch Committee, *The Moscow Helsinki Monitors: Their Vision, Their Achievement, The Price They Paid, May 12, 1976–May 12, 1986* (New York: U.S. Helsinki Watch Committee, 1986), 5.

22. We should also note that repression of human rights activists in CSCE countries was not entirely restricted to the Soviet bloc. For example, in Turkey, twenty-three members of the Executive Committee of the Turkish Peace Association, formed in response to the security provisions of the Helsinki accords, were imprisoned for their activities.

23. Jack Donnelly, "Human Rights in the New World Order," *World Policy Journal* 9 (spring 1992): 249–77.

24. Robert O. Keohane and Joseph Nye, *Power and Interdependence: World Politics in Transition* (Boston: Little Brown, 1977).

25. In fact, repression of the Kurds is not even mentioned in Security Council Resolution 687, the principal cease-fire document. Resolution 688, passed two days later, did address the issue of human rights violations in general terms, and the specific case of Kurds. The explicit context, however, was the threat to international peace and security posed by Kurdish refugees. The resolution explicitly disavowed any intention to interfere in the internal affairs of Iraq. Both the United Nations and the United States went out of their way to discourage any interpretation that this was a precedent for multilateral humanitarian intervention.

CHAPTER SEVEN ENVIRONMENTAL PROTECTION,
INTERNATIONAL NORMS, AND STATE SOVEREIGNTY

1. John Perlin, *A Forest Journey: The Role of Wood in the Development of Civilization* (Cambridge: Harvard University Press, 1991), 46.

2. Zuo Dakang and Zhang Peiyuan, "The Huang-Huai-Hai Plain," in B. L. Turner II et al., eds., *The Earth as Transformed by Human Action* (New York: Cambridge University Press, 1990).

3. Peter Brimblecombe, *The Big Smoke: A History of Air Pollution in London Since Medieval Times* (London: Methuen, 1987).

4. World Commission on Environment and Development, *Our Common Future* (New York: Oxford University Press, 1987), 1; emphasis added.

5. See, for example, *Managing Planet Earth: Readings from "Scientific American"* (New York: Freeman, 1990).

6. For an account of colonial and neocolonial rule in Latin America stressing control of natural resources, see Eduardo Galeano, *Open Veins of Latin America: Five Centuries of the Pillage of a Continent* (New York: Monthly Review, 1973).

7. See Ronnie D. Lipschutz and Judith Mayer, "Property Rights, Constitutive Rules, and the Renegotiation of Resource Management Regimes," in Ronnie D. Lipschutz and Ken Conca, eds., *The State and Social Power in Global Environmental Politics* (New York: Columbia University Press, 1993).

8. This point is discussed in Ken Conca, "In the Name of Sustainability: Peace Studies and Environmental Discourse," *Peace and Change* 19, no. 2 (1994).

9. Lipschutz and Conca, eds., *State and Social Power.*

10. Frederick H. Buttel, Ann P. Hawkins, and Alison G. Power, "From Limits to Growth to Global Change," *Global Environmental Change* 1 (Dec. 1990): 57–66.

11. Donella H. Meadows et al., *The Limits to Growth* (New York: Universe Books, 1972).

12. The preamble to the Stockholm Declaration does acknowledge that "[a] growing class of environmental problems, because they are regional or global in extent or because they affect the common international realm, will require extensive cooperation among nations and action by international organizations in the common interest." But among the principles of the declaration only Principle 24, which makes a general call for "co-operation through multilateral or bilateral agreements," addresses this point explicitly. See UN Environment Programme, *Taking a Stand: From Stockholm 1972 to Nairobi 1982* (Nairobi: UNEP, 1982).

13. For a discussion of the various debates surrounding the Stockholm conference, see Lynton Caldwell, *International Environmental Policy: Emergence and Dimensions* (Durham, N.C.: Duke University Press, 1984).

14. On the growth of scientific understanding see M. K. Tolba et al., eds., *The World Environment 1972–1992: Two Decades of Challenge* (London: Chapman and Hall, 1992), especially chap. 20.

15. See, for example, National Academy of Sciences, *One Earth, One Future: Our Changing Global Environment* (Washington, D.C.: National Academy, 1990).

16. For a discussion of the problems and prospects facing environmental groups in the developing world, see World Resources Institute, "Policies and Institutions: Nongovernmental Organizations," in *World Resources 1992–93* (New York: Oxford University Press, 1992). For various perspectives on North-South linkages between environmentalists, see Alan Durning, "People Power and Development," *Foreign Policy* 76 (1990): 66–82; Vandana Shiva, *Ecology and the Politics of Survival: Conflicts over Natural Resources in India* (Newbury Park, Calif.: Sage, 1991); David Korten, *Getting to the Twenty-first Century: Voluntary Action and the Global Agenda* (West Hartford, Conn.: Kumarian, 1990); and Ronnie D. Lipschutz, "Reconstructing World Politics: The Emergence of Global Civil Society," *Millennium: Journal of International Studies* 21 (winter 1992): 389–420.

17. B. L. Turner et al. discuss this distinction in terms of "systemic" versus "cumulative" processes. See B. L. Turner et al., "Two Types of Global Environmental Change: Definitional and Spatial-Scale Issues in Their Human Dimensions," *Global Environmental Change* 1, no. 1 (1990): 14–22.

18. Piers Blaikie, *The Political Economy of Soil Erosion in Developing Countries* (London: Longman, 1985).

19. International Union for Conservation of Nature and Natural Resources, *World Conservation Strategy: Living Resource Conservation for Sustainable Development* (n.p.: IUCN, 1980). The World Conservation Strategy was prepared by IUCN along with the UN Environment Program, the World Wildlife Fund, the UN Food and Agriculture Organization, and the UN Economic, Scientific, and Cultural Organization.

20. Food and Agriculture Organization, *Tropical Forestry Action Plan* (Rome: FAO, 1985).

21. See Richard E. Benedick, *Ozone Diplomacy: New Directions in Safeguarding the Planet* (Cambridge: Harvard University Press, 1991).

22. World Commission on Environment and Development, *Our Common Future*, 348–51.

23. H. A. Smith identifies sovereignty, collective action, and information sharing as the principles underlying what he sees as an emerging "meta-regime" for environmental protection. See H. A. Smith, "An Environmental Meta-Regime" (paper presented at the International Studies Association Meeting, Atlanta, Apr. 1992). Smith identifies two additional principles: the integral role of science, and the interrelationship of human and environmental health.

24. See Buttel, Hawkins, and Power, "From Limits to Growth." This has been one of the principal criticisms of the concept of sustainable development; see David C. Korten, "Sustainable Development," *World Policy Journal* 9, no. 1 (1991–92): 157–90.

25. On environmental regime building, see Oran R. Young, "The Politics of

International Regime Formation: Managing Natural Resources and the Environment," *International Organization* 43, no. 3 (1989): 349-75; Karen Litfin, "Eco-regimes: Playing Tug of War with the Nation-State," in Lipschutz and Conca, eds., *State and Social Power;* Veit Koster, "From Stockholm to Brundtland," *Environmental Policy and Law* 20, no. 1/2 (1990): 14-18. For a list of international environmental agreements, see U.N. Environment Programme, *Register of International Treaties and Other Agreements in the Field of the Environment,* Document UNEP/GC.16/Inf.4 (Nairobi: U.N. Environment Programme, 1991).

26. According to the World Bank, tropical moist forests cover an area of 15 million square kilometers, two-thirds of which is found in Latin America. The remainder of the world's forest cover consists of temperate-zone forests (16 million square kilometers, three-quarters of which is found in the developed countries) and tropical dry forests (15 million square kilometers, 75 percent of which is found in Africa). Two-thirds of the tropical moist forest area is said to represent primary forest, which has been disrupted only minimally by human activity. The remaining one-third falls into the category of "degraded forestland." See World Bank, *The Forestry Sector: A World Bank Policy Paper* (Washington, D.C.: World Bank, 1991), 26-28.

27. Robert Repetto presents the following regional estimates for percentage change in forest and woodland cover between 1850 and 1980: North Africa and the Middle East, minus 60 percent; South Asia, minus 43 percent; China, minus 39 percent; tropical Africa, minus 20 percent; Latin America, minus 19 percent; Southeast Asia, minus 7 percent. The corresponding estimates for developed regions were North America, minus 3 percent; Europe, plus 4 percent; Soviet Union, minus 12 percent; Pacific developed countries, minus 8 percent. See Robert Repetto, "Overview," in Robert Repetto and Malcolm Gillis, eds., *Public Policies and the Misuse of Forest Resources* (Cambridge: Cambridge University Press, 1988).

28. Norman Myers, "Deforestation Rates in Tropical Forests and Their Climatic Implications: A Friends of the Earth Report" (San Francisco: Friends of the Earth, 1989), 1. The World Bank estimates that tropical deforestation (including both moist and dry forests) claims 170,000 to 200,000 square kilometers annually; see World Bank, *Forestry Sector,* 10. Note that in calculating the annual percentage loss Myers uses a very different baseline than that presented in note 26 above; he estimates the total current extent of tropical moist forests to be only 8 million square kilometers.

29. Myers, "Deforestation Rates," 1.

30. The World Bank estimates that 60 percent of the annual clearing of tropical moist forests is for agricultural settlement, with the remaining 40 percent divided almost evenly between logging and "other purposes such as roads, urbanization, and fuelwood." See World Bank, *Forestry Sector,* 10.

31. William B. Wood, "Tropical Deforestation: Balancing Regional Development Demands and Global Environmental Concerns," *Global Environmental Change* 1 no. 1 (1990): 23-41.

32. See Jan G. Laarman, "Exports of Tropical Hardwoods in the Twentieth Century," in John F. Richards and Richard P. Tucker, eds., *World Deforestation in the Twentieth Century* (Durham, N.C.: Duke University Press, 1988).

33. World Bank, *Forestry Sector,* 5.

34. See, for example, Shiva, *Ecology and the Politics of Survival;* Chico Mendes

with Tony Gross, *Fight for the Forest* (London: Latin America Bureau, 1989); Seth Zuckerman, *Saving Our Ancient Forests* (Los Angeles: Living Planet, 1991).

35. On biodiversity and species extinction, see E. C. Wolf, *On the Brink of Extinction: Conserving the Diversity of Life*, Worldwatch Paper 78 (Washington, D.C.: Worldwatch Institute, 1987); Edward O. Wilson, *The Diversity of Life* (Cambridge: Harvard University Press, 1992).

36. Exactly how much is a matter of some controversy, particularly in light of the widely variable estimates of current deforestation rates. A 1990 study by the World Resources Institute estimated that the third world accounted for 48 percent of global carbon dioxide emissions. The study has been criticized on several counts, however, including the deforestation data on which it is based and its failure to calculate emissions on a per-capita basis. See "Global Warming in an Unequal World: A Case of Environmental Colonialism," *Earth Island Journal*, spring 1991, 39–42.

37. Many of these issues emerged in the debate on forests prior to and during the Earth Summit. See "Forest Talks Yield Little Agreement," *NGO Networker*, no. 15 (winter 1992): 1–2; Wood, "Tropical Deforestation"; Ann Hawkins, "Contested Ground: International Environmentalism and Global Climate Change," in Lipschutz and Conca, eds., *State and Social Power*.

38. Andrew Hurrell, "Brazil and the International Politics of Amazonian Deforestation," in Andrew Hurrell and Benedict Kingsbury, eds., *The International Politics of the Environment* (New York: Oxford University Press, 1992).

39. The Amazon forest should not be confused with the Amazon River basin, which covers an even larger area (roughly 7 million square kilometers). Although most of the forest lies within the basin area, the forest does extend beyond the basin area to the north, and not all of the basin area consists of rainforest ecosystems. Nor should it be confused with the nine-state region of Brazil known as legal Amazônia. About three-fourths of legal Amazônia is dense and nondense forest growth, but the region also includes savannah, natural fields, secondary vegetation, pasture and agricultural land, and human settlements. The Brazilian government estimates the current population of legal Amazônia, which accounts for 60 percent of Brazilian national territory, to be 16.7 million people, 170,000 of whom are said to be indigenous people. See *The Challenge of Sustainable Development: The Brazilian Report for the United Nations Conference on Environment and Development* (Brasília: Press Secretariat of the Presidency of the Republic, 1992), 89–90.

40. Government data show an average annual rate of deforestation of 22,000 square kilometers (an area roughly the size of Massachusetts) for 1977–88 and declining rates since then (19,000 square kilometers in 1988–89 and 13,800 square kilometers in 1989–90). Other observers have challenged these figures, however, arguing that they understate both the extent of deforestation and the current rate of change. Norman Myers, for example, estimated an annual rate of roughly 50,000 square kilometers circa 1989; see Myers, "Deforestation Rates," 14–18.

41. For a review and critique of the literature see Andrew Hurrell, "The Politics of Amazonian Deforestation," *Journal of Latin American Studies* 23 (Feb. 1991): 197–215.

42. As Hurrell points out, this latter argument has been put forward by the Brazilian government itself. See ibid., 205–6. On the role of foreign capital, see

Stephen G. Bunker, *Underdeveloping the Amazon: Extraction, Unequal Exchange, and the Failure of the Modern State* (Urbana: University of Illinois Press, 1985). For an interpretation stressing geopolitics and the military, see Susanna Hecht and Alexander Cockburn, *The Fate of the Forest: Developers, Destroyers, and Defenders of the Amazon* (London: Verso, 1989). On The Amazon as a social safety valve, see José de Souza Martins, "The State and the Militarization of the Agrarian Question in Brazil," in M. Schmink and C. Wood, eds., *Frontier Expansion in Amazonia* (Gainesville: University of Florida Press, 1984). For an interpretation stressing the dynamic of the frontier, see Anna Luiza Ozorio de Almeida, *The Colonization of the Amazon* (Austin: University of Texas Press, 1992).

43. The Constitution of 1946 called for a comprehensive plan for Amazonian development, and a regional planning agency, the Superintendência do Plano de Valorização Económica da Amazônia (SPVEA), was formed in 1953. The SPVEA was "beleaguered by political problems from the start," however, and the military regime replaced it with the Superintendency for the Development of the Amazon (SUDAM) in 1966. See J. O. Browder, "Public Policy and Deforestation in the Brazilian Amazon," in Repetto and Gillis, eds., *Public Policies and the Misuse of Forest Resources*, 256. On the role of the state in Amazonian development, see Dennis J. Mahar, "Deforestation in Brazil's Amazon Region: Magnitude, Rate, and Causes," in G. Schramm and J. Warford, eds., *Environmental Management and Economic Development* (Baltimore: Johns Hopkins University Press, 1989); Marianne Schmink and Charles H. Wood, *Contested Frontiers in Amazonia* (New York: Columbia University Press, 1992); and Browder, "Public Policy and Deforestation."

44. J. O. Browder concludes that "[n]early half the rain forest destruction in the Brazilian Amazon thus far is directly attributable to four government subsidy programs: the SUDAM program for developing the Brazilian Amazon, the Brazilian Central Bank's rural credit program, the National Integration Program in the Transamazon, and the semi-directed program of small farmer settlement in the state of Rondônia." See Browder, "Public Policy and Deforestation," 284.

45. Data published in late 1989, for example, indicated that the combined gross product of the Amazon from agriculture, extractive activities, mining, and fishing came to roughly $4.5 billion for that year, whereas a free-trade manufacturing zone in the Amazonian city of Manaus accounted for $5 billion. See "O Brasil anfíbio," in "Amazônia: Guerra e Paz" (special edition), *Globo Rural*, Oct. 1989. In contrast, one estimate of state investment suggests that the directed colonization program alone (including costs such as settlements, road building, and land titling) cost $7.5 billion; see Ozorio de Almeida, *Colonization of the Amazon*, 112.

46. Alfred W. Crosby, *Ecological Imperialism: The Biological Expansion of Europe 900–1900* (London: Cambridge University Press, 1986).

47. Elizabeth Dore has written that "[t]he moment Columbus set foot on Hispaniola, mining replaced food security as the organizing principle of society." Elizabeth Dore, "Open Wounds," *Report on the Americas* 25, no. 2 (Sept. 1991): 15. See also Sidney W. Mintz, "A Bittersweet Tale," ibid., 25, no. 2 (Sept. 1991).

48. On the debate over the size of the "pre-contact" Amazonian population, see Hecht and Cockburn, *Fate of the Forest*, 12 n. 3.

49. Ibid., chaps. 4–5.

50. Ibid., 56–61.

51. Ibid., 66–68.

52. See Ronald M. Schneider, *Order and Progress: A Political History of Brazil* (Boulder, Colo.: Westview, 1991), chaps. 2–4.

53. On dependent development in Brazil, see Peter Evans, *Dependent Development: The Alliance of Multinational, State, and Local Capital in Brazil* (Princeton: Princeton University Press, 1979).

54. Hecht and Cockburn, *Fate of the Forest*, chap. 5.

55. This point is made in José Goldemberg and Eunice Durham, "The Amazonia and National Sovereignty" (University of São Paulo, n.d.).

56. Martins, "State and Militarization."

57. The groups mounting the campaign included the Environmental Defense Fund, the Environmental Policy Institute, the National Wildlife Federation, the Natural Resources Defense Council, the Rainforest Action Network, and the Sierra Club. See Pat Aufderheide and Bruce Rich, "Environmental Reform and the Multilateral Banks," *World Policy Journal* 5, no. 2 (spring 1988): 301–21; Barbara J. Bramble and Gareth Porter, "Non-Governmental Organizations and the Making of US International Environmental Policy," in Hurrell and Kingsbury, eds., *International Politics of the Environment*.

58. On the complex history of rural social movements in the Amazon, see José de Souza Martins, "The Political Impasses of Rural Social Movements in Amazonia," in David Goodman and Anthony Hall, eds., *The Future of Amazonia: Destruction or Sustainable Development* (London: Macmillan, 1990). Martins argues that the efforts of the military regime to undermine rural peasant organization and depoliticize local land conflicts had the opposite effect. For a general overview of the emergence of the domestic environmental movement in Brazil, see Nira Broner Worcman, "Brazil's Thriving Environmental Movement," *Technology Review*, Oct. 1990.

59. David Treece, "Indigenous Peoples in Brazilian Amazonia and the Expansion of the Economic Frontier," in Goodman and Hall, eds., *Future of Amazonia*, 285.

60. Margaret Keck and Kathryn Sikkink, "International Issue Networks in the Environment and Human Rights" (paper prepared for the Seventeenth International Congress of the Latin American Studies Association, Los Angeles, Sept. 24–27, 1992).

61. Susanna Hecht and Alexander Cockburn have argued that international environmental groups exploited the rubber tappers' movement by distorting their message, presenting them as nonpolitical environmentalists rather than the trade-union activists that they are. See Hecht and Cockburn, "Defending the Rainforest and Its People," *Nation*, May 22, 1989.

62. For this action, the two Kayapó and the American anthropologist accompanying them were charged under Brazil's "Law of Foreigners" with having "denigrated the image of Brazil abroad." See Survival International, "Urgent Action Bulletin," BRZ/14/NOV/88, cited in Treece, "Indigenous Peoples," 280. The charges were later dismissed.

63. *Challenge of Sustainable Development*, 156.

64. Changes in the World Bank's policy have been accompanied by changes in its organization, including the establishment of an Environment Department and the addition of environmental analysts in the bank's regional and sector groups. For a critical view of these and related reforms, see Bruce Rich, "The Emperor's New

Clothes: The World Bank and Environmental Reform," *World Policy Journal* 7, no. 2 (1990): 305–29.

65. Rich, "Emperor's New Clothes," 312–13.

66. "Brazil, Smarting from the Outcry over the Amazon, Charges Foreign Plot," *New York Times*, Mar. 23, 1989.

67. "G-7 Support for Rainforest Project," *Latin American Regional Reports: Brazil*, no. RB-91–07, Aug. 15, 1991.

68. As David Treece points out, the European Coal and Steel Community played a key role in providing financing for the Grande Carajás mining complex in the eastern Amazon. See Treece, "Indigenous Peoples," 275–82.

69. On the Calha Norte program, see João Pacheco de Oliveira Filho, "Frontier Security and the New Indigenism: Nature and Origins of the Calha Norte Project," in Goodman and Hall, eds., *Future of Amazonia*.

70. The Rural Democratic Union (UDR), an organization of rural landowning elites, was along with the military perhaps the most effective lobbying force in the Constituent Assembly, successfully weakening several proposals that threatened the interests of large landowners.

71. "Brazil Charges Foreign Plot." For a general discussion of the nationalist backlash against international pressures, see Hurrell, "Brazil and the International Politics of Amazonian Deforestation."

72. "Brazil Charges Foreign Plot."

73. "Brazilian Announces Plan to Protect the Amazon," *New York Times*, Apr. 7, 1989.

74. See for example "Brazil's New Chief Raises Doubts on Amazon," *New York Times*, Dec. 25, 1989, p. A-4.

75. See also Hurrell, "Brazil and the International Politics of Amazonian Deforestation."

76. "Lutzenberger to Head New Secretariat," *Gazeta Mercantil* [international edition], Mar. 12, 1990, 5; "Amazon Advocate's Unsettling Vision," *New York Times*, Apr. 30, 1991, B-6.

77. "Collor Open to Criticism of Policy in the Amazon," *New York Times*, Feb. 12, 1990, A-13.

78. "Debt Swaps: The Greening of Collor," *Nature* 352 (July 1991): 6.

79. The Brazilian proposal was in response to a general commitment to Amazonian preservation expressed by the G-7 at their 1990 annual meeting. See Hurrell, "Brazil and the International Politics of Amazonian Deforestation," 411.

80. Ben Ross Schneider, "Brazil under Collor: Anatomy of a Crisis," *World Policy Journal* 8, no. 2 (1991): 321–47. As Schneider points out, the Collor program reflected more than anything else an underlying political pragmatism, blending elements of classical neoliberalism, social democracy, and conservative modernization in complex fashion.

81. Calha Norte was essentially completed by the time Collor took office. "Calha Norte, quase concluido, recebe Collor e Lutzenberger," *Jornal do Brasil*, Mar. 23, 1990, 15.

82. By 1990 there were an estimated one thousand environmental organizations in Brazil, most operating on a local level. See Worcman, "Brazil's Thriving Environmental Movement."

83. Sarney himself signed a decree creating three extractive reserves just before leaving office. "Three New Reserves in Amazon Region," *Gazeta Mercantil* (international edition), Mar. 19, 1990, 12.

84. President Sarney announced an ambitious land reform proposal early in his tenure, but failed to deliver. See Frances Hagopian and Scott Mainwaring, "Democracy in Brazil: Problems and Prospects," *World Policy Journal* 4, no. 3 (1987).

85. This distinction, attributed to Michael Mann, is discussed in chap. 1 of John A. Hall and G. John Ikenberry, *The State* (Minneapolis: University of Minnesota Press, 1989).

86. Ibid., 13.

87. "Um grito do fundo da selva," *Veja,* Aug. 25, 1993, 27; my translation.

CHAPTER EIGHT   SOVEREIGNTY AND COLLECTIVE INTERVENTION

1. The Geneva Protocol was not the first attempt to control chemical and biological agents. In 1899, twenty-seven nations ratified the Hague Gas Declaration as part of the Hague Convention; the declaration committed its signatories to refrain from the use of artillery carrying "asphyxiating or deleterious gases." The use of various poisons and poisoned bullets also was banned in the Hague Convention of 1907. Only a minority of the large powers acceded to these agreements, however, and the ban on chemical and biological weapons was ignored during World War I. The Geneva Protocol, which replaced these earlier agreements, currently has 125 signatories. It is bolstered by the Convention on the Prohibition of the Development and Stockpiling of Bacteriological (Biological) and Toxin Weapons and on Their Destruction, which went into effect in 1975, and by various export controls on chemical weapons. For further analysis, see Barend ter Haar, *The Future of Biological Weapons* (New York: Praeger, 1991); Victor Utgoff, *Chemical Weapons* (London: Macmillan, 1989); and the section on chemical and biological weapon control below.

2. International military restraint arrangements vary in the degree to which they seek to prohibit particular military capabilities or limit them more selectively. The biological weapons convention is the only existing agreement that seeks the actual elimination of weapon stockpiles and production capabilities, although this is also a goal of the chemical weapons convention currently under negotiation. Both the biological and chemical weapon conventions declare the use of these weapons to be illegitimate a priori, an element missing in the arrangements for the control of nuclear weapons, missiles, or other conventional weapons.

3. See, for instance, Gary Milhollin, "Building Saddam Hussein's Bomb," *New York Times Magazine,* Mar. 8, 1992, 30. For a list of the U.S. companies alleged to have assisted Iraq's weapons development, see Gary Milhollin and Diana Edensword, "Iraq's Bomb, Chip by Chip," *New York Times,* Apr. 24, 1992, A35.

4. In 1991, the discovery that Iraq was using 1950s-vintage calutrons to develop weapons-grade nuclear materials highlighted the fact that technologies that were considered too outdated or too commercial in nature to warrant inclusion in a control regime could materially aid a country's military ambitions.

5. After Iraq, the North Korean nuclear program has emerged as an example of the weaknesses of existing controls. In addition, there are concerns that North Korea could soon become a source of exports of nuclear weapons materials, even

though North Korea has recently signed a nuclear safeguards agreement. See Don Oberdorfer, "N. Korea Seen Closer to A-Bomb," *Washington Post,* Feb. 23, 1992, A1, A26; and George D. Moffett III, "Last Remaining Hot Spot of the Cold War Asked to Cool Its Desire for Nuclear Weapons," *Christian Science Monitor,* Feb. 14, 1992, 3.

6. The spread of democracy and the formation of new states throughout the region has prompted U.S. efforts to persuade these countries to abide by all international nonproliferation regimes. In addition, it is hoped that initiatives to employ former Soviet scientists in international research bodies engaged in peaceful activities may attenuate the risks posed by the migration of weapons expertise, although this has yet to be seen. See, for instance, Kurt Campbell et al., *Soviet Nuclear Fission* (Cambridge, Mass.: Center for Science and International Affairs, Studies in International Security, 1991).

7. In addition to the United States, many other countries exhibited more pronounced concern about weapons proliferation in the early 1990s. Illustratively, China and France pledged to join the NPT, as did several former Soviet republics. Argentina and Brazil agreed to conduct joint inspections of one another's nuclear installations with assistance from the International Atomic Energy Agency, and for now appear to have put their nuclear weapons programs on indefinite hold. South Africa, which had an active nuclear weapons program for two decades, signed the NPT and negotiated an inspection agreement with the IAEA at the end of 1991. In February 1992, the Pakistani government, while admitting that it had sufficient materials to assemble one nuclear device, stated that it had stopped the production of highly enriched uranium and pledged not to export nuclear technology. And Iran, which apparently has been importing nuclear technology from China, invited IAEA inspectors to inspect its facilities; the inspectors confirmed in early 1992 that none of the facilities they visited was being used for the development of nuclear weapons. See, for instance, R. Jeffrey Smith, "Pakistan Official Affirms Capacity for Nuclear Device: Foreign Minister Vows to Contain Technology," *Washington Post,* Feb. 7, 1992, A18; Michael Z. Wise, "Atomic Team Reports on Iran Probe: No Weapons Research Found by Inspectors," ibid., Feb. 15, 1992, A29–A30; and "Atom Agency Finds No Threat at Iran's Sites," *New York Times,* Feb. 13, 1992, A17.

8. Similarly, ballistic missiles are viewed as destabilizing in regional contexts but are not likely to be eliminated from the arsenals of industrial countries in the near future. The 1987 Intermediate-Range Nuclear Forces Treaty between the United States and the Soviet Union did set a precedent in this regard by renouncing all missiles that fell into a specified range.

9. For a series of essays on collective intervention in defeated states, see Fred Tanner, ed., *From Versailles to Baghdad: Post-War Armament Control of Defeated States,* United Nations Institute for Disarmament Research, GV.E.92.0.26 (New York: United Nations, 1992).

10. An important distinction, however, is that UN Resolution 687 allows Iraq a degree of sovereignty that the Germans were denied. Whereas the Versailles Treaty only permitted as many forces as were necessary to provide for German "safety," presumably meaning internal security, United Nations–sponsored collective intervention in the Gulf allows Iraq to maintain unlimited conventional forces, a move that is clearly intended to avoid pushing Iraqi armament efforts further underground. See Johan Molander, "The United Nations and the Elimination of Iraq's

Weapons of Mass Destruction: The Implementation of a Cease-Fire Condition," in Tanner, ed., *From Versailles to Baghdad*, 155.

11. Japan's position on obtaining nuclear weapons has become more ambiguous, particularly as North Korea's rejection of routine IAEA inspections has become more threatening. The Japanese government refused to publicly support the open extension of the Nuclear Non-Proliferation Treaty early in 1993, but then Prime Minister Morihiro Hosokawa later reversed that position. See Charles A. Radin, "In Japan, Quiet Talk of Nuclear Arms," *Boston Globe*, Sept. 19, 1993, 10; and Jacob Schlesinger, "Japan Supports Open Extension of Nuclear Treaty," *Wall Street Journal*, Sept. 28, 1993, 14.

12. Article 9 of the Japanese Constitution renounces the use of war as an exercise of national sovereignty. See Takako Ueta, "Japan: A Case of a Non-Control Regime," in Tanner, ed., *From Versailles to Baghdad*, 101–2.

13. Seymour Hersh alleges repeated instances of U.S. support for Israel's nuclear ambitions over the course of several administrations, motivated in part by the belief that the possession of nuclear weapons by this close ally would prove to be in the U.S. interest in the region. See Hersh, *The Samson Option* (New York: Random House, 1991).

14. With a measure known as the Pressler Amendment, Congress amended the Foreign Assistance Act of 1961 to require the suspension of all economic and military aid to Pakistan if the executive branch could not certify that Pakistan was not pursuing nuclear weapons development. After years of formal fiction, even a modified certification proved impossible in 1990, and U.S. aid was terminated. Still, the Bush administration chose to interpret the aid cut-off as not covering commercial sales, and continued to provide dual-use equipment such as spare parts for Pakistan's F-16 (nuclear-capable) fighter aircraft. See, for instance, Steven Greenhouse, "Senators Seek Full Cutoff of Arms to Pakistan," *New York Times*, Mar. 8, 1992, A12.

15. The most significant instances of circumvention of NPT controls have involved technology cooperation agreements between third world clients that were perceived as benign and the advanced nuclear power states, including parties to the NPT. The United States, Canada, and Britain helped India in its nuclear and missile programs, for example; France and the United States assisted Israel to develop nuclear and high-performance missile capabilities; and Germany, France, and the Soviet Union assisted Iraq in chemical, nuclear, and ballistic missile development. Countries that openly violate the regime, such as China, suggest that they know that the penalties will be minor or nonexistent, a point reinforced when the Bush administration lifted trade sanctions before China had demonstrated any good faith effort to abide by international norms.   •

16. Michael R. Gordon, "C.I.A. Sees a Developing World with Developed Arms," *New York Times*, Feb. 10, 1989, A3.

17. The Atoms for Peace program was institutionalized internationally in 1957, as a body affiliated with the United Nations and known as the International Atomic Energy Agency. The IAEA, which currently has more than one hundred members, embodied the two objectives of the Eisenhower policy: to promote international access to peaceful uses of nuclear technology and to ensure that nuclear materials are not diverted to weapons development. By promoting nuclear applications in the fields of agriculture, medicine, and energy, the IAEA largely fulfilled its first objec-

tive. Despite an elaborate system of inventories, inspections, and other safeguard mechanisms, however, the agency has been unable to accomplish its second objective.

To complement the work of the IAEA, supplier states have created mechanisms such as the Zangger Committee, a 1974 agreement among ten industrial countries to compile a list of components and technologies that could be used in nuclear weapons development and whose export would require application of IAEA safeguards. Such cartel arrangements have been intended to discourage states from succumbing to the temptation to weaken or circumvent safeguard requirements in the interest of commercial advantage, and to improve international coordination of exports on behalf of nonproliferation objectives. Trigger lists, based on arduous analyses of items deemed critical for the development of particular weapons, are central to various other control arrangements, including the Chemical Weapons Convention, the MTCR, and the Coordinating Committee on Multilateral Export Controls (COCOM).

18. The treaty was signed by 62 countries in 1968; it entered into force in 1970, and as of 1993 had 148 signatories.

The NPT divides countries into two categories, each with distinct obligations. States with nuclear weapons (defined as those that had detonated a nuclear weapon before 1967) were expected not to assist any state that lacked nuclear weapons to acquire nuclear materials and equipment for the development of weapons (Article I), agreed to promote access to civilian nuclear technology under strict safeguards (Article III), and agreed to negotiate "in good faith" toward ending the nuclear arms race and toward global disarmament (Article VI). States without nuclear weapons, in turn, agreed not to acquire or produce such weapons (Article II) and to accept "full-scope" IAEA safeguards on their civilian nuclear programs (Article III).

NPT signatories are obligated to accept comprehensive safeguards covering all of their declared peaceful nuclear programs, in the form of inspections, inventories, and data collection conducted by the IAEA. This agency inspects an estimated seven hundred installations in fifty countries annually. See Leonard S. Spector, *The Undeclared Bomb* (Cambridge, Mass: Ballinger, 1988), app. C.

19. Until 1991, the United States insisted that it had to retain a chemical weapons stockpile until all states had ratified the Chemical Weapons Convention banning the production and use of these weapons.

20. Every five years, NPT review conferences have revealed the highly fractious nature of the NPT regime, bringing to light the very different interests of the various categories of signatories. At the last review conference in 1990, for example, a perennial dispute between industrial and nonindustrial states resurfaced, vitiating agreement on a final declaration. Led by the Mexican delegation, the nonaligned countries attacked the legitimacy of the NPT, criticizing the two superpowers for not upholding their commitment under Article VI to pursue nuclear arms control, and demanding that any final declaration include a commitment to a comprehensive nuclear test ban (CTB). The United States refused to link the NPT's extension to an agreement to pursue a CTB, and the review conference ended in deadlock. For additional discussion, see Charles Van Doren and George Bunn, "Progress and Peril at the Fourth NPT Review," *Arms Control Today* 8 (Oct. 1990): 8–12.

21. Pending an agreement on a global ban, states have relied on supplier export controls on chemical materials and an eroding international taboo against use of these weapons. After Iraq used chemical weapons against Iran in 1982, fifteen West-

ern countries led by Australia began working on a voluntary system of controls that were more stringent. Known as the Australia Group, participants agreed in 1984 to restrict and coordinate their transfers of chemical weapons precursors. Chemical weapon precursors are materials that have legitimate uses but can be diverted to use in developing munitions. Any state using 1950s technology in various civilian enterprises, such as pesticides, can in principle develop chemical weapon agents. Members compiled a "warning list" of fifty chemicals useful in the manufacture of chemical weapons. Nine of these chemicals made up the "core list" of items that were to be subject to export restrictions in all Australia Group states. Remaining items are subject to voluntary restrictions imposed by industry. Today, the Australia Group has twenty members, including Australia, Austria, Canada, the Commission of the European Community and the members of the European Union (Belgium, Denmark, Germany, France, Ireland, Italy, Luxembourg, the Netherlands, Portugal, Spain, and Britain), Japan, New Zealand, Norway, Switzerland, and the United States. The group maintains a secretariat in the Australian embassy in Paris. See, for instance, Zachary Davis, "Non-Proliferation Regimes: A Comparative Analysis of Policies to Control the Spread of Nuclear, Chemical, and Biological Weapons and Missiles," Congressional Research Service, CRS Report for Congress, 91–334ENR, Apr. 1, 1991.

22. Whatever its limitations, the CWC has several features that enhance its prospects for success. One of these has been its ability to elicit the cooperation and support of industry, without which control guidelines would have been impossible to devise and even less possible to enforce. The U.S. chemical industry has been serving as a vital source of expertise for negotiators, identifying technologies and inputs to include in the treaty and helping to devise practical verification schemes.

23. See the *Convention of the Prohibition of the Development, Production, and Stockpiling of Bacteriological (Biological) and Toxin Weapons and on Their Destruction*, in U.S. Arms Control and Disarmament Agency, *Arms Control and Disarmament Agreements* (Washington, D.C.: U.S. Government Printing Office, 1975).

24. At the time the BWC was negotiated, it was widely assumed that the combination of a strong moral taboo against biological weapons and the limited military utility of these weapons would be sufficient to ensure compliance. Recently, however, it has been estimated that as many as eleven nations, including Iraq, Syria, Egypt, Libya, Israel, the former Soviet Union, China, North Korea, Vietnam, Laos, and possibly Taiwan, may have biological weapons development or production programs. See David Fairhall, "Eleven Countries' Defying Ban on Germ Weapons," *Guardian*, Sept. 5, 1991, 1.

25. Controversy erupted over the Soviet Union's possible violation of the BWC in the 1970s, when it was accused of helping Vietnam to use toxin weapons against Laos and Cambodia; in 1980, when there were similar accusations of Soviet use of toxins in Afghanistan; and later that year, when an anthrax epidemic hit the city of Sverdlovsk, the site of a suspect biological research facility. See ter Haar, *Future of Biological Weapons*, 22–31.

26. See Antonia Handler Chayes and Abram Chayes, "Improving Non-Proliferation Regimes" (draft for Aspen Strategy Group, Nov. 1991), 20–21; and ter Haar, *Future of Biological Weapons*.

27. If it ever did serve to dissuade states from going the route of nuclear weapons

development, access to nuclear energy is certainly not now a sufficient inducement. Concerns about safety, environmental effects, the vulnerability of installations to attack, and high costs have combined to make nuclear energy far less compelling to all but a few states.

28. See Lawrence Scheinman, *Assuring the Nuclear Non-Proliferation Safeguards System*, Occasional Paper (Washington, D.C.: Atlantic Council of the United States, 1992), v.

29. In addition to intrusive mechanisms, numerous noncoercive initiatives to improve the effectiveness of nonproliferation efforts were considered or implemented in the early 1990s. With modern technology, it is possible to discuss new techniques of verification, such as aerial inspections, to add to the IAEA's toolbox of verification capabilities. In an effort to stem the risks posed by the migration of nuclear expertise, the United States and the European Community agreed in 1992 to develop an International Science and Technology Center to provide jobs for Russian scientists trained in the Soviet military-industrial complex. And in early 1992, Germany's foreign minister, Hans-Dietrich Genscher, proposed a nuclear nonproliferation plan calling for governments to make it illegal for their nationals to participate in the production of weapons of mass destruction abroad. See, for instance, David Hoffman, "Atom Scientists at Ex-Soviet Lab Seek Help: Baker Hears Appeals on Tour of Arms Complex," *Washington Post*, Feb. 15, 1992, A1; "Genscher Launches Nonproliferation Initiative," *Handelsblatt*, Jan. 20, 1992, 4, reprinted in *FBIS Report on West Europe*, FBIS-WEU-92-013, Jan. 21, 1992, 14–15.

30. Johan Molander, "The United Nations and the Elimination of Iraq's Weapons of Mass Destruction," in Tanner, ed., *From Versailles to Baghdad*, 137–157.

31. Scheinman, *Assuring the Nuclear Non-Proliferation Safeguards System*, 10–14.

32. See Leonard S. Spector, "Repentant Nuclear Proliferants," *Foreign Policy*, no. 88 (fall 1992): 23.

33. There is continued controversy about the degree to which the IAEA has the authority to conduct challenge inspections, and about whether the NPT regime will need treaty amendments or an augmented role for the United Nations. See Chayes and Chayes, "Improving Non-Proliferation Regimes," 13; and interview with IAEA director Hans Blix: "Keeping an Eye on a Nuclear World," *Arms Control Today* 21 (Nov. 1991): 3–6.

34. Firms in West Germany, France, the United Kingdom, and even the United States have assisted Pakistan, India, Brazil, and Iraq in acquiring nuclear programs. See Davis, "Nonproliferation Regimes," 10–11; and later sections of this paper.

35. For further discussion, see Leonard S. Spector with Jacqueline R. Smith, *Nuclear Ambitions* (Boulder, Colo.: Westview, 1990), app. A.

36. Current financial commitments to the IAEA are inadequate to meet the agency's existing requirements, let alone the new requirements that may be imposed upon it. The IAEA has been operating on a zero-growth budget while burdening its staff with new initiatives, from facilitating the Argentinean-Brazilian joint inspection agreement to establishing a safeguards system in South Africa.

37. Resolution 687 has received its share of criticism as an unwarranted violation of the basic sovereignty and territorial integrity of Iraq. Questions have been raised about the legality of the operation; these range from the question of whether it is

correct to assert that possession of weapons-grade material is a threat to peace, as implied by Resolution 687, to the question of whether the operation is a violation of NPT Article 4, which provides for signatories' "inalienable right" to pursue peaceful nuclear activities. See, for instance, Ambassador Ryukichi Imai and Yasuhide Yamanouchi, *International Transfer of Weapons and Related Technologies*, International Institute for Global Peace, Policy Paper 79 E, Jan. 1992, 8.

38. The draft of the treaty specifies various levels of controls on chemical weapons and precursor materials, and provides for the destruction of these items within ten years after the treaty enters into force.

39. Critics argue that there are other ways to protect against the compromise of national security or of proprietary information in the conduct of inspections. A British proposal for "managed access" to suspect sites, which would permit parties to shroud sensitive items, is a more popular alternative, which retains the advantages of intrusive, short-notice inspections while minimizing their risks. For further discussion, see, for instance, Amy E. Smithson, "Chemical Inspectors: On the Outside Looking In?" *Bulletin of the Atomic Scientists* 47, no. 8 (1991): 23–25.

40. In the early 1960s, some Western analysts warned that within two to three decades there would be up to twenty countries with nuclear weapons. There are still only five declared nuclear-weapons states, to which have been added four de facto nuclear-weapons states, Israel, India, Pakistan, and South Africa, as well as several "threshold" countries, including Argentina, Brazil, South Korea, Taiwan, North Korea, and Iraq before Desert Storm. See Spector with Smith, *Nuclear Ambitions*, chap. 1.

41. In the 1950s, predictions of the likely number of new nuclear-weapons states over the next two to three decades typically exceeded a dozen.

42. Although obligated to do so, not all NPT states completed a comprehensive safeguards agreement with the IAEA. North Korea, for example, signed the NPT in 1985 but only recently signed a full-scope safeguards agreement, which it has yet to implement. Syria, an NPT signatory since 1969, has for years conditioned its acceptance of comprehensive safeguards on inspections of Israeli nuclear facilities, although it has since agreed to permit IAEA inspections. See Davis, "Non-Proliferation Regimes," 8–9; and "Syria, IAEA to Negotiate Nuclear Accord," *Washington Post*, Feb. 11, 1992, 16.

43. Facing the threat of renewed military action, Iraq agreed in March 1992, after several weeks of stalemate, to allow inspections of its missile facilities. This concession was still greeted with suspicion by UN officials, however, and did not include any concession on nuclear or chemical installation inspections. See, for instance, Trevor Rowe and R. Jeffrey Smith, "Iraq Makes New Concession to UN; U.S. Officials View Move Skeptically," *Washington Post*, Mar. 21, 1992, A1.

44. In a series of discussions beginning in late 1991, the Koreas reached agreement on a wide range of security measures, including a pledge to rid the peninsula of nuclear weapons. With the support of Pakistan, the United States is helping to promote multilateral security consultations in South Asia which include India, Pakistan, China, and Russia. The United States, in conjunction with the United Nations, also is proposing a variety of arms control measures for the Middle East. These initiatives have yet to yield concrete results but are seen by many as indications of growing regional interest in military restraint. See, for example, Michael Z.

Wise, "U.N. Nuclear Team to Inspect Iranian Sites: Efforts to Curb Weapons Proliferation Are Broadened in Wake of Persian Gulf War," *Washington Post,* Feb. 7, 1992, A18.

45. The Treaty of Tlatelolco has not yet taken full effect, since not all Latin American nations have signed and ratified the agreement. Recently, however, progress has been made toward finalizing the treaty. See "Official Discusses Regional Nuclear Ban," interview on the Tlatelolco Treaty with Ambassador Jorge Morales by Barbara Bethancourt in Havana, date not given, recorded from Havana Radio, Havana, Cuba, in Spanish, Oct. 30, 1991, printed in *Proliferation Issues,* JPRS-TND-91-018, Nov. 18, 1991, 7–8.

46. With few stakes in preserving an inequitable system of this kind, India and Israel began their nuclear programs in the 1960s, for example, and were assisted by industrial states that put commercial advantage ahead of their stated nonproliferation objectives.

CHAPTER NINE   SOVEREIGNTY IN A TURBULENT WORLD

1. The shift from the sovereignty of kings to the sovereignty of the people provides a good measure of the time scale that may be involved in the processes whereby conceptions of sovereignty undergo transformation during the times between the intermittent periods in which a widely shared consensus prevails. Popular sovereignty can be fairly said to have originated with the American and French Revolutions, but it did not culminate in worldwide acceptance until 1945, when it was incorporated in Article 1 of the United Nations Charter. For a cogent analysis of how the protection of the "sovereign's sovereignty" in international law changed to protection of the "peoples' sovereignty," see W. Michael Reisman, "Sovereignty and Human Rights in Contemporary International Law," *American Journal of International Law* 84 (Oct. 1990): 866–76.

2. For a cogent analysis of why the processes of globalization may be irreversible, see Walter B. Wriston, "Technology and Sovereignty," *Foreign Affairs* 67 (winter 1988/89): 63–75; and David Webster, "Direct Broadcast Satellites: Proximity Sovereignty and National Identity," ibid., 62 (summer 1984): 1161–74.

3. Benjamin R. Barber, "Jihad vs. McWorld," *Atlantic Monthly,* Mar. 1992, 54–55.

4. For a cogent analysis of how sovereignty serves deep-seated psychological needs, see Gordon Pocock, "Nation, Community, Devolution, and Sovereignty," *Political Quarterly* 61 (July–Sept. 1990): 318–27.

5. Stephen D. Krasner, "Sovereignty: An Institutional Perspective," *Comparative Political Studies* 21 (Apr. 1988): 88, 90. For another expression of the difficulty of envisioning "a politics sans sovereignty," see Jean Bethke Elshtain, "Sovereignty, Identity, Sacrifice," *Social Research* 58 (fall 1991): 545–64.

6. John Gerard Ruggie, "'Finding Our Feet' in Territoriality: Problematizing Modernity in International Relations" (photocopy, Aug. 1991), 5. For another extended discussion of the problems involved in employing the concept of sovereignty in the context of rapid change, see R.B.J. Walker and Saul H. Mendlovitz, "Interrogating State Sovereignty," in R.B.J. Walker and Saul H. Mendlovitz, eds., *Contending Sovereignties: Redefining Political Community* (Boulder, Colo.: Rienner, 1990), 1–12.

7. James N. Rosenau, *Turbulence in World Politics: A Theory of Change and Continuity* (Princeton: Princeton University Press, 1990), chap. 2.

8. The distinction between these two contexts is elaborated in James N. Rosenau, *The United Nations in a Turbulent World* (Boulder, Colo.: Rienner, 1992), 61–64.

9. Robert H. Jackson, *Quasi-States: Sovereignty, International Relations and the Third World* (Cambridge: Cambridge University Press, 1990), 27–30. For the descriptions of negative sovereignty as "formal-legal" and an "absolute condition," see 27 and 29, respectively.

10. The model is set forth in Rosenau, *Turbulence in World Politics.* For other applications of the model, see the following papers I have written: "Armed Force and Armed Forces in a Turbulent World" (paper presented at the Symposium on Armed Force in a Multi-Centric World, Texas A&M University, College Station, Tex., Apr. 23–24, 1992); "Normative Challenges in a Turbulent World," *Ethics and International Affairs* 6 (1992): 1–19; "Constitutions in a Turbulent World" (paper presented at the Conference on Unification of Multi-System Nations, Taipei, Taiwan, Sept. 27, 1991); and my *United Nations in a Turbulent World.*

11. For an elaboration of this conception of autonomy, see James N. Rosenau, "The New Global Order: Underpinnings and Outcomes" (paper presented at the Fifteenth World Congress of the International Political Science Association, Buenos Aires, July 24, 1991). For a subsequent development that translated this conception into an operative (albeit short-lived) political principle, see the agreement reached among ten Soviet republics and Mikhail Gorbachev to preserve a modicum of union. In that emergency plan each republic was guaranteed a right to "independently determine the form of its participation in the union." Francis X. Clines, "A Gamble with Chaos," *New York Times*, Sept. 2, 1991, 1.

12. The analysis that concludes that the system's parameters are undergoing their first profound transformation since 1648 can be found in Rosenau, *Turbulence in World Politics*, chap. 5.

13. Ibid., 10–11. For a formulation that identifies six parameters, see Mark W. Zacher, "The Decaying Pillars of the Westphalian Temple: Implications for International Order and Governance," in James N. Rosenau and Ernst-Otto Czempiel, eds., *Governance without Government: Order and Change in World Politics* (Cambridge: Cambridge University Press, 1992), chap. 3.

14. An extensive discussion of the nature of the various dimensions of the skill revolution can be found in Rosenau, *Turbulence in World Politics*, chap. 9; an analysis of various types of evidence indicative of the breadth and depth of the skill revolution is presented in chap. 13 of that volume.

15. For an interesting historical comparison of the mid-nineteenth-century and late-twentieth-century situations, see Sidney Tarrow, "The Globalization of Conflict: 'Isn't This Where We Came In?'" (paper presented at the Annual Meeting of the American Political Science Association, Washington, D.C., Aug. 31, 1991).

16. James N. Rosenau, "The Relocation of Authority in a Shrinking World," *Comparative Politics* 24 (Apr. 1992): 253–72.

17. "The Columbo family civil war . . . is solid evidence of a widespread phenomenon: the breakdown of autocratic leadership and dissension in the lower ranks. . . . The system of dictatorial control and unflinching loyalty in all of the families . . . is fracturing in the same way that the Soviet Union suddenly collapsed." Selwyn Raab, "In the Mafia, Too, a Decline in Standards," *New York Times*, Jan. 19, 1992, sec. 4, p. 6.

18. See Rosenau, "Armed Force and Armed Forces in a Turbulent World."

19. Rosenau, *Turbulence in World Politics*, chaps. 1, 5, 10, 13.

20. For an explanation of why the terms *sovereignty-free* and *sovereignty-bound* seem appropriate to differentiate between state and nonstate actors, see Rosenau, *Turbulence in World Politics*, 36. A graphic elaboration of the attributes that differentiate the state-centric and multi-centric worlds can be found in the same source (p. 250).

21. William Wallace, "What Price Independence? Sovereignty and Interdependence in British Politics," *International Affairs* 62 (summer 1986): 367.

22. Piotr Sztompka, "The Global Crisis and the Reflexiveness of the Social System," *International Journal of Comparative Sociology* 25 (1984): 45.

23. For an extended discussion of how the "cascade" has superseded the "event" as the central process of world politics, see Rosenau, *Turbulence in World Politics*, 298–395.

24. Francis X. Clines, "Ex-Soviet States Allow Separate Armies," *New York Times*, Dec. 31, 1991, A5.

25. Adam Bryant, "Views on Foreign Cars Cost Salesman His Job," *New York Times*, Feb. 23, 1992, 16.

26. Serge Schmemann, "A Nation Unified in an Identity Crisis," *New York Times*, Feb. 25, 1992, B10.

27. Alan Cowell, "Now, After 1,600 Years, Time to Join the World," *New York Times*, Feb. 26, 1992, A4.

28. Geoffrey Hosking, "The Roots of Dissolution," *New York Review of Books*, Jan. 16, 1992, 36.

29. John F. Burns, "Sovereign Quebec Needn't Be Separate," *New York Times*, Feb. 21, 1992, A4.

30. Ibid.

31. Serge Schmemann, "With Seeds of Nation Slow to Flower, Ukrainians Blame Shadow of Russia," *New York Times*, Mar. 9, 1992, A4.

32. Serge Schmemann, "Free, Yes, but Estonians Are Also Shivering," *New York Times*, Jan. 24, 1992, 1.

33. "Russia and Ukraine Try to Settle Military Dispute," *New York Times*, Jan. 12, 1992, 3.

34. For a lengthy discussion of the possibility that orientations toward systemic and subsystemic levels of authority may be rooted in cyclical dynamics, see Rosenau, *Turbulence in World Politics*, 454–59.

35. Thomas J. Biersteker, "The 'Triumph' of Neoclassical Economics in the Developing World: Policy Convergence and Bases of Governance in the International Economic Order," in Rosenau and Czempiel, eds., *Governance without Government*, chap. 4.

36. For an analysis of how the momentum surged with respect to monetary union in Europe, see Ian Harder, "Sovereignty and the Eurofed," *Political Quarterly* 61 (Oct.–Dec. 1990): 402–14.

37. For an example of how one nongovernmental organization has successfully championed movement toward the states-are-obliged-to-go-along extreme of the sovereignty continuum, see Howard Tolley Jr., "Popular Sovereignty and International Law: ICJ Strategies for Human Rights Standard Setting," *Human Rights Quarterly* 11 (Nov. 1989): 561–85.

38. For an extensive analysis of the emergent role played by social movements in world politics, see R.B.J. Walker, *One World, Many Worlds: Struggles for a Just World Peace* (Boulder, Colo.: Rienner, 1988).

39. Fund-raising letter from John G. Healy, executive director, Amnesty International USA, Dec. 5, 1991, 3 (italics in the original).

40. John G. Healy, quoted in Barbara Crossette, "State Department's Human Rights Office Grows in Influence," *New York Times*, Jan. 19, 1992, A9.

41. It is intriguing to speculate that the momentum toward change in the legal foundations of sovereignty may also be spurred and sustained by academicians as well as politicians and publics. Perhaps it is not mere coincidence that the conference for which this paper was originally prepared—at Dartmouth College during May 1992—was only one of three on the same subject—the changing nature of sovereignty—being held within weeks of each other. One of the others was sponsored by the MacArthur Foundation, and the third was scheduled by the InterAmerican Dialogue, which describes its purpose of redefining sovereignty as stemming from "the increasingly active roles of international organizations, nongovernmental groups and national governments in promoting economic integration and reducing social inequities in the region, a new trend in an area where national sovereignties were once jealously guarded." *New York Times*, Mar. 1, 1992, A10. Could it be that this convergence of shared concerns derives from the analytic skills of research scholars, who are among the first to recognize that changes are at work and thereby to clarify the intellectual foundations of them, all of which adds impetus to their evolution? To answer the question in the affirmative one need only cite the example of two philosophers, Jean Bodin and Thomas Hobbes, whose writings were central to shaping the evolution of sovereignty as a concept related to the prerogatives of kings.

42. Cf. Reisman, "Sovereignty and Human Rights in Contemporary International Law," 868.

43. Robert Pastor, as quoted in Crossette, "State Department's Human Rights Office Grows in Influence," 9.

44. Edward A. Gargan, "Afghan President Agrees to Step Down," *New York Times*, Mar. 19, 1992, A3.

45. Paul Lewis, "U.N. Says Iraq Defies Order to Destroy Weapons," *New York Times*, Feb. 28, 1992, A5.

46. Paul Kennedy, *The Rise and Fall of the Great Powers: Economic Change and Military Conflict from 1500 to 2000* (New York: Random House, 1987), 440.

47. Anthony Giddens, "Review Symposium: Comments on Paul Kennedy's *The Rise and Fall of the Great Powers*," *British Journal of Sociology* 39 (1988): 331.

48. For another formulation that also challenges the question as deceptive, even as "a red herring," see Jarat Chopra and Thomas G. Weiss, "Sovereignty Is No Longer Sacrosanct: Codifying Humanitarian Intervention," *Ethics and International Affairs* 6 (1992): 95–117.

49. For inquires that focus on these new forms of global structure, see Kenichi Ohmae, *A Borderless World* (New York: Harper's, 1990); Robert B. Reich, *The Work of Nations: Preparing Ourselves for Twenty-first Century Capitalism* (New York: Knopf, 1991); Joseph Grunwald and Kenneth Flam, *The Global Factory: Foreign Assembly in International Trade* (Washington, D.C.: Brookings Institution, 1985); Jonathan David Aronson and Peter Cowhey, *When Countries Talk: International*

Trade in Telecommunications Services (Cambridge, Mass.: Ballinger, 1987); Katrina Burgess and Abraham F. Lowenthal, eds., *The California-Mexico Connection* (Stanford: Stanford University Press, 1993); and Joel Havemann, "Neither a State nor International Organization," *Los Angeles Times,* Feb. 4, 1992, H9.

50. The expectation that the future of world politics will continue to be marked by turbulence is set forth in Rosenau, *Turbulence in World Politics,* 453–54.

CHAPTER TEN   SOVEREIGNTY AND INTERVENTION

1. See, for instance, Richard Cooper, *The Economics of Interdependence* (New York: McGraw-Hill, 1968); Robert Keohane and Joseph Nye, *Power and Interdependence* (Boston: Little, Brown, 1977); Edward Morse, "The Transformation of Foreign Policies: Modernization, Interdependence, and Externalization," *World Politics* 22 (Apr. 1970); James Rosenau, *Turbulence in World Politics: A Theory of Change and Continuity* (Princeton: Princeton University Press, 1990); James Lee Ray, "The Abolition of Slavery and the End of International War," *International Organization* 43, no. 3 (1989): 405–40.

2. Michael Webb, "International Economic Structures, Government Interests, and International Coordination of Macroeconomic Adjustment Policies," *International Organization* 45 (summer 1991).

3. Francis Fukuyama, *The End of History and the Last Man* (New York: Free Press, 1992).

4. Stanley Hoffmann, "The Problem of Intervention," in Hedley Bull, ed., *Intervention in World Politics* (Oxford: Clarendon, 1984).

5. Joseph Gagliardo, *Germany under the Old Regime, 1600–1790* (London: Longman, 1991), 16–17.

6. Joseph Gagliardo, *Reich and Nation: The Holy Roman Empire as Idea and Reality, 1763–1806* (Bloomington: University of Indiana Press, 1980), chap. 2.

7. E. A. Beller, "The Thirty Years' War," in *The New Cambridge Modern History,* vol. 4, *The Decline of Spain and the Thirty Years War 1609–48* (Cambridge: Cambridge University Press, 1970), 345–46, 357.

8. "Treaty of Osnabrück," in Clive Perry, ed., *The Consolidated Treaty Series,* vol. 1, *1648–49* (New York: Oceana, 1969), 219–225.

9. Ibid., 229.

10. Ibid., 229.

11. Ibid., 226.

12. Ibid., 217.

13. Ibid., 234.

14. "Treaty of Münster," in Fred Israel, ed., *Major Peace Treaties of Modern History, 1648–1967* (New York: McGraw-Hill, 1967), vol. 1, sec. 77.

15. A. C. Macartney, *National States and National Minorities* (London: Oxford University Press, 1934), 161–63.

16. Ibid., 164–65.

17. Inis L. Claude Jr., *National Minorities: An International Problem* (Cambridge: Harvard University Press, 1955), 2; and Macartney, *National States,* 166–67.

18. Macartney, *National States,* 170; Claude, *National Minorities,* 5; and Alan Sharp "Britain and the Protection of Minorities at the Paris Peace Conference, 1919,"

in A. C. Hepburn, ed., *Minorities in History* (New York: St. Martin's Press, 1979), 171.

19. Claude, *National Minorities*, 16; and Dorothy V. Jones, *Code of Peace: Ethics and Security in the World of the Warlord States* (Chicago: University of Chicago Press, 1991), 45.

20. Macartney, *National States*, 275, 278, 297; and Claude, *National Minorities*, 14.

21. See Macartney, *National States*, 502-6, for the text of the treaty.

22. Claude, *National Minorities*, 20-28; and Sharp, "Britain and the Protection of Minorities," 174.

23. Quoted in Macartney, *National States*, 238.

24. Claude, *National Minorities*, 17.

25. Macartney, *National States*, 252; and Sharp, "Britain and the Protection of Minorities," 181-83.

26. Claude, *National Minorities*, 32-35.

27. Ibid., 30.

28. Ray, "Abolition of Slavery," 409.

29. Leslie Bethell, *The Abolition of the Brazilian Slave Trade: Britain, Brazil, and the Slave Trade Question, 1807-1869* (Cambridge: Cambridge University Press, 1970), 10.

30. Ibid., 11-15, 20.

31. Ibid., 20 and 96.

32. Ibid., 7-9, 13, 164.

33. Ibid., 60-61.

34. Ibid., 60-61 and chap. 3.

35. Ibid., chap. 12.

36. Quoted in ibid., 338.

37. Quoted in A. Thomas and A. Thomas, *Non-Intervention: The Law and Its Import in the Americas* (Dallas: Southern Methodist University Press, 1956), 8.

38. Goronwy J. Jones, *The United Nations and the Domestic Jurisdiction of States: Interpretations and Applications of the Non-Intervention Principle* (Cardiff: University of Wales Press, 1979), 2; Thomas and Thomas, *Non-Intervention*, 10; and R. Vincent, *Nonintervention and International Order* (Princeton: Princeton University Press, 1974), 84.

39. Jones, *United Nations*, 2; and Vincent, *Nonintervention*, 80.

40. Jones, *United Nations*, 3.

41. M. S. Anderson, *The Eastern Question, 1774-1923: A Study in International Relations* (London: Macmillan, 1966), 60-62; H. Temperley, *The Foreign Policy of Canning, 1822-27* (Hamden, Conn.: Archon, 1966), 320-21; Schwartzberg, "The Lion and the Phoenix," *Journal of Middle Eastern Studies* 24, nos. 2 and 3 (1992): 139-77, 287-311; and Vincent, *Nonintervention*, 77-79, 86-87.

42. Vincent, *Nonintervention*, 91-95.

43. The material in this paragraph and the two that follow is from J. Leurdijk, *Intervention in International Politics* (Leeuwarden, Netherlands: Eisma B.V., 1986), app. 1.

44. Thucydides, *The Peloponnesian Wars* (London: Penguin, 1954), 402.

45. John G. Ruggie, "International Regimes, Transactions, and Change: Em-

bedded Liberalism in the Postwar Economic Order," in S. Krasner, ed., *International Regimes* (Ithaca: Cornell University Press, 1983).

1. The evidence that comes closest involves Jack Donnelly's discussion of the European human rights regime, in which he finds a "significant transfer of authority from states to a regional community of states" (see chapter 6, above). He cautions, however, that the European experience in this area is exceptional owing to existing high levels of political and economic cooperation regionally, and to generally excellent human rights records. One should not expect the European experience to be replicated in other regions, or for the European powers to accept at the global level the constraints they accept regionally as part of their ongoing integration project.

2. See also David E. Pitt, "Accord Is Reached on Use of Forests," *New York Times,* Jan. 23, 1994, 7.

3. See, for example, Security Council Resolution 688, Apr. 1991, in the case of Iraq; Security Council Resolution 757, May 30, 1992, in the case of Bosnia; and Security Council Resolution 794, Dec. 3, 1992, in the case of Somalia.

4. As described in chapter 1, efforts by the international community to constrain sovereignty could take the form of intervention, isolation, or influence. Conca's discussion suggests that in the case of implementing international environmental standards, influence is more likely than intervention to emerge as the instrument of choice.

5. Weiss and Chopra similarly observe the disjuncture between norms and procedures in the area of humanitarian assistance: "125 years of practice by the International Committee of the Red Cross (ICRC) and four decades of the passage of human rights treaties within the United Nations" have led to "the possibility of and the need for the implementation of norms."

6. See, for example, Geraldine Brooks, "Peacekeeping Missions of the U.N. Are Pursued on a Wing and a Prayer," *Wall Street Journal,* Dec. 28, 1993, A1; and Brian Hall, "Blue Helmets, Empty Guns," *New York Times Magazine,* Jan. 2, 1994, 18–43.

7. This limited willingness on the part of member countries and the intractability of many of the conflicts in which the United Nations is currently involved have led some observers to advise that the United Nations and the international community act with greater prudence and selectivity when contemplating intervention. See, for example, Ernst Haas, "Beware the Slippery Slope: Notes toward the Definition of Justifiable Intervention," in Laura W. Reed and Carl Kaysen, eds., *Emerging Norms of Justified Intervention* (Cambridge, Mass.: American Academy of Arts and Sciences, 1993), 63–88. Haas mistakenly cites our work as advocating a "hugely expanded scope" for UN intervention (Haas, "Slippery Slope," n. 6); that is clearly not our intention.

8. An earlier version of this discussion appeared in Gene M. Lyons and Michael Mastanduno, "International Intervention, State Sovereignty, and the Future of International Society," *International Social Science Journal* 138 (Nov. 1993): 517–32.

9. Thucydides, *The Peloponnesian War,* trans. Rex Warner (Baltimore: Penguin, 1954), 400–408.

10. Edward Luttwak, "Intervention and Access to Natural Resources," in Hedley Bull, ed., *Intervention in World Politics* (Oxford: Oxford University Press, 1984), 79–94.

11. Hedley Bull, "Conclusion," in Bull, *Intervention in World Politics,* 185.

12. See Marc Trachtenberg, "Intervention in Historical Perspective," in Reed and Kaysen, eds., *Emerging Norms of Justified Intervention,* 23.

Contributors

JARAT CHOPRA is a research associate at the Thomas J. Watson Institute for International Studies, Brown University, Providence, Rhode Island.

KEN CONCA is assistant professor of government and politics at the University of Maryland, College Park, Maryland.

JACK DONNELLY is professor of political science at the University of Denver, Denver, Colorado.

ROBERT H. JACKSON is professor of political science at the University of British Columbia, Vancouver, British Columbia.

STEPHEN D. KRASNER is Graham H. Stuart Professor of International Relations at Stanford University, Stanford, California.

FRIEDRICH KRATOCHWIL is professor of political science at the University of Pennsylvania, Philadelphia, Pennsylvania.

GENE M. LYONS is professor emeritus of government at Dartmouth College, Hanover, New Hampshire.

MICHAEL MASTANDUNO is associate professor of government at Dartmouth College, Hanover, New Hampshire.

JANNE E. NOLAN is senior fellow at the Foreign Policy Studies Program at the Brookings Institution, Washington, D.C.

NICHOLAS ONUF is professor of international relations at Florida International University, Miami, Florida.

JAMES N. ROSENAU is University Professor of International Affairs at the George Washington University, Washington, D.C.

THOMAS G. WEISS is associate director of the Thomas J. Watson Institute for International Studies, Brown University, Providence, Rhode Island.

Index

Library of Congress Cataloging-in-Publication Data

Beyond Westphalia? : state sovereignty and international intervention
  / edited by Gene M. Lyons and Michael Mastanduno.
        p.   cm.
      Includes bibliographical references (p.   ) and index.
      ISBN 0-8018-4953-5 (hardcover : acid-free paper). — ISBN
  0-8018-4954-3 (pbk. : acid-free paper)
        1. Sovereignty.   2. Intervention (International law)
  3. International relations.   I. Lyons, Gene M.   II. Mastanduno,
  Michael.
  JX4041.B49   1995
  341.5'84—dc20   94-32440

Printed in the United States
6247